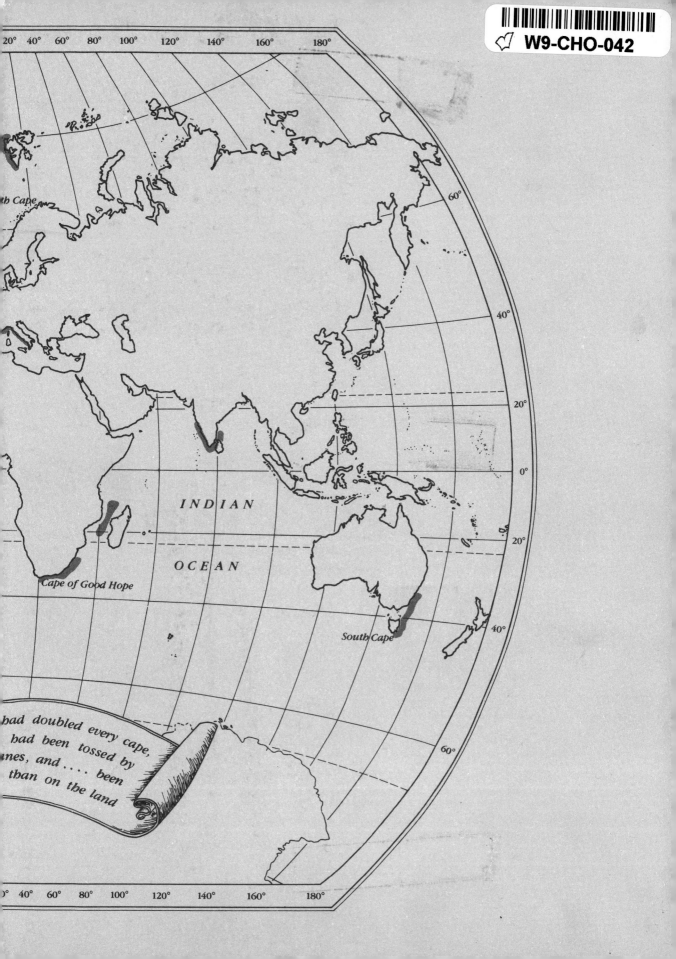

60°

th Cape

40°

20°

0°

I N D I A N

20°

O C E A N

Cape of Good Hope

40°

South Cape

had doubled every cape,
had been tossed by
anes, and . . . . been
than on the land

60°

Arthur Phillip

1738-1814

HIS VOYAGING

Arthur Phillip

1738-1814

HIS VOYAGING

ALAN FROST

Melbourne
OXFORD UNIVERSITY PRESS
Oxford Auckland New York

OXFORD UNIVERSITY PRESS
Oxford New York Toronto Delhi Bombay Calcutta
Madras Karachi Petaling Jaya Singapore Hong Kong Tokyo
Nairobi Dar es Salaam Cape Town Melbourne Auckland
and associated companies in
Beirut Berlin Ibadan Nicosia

National Library of Australia
Cataloguing-in-Publication data:

Frost, Alan, 1943– .
Arthur Phillip, 1738–1814 His Voyaging

Bibliography.
Includes index.
ISBN 0 19 554701 2.

1. Phillip, Arthur, 1738–1814. 2. Great Britain. Navy—
Biography. 3. New South Wales—Governors—Biography.
4. New South Wales—History—1788–1851. 5. Great
Britain—History, Naval—18th century. I. Title.

994.402'092'4

Maps by Mary Hutchinson
Designed by Guy Mirabella
Typeset by Asco Trade Typesetting Ltd, Hong Kong
Printed by Impact Printing, Melbourne
Published by Oxford University Press, 253 Normanby Road, South Melbourne
OXFORD is a trademark of Oxford University Press

We each have woven selves from skeins of early
dreaming. You played among these terraces,
scaled the Moors' intractible ramparts.
High in this castle you saw your caravels
reach India, heard poets hallow the dead.

Past your world's edge, I knew a hemisphere
where parrots blossomed on the littoral,
crustaceous frangipani fringed the sea.
From mangoed shades, I plundered continents,
at last returned with gold, and furled old sails.

Two hundred years ago, when Phillip touched
antipodes, Sintra drew wanderers.
Then, they did not walk among cool eucalypts,
nor had they you, come briefly home,
to lead them through the palaces and gardens.

Contents

Conversion Table

In some instances, imperial measurements have been retained in the text in the interests of historical accuracy. The following are approximate conversions.

1 inch	2.5 centimetres	£1	$2	1 gallon	4.5 litres
1 foot	0.3 metre	1s	10c	1 pint	600 millilitres
1 yard	0.9 metre	1d	8c	1 ounce	28 grams
1 mile	1.6 kilometres			1 pound	450 grams
1 acre	0.4 hectare			1 ton	1 tonne
1 fathom	1.8 metres				

Acknowledgements

The research which underlies this study and which has spread over five continents has led me into many obligations.

I have first warmly to thank the directors and staff of the institutions listed in the Key at the head of the Bibliographies and Notes, and also those of the Bank of England. The Marquis of Normanby, Mr Victor Montagu, Dr Francisco Olazabal, Sr Marcos Carneiro de Mendonça, Sir George and Lady Raper, and two others who wish to remain anonymous have granted me access to material in their possession. They and the directors and trustees of the various institutions have also given permission for me to cite and quote from, and in some instances reproduce, original materials.

I have to specify permissions from: the Trustees of the State Library of New South Wales; the Trustees of the British Museum (Natural History); the Trustees of the National Maritime Museum; the Controller of Her Majesty's Stationery Office and the Keeper of Public Records and the Hydrographer of the Navy; William Heinemann Ltd (for the Henry Handel Richardson passage on p. 219).

For help with wide-ranging enquiries or access to uncatalogued materials, I have particularly to thank Dr N.A.M. Rodger, Assistant Keeper, the Public Record Office; Dr R.J.B. Knight, Head of Documentation and Research, National Maritime Museum; Mr A.P. Harvey, Director of Library Services, British Museum (Natural History); and Mr John C. Dann, Director, William L. Clements Library.

Miss Isabel Moutinho, who speaks all the languages that Arthur Phillip spoke, has given invaluable help in locating relevant materials in European and South American archives. Mr M. Yelland kindly pursued Phillip's family connections in England, and Mrs B. Cubbon the Whiteheads'. The following answered specific queries: Professor Dauril Alden, Mr H.B. Carter, Professor Robert Darnton, Commander Andrew David, Dr H.E.S. Fisher, Dr T.A.

Heathcote, Professor E.L. Jones, Dr Dámaso de Lario, Brigadier R.T. Lewendon, Dr Campbell Macknight, Sir Robin Mackworth-Young, Mr A.H. Pearsall, Comandante Estácio dos Reis, Emeritus Professor Bernard Smith, Mr Colin Tubbs, Mr John Vivian, Sir James Watt. Acknowledgements of other specific debts appear in the notes.

Inevitably, the research for a project such as this requires some courteous introductions. Sir Geoffrey Yeend, Secretary of the Department of Prime Minister and Cabinet, Mr R.H. Robertson, formerly Deputy Australian High Commissioner to Britain, Mr G.V. Brady, formerly Australian Ambassador to Portugal, and Mr P.C.J. Curtis, Australian Ambassador to France, each helped me to gain access to public and private collections.

Such research also requires much time and money. Twelve months' leave from La Trobe University in 1981–82 enabled me to lay the basis of the study; and La Trobe University has also given incidental grants to meet some expenses, and a grant towards publication. A series of larger grants from the Australian Research Grants Scheme enabled me to travel to the various archives and libraries, to have some assistance with the research, and to obtain photocopies of various materials. Reflecting a welcome sense of the importance of recovering and preserving the past, the Government of New South Wales under Premier Neville Wran also contributed generously to the cost of research. I drafted the study during six pleasant months at the Humanities Research Centre, Australian National University; and I have since drawn on the resources of La Trobe University's History Department and its efficient staff, particularly Mrs Merelyn Dowling.

Many others have of course helped in the completion of this work. All will know privately how grateful I am, but it behoves me to acknowledge explicitly my debt to three amongst this group. For many years now, I have had the great pleasure of discussing the British expansion into the Pacific Ocean with Professor Greg Dening, Emeritus Professor O.H.K. Spate, and Professor Glyndwr Williams, each of whom has contributed distinctly to my perspectives and made me aware of the importance of generous and disinterested scholarship. Professor Spate and Professor Williams have also commented in detail on my penultimate draft.

Preface

Some people—those who perceive their own significance, or those who understand that they live in momentous times—record for posterity the details of their lives in studied ways which are, then or later, open to rational interpretation. Whether Arthur Phillip did so it is now impossible to know, for his private papers have seemingly not survived. While this is a considerable impediment to the biographer, it is not a final one, for there are other ways of knowing the meaning of experience and the importance of events, ways that involve images and motifs (e.g., those of confinement and the voyage) which not only suggest but actually are the habitual modes of the Western imagination's understanding. Accordingly, as well as on those papers of Phillip which are extant, I have drawn on contemporary or near-contemporary descriptions and illustrations, and on modern perceptions, to recreate those landscapes and seascapes through which Phillip moved. My intention has been to present a panorama of his life and times, in which are highlighted those events and circumstances of most significance, to him or to posterity. This method may give a greater unity to Phillip's life than he himself would have understood it to have had: that is a necessary risk; but it is impossible that it should not convey something of his own sense of himself and his age—and then, biography is more than self-perception.

TRAINED UP TO
A SEAFARING LIFE, 1738–53

This excellent Charity . . . is calculated for the double purpose of providing for the sons of poor Seamen and making them useful to their country, by training them up to a Seafaring life.

An Historical Account of the Royal Hospital for Seamen at Greenwich

On 29 November 1728, John Herbert went to the Archdeacon of London's Court and 'alleged' that he would marry Elizabeth Breach. Obtaining church permission to marry via an allegation rather than via the publication of banns was a path preferred by those whom time urged to an immediate ceremony, or who found prosperity's decorum irrelevant. John Herbert and Elizabeth Breach were of this second sort. He was twenty-three years old, and lived in the parish of St Paul Shadwell, the area on the north bank of the Thames adjacent to the various docks that was the haunt of watermen and sailors. She was 'twenty-one years and upwards', one of a numerous family based in the parish of St Botolph without Aldgate, in Stony Lane near the Everitts, to whom they were linked by circumstance and marriage.[1]

John Herbert and Elizabeth Breach's world was a hard one. The metropolis they inhabited was notoriously unhealthy. One in three children born there died in their first two years. Others died before they were five. Those who survived this early period might expect to live to about fifty, but pain and disease were their constant companions. Teeth rotted until decayed enough to justify removal, broken bones were not set properly, surgery was performed without anaesthetics. There was little personal or public hygiene, and the

Thames was an open sewer. Typhoid, typhus, and smallpox periodically ravaged the community. Gastric disorders resulting from the consumption of rotten food were prevalent, and the poor diet meant that scurvy was endemic in winter, when those unable to afford coal also froze.

The life of the community was turbulent. Children began to work at five or six, with not more than half the boys and fewer than a third of the girls receiving any formal education. Masters and mistresses beat their servants, and servants robbed their masters and mistresses. Thugs beat and robbed in daylight with impunity, and the poor actively resisted the authorities' minimal attempts to enforce order. Women pregnant by their masters lost their positions, and prostitution was rife. The working class and poor found diversion in drinking, and in such 'sports' as bull- and bear-baiting, and public punishments. Persons confined to the stocks might lose eyes to the rocks included in the hails of refuse and rotten food directed at them. Crowds flocked to executions, and after the hangings the friends of the dead might need to fight for the body with the gangs which supplied the anatomy schools.

John Herbert and Elizabeth Breach were married in the Church of St Mary Aldermanbury, within the City of London, on 30 November.[2] Their union seems not to have resulted in children. On 6 February 1729, considering 'the Perrills & Dangers of ye Seas & other Uncertainties of this Transitory life',[3] Herbert swore a will.[4] This was a mandatory action for men serving in the Royal Navy, for if they died at sea their families might otherwise not recover the pay due to them. It is therefore likely that in 1729 Herbert sailed on a King's ship, but the details are unknown. On 19 June 1730, however, he entered the *Tartar*, a 32-gun frigate carrying a crew of 135 men. He joined the ship as an ordinary seaman at Sheerness, one of the Thames dockyards, where she was fitting for cruising duty in the Caribbean.[5] In August, she proceeded to Spithead, where she continued fitting, and from where she sailed on 3 October. Calling at Madeira en route, after a quick and uneventful voyage she reached Barbados on 24 November, and Port Royal, Jamaica, two weeks later.[6]

For the next twelve months, the *Tartar* patrolled the Jamaica station, returning at intervals to Port Royal to refit and refresh her crew. The service was both arduous and unhealthy. When the ship docked in August 1731, she needed several months' repair to fit her for return to England; and as the artificers worked on her, many of the crew fell ill. Among them was John Herbert, who died in the naval hospital on 18 October. Elizabeth Herbert would probably have learned of his death upon the *Tartar*'s arrival in England early in June 1732; and whatever may have been her grief then, hers was a lot only too common amongst the wives of seamen. Quickly taking the steps necessary to realize her husband's meagre effects, she obtained probate on his will on 1 August.[7]

Elizabeth Herbert next appears in 1737 as the wife of Jacob Phillip. Almost all about Phillip is obscure. Eighteenth-century accounts identify him as a 'native of Frankfort', and a teacher of 'the languages'.[8] His birth date is unknown, as is that of his death, and the circumstances thereof. He is as transient in history as one of the great albatrosses with whom old sailors shared their ocean passages, and is now redeemed briefly from time's oblivion by the activities of one of his children.[9] We do not know where and when he and Elizabeth Herbert met and married. Phillip might have come to London to teach languages, or he may have come as a sailor. Their taking up residence in or near Bread Street in the City, in the second half of 1736, and the baptism of their child in the parish church of All Hallows in mid-1737, together suggest that they married in the summer or autumn of 1736; but there are no firm details. In 1737 a daughter, Rebecca, was born to the Phillips and baptized on 26 June. A son, Arthur, followed the next year, born on 11 October, and baptized a month later.[10] There is no record of any subsequent children.

The family seems to have been in reasonably comfortable circumstances in the late 1730s. As the occupant of Martha Meredith's house, Phillip paid 19s 6d to the parish's Poor fund in 1736–37, and £1 19s in 1737–38 and 1738–39. Though not the highest, these contributions were somewhat above the average.[11] The absence of Jacob's name from the Poor Rate register after 1739 suggests that the Phillips moved in this year; and their history in the 1740s is almost totally obscure. If Arthur's admission to the Charity School of the Royal Hospital for Seamen at Greenwich in 1751 can be taken to bespeak the family's reality, one might assume that Jacob served in the Royal Navy; that one parent, most likely Jacob, died; and that the family then fell on hard times.

There are hints to give this hypothesis some plausibility. The Greenwich Hospital School was a charity for the sons of seamen. In the Entry register, Arthur Phillip's father is identified as a 'Steward' (i.e., a purser's steward), in the Binding Out one as an 'Able Seaman'.[12] As Elizabeth Phillip was seemingly still living in 1756, it appears that Jacob died prior to 1751, perhaps while at sea. It is also possible that the circumstance linking all these others was the commencement of war with Spain in 1739. This led to great recruitments to man the fleets, and to the establishment of six marine regiments. Typhus was soon raging through the men on the ships, its ravages intensified by the winter of 1739–40, which was perhaps the most severe of the eighteenth century.

A later comment by the Viceroy of Brazil that Arthur Phillip had begun serving on the warships of his country from the age of nine again suggests that he had a close relative in the Navy.[13] Less clear, however, is the capacity in

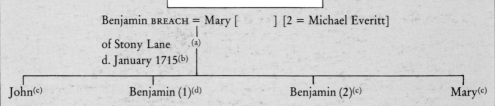

BREACH FAMILY

Benjamin BREACH = Mary [   ] [2 = Michael Everitt]

of Stony Lane   (a)

d. January 1715[b]

| John[c] | Benjamin (1)[d] | Benjamin (2)[c] | Mary[c] |

a The date of the couple's marriage has not appeared.

b St. Botolph without Aldgate, Burial register, Guildhall ms 9232/1. His will was proved 21 March 1715—Archdeacon of London's Court, Wills and Administrations, Guildhall ms 9050/20.

c In her will, which was proved in the Archdeacon of London's Court 1 March 1726, Guildhall ms 9051/13, Mary Breach/Everitt indicated that the then-living children of her first marriage were John, Benjamin, and Mary Breach, and of her second one, Michael and William Everitt.

d St Botolph's without Aldgate, Burial registers, Guildhall ms 9232/1, records that Benjamin (1) was buried 12 March 1714. The Baptismal register, Guildhall ms 9225/2 records that Benjamin (2) was baptised 29 January 1715. Both entries give the father's address as Stony ('Stoney') Lane.

Still to be determined is the precise relationship of Elizabeth to Benjamin and Mary Breach. Her 1728 marriage allegation states that she was 'twenty one years and upwards' (Archdeacon of London's Court, Marriage Allegations, Guildhall ms 10091/68), so that she appears to have been born in or about 1707. It seems reasonable to suppose that she was the daughter of an elder brother of Benjamin Breach, and therefore his and Mary's niece. There are the following possibilities (which still leave unresolved the relation of the men):

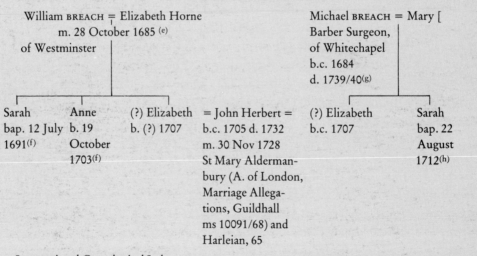

William BREACH = Elizabeth Horne

m. 28 October 1685 (e)

of Westminster

Michael BREACH = Mary [   ]

Barber Surgeon,

of Whitechapel

b.c. 1684

d. 1739/40[g]

| Sarah bap. 12 July 1691[f] | Anne b. 19 October 1703[f] | (?) Elizabeth b. (?) 1707 | = John Herbert = b.c. 1705 d. 1732 m. 30 Nov 1728 St Mary Aldermanbury (A. of London, Marriage Allegations, Guildhall ms 10091/68) and Harleian, 65 | (?) Elizabeth b.c. 1707 | Sarah bap. 22 August 1712[h] |

e International Genealogical Index.

f St Martin in the Fields, Baptismal register, Westminister Archives, vol. 9.

g Barber Surgeon Company, Admissions to Freedom 1665–1704, Guildhall ms 5265/2; Quarterage Books, 1739–40, Guildhall ms 9815/8.

h St Mary, Whitechapel, Baptismal register, Greater London Record Office P 93/MRY1/7.

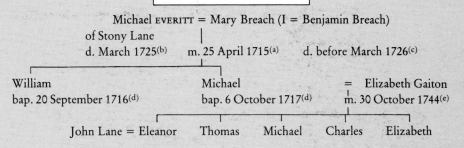

EVERITT FAMILY

Michael EVERITT = Mary Breach (I = Benjamin Breach)
of Stony Lane
d. March 1725[b]   m. 25 April 1715[a]   d. before March 1726[c]

William
bap. 20 September 1716[d]

Michael
bap. 6 October 1717[d]   = Elizabeth Gaiton
m. 30 October 1744[e]

John Lane = Eleanor   Thomas   Michael   Charles   Elizabeth

[a] International Genealogical Index.

[b] Michael Everitt Senior's will was proved 21 March 1715—see Archdeacon of London's Court, Wills and Administrations, Guildhall ms 9050/22.

[c] Mary Everitt's will was proved 1 March 1726—see ibid., Guildhall ms 9051/13.

[d] St Botolph without Aldgate, Baptismal register, Guildhall ms 9225/2.

[e] St Thomas, Portsmouth, Phillimore's Hampshire Parish Registers (Marriages), 15.

PHILLIP FAMILY

Jacob PHILLIP = Elizabeth Breach (1 = John Herbert)
m. (?) 1736[a]

Rebecca
bap. 26 June 1737[b]

Arthur
born 11 October 1738[b]   = (1) John Denison
m. 14 August 1759[c]

[   ] Dove =

= (1) Charlott Denison
m. 19 July 1763[d]

= (2) Isabella Whitehead
m. 8 May 1794[e]

[a] Despite extensive searches, the date and place of Phillip's parents' marriage are unknown.

[b] All Hallows Bread Street, Baptismal register, Guildhall ms 5033.

[c] 14 August 1759, *Gentleman's Magazine*, 29 (1759), 392.

[d] St Augustine, Watling Street, Marriage register, Guildhall ms 8875/1.

[e] St Mary le Bone, Middlesex, Marriage register, Harleian, 53.

Unclear also is the precise link between the Lane family and Arthur Phillip. Circumstances suggest that this was a strong one. The Lane family firm (Lane, Son & Fraser, of 11 Nicholas Lane) acted as banker for both Michael Everitt and Phillip. Phillip was close to John Lane and Eleanor Everitt and their immediate family throughout his life. In the later 1780s, after Michael Everitt's death, Elizabeth Gaiton Everitt lived close to her daughter in Nicholas Lane, and about this time she commissioned from Francis Wheatley the portrait of Arthur Phillip now in the National Portrait Gallery, which she subsequently gave to Isabella Phillip. Isabella then bequeathed this to Eleanor Lane 'of Peckham'. In the later nineteenth century, the Lane house at Peckham passed to the Gaiton family.

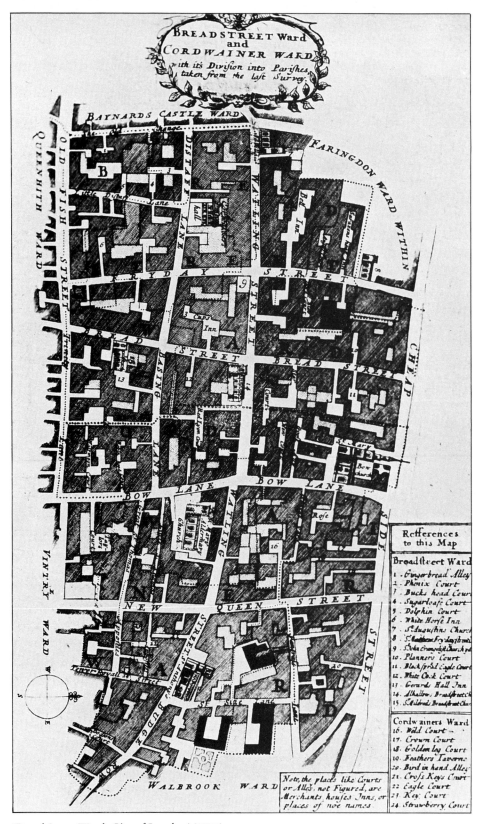

'Bread Street Ward, City of London' (1734)

which the boy might have served. The Viceroy's identification is 'guarda de Pavilhão' ('guard to the flag'), which is the Portuguese equivalent of the French 'Garde de la Marine' ('ensign'). There was then formally no such position in the Royal Navy, but it is not impossible that a friendly marine commander might have created one to give a boy a sense of purpose. Nor do we know the ships on which either Jacob or Arthur Phillip sailed in the 1740s. Later circumstances suggest that his mother's relative Michael Everitt, who became a post captain in late 1747, may have begun to prepare the boy for a naval career, but again, there is no record in the relevant musterbooks of Arthur Phillip's presence in the ships which Everitt commanded in the next years.

Whatever his early circumstances were, Arthur Phillip was admitted to the Greenwich Hospital School on 22 June 1751.[14] The school was 'calculated for the double purpose of providing for the sons of poor Seamen and making them useful to their country, by training them up to a Seafaring life'. The boys admitted were 'the Sons of disabled Seamen, or whose Fathers were slain, kill'd, or drown'd in the Sea Service', and who were 'objects of charity'. They were between eleven and thirteen years of age on admission, in good health and able to read, and they departed at fourteen into a seven-year apprenticeship in a branch of the merchant navy where they continued their nautical education.[15]

Phillip began his formal education on 24 June. On entry, he received a blue cloth jacket and breeches, a blue serge waistcoat, leather breeches to wear on weekdays, a number of checked shirts, blue worsted stockings, and a small round hat; a Bible and a Common Prayer Book; and the books and instruments he needed for his studies. For the next two and a half years he followed an exacting regimen designed to fit him for the sea. He took his meals together with his fellow students at a single table in the Hospital's dining hall. For breakfast each day he had 4 ounces of bread and 1 ounce of cheese, and a half-pint of beer. Dinners varied, with meat on some days; and these meals he washed down with a pint of beer. For supper, he had 5 ounces of bread, 1 ounce of cheese, and another half-pint of beer. He washed his hands and face each morning before school, his feet every Saturday night before bed, and put on clean clothes every Sunday morning before Divine Service. The school's nurse daily attended to his hair with a fine comb. He was allowed out of the hospital precincts only to go to the school, where he learned writing, mathematics, navigation, and drawing.[16]

Phillip learned the mariner's craft in an ethos permeated with the nation's naval traditions. The Seamen's Hospital was founded in 1694, on the south bank of the Thames, 8 kilometres downstream from London Bridge, where the Stuarts had built a summer residence (1616–29), and the Royal Observatory

(1675–76). Here, between 1696 and 1745, William and Mary, Anne, George I, and George II raised the four matching hospital buildings, surrounding a large square, from which the pensioners could see the merchant traffic passing along the river and the warships which came to refit and load at the Thames yards, and which offered to viewers from the river an imperial vista to the Queen's House and beyond to the Observatory.

The hospital's adornments intensified this ethos. The Painted Hall, which the boys saw on ceremonial occasions, was lavishly decorated with zodiacs and the rivers of the earth, allegorical figures of the four elements and the four seasons, of Time, Truth and Fame, and of the Arts and Sciences giving rise to navigation. There were depictions of Copernicus and his planetary system and of Newton. A central focus was 'the *Blenheim* man of war, with all her galleries, port holes open, &c to one side of which is a figure of Victory flying with spoils taken from the enemy, and putting them on board the English [ship]'. The whole was designed to raise in the viewer 'the most lively images of Glory and Victory'; and contemporaries found they could not view it without 'much passion and emotion'.[17]

Though so grandly conceived and lavishly decorated as to be considered by some 'too magnificent for a place of charity',[18] the hospital fulfilled the need for which it was founded. In the mid-eighteenth century its corridors were crowded with men whose bodies had been seared by privation, disease, and flame, who had fallen from rigging, or lost limbs and sight to ensnaring cables, splintering timber, and marauding shot. The nation's achievement was founded on the mute endeavours of such sailors as these pensioners; yet at the same time as they testified with their shattered bodies to this achievement's cost, they told of the magical places and stirring experiences from which it sprang. In Arthur Phillip's time some of the pensioners had savoured the sensuous welcome of the Mediterranean ports; others had cruised the Spanish Main; a few had rounded the world with Anson and returned triumphant. His later inclinations indicate to which reality the boy attended.

Having been bound to an apprenticeship, Phillip left the Greenwich Hospital School on 1 December 1753.[19] He took with him the books and instruments he had used, and he received what he would need at sea: a suit of flock bedding; a double-breasted pea jacket, and a coarser one; a serge and a blue Kersey waistcoat; a pair of good cloth breeches, and a pair of ordinary shag ones; a drugget coat and a matching pair of breeches; two white shirts and three checked ones; three silk handkerchiefs; two pairs of yarn stockings, and one pair of worsted ones; two pairs of shoes; one hat and one cap; and a sea-chest in which to transport and store this bounty.

The western entrance to the hospital, near to the ships' stairs, was dominated by two large stone globes that surmounted the gates. On the celestial one were inlaid the meridians, the equinoctial, ecliptic, tropic, and polar circles, and a multitude of stars in their relative positions. The terrestrial one exhibited the equator, the tropics, and the polar circles, showing every tenth latitude; the shapes of the continents; and the track of Anson's *Centurion*. Had Arthur Phillip been possessed of foresight, he would, as he left to begin his voyaging, have sensed that these globes bespoke his life's reality, for he too was destined to see battle in western seas, to range the coast of South America, and to reach beyond the world's great capes to India and the Antipodes.

1

About Northern Capes

The Arctic and Atlantic Oceans, the Mediterranean and Caribbean Seas, 1754–63

Valeu a pena? Tudo vale a pena
Se a alma não é pequena.
Quem quer passar além do Bojador
Tem que passar além da dor.
Deus ao mar o perigo e o abysmo deu,
Mas nelle é que espelhou o céu.

Was the effort worthwhile? Everything is worthwhile,
so long as the spirit dreams of great things.
Whoever aspires to pass Cape Bojador must endure pain.
God gave the sea perils and abysses,
but he also made it the mirror of heaven.

Fernando Pessoa, 'Mar Portuguez'

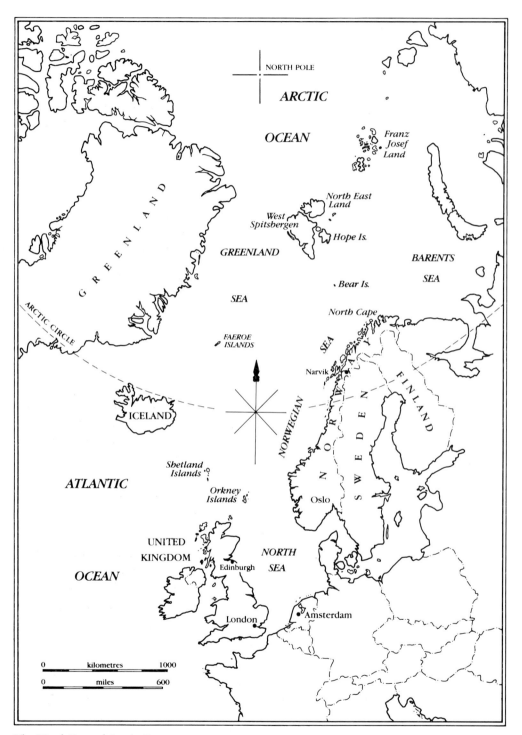

The North Sea and Arctic Ocean

The Arctic Ocean, 1754

Our ship is well-rigged and she's ready to sail,
The crew they are anxious to follow the whale,
Where the ice-bergs do float and the stormy wind blow,
Where the land and the ocean are covered with snow.

Whalemen's Song

On 1 December 1753, with his 'voluntary and free Consent', the governors of Greenwich Hospital apprenticed Arthur Phillip for seven years to William Readhead, mariner, who agreed to instruct him 'the best Way and Manner for making him an able Seaman and as good an Artist as he can'—and not to 'immoderately beat or misuse' him.[1]

Readhead was the master of the *Fortune*, a 210 ton vessel built for the Greenland whale fishery. 'Greenland' is a slight misnomer, for while Europeans hunted for whales in the general area of the Greenland Sea, rather than the island's coastal waters, the areas they frequented were Spitsbergen or 'East Greenland', the edge of the pack-ice to the northwest, and across the East Greenland current along which the whales migrated. The British had opened this northern fishery at the beginning of the seventeenth century, after Muscovy Company adventurers had encountered the Right whale (*Balaena mysticetus*) in the course of their voyages to the northeast, but through lack of accumulated skills and poor management, by the end of the century they found themselves supplanted by the Dutch and Germans. With demand for whale oil increasing, in 1724 the South Sea Company began a concerted effort to re-establish a British presence, recruiting skilled masters, seamen, harpooners, and blubber-cutters from Germany and Holland. After eight years, however, the company was showing an accumulated loss of £178 000. To encourage the industry, and thus to ensure the nation a continuance of a 'nursery of seamen' and a resource of ships, in 1733 Parliament granted a bounty on whaling vessels, but the industry languished until 1749, when Parliament raised the bounty for ships of more than 200 tons to £2 per ton. Though the intention of the owners may have been as much 'of catching the bounty as of catching fish',[2] this led to an immediate increase in activity, with an average of forty-three ships sailing from London each year in the 1750s, to hunt either in the bays and among the islands of Spitsbergen, or at the edge of the pack-ice.

The ships of this fleet would leave the Greenland Dock together about the beginning of April, with the masters usually calling at Lerwick, in the Shetland Islands, to take on board fresh provisions and any additional men they might lay their hands on, and to allow the crews to buy mittens, caps, and other heavy woollens. From here, they would sail directly north, usually reaching their destination by the end of the month. They would then hunt for two months. By the first week in July, they would gather and turn south, so as to make port together three or four weeks later. Safety was one reason for this joint return, but more pressing was the need to avoid arriving after the bulk of the fleet, and therefore find the market for oil satisfied. On reaching London, the masters turned their catches over for processing, and paid their crews off.

Spitsbergen is the general name of a series of granite peaks and islands which lie between 76° and 80°N latitude. The islands have no springs of fresh water, but they do possess some vegetation—lichens, dwarf willows less than a metre tall, 'scurvy' grasses, Arctic poppies. One who sailed among them wrote: 'The general aspect of this gloomy and sterile country, affords a scene truly picturesque and sombre. The shores are rugged, bold, and terrific, being in many places formed by lofty, black, inaccessible rocks, some of which taper to exceedingly high points, and are altogether bare, and almost destitute of vegetation. The entire face of the country exhibits a wild, dreary landscape, of amazingly high sharp-pointed mountains, some of which rear their summits above the clouds, and are capped with strata of snow, probably coeval with the creation of the world.'[3] But if these forbidding rocks offered small welcome to the mariner, they and their surrounding waters abounded with animal life. Reindeer and arctic foxes which crossed the ice from the northern edge of Europe inhabited them; fat ducks crowded their bays; polar bears ranged the ice floes; seals, walruses, and whales swam in the sea; countless birds swarmed about.

On reaching a suitable situation, the crew would anchor in a bay, or fasten the ship to an iceberg, and first enact a barbaric ritual known as 'hoisting the

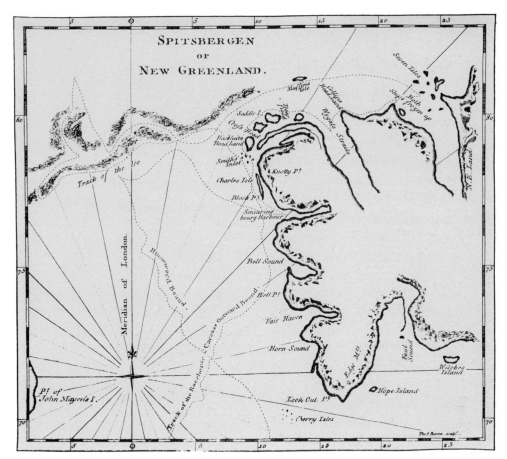

'Spitsbergen' (1773)

Garland'. The 'garland' consisted of three small hoops formed into a globe, covered with ribbons. The man most recently married hung it from the main-topgallant stay, and his companions, their faces blackened with grease and soot, danced round the deck to a pandemonium of beaten frying-pans, kettles, fire-irons, and whatever else might produce a sound. The celebration ended with the master ordering an ample allowance of grog.[4]

With the distant gods of fertility and the chase propitiated, the men then entered on the business of whaling. They hunted from small boats, each of which was equipped with a line 720 fathoms long, harpoons of 8½ feet with 2-foot-long blades, and lances 6 feet long. A typical boat's crew consisted of a harpooner, a steerer, a line-manager, and three or four men. On 'striking' a whale, the crew would hoist a small flag. Observing this sign of a 'fall', their companions would rush to join them at where they expected the whale to rise; and all would harpoon the unfortunate animal again and again until it died, often twelve or more hours later, amid a lather of blood-stained water and an escort of scavenging sharks. If they were hunting in a bay or in open sea, the crews would tow the carcass to the ship to flense its blubber; or, if they were hunting at the edge of the ice, they flensed it on the spot. The final task was to cut the blubber into small pieces and stuff it into casks, for boiling down on return to port.

It was arduous work, and dangerous. Sudden shifts in the ice might trap or crush a ship. The ropes which ran out from the boats as the struck whales sounded might catch and mutilate limbs. A desperate animal rising might overturn or shatter a boat, and its crew freeze or drown. Ropes from two or more boats hunting in the same area might tangle in the chase, with the same effects. Stripping the blubber was the most difficult aspect of the whole. It was hard enough when working beside the ship for the flensers to keep a precarious balance on the pitching carcass as they carved at it with their razor-sharp knives and spades and tore off its blubber. Against the pack-ice, this work was worse, for the small boats into which the flensers passed their harvest pitched as much as the carcass, and wind and flying water froze the workers. Accordingly, crews suffered frequently from colds, fractured and frost-bitten limbs, and scurvy.

To make the work worse, ship owners provided only an austere ration, which crews had to supplement by gathering birds' eggs and 'scurvy grass', and by shooting ducks and the odd reindeer. Each man brought his own supply of tea and coffee, with masters serving beer or spirits on extraordinary occasions. To relieve the tedium of whaleless days, the men sang and danced, wrestled on the ice, and picked the white poppy to put about their caps. Occasional chases after polar bears, whose hides were in demand as carriage seat covering, gave another interest, as did contact with Russians, who camped year long on the islands, living off seal blubber and hunting bears and foxes.

When not engrossed by the hunt, the whalers found themselves in an unnatural world. One day might be filled with eerie silence, while in the next the noise of splitting, falling, and grinding ice was enough to deafen. Some days the heat was such as to melt the pitch on cordage and deck, and cause the crew to work naked; and on these days the snow on the peaks would run with the colours of the minerals beneath. But then, high winds, snow, and frost might sweep the warmth away in a moment. On other days, the cold might be so intense as to double the thickness of the ropes with a casing of ice and make them like metal to work; and the sea freeze to a meadow where seals sported by the hundreds. Sometimes, the waves would glow with different colours, and the plankton the whales fed on might turn them phosphorescent at night. Drifting icebergs offered strange shapes and stunning aspects. These might appear as plateaus or tables, as Nile temples or Gothic cathedrals. When salt had formed over freshwater ice, and snow encased the whole, the mass dazzled with the colours of the spectrum, being emerald from one angle and sapphire from another, ruby from a third. A companion of Constantine John Phipps in 1773 wrote of one fine day: 'the air being perfectly serene, and the weather moderate, the fishes seemed to enjoy the temperature, and to express it by their sporting. The whales were seen spouting their fountains towards the skies, and the fin fish following their example. They likewise ... saw dolphins; the whole prospect in short was more pleasing and picturesque than they had yet beheld in this remote region. The very ice in which they were beset looked beautiful, and put forth a thousand glittering forms, and the tops of the mountains, which they could see like sparkling gems at a vast distance, had the appearance of so many silver stars illuminating a new firmament.'[5] In all this strangeness, night was scarcely distinguishable from day. The early summer sun would scarcely dip below the horizon at about 10 p.m., and light cabins again at 1 or 2 a.m. On clear evenings, there were the mysterious splendours of the *aurora borealis*. Appearing on the horizon at twilight, these northern lights might continue a dull yellow for some hours, then burst into a myriad quickly changing shapes and colours, from dusk grey to blood. Often, they would cover the whole sky and horizon in a bewildering display of form and colour, breaking out in previously dark areas, skimming the heavens, suddenly dying, then bursting forth again in wild profusion.

For four months in the spring and summer of 1754 Arthur Phillip, aged fifteen, learned the business of whaling in Arctic waters. On 1 April his master William Readhead signed on a crew of thirty for the voyage; and soon after the *Fortune* sailed in company with more than thirty other whalers. They returned by 20 July, when Readhead paid the crew off.[6] There is no record of what Phillip thought of the experience. However much he may have been struck by the strange qualities of the Arctic world, he could scarcely have found the work pleasant. To him as apprentice would have fallen the worst part of it, that of managing the boat into which the flensers passed the blubber; and it may be that the origin of his repeated ill-health in later life lies in the privation of this regimen. But, whether pleasant or not, the experience appears to have had some lasting influence on his outlook. Twenty years later, he was to take an interest in Portuguese whaling in Brazilian waters; and another twenty years on, he was to see whaling as offering a considerable resource to a struggling colony in New South Wales. As a thoughtful man, he made connections: 'Should a fishery ever be established on this coast, and which I should suppose likely to answer as well as the one which has been established many years in the Brazil (at Sta Catharina and Rio de Janeiro), I think it would be found to answer best if carried on in small vessels, as it is from Rio de Janeiro; and with respect to the currents, I believe they are neither more frequent nor stronger than what they are on the Brazil coast.'[7]

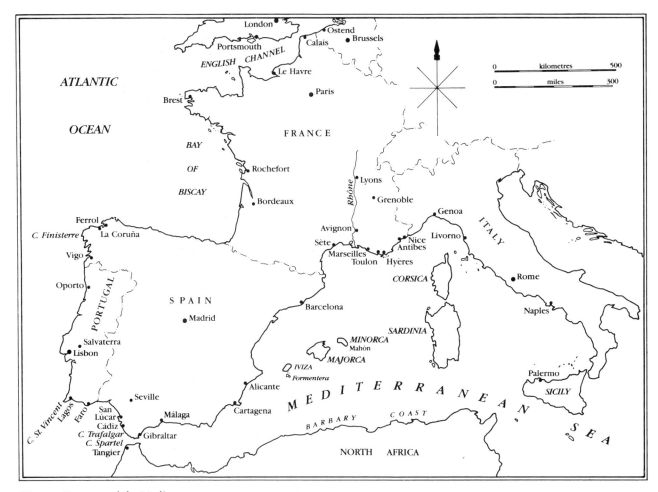

Western Europe and the Mediterranean

The European Coasting Trade, 1754–55

In 1754, the London whalers returned with one polar bear skin, and blubber which produced 1290 tons of oil.[2] With oil bringing £29 per ton, together with the shipping bounty, it represented an adequate, if not ample, return. At this price, though, only a rich or an indulgent owner might afford to keep his ship idle until the next season; and in common with most of his fellows Readhead was soon engaged in another venture.

    The usual off-season employment for whaling ships was in charter or independent ventures in the southern European coasting trade. With demand growing for whaling products—oil for lamps and soap, bone for stays—some of the trade was directly in the whalers' catch: in 1754, Britain exported about 300 tons of oil. But as the Dutch and Germans provided these products more cheaply, they constituted only a small part of Britain's trade to southern Europe. Much more prominent in the trade were grain, cloths, and other manufactures outwards; and silks, wines, fruits, wool, and bullion in return. This made for another, if indirect, connection between the whaling industry and British exporters, for textile manufacturers used whale oil to process the yarns from which they made their coarser cloths. (Since whale oil discoloured and stiffened finer yarns, rape or olive oil was used to process these.)

The trade in textiles was central to the whole. By the mid-eighteenth century, with increasing demand in Europe, and with the technological innovations that were soon to give rise to the Industrial Revolution emerging, British textile manufacturing was expanding rapidly. In Yorkshire and Lancashire, in the West Country, and in and about London, entrepreneurs and merchants employed vast networks of spinners and weavers to produce a great variety of cloths. From the western regions of Yorkshire and from Devon and Somerset came woollens, serges, and worsteds ('long ells, tammies, long bays, shallons'). In and about Preston, Blackburn, and Lancaster an army of handloom weavers produced calicoes and linens. Often, these cloths were shipped directly from local ports to their European destinations; but equally, they might be sent to London first, sometimes for dyeing. The British merchants sold most of their production to Portugal and Spain, either for consumption there, or for transshipment to these nations' colonies in the Americas.

Britain also exported other products to the Iberian peninsula—iron and brass manufactures; small quantities of lead and tin from Cornwall and coal from Wales; some pepper; quantities of fish, especially Newfoundland cod; and increasing quantities of grain. In return, merchants brought in olive oil, fruit, wool and dyes from Spain; and fruit and wine from Portugal. The balance of the trade was decidedly in Britain's favour, so that the Iberians paid for much of it with the bullion they drew from their American mines. This was particularly the case with the Portuguese, so much so that the carrying of bullion from Lisbon, either directly to England, or to other European centres, was in itself a distinct and profitable trade.

To promote their trade, British merchants maintained subsidiary houses or employed agents in the main European ports; and by the mid-eighteenth century, some of these arrangements had taken on a distinctive character. The British 'factories' in Lisbon and Oporto, for example, were made up of persons who, while often having family connections with the home principals, might reside there most or all of their adult lives. They formed closely-knit enclaves in a foreign country, they had their own rules and procedures, and they enjoyed a favoured position in Portuguese law. While their first loyalty was to their principals, they also bought and sold on behalf of other firms, and on their own account. And they participated more or less directly—sometimes illicitly—in Portugal's trade with Brazil. In Spain, where only nationals were permitted to trade to the colonies, British merchants often maintained houses for the purposes of the European trade, but employed Spanish agents or Jewish intermediaries to further that to the colonies. The British government

Antonio Canaletto, 'Greenwich Hospital'
(1751–56)

Charles Brooking, 'Fishing for whales at the
Edge of the Pack-Ice' (*c.* 1755)

Claude-Joseph Vernet, 'Marseilles Harbour' (1754)

Claude-Joseph Vernet, 'Antibes Bay' (1756)

maintained consuls at many ports, to keep statistics on the trade, to see that it went smoothly, and to advise about how it might be increased.

The trade to the Iberian peninsula was inextricably linked with that to the Mediterranean. This was partly because speculating merchants and roaming ships' masters would take cargoes wherever they thought they might make a profit, so that, for example, the British exported large quantities of red herrings, some cloths, and small quantities of pepper, lead and tin to Italy. But the link was equally a result of the circumstances of Portugal's trade with the countries surrounding the Mediterranean. Portugal imported grains from the Levant, Italy, Sicily, and France; silks and other luxury goods from Italy; and olive oil, cattle, and cheap velvets from Spain. To these countries she sent quantities of Brazilian diamonds, sugar, tobacco, and hides; ivory from her African colonies; and cotton, coffee, and pepper from India. As Portuguese nationals played very little part in the actual movement of these goods, British ships carried a large proportion of the trade. And once in the Mediterranean, masters might find cargoes to carry backwards and forwards across it—in Italy, salt for southern France, and grains and cloths for Portugal; in Spain, fruits and hides for Italy; in France, grain for Portugal. From these countries, they might gather cargoes of raw silk and silk yarn, wool, raisins and currants, olive oil, and fresh fruits for England; or salt and fruits for other northern countries.

Much of the British trade with the Iberian peninsula and the Mediterranean was conducted from late summer into winter, according to the availability of return cargoes. Ships would load outward cargoes of cloths, grain, fish, manufactures, minerals, or provisions and, clearing the Channel, cross the Bay of Biscay, pass Cape Finisterre, and run down the coast of Portugal. If laded specifically for the Portugal trade, they would then call either at Lisbon or Oporto, dispose of their cargoes, and obtain return ones of wine, fruit, and bullion.

If laded more generally for the Mediterranean trade, they would continue south past Lisbon, rounding Cape St Vincent, whose high and bleak escarpments and isolated position make it more truly than Finisterre the end of Europe, and run either to Cádiz, or through the narrow straits to Gibraltar. Formed by a beetle's leg of land that probes the Atlantic, Cádiz was a focus of the southern carrying trade. In the mid-eighteenth century, it was also—as the substantial buildings that shimmered in the abundant sunlight and the rising new cathedral testified—the port from which Spanish fleets sailed with European manufactures and to which they returned with the riches of the New World. Gibraltar was similarly a focus of the trade; and there the northern

European encountered the Mediterranean. To its bay came the merchants and sailors of many nations, so that its narrow streets were lit by the costumes of soldier and sailor, of Moor and Spaniard, Corsican and Greek. Across the bay, Algeciras gleamed like a pearl in an oyster of blue sea and brown hills. In the clear evenings witches' fires etched the coasts of the opposing continents, and phosphorescent plankton lit the sea.

If carrying government provisions and munitions, from Gibraltar the trader might cross to Minorca, which the British had held since 1708, and where they had built an important naval base at Port Mahon. If otherwise laded, from Cádiz or Gibraltar, she might proceed up the Spanish coast to Málaga, Alicante, or Barcelona for raisins and white wine; or she might sail across the Mediterranean to the ports of Sicily and Italy—to Palermo or Naples; to Leghorn (Livorno), then an important entrepôt; to Genoa, where she might unload her cargo and pick up an intermediate or return one of grain, salt, currants, olive oil, or silk. At the French ports of Nice and Antibes, Toulon, Marseilles and Sète, she might unload salt, and gather olives and grain. Heading out of the Mediterranean, she would edge past Tarifa, by Cape Trafalgar, where the sweep of the Atlantic waves against the long beaches sounded like distant cannon. Perhaps she might call at Cádiz, to find some indigo and cochineal from America, and the dark sherries of the heat-filled hinterland; or, and especially at San Lúcar, on the broad estuary of the Guadalquivir River further along the coast, the luscious fruits of the Seville region. Or she might land her grain at the small southern Portuguese ports of Faro, Albufeira, or Lagos, and take on citrus fruits. From these, she might proceed to the northern European ports, to Le Havre and Calais, Ostend, Rotterdam, Amsterdam, and Hamburg to unload her fruit; or she might return directly to London.

William Readhead signed on a crew of twelve for a trading voyage to the Mediterranean on 24 August 1754. The pass which he obtained from the Admiralty gave his first destination as Barcelona, the second as Leghorn; and *Lloyd's List* records his returning via Sète and Rotterdam.[3] These destinations allow us to surmise that the *Fortune* may have collected raisins at Barcelona; delivered herring at Leghorn and taken on currants and perhaps some salt; dropped off the salt at Sète, and taken on some grain; unloaded the grain at one of the southern Spanish or Portuguese ports; and taken on citrus fruit for Rotterdam. She reached London again on 20 April 1755, and Readhead paid the crew off two days later.

What precisely Arthur Phillip thought of his Iberian and Mediterranean initiation is again unknown. Still, as did the whaling, it seems to have made a lasting impression. Decades later, in an austere time, he was to remember with relish the figs he had eaten in Portugal and Spain; and this voyage gave him his first acquaintance with coasts and ports that he would later return to repeatedly. And there were strategic aspects to the knowledge which he gained. Cádiz was Spain's principal Atlantic naval base. The great fortress of Gibraltar was the key to naval control of the Mediterranean, with Port Mahon also of distinct significance. Toulon was the French navy's Mediterranean base. British fleets needed access to Lisbon to operate successfully about Europe's Atlantic coasts. In sailing the waters about these bases, in seeing at least some of them, Phillip must have begun to see the world in a strategic light.

He may also have begun to see it in another way. In 1755, most of Arthur Phillip's voyaging lay before him; and, naively hopeful or ambitious as he may have been, he could scarcely have truly suspected how extensive this voyaging was to be. For him then, Brazil was still a large hemisphere away, India a mirage bounded by wastes of land and sea; and it would be fifteen years before James Cook would chart the east coast of New Holland and call it New South Wales. But if his father had not already taught him the lessons, Portugal and Spain, Italy and France would have shown him how others lived differently, and the utility of knowing their languages. By the summer of 1755, Phillip's youthful experience had begun to offer that sense of the world's expanse and variousness, of the diversity of men and their societies, that distinguishes the true voyager. It was to be this sense, more than any other single attribute, that would one day bring him safely through a scarcely-travelled sea.

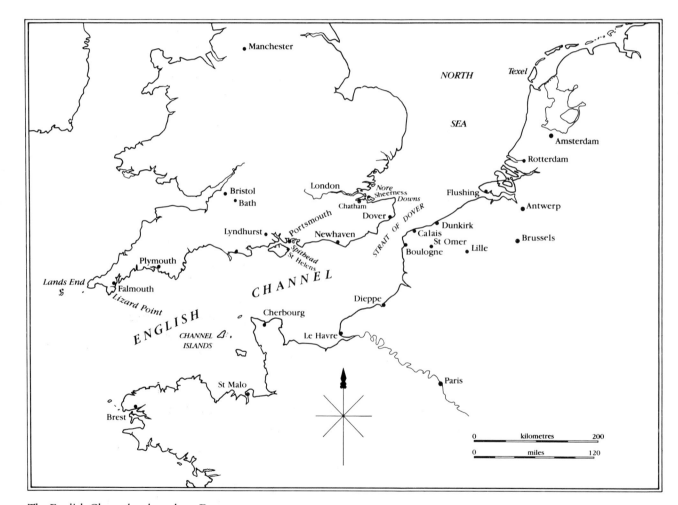

The English Channel and northern European ports

The Seven Years War: Europe, 1755–60

West gallantly charg'd in the van, sir,
Without dismay or fear;
    But Byng, who would not risk a man, sir,
Kept cautiously snug in the rear.
    Sing, sing, great Rear-Admiral Byng.

At length the French run away, sir,
As Frenchmen are apt to do:
    But he scorn'd to give them foul play, sir,
So *he* civilly run away too.
    Sing, sing, generous Admiral Byng.

For behaving so well in the ocean,
At least he deserves well a string;
    And if he wou'd sue for promotion,
I hope they will give him his swing.
    Swing, swing, O rare Admiral Byng!

'A Rueful Story, Admiral B-g's Glory, or
Who Run Away First'

William Readhead signed on thirty men for another Greenland voyage on 28 April 1755, and the *Fortune* sailed immediately. She returned to London on 27 July, and Readhead paid the crew off the next day.[1] Readhead and his ship now drop from sight, as Arthur Phillip did not continue his association with either. Why Phillip did not complete his apprenticeship is unclear. Perhaps Readhead died; or perhaps Phillip's relatives, sensing that war was imminent, secured his release so as to set him on his intended career in the Royal Navy.

In 1755, Britain and France were moving steadily towards war. The uneasy peace that had followed the conflict of the previous decade was broken first in North America. There, in the early 1750s, wishing to establish a line of communication between their Canadian settlements and that in Louisiana, seeking access to the lucrative fur trade of the interior, and intending to hem the British in to their already settled areas on the eastern seaboard, the French began constructing a series of forts in the Great Lakes region and along the Ohio Valley. In July 1754, beginning the 'French and Indian War', George Washington led a force of Virginians against the French outposts. When this attack failed, the British government sent General Braddock with 800 regular soldiers and artillery to make another attempt in conjunction with the colonial militia. Learning of Braddock's despatch, the French in turn began assembling a force of 3000 troops for Canada. At this, the British placed the Navy on a war footing, and sent Admiral Boscawen with ten line-of-battle ships and a large frigate to intercept the French reinforcements off Louisbourg, the great fortress on Cape Breton Island that commanded the St Lawrence seaway. The French force sailed from Brest in early May; and when the British found that nineteen ships of the line and six frigates were carrying the troops, they sent another six ships of the line to reinforce Boscawen's squadron.

Boscawen did both too little and too much. Capturing only two of the French ships, he failed in his attempt to cripple the enemy's navy before hostilities were declared; and on the other hand, his attack made war inevitable. In July, the Admiralty ordered Sir Edward Hawke to cruise with a large squadron in the Bay of Biscay, across the routes to the northern French ports. Rather than mounting a general offensive against French shipping, Hawke was to capture only battleships, and bring these into port for the British to hold as 'securities' for the redress of French 'encroachments' in America. Hawke put to sea on 24 July. On 6 August, the ministry altered his orders so that these comprehended the taking of 'all French ships and vessels, as well men of war and privateers as merchantmen'. The nations were effectively at war.[2]

On 16 October 1755, just after his seventeenth birthday, Arthur Phillip joined the *Buckingham*, a 68-gun battleship, and one of Hawke's Western Squadron. Her captain was Michael Everitt; and Vice-Admiral Temple West sailed on her. These commanders had first come together more than twenty years earlier, when they had served on the *Dursley Galley*. Being one of the Temple–Grenville cousins, West had advanced a good deal more rapidly than Everitt, who was made post captain in 1747. He received the command of the *Buckingham* in February 1755, as the Navy prepared for war. It was customary for captains to have under their protection boys training to become officers; and Everitt was no exception, for he had on board his sons Robert and George, and West's sons Temple and Thomas.[3] In June, he asked the Admiralty for a schoolmaster to assist in the naval education of these 'Young Gentlemen'.[4] In October, he extended his patronage to his relative Arthur Phillip, for Phillip's entering his ship as a 'captain's servant' indicates that he became one of the group that Everitt was training.

Phillip joined the *Buckingham* at Plymouth, where West had brought the ships of his division at the end of September to have them cleaned.[5] They put to sea again on 7 November, with Admiral John Byng replacing Hawke in the overall command of the squadron. Five days later, the *Buckingham* captured a

French 74-gun ship of the line but, unable to 'keep her above Water', Everitt was forced to burn his prize; and he put into Plymouth with the French crew on 13 November. On 23 November, Phillip's rating was changed to 'Able Bodied', and on 31 December to 'Corporal', changes which indicate only that he was broadening his experience of a warship. After the usual winter confinement to port, the *Buckingham* sailed with the squadron again on 2 February 1756. Two weeks later, she was ordered into Spithead to be fitted for more distant service.

The British had for some time been receiving reports that the French were preparing a force at Toulon to send against Minorca. In March, to counter this threat, the Admiralty ordered Byng and West to take part of the squadron, together with troops and munitions, to the Mediterranean. With his ten ships of the line inadequately prepared and manned even after much delay, Byng sailed on 6 April, passing Cape St Vincent on 28 April after a rough passage down the Atlantic and reaching Gibraltar on 2 May. There, he and the land commanders learned that a French army of 15 000 had occupied all of Minorca except for Fort St Philip, into which the British garrison had retreated, and that the French squadron of twelve line-of-battle ships and some frigates was superior in condition, numbers of crew, and weight of guns.

With his squadron augmented by the small Mediterranean one, but also with his crews sickening, Byng sailed again on 8 May. That the health of the crews should be deteriorating only four weeks after they had left port reveals a number of circumstances about eighteenth-century naval service. Having been taken from naval hospitals, or by reason of drunkenness or disability having been unable to escape the press gangs, numbers of the crews were in poor health to begin with, and had entered the ships 'badly clothed and with no bedding'.[6] Naval food was often not such as to lead to any improvement in their health. The average ration was 2 pounds of salt beef and 1 pound of salt pork twice a week; 12 ounces of cheese and 8 ounces of butter a week, together with 2 pints of peas and 3 pints of oatmeal or flour; and 1 pound of ship's biscuit and 1 gallon of beer daily. A daily ration of spirits was added at sea.[7] All too often these foods were unwholesome. The salt meats might be mostly bone, fat, or gristle, or bad; the biscuit infested with weevils; the cheese and butter rancid. The supplements to this basic ration might be no better, as Hawke's complaint about one offering illustrates: 'The sugar is extremely black, coarse, and ready to run into molasses, and the fruit in general mouldy and so masked and clotted that it is scarce possible to determine the species it was of. The sago, or rather what was put up for it, full of dust and musty. The cinnamon very coarse and having neither spicy taste nor flavour... Instead of shallots and garlick ... there is in each box a few ounces of chocolate ...'[8]

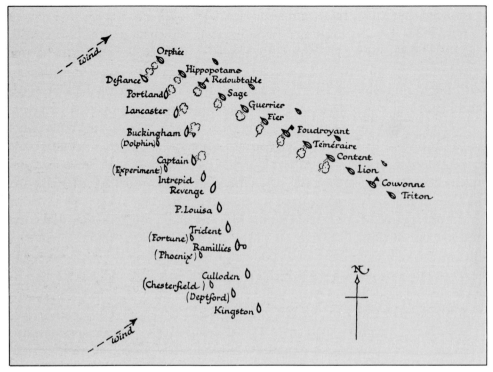

THE BATTLE OFF MINORCA (1756)

2.45 p.m.
The English van commences action, while the rearward ships, including Byng's *Ramilles*, are too far from the French line to engage.

The circumstances of labour in wet, cold, or unhygienic conditions, high intakes of salt, alcohol, and tobacco, and the absence of new supplies from fresh foods all combined to diminish the body's store of vitamins, which, in persons sick or pressed immediately on the conclusion of a voyage, was in any case likely to be depleted. Sailors were therefore easy prey to vitamin B deficiency-related diseases and especially to scurvy, the vitamin C deficiency-related one whose symptoms include dizziness, swelling of limbs and gums, haemorrhages, and loss of energy. In 1747 the naval surgeon James Lind conducted a controlled experiment which showed that orange and lemon juices were effective in the treatment of scurvy; and subsequently he came to perceive the importance of fresh vegetables and of hygiene, both personal and in cooking. While it was to be fifty years before the Royal Navy accepted that citrus juices were efficacious in the prevention and treatment of scurvy, captains and surgeons who followed Lind's general regimen for the maintenance of health at sea kept their crews in better condition than those who did not. This regimen included:

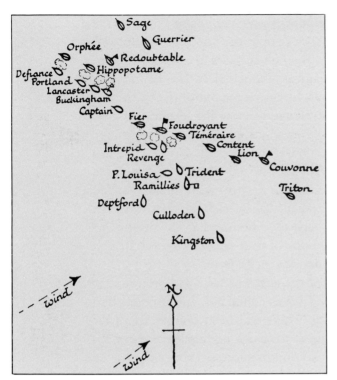

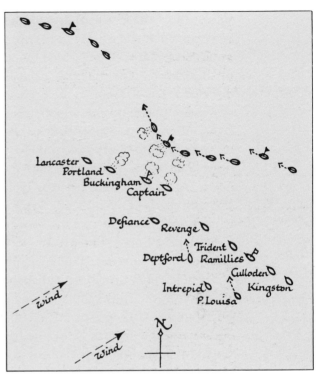

3.20 p.m. (frigates left out)
The English van has driven off the French one,
but the rearward ships are still distant.

4.50 p.m. (frigates left out)
The French centre and rear ships also break off
action, to rejoin their van.

personal hygiene (cold bathing, skin friction, exercise); ship hygiene (cleanliness, ventilation, fumigation); clean, warm, dry conditions (in clothes, hammocks, bedding, and generally in the ship); medical hygiene (large sick bay, the isolation of those with infectious diseases); distillation and purification of water; the baking of wheat bread and the growing of greens on board; bottled fruits and salted antiscorbutic vegetables; fresh meats and vegetables whenever possible; reduced spirits, with wine, cider, and fruit drinks instead; and oranges and lemons.

These measures were not widely followed in the ships of Byng's squadron, and it was accordingly weakened by illness by the time it arrived off Minorca on 19 May. The admiral's first move was to send Augustus Hervey in the *Phoenix* to assess the possibility of running into Port Mahon past the French forces besieging Fort St Philip, but before Hervey was able to make contact with the British garrison, the French warships appeared. The squadrons came together in the early afternoon of 20 May, with the leading British ships much closer to the

French line than the rearward ones; and the battle has been controversial ever since. The British van of five under Temple West's command engaged the enemy at once, and a fierce fight ensued. At one point, the *Buckingham* and two of her sister ships were opposed by nine of the French van and centre, with two of the British ships suffering extensive damage. Nonetheless, the British also inflicted severe damage on the French ships, forcing some out of the battle, but they were unable to press home their advantage because the leading ships of Byng's division took more than an hour to draw close enough to the French line to begin firing. Indeed, two of this division never joined in the battle at all, and others, including Byng's flagship *Ramilles*, did so only briefly. After three hours, when they were perhaps in a position to destroy the British van, the French surprisingly sailed off. Byng then persuaded his captains that it was of greater importance to take the squadron back to Gibraltar than to continue to try to relieve Fort St Philip; and, with its hope of help sailed away, the British garrison there surrendered after a gallant defence on 28 June.

On learning that Byng had abandoned the task which he had been sent to accomplish, the Admiralty superseded him in his command, and brought him home to face a charge of neglect of duty. There had been doubts about his enthusiasm for the task before he had sailed, to which he himself had contributed by pessimistic appraisals of the likelihood of success. From the time he reached Gibraltar, he had shown himself unable to act decisively; so that his failure lay not so much in the manner he had conducted himself in the battle, curious as this was, as in his reluctance to take all measures to relieve the Port Mahon garrison and drive the French from Minorca. It was unfortunate for him that, whereas the naval code said nothing about the failure to relieve castles, it clearly comprehended 'cowardice, negligence, or disaffection' in battle. With the administration of the day determined that he should suffer an exemplary punishment, the court martial rather reluctantly convicted him, under the twelfth Article of War, of neglect of duty. This conviction carried a mandatory death sentence; and Byng was shot on the quarterdeck of the *Monarch* in Portsmouth harbour on 14 March 1757.

The circumstances of the battle, the loss of Minorca, and Byng's court martial and sentence aroused great and opposing passions at the time. Byng had friends and supporters, but these lacked the political influence to save him. Like them, historians have tended to see the unhappy admiral as, even if excessively cautious and indecisive, principally the victim of political machinations. But just as time may lead to kinder judgements of men in their moments of weakness and failure, so too may it distort the quality of those moments; and it is now difficult to determine the most judicious balance of this one's conflicting elements. Certainly, for someone young and ardent, the view of Admiral Byng from the deck of the *Buckingham* in the heat of the battle off Minorca was unsympathetic in the extreme. Arthur Phillip was in no doubt as to the cause of the British squadron's not gaining a glorious victory over the French one and relieving the island. Describing the action to his sister, he wrote:

When Admiral Byng hoisted the Red Flagg a signal to Engage, We w.th our Division bore down to the Enemy, and with Six Ships engaged their Van, (as we led the Van) which He (ie., Admiral Byng) instead of doing the Same with the Rear, layed his Main Top-Sails aback, then all his Division was obliged to do the like.

The French began fireing at us, Some time before we fired at them, as their aim was to engage at a distance, and ours to engage them as close as we could. But when we began, we played upon [them] very briskly, and Soon drove the 4.th and 5.th Ships out of the line & Raked them fore & aft as they went. One of them was their Rear Admiral, whose Stern was Shattered very much, & by this time our Van had a very great advantage over theirs, which we was hinder'd from making use of, by their Rear coming up. For all this time Admiral Byng lay with his Top Sails aback, and only fired now & then, & that at too great a distance to doe, or Receive any damage. But we gave them So brisk a fire that they declined coming to a close engagem.t tho' they had it in their power; So they filled their Sails and edged away to the rest of the Fleet, who altogether Stood towards the Island of Minorca, and Soon after we tacked, and lay too.

We received but very little damage considering what a hot Fire we was exposed to,... But then we can give very good reasons for it, every man in our Fleet burned with the greatest ardour imaginable, and theirs by their behaviour i.e. the French with a great dastardness, for their not coming to a close engagem.t when they had Such Odds as their Whole Fleet against our [Division]. Plainly Shewed that most of them had rather Run than Fight. And it is very certain, that their fear kept them from taking proper Aim, which Saved Us a great many Men, as well as our Masts and Rigging. I need not mention the great Courage & conduct of our Admiral [ie. West] and Captains Shewed that Day in our Division, nor the Cowardice of the Only person Admiral Byng, that kept the French Fleet from being Distroyed, and the Island from being relieved. For no doubt all England will Soon be convinced of the merit of Admiral West, and the downright Cowardice of Admiral Byng.9

The squadron returned to Gibraltar on 20 June, where Byng was superseded by Sir Edward Hawke, and sent home. On 3 July, Michael Everitt was also superseded and, with other captains, ordered home to give evidence at the coming court martial. Upon this, Phillip transferred to the *Princess Louisa*, a 60-gun ship of the line, for three days as an able bodied seaman, thereafter as a captain's clerk. With Britain and France having formally declared war on 28 May, and with the conflict soon to involve other European nations, the squadron sailed again on 10 July. For the next three months, it cruised the western Mediterranean, from time to time giving chase to suspicious ships, but seeing no real action. After a week's respite at Gibraltar in early October, it passed the Straits, and cruised off Cape St Vincent and Cádiz until 20 November, when it returned to Gibraltar.[10] Phillip then transferred as able bodied seaman to the *Ramilles*, which was returning to England. She sailed on 9 December, and after a passage made noteworthy only by the meeting with the returning East India fleet at the entrance to the Channel, she anchored at Spithead on 14 January 1757.[11]

Phillip left the *Ramilles* on 2 February. The next day, he entered the *Neptune*, the 98-gun battleship to which Temple West and Michael Everitt had gone the previous November. Not only did he thereby regain the company of his cousins and the young Wests, with whom he had shared the danger and excitement off Minorca, he also benefited from the renewal of Everitt's patronage, for he entered in the capacity of midshipman, that first rung on the ladder of officer rank. As midshipman, he was occupied with details of the running of the ship, and supervised the men at their various tasks. His wage was £2 5s per month. If he was pleased by this promotion, though, he could scarcely have been satisfied with the service he saw on the *Neptune*. The ship left Portsmouth harbour only for Spithead, where she remained idle into July. The only notable circumstance during these months was the untoward weather in the first days of April, when 'Gales with Snow' swept over the ship.[12]

On 14 July 1757, Phillip was discharged from the *Neptune* as 'unserviceable'. This notation presumably indicates the onset of one of the bouts of ill health that he was henceforth to endure repeatedly. How long this one lasted is unclear, for it is not possible to trace his movements precisely for the next twenty-two months, until he again appears in the Navy's musterbooks. It may be that the duration of the illness was not as great as this gap in the records indicates, and that Phillip was at sea in a private capacity for part of this time. A nineteenth-century source states that he was on the *Union* while Michael Everitt commanded it between August 1757 and November 1758. His name does not appear in the ship's musterbooks, but, given his link with Everitt, it is possible that he may have been among the captain's personal 'followers'. A 90-gun battleship, the *Union* was one of the Western Squadron. She made a series of cruises across 1758, including a most arduous winter one, interspersed with periods of refitting at Plymouth and Portsmouth, without seeing any action of consequence. As Everitt left her at the end of November 1758, it can be assumed that any period Phillip spent aboard her also ended at this time.[13]

Phillip next appears definitely in mid-1759, when he was listed among the *Jason*'s supernumeraries from 26 May to 16 June as belonging to 'no ship'.[14] On 17 June, he entered the *Aurora*, a 36-gun frigate, at Spithead, in the capacity of midshipman. On 2 July, this sailed as one of the escort to thirty-nine merchantmen and supply ships destined for Gibraltar. In an uneventful passage, the ships passed Cape St Vincent on 21 July, and reached their destination four days later. On 1 August, the *Aurora* sailed with a return fleet of thirty-six merchant-men and, after another uneventful passage, reached Spithead again on 10 September. From 1 October, she cruised with the Channel squadron. She was off Flushing, on the Dutch coast, from 16 to 21 October, in the Downs to 28 November, then off Calais from 1 to 5 December. She next retired to the Downs, staying until 17 December when she shifted to Sheerness. The service was of that difficulty usual at the edge of winter, but otherwise unremarkable. On 31 January 1760, the *Aurora* moved out to the Nore, where Phillip left her on 18 February.[15]

By the end of 1759 the positions which Arthur Phillip had held in the Royal Navy, of captain's servant, corporal, able bodied seaman, and captain's clerk had given him much practical experience of a large warship's operation. While in these positions, and more particularly while serving later as a midship-man, he had learned to draw coastal profiles, how to calculate latitude and longitude from solar and astronomical observation, the intricacies of navigation in a great variety of oceanic and atmospheric conditions, and techniques of battle. He had also begun to learn the rhythm of naval operations about Europe, which arose conjointly from warships' need of bases and supplies, the conditions prevailing in the different seasons, and the more general strategic need to balance prospects of harming the enemy against those of meeting reverses that would leave vulnerable one's own national endeavour. The European navies cruised out of the ports about the English Channel in winter only in urgent circumstances, for otherwise the small deterrent benefit obtained did not outweigh the wear to the ships. The British squadrons operating about the Iberian peninsula and in the Mediterranean might hinder France's and Spain's war efforts by blockading squadrons in Toulon or Cartagena or Cádiz harbours, or by defeating them at sea: but if they themselves were beaten, then Gibraltar and the naval control of the Mediterranean, and Britain's valuable trade with Portugal and India, were imperilled. Such knowledge was essential to someone setting himself on a career in the Royal Navy. As Europe was but part of the world in which the Navy operated, Phillip still had much necessary learning before him before he might become a fully competent officer.

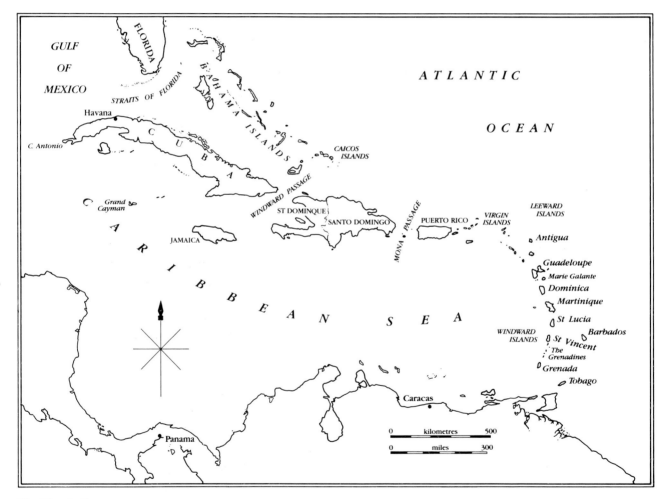

The West Indies

The Seven Years War: West Indies, 1760–63

The Spaniards judg'd the Moro's fort the Briton's strength would banter,
But when we blew it up i' the air, they tuned another chanter.
Bold Harvey with three noble ships their walls by sea did batter,
While we bombarded it on land, and did their out-works clatter.

But never was heard such woful thuds as the *Cambridge* and *Marlborough*
  [did give 'em]
The *Dragon* fired as brisk as they, but for smoak none could perceive them.
The *Cambridge* got her captain shot, and a hundred more beside him,
Brave Harvey then his station quit, for five long hours he try'd them.

'A New Song on the Taking of Havannah'

It was again to join his fortune to Michael Everitt's, and to see more distant service, that Phillip quitted the *Aurora*. On 19 February 1760, he entered the *Stirling Castle*, to which Everitt had moved fourteen months before. As it was customary for ships to carry more than their complement of midshipmen by recording some in other positions, Phillip's entering in the capacity of able bodied seaman does not indicate a demotion.[1] Phillip joined his new ship at Spithead, but she immediately shifted to Woolwich, where for the next four months she was fitted for service in the West Indies.[2] This fitting out then continued at Spithead until 6 September, when the *Stirling Castle* sailed in convoy. She passed Madeira, that island of legendary wines that basks like a siren in the warm Atlantic, on 1 October, and on 25 October reached Antigua, where the Leeward Island squadron was based. The only notable occurrence on the voyage was the capture of a small French brig on 12 October.

The British Navy pursued a twofold endeavour in the West Indies at this time, the first of which was the protection of the nation's trade. From the lush tropical islands planters sent large quantities of sugar and its derivative rum to North America and England, and smaller quantities of cotton, coffee, pimento, ginger, drugs, and mahogany. To them came American flour and timber, British manufactures and Portuguese wines, and large numbers of African slaves. French privateers, based principally on Martinique, were as eager to plunder the small ships that carried this trade between the islands as were French squadrons to raid the great convoys that bore it to and from Europe.

The second aim was to further the nation's general war effort. Her sea separation from the European mainland had from early times led Britain to emphasize naval development; and in the first decades of the eighteenth century, with her colonial empire expanding and her overseas trade of ever-increasing importance to her economy, those who directed her affairs began to follow a policy of gaining control of the sea as the central plank of her warfare. In the Seven Years War, William Pitt (later Earl of Chatham) developed this policy into a distinctive strategy of subsidizing allies to engage enemies on the continent, while British squadrons destroyed these enemies' navies and plundered their trade, and British expeditions moved against their colonies.[3] In July 1758, British forces captured Louisbourg which, together with Quebec, taken in September 1759, gave them command of Canada. Anxious to retain this domain, and as well to regain Minorca, the British sought to capture France's West Indian islands, as counters to bargain in negotiations for peace. British forces took Guadeloupe in the spring of 1759, but an attempt on Martinique, the richest of the French sugar islands, failed.

Avoiding the last of the hurricane season, the *Stirling Castle* stayed in St John's Road, Antigua, until 5 December 1760, when she began patrols. For the next four weeks, she cruised south of Guadeloupe, among the Windward Islands of Dominica, Martinique, St Lucia, Barbados, St Vincent, and Grenada. Of volcanic origin, and constituting part of the group known as the Lesser Antilles which arcs for 800 kilometres between the Atlantic Ocean and the Caribbean Sea, these small islands display a common configuration of central ranges (then heavily forested), valleys through which flow rapid streams, coastal plains, beaches of white sand, coral and shell, and lagoons bounded by reefs.

To Europeans, these islands were another world. There were no seasons as the northerners knew them, and no cold. The brooding greens of the tropical vegetation filled the whole year; and only the trade winds prevailing from the north and east made the days tolerable. Only the burgeoning of such richly flowered shrubs and trees as frangipani, poinciana, and jacaranda, and the onset between June and October or November of the prodigious rains with their attendant hurricanes, distinguished one period from another. On these emeralds set in a sapphire sea, nature of her bounty offered such Old World fruits as oranges, lemons, and citrons, and such exotic New World ones as pineapples, bananas, custard apples, guavas, coconuts, and melons. Bright parrots and the

Richard Wilson, 'Captain Michael Everitt'
(c. 1747–48)

Richard Paton, 'The Naval Bombardment of El
Morro Castle, 1 July [1762]'

George James, 'Lieutenant
Arthur Phillip' (1764)

George James, 'Charlott Phillip'
(1764)

startling macaw lit the forests. Planters worked their slaves to produce the sugar for which Europe hungered, and such other desirable commodities as coffee, cotton, and indigo; and they raised horses, cattle, pigs, and a multitude of fowls.

With nothing to show for her work but battering from rough weather, the *Stirling Castle* returned to Antigua again on 10 January 1761, this time to English Harbour, where she remained for the next six weeks. She began another cruise on 1 March, spending some days in Carlisle Bay, Barbados, at the beginning of April, capturing a small French prize on 15 April, passing a week in Prince Rupert's Bay, Dominica, then sailing off Guadeloupe in May, and Puerto Rico in July. She continued to cruise in this fashion until early August, when, with the onset of the hurricane season, she returned to English Harbour. Though there was little to show for the cruise, Phillip would have been pleased with one circumstance, for on 7 June Sir James Douglas, the commodore of the Leeward Island station, appointed him fourth lieutenant of the ship. With this promotion he came to share the responsibility for keeping watches, supervising practice with arms, and navigating the ship.[4]

After two months' respite, the *Stirling Castle* resumed cruising on 8 October.[5] On 25 November, she joined Douglas' squadron, which united with that under Admiral George Rodney at Carlisle Bay on 21 December. Rodney had come from England with orders to capture Martinique and other of the French islands. Lying midway between Barbados and Guadeloupe, Martinique is 100 kilometres long and 50 at its widest, and its coastline is indented with a large number of creeks and harbours. It has the formation and relief common to the others; and its planters then produced sugar, indigo, coffee, cotton, ginger, and pimento. The surrounding waters abounded with fish and turtles. Its population consisted of 10 000 whites and 40 000 slaves. Its principal towns were St Pierre and Fort Royal, which was the seat of French administration in the Caribbean, and whose harbour offered good protection.

After a fortnight of unseasonable rain, Rodney sailed with a combined squadron of eighteen line-of-battle ships and 120 support vessels carrying 12 000 soldiers to begin his task. Part of this massive force, the *Stirling Castle* anchored in St Anne's Bay on the southern tip of the island on 8 January 1762. On 11 January she bombarded the batteries at Grand Anse d'Arle Bay, to the south of Fort Royal Bay. Ten days later, she joined in the disembarking of the army at Cas Navire Bay, just to the north of Fort Royal Bay, returning to St Anne's Bay on 3 February. The British forces took the Fort Royal settlement between 4 and 7 February, and the French governor surrendered the island one week later. Rodney then moved against St Lucia, St Vincent, and Grenada, but the *Stirling Castle* did not participate in these smaller operations. Instead, on 9

February, she resumed cruising among the Windward and Leeward Islands. Late in March, so as to return to England, Michael Everitt gave up her command, and was succeeded by Captain James Campbell.

Phillip elected to stay with the *Stirling Castle*, and consequently was soon participating in the siege and capture of Havana. Located on the northwestern coast of Cuba, Havana was built around a good harbour, which the Spanish had fortified very strongly. It was the link between metropolitan Spain and her American colonies, and through it passed the riches of the New World and the manufactures of the Old. The British decision to move against this hub of the Spanish empire followed on Spain's making a secret alliance with France at the end of 1761 and on Britain's consequent declaration of war on 2 January 1762. On 6 January, deciding to pursue against Spain the naval and colonial strategy that was proving so successful against France, the British ministry resolved to send expeditions against Havana, Louisiana, and Manila. Across January into February, authorities gathered forces from Europe, North America, and the West Indies for the assault on Havana. Lord Albemarle received the command of the 16 000 troops; and Sir George Pocock that of the naval forces, with Augustus Keppel his second-in-command. Cabinet ordered the generals and governors in North America and the West Indies to supply additional personnel including blacks used to labouring in the climate, and Rodney and Douglas to send ships from their squadrons.

On receiving details of the expedition, Douglas sent eleven ships, including the *Stirling Castle*, under the command of Augustus Hervey, to blockade the French squadron of fourteen ships at Cap François on St Domingue (now Haiti), so as to prevent it from either attacking Jamaica or reinforcing the Spanish at Havana. In mid-May, having done its work well, Hervey's division joined the main force off Cap St Nicolas, and then proceeded west along the northern coast of Cuba. As it was usual for ships to approach Havana from the west, the British arrival from the east on 6 June took the Spanish by surprise.

Although by these moves the British succeeded in confining the powerful Spanish squadron to Havana harbour and in preventing the authorities there from gathering reinforcements from about the Americas, formidable obstacles remained to be overcome before the city might be taken. The natural features of the site and the position and design of the fortifications meant that they could not surround the town immediately. To capture it, they had first to capture the fort of El Morro, which guarded the eastern approach to the harbour. Built above high cliffs, El Morro was a prospect to daunt even the hardiest would-be conqueror. Its walls were metres thick, and in the rock around it the Spanish had cut a 10-metre deep trench. The fort had its own supply of water, and the

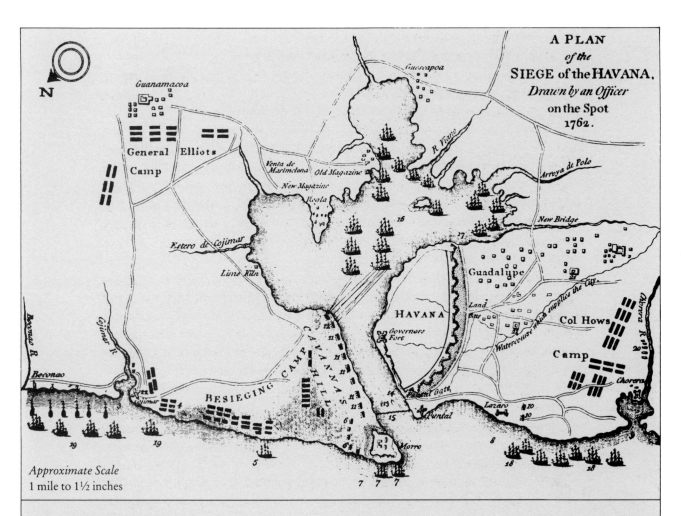

A PLAN
of the
SIEGE of the HAVANA,
Drawn by an Officer
on the Spot
1762.

Approximate Scale
1 mile to 1½ inches

LEGEND

1. Place where the troops landed 7 June.
2. March of the Army after landing.
3. The *Dragon* against Coximar.
4. Where the Army first encamped.
5. Where the cannon &c. were landed.
6. Batteries against El Morro.
7. The *Dragon*, *Cambridge* and *Marlborough* against El Morro.
8. The bombs against La Punta.
9. *Belleisle* against Chorea fort.
10. Batteries against La Punta.
11. Batteries against the La Cabaña.
12. Howitzers against the shipping.
13. Three Spanish men-of-war sunk.
14. One Company's ship overset.
15. The chain and boom.
16. Spanish Admiral and Fleet.
17. Two ships on the stocks.
18. Admiral Pocock, with the men-of-war and transports.
19. Commodore Keppel, with ditto.
20. Camp at the watermills.
21. Fortified houses.
22. Headquarters.

The Siege of Havana (1762)

authorities in the town rotated the garrison every four days, in order to keep it at full strength.

The British were soon able to capture the high ground to the east and south of El Morro, which they needed to control in order to besiege the fort, but its reduction proved an extremely difficult task. The army had to haul the siege guns from the landing at Coximar River, about 7 kilometres away, and, as the high ground offered no water, so too did this essential article have to be carried up. The Jamaican authorities had found very few blacks willing to enlist, and fewer planters willing to lend their slaves, so that these arduous tasks fell to the regular soldiers. Unused to the heat, with strictly limited rations of food and water, these quickly became enervated, and then sickened; and the commanders had to turn to the Navy for help. Phillip recorded in his journal for 21 June, that the *Stirling Castle* 'sent ashore a Lieut. and 40 men to hawl Cannon', and his entries for 24, 25, and 26 June are similar.

The work of reducing El Morro proceeded slowly through June. The sites chosen for the siege guns by Jacques Funck's engineers were on bare rock, and were open to fire from the fort, from Havana's batteries, and from the Spanish warships in the harbour; and as the ravages of the work, climate, and yellow fever became every day more apparent, the capture of the fort became increasingly urgent. At the end of the month, Augustus Hervey obtained permission from the commodores to try his idea of bombarding it from the sea. With the land batteries opening a distracting fire at dawn, on 1 July Hervey in the *Dragon* led the *Cambridge*, *Marlborough*, and *Stirling Castle* along the cliffs towards El Morro, his plan being for the *Stirling Castle* to pass it first so as to draw its fire while the other ships positioned themselves under its walls, and then to return to support the others in the bombardment. The attack went badly from the start. The *Stirling Castle* failed to perform her part; and the other ships were unable to raise their guns enough to bear on the fort's walls, so that their shot fell harmlessly against the cliff. In the middle of the action, the *Dragon* grounded, and became an easy target for the Spanish gunners. While the British ships thus did only very slight damage to the fort, the Spanish severely injured them in their masts, spars, and rigging. The captain of the *Cambridge* was killed, and there were many casualties amongst the crews. After three hours, Keppel ordered the ships to withdraw.[6]

Severe as the damage to the ships was, that to naval honour was greater. By unloading many of his lesser spars and sails before the action, and by keeping his main and sprit sails furled, Campbell had ensured that, instead of leading the attack, the *Stirling Castle* fell much behind the other ships. On this, the incensed Hervey had first ordered him repeatedly to take up his allotted position.

Then, with the *Dragon* aground and under heavy fire, Hervey had sent Captain Lindsay of the *Trent* to order Campbell to help free her. Instead of obeying this order, Campbell had sailed past the attacking ships to a safe distance, and merely sent a boat with a light anchor to assist Hervey. And when Hervey had then ordered him to take the disabled *Cambridge* in tow, Campbell had instead come on board the *Dragon*. So, for a second time, Arthur Phillip found himself involved in a dangerous action where a superior brought disrepute upon himself by strange, not to say cowardly, behaviour. We do not know his private feelings, but these could hardly have been different from those he had earlier had towards Byng, or those implied in Hervey's bitter comment to Keppel that the *Stirling Castle*'s officers would 'represent' their captain's behaviour more than adequately.[7] There is no record of these officers' testimony to the court martial presided over by Hervey, but as Campbell was dismissed from the service, their representations must have been damning.[8]

While Hervey's attack failed to damage El Morro, it did cause the Spanish there to shift guns from the landward bastions. This enabled the British siege batteries to gain an advantage, and dismount all but two of the Spanish guns opposing them. In the next days, the British tried desperately to press this advantage home, but in the searing heat unrelieved by rain, the army wilted. Pocock wrote how 'Soldiers and Seamen fall down in great Numbers by Sickness in this very unhealthy Season',[9] but this general description does not adequately convey a sense of the agony. An officer recorded how 'the fatigues on shore were excessive, the bad water brought on disorders, which were mortal, you would see the men's tongues, hanging out parched like a mad dog's, a dollar was frequently given for a quart of water; in short by dead, wounded, and sick the army were reduced'.[10]

In this extremity, the commanders looked further to the Navy, drawing cannon from the ships for additional batteries, and seamen to man them. On 8 July, Keppel sent some 24-pounders from the *Stirling Castle*; and he recorded in his journal the next day: 'Moderate and cloudy weather. The sea detachment employed in assisting to raise new batteries and in carrying up to them cannon, ammunition, and stores. The ships' companies as well as the troops begin to fall sick very fast. Vessels continually employed supplying the army with water from the Chorera, and their want of that article is frequently so pressing that we are obliged to land water from the ships.'[11] Eight days later, Pocock reported to the Admiralty that 'the seamen have performed extremely well at the batteries. They have managed one of four 32-pounders for some days, and another of the same number of guns opened this day. They have been commanded by the Captains Lindsay and Douglas and lieutenants of the men-of-war'.[12]

Phillip's work continued to be of this sort until 30 July when, reinforced by 3000 troops newly arrived from North America, the army stormed and over-ran El Morro. From it, they then bombarded Havana until the governor surrendered the city on 13 August. It was a rich conquest. The value of the various prizes amounted to £770 000; and the ten line-of-battle ships and twelve frigates in the harbour constituted a fifth of the Spanish navy. But it was also a conquest gained at great cost. By mid-August, 5000 British soldiers and 3000 sailors were sick or dead. The mortality rose sharply with the onset of the wet season. By mid-October, 5400 soldiers were dead, and thousands more ill; 800 sailors and 500 marines were dead, and another 3000 ill; and hundreds of these sick were subsequently to die. To carry on to Louisiana was clearly out of the question.

Knowing this, the British commanders moved to repatriate their forces as quickly as possible. This was again no easy matter, for the service had told greatly on the ships, with many being in need of repair before they might make an ocean crossing. The *Stirling Castle* was so decrepit that she could only with difficulty be kept afloat during the unloading of her stores and provisions; and after a survey showed her to be 'so bad that it was quite impracticable to repair her without a dock so as to be safe to proceed to sea', Pocock ordered that she be sunk in the harbour.[13] He transferred her company to the *Infanta*, one of the ships taken with the town. This was a new 70-gun line-of-battle ship in good condition; and the Admiralty subsequently endorsed Pocock's action by buying her for the Navy.

Phillip was on board the *Infanta* from 15 September 1762. After six weeks of preparation, she sailed in convoy for England on 3 November. She had a rough passage, losing her main and mizzen masts in a hurricane on 11 November, and running through Atlantic storms. After sheltering on the Irish coast from 4 January to 28 February 1763, she reached Spithead on 11 March, and moved into Portsmouth Harbour three days later. The Navy Board confirmed Phillip's appointment as lieutenant on 24 March and, the nations having concluded the Peace of Paris the previous month, he ceased active service one month later, when the *Infanta*'s crew was paid off.[14]

There are no documents which provide any assessment by Phillip of the importance of his West Indian experience, but there are hints which point to its having been central in his development as an officer and a man. Its relevance to his emergence as an officer is the more readily apparent. It was in the Caribbean that he received his first important appointment, as fourth lieutenant of a man-of-war. In this capacity, he began to have a substantial hand in the management of a large ship. Not only did he therefore help to direct its daily functioning and navigation, he also came to know how it might be well, or badly, equipped for operations in a distant theatre, where conditions were very different from those in Europe. In the warm waters ships quickly grew foul as barnacles and sea-weeds sprouted from their bottoms, and were much slower in their sailing and much more difficult to steer. The marine borer known as the Teredo 'worm' ate into their planks, reducing their soundness. Hurricanes shattered their masts, spars, rigging, and sails, and strained their hulls. Captains were able to have some of these effects repaired in the substantial dockyards at Antigua and Jamaica; but few ships were able to stay in the West Indies for more than a year without their efficiency being severely impaired. Sometimes, as in the case of the *Stirling Castle*, extended service on the station left a ship so decrepit that she was no longer capable of making the ocean return to Europe.

The islands were also notoriously unhealthy. Because captains were able to obtain fresh foods for their crews, scurvy was not here the problem it was elsewhere. Much greater scourges were typhus fever, spread by the lice-ridden rats that infested the ships; and, especially, malaria and yellow fever, trans-mitted by mosquitos. In the infant state of medical science, it was known that quinine ('Peruvian bark') was effective against malaria; but the most doctors could do to combat yellow fever was to regularize diet and enforce cleanliness, and trust to the patient's natural resilience. Often, as the island's extensive cemeteries showed, in bodies exhausted by a lifetime of privation or by un-accustomed labour in the tropical heat, the benefit of quinine came too late, and natural resilience was quite inadequate. Still, the application of Lind's principles offered a general regimen for the maintenance of health at sea; and Phillip's later actions show that the West Indies taught him something of the need.

It was as lieutenant, too, that Phillip first began to exercise a real authority over men. To obtain a co-operative effort from a group of persons very different in temperament, sensibility, education and privilege is a complex business, one always liable to the impediments raised by clashes of opposing wills. The Royal Navy obtained the cohesion necessary to operate its ships by the exercise of a rigid, not to say barbarous, code of discipline. The boyish midshipmen were permitted to beat men, some of them decades their seniors in age, so as to obtain greater effort from them. Drunkenness, failure to obey orders, dereliction of duty, desertion, and deviant sexuality were punishable by flogging, to varying degrees of severity according to the extent of the offence and the dispositions of the captain and the officers who formed courts martial. The punishment for a recalcitrant sailor's striking an officer, or for outright mutiny, was death.

The litany of offences recorded by Phillip in 1761–62 shows that the *Stirling Castle* was no different from most other Navy ships, having on board the usual complement of difficult and unsavoury characters. And Michael Everitt's punishments were frequent and severe. On 14 August 1761, John Tead received 200 lashes, John Green 400 lashes, and Samuel Price was hanged, all for desertion. These punishments not having the salutary effect desired, on 27 August Thomas Riley was sentenced to 600 lashes for desertion, receiving half the next day, and the second lot on 3 September. On 9 February 1762, when the work at Martinique had made the crew fractious, Everitt again dispensed heavy punishments for drunkenness, neglect of duty and, in one case, suspected sodomy.

As lieutenant, Phillip noted offences and oversaw punishments; and perhaps his family connection with Everitt allowed him to obtain an intimate insight into the captain's reasons for punishing as he did. Since a brutal captain might drive his crew to rebellion, as Captain Pigot of the *Hermione* did in 1797, an important part of the maintenance of discipline was to know when not to punish further, and sometimes, when not to punish at all. Phillip's later actions show that while he certainly knew when to be strict, he also knew when not to punish as legally he might have done. How to keep the precarious balance between exemplary justice and understanding mercy, and thereby obtain a communal effort, was one of the most important lessons that he ever learned. He began discernibly to do so in the West Indies.

There, too, Phillip came to understand that illness, climate, and lack of food and water placed limits on physical endeavour. Particularly was this true on the bare ground about El Morro, where the labour of the soldiers and sailors was constrained more by heat, thirst, and yellow fever than by the depredations of the enemy; and where the commanders had to tailor their expectations according to the men's diminishing ability to work. Again, Phillip's later actions show that he learned this point well.

Phillip's time in the West Indies is also significant for its bringing him into proximity with Augustus Hervey. The relationship between the two is tantalizing in its obscurity. Their paths crossed repeatedly in the Seven Years War—off Minorca; in the Channel and the Bay of Biscay; at Martinique and Cap François. But unless there was some private connection between them that is now lost to sight, it is unlikely that they would have had anything to do with each other. Hervey sailed as the scion of that noble and influential family, the Earls of Bristol, Phillip as a poor boy from inner London via the Charity School at Greenwich Hospital; and they were never to be on the one ship together. Yet ten years later, Hervey was to become Phillip's patron, commending him in such terms as to indicate a developed sense of his worth. What seems most likely is that the great man was impressed by the lieutenant's conduct at the siege and during the bombardment of El Morro, and remembered his merit.

In the West Indies, too, Phillip saw for the first time how European colonization might flourish, and what benefits it might bring to the metropolitan power. The English settlements of Antigua, Barbados, and Jamaica, the French ones of Guadeloupe, Martinique, and St Domingue, and the Spanish one of Cuba were impressive endeavours, involving the successful establishment of branches of the home culture in an exotic environment. Though many of the colonists were vulgar in their personalities and brutal in their treatment of others, the towns they raised were substantial, and the wealth they produced on their plantations considerable. By the 1750s, Britain's trade with her colonies in the Americas constituted a third of her whole trade; and in 1756, the merchants of Nantes considered the West Indian trade to be the keystone of France's entire economy.

By the time he left the lavish islands, though, Phillip had come to see that behind their gleaming skin lurked a gruesome skull. The Europeans had raised their colonies on an odious base. Quickly finding that the Caribs made unsatisfactory workers, the first planters had substituted black slaves from West Africa. Transported across the Atlantic in appalling conditions, inadequately fed, brutally worked, and arbitrarily flogged, dislocated in their family and cultural life and sexually abused by their masters, the Africans lived an average of seven years on a sugar island, and their fertility was much diminished. Perpetuating cycles of exploitation and misery, British, French, and Dutch slave traders were bringing tens of thousands of replacements each year by the middle of the eighteenth century.

This evil commerce and the lot of the slaves made an abiding impression on Phillip. Twenty-five years later, when about the business of founding a colony, and conscious of Lord Mansfield's historic judgement abolishing the holding of slaves in England, he commented that 'there can be no Slavery in a Free Land—& consequently no Slaves'.[15] In saying this, he implicitly condemned those of his countrymen who cheerfully claimed the benefits of English freedom and yet in distant colonies deprived others utterly of their liberty.

Arthur Phillip ended the Seven Years War much richer in experience than he began it. Learning principles of navigation and modes of warfare, and surviving battle, across these years he opened the career he desired in the Royal Navy. Laying the basis of some of his most significant mature perceptions as he grew into his manhood, he also enlarged his imagination. He gained these benefits at some cost. The rigours he endured between 1753 and 1763 certainly impaired his health. Perhaps service at sea stunted his personal development in one particular, too, for while his emotional life remains largely a blank, it seems that he was incapable of romantic love of women. This is not to hint at any homosexual leaning, of which there is not the slightest evidence.[16] But it may be that through circumstance he came to find whatever need he had of companionship or intimacy satisfied by shipboard relations of an asexual nature. And if not, he must by this time have already begun the habit that marks his maturity, of guarding his inner self closely. Though there is much that is impossible to know, by 1763, when he was twenty-four, Phillip's mature personality must already have been substantially shaped.

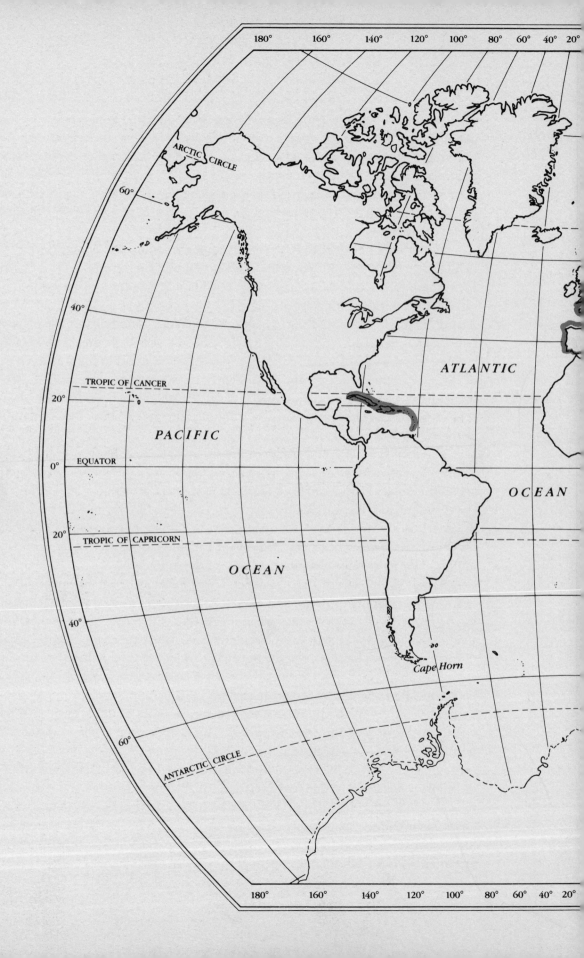

0° 20° 40° 60° 80° 100° 120° 140° 160° 180°

60°

40°

North Cape

20°

0°

INDIAN

20°

OCEAN

Cape of Good Hope

40°

South Cape

60°

0° 20° 40° 60° 80° 100° 120° 140° 160° 180°

PEACETIME PURSUITS: LONDON, NEW FOREST, FRANCE, 1763–74

Peace, with its blessings, was restored in 1763. And Phillip now found leisure to marry; and to settle at Lyndhurst, in the New Forest, where he amused himself with farming, and like other country gentlemen, discharged assiduously those provincial offices, which, however unimportant, occupy respectably the owners of land, who, in this island, require no office to make them important.

Anecdotes of Governor Phillip

Navy officials confirmed Arthur Phillip's appointment to the fourth lieutenancy of the *Stirling Castle* on 24 March 1763, and entered his name in the Half Pay register from 25 April.[1] As a junior lieutenant he was eligible for two shillings per day, so that at this time Phillip received approximately fourteen shillings per week for having proved his competence in the business of war at sea. To this small regular income, he was initially able to add £130—a lieutenant's share of the squadron's half of the enormous prize (£385 000) arising from the capture of Havana.[2]

These less than handsome means were quite insufficient for a young man eager to make his way in the world and to establish himself as a gentleman; and with the European nations temporarily weary of war, Phillip could not hope to do so quickly via his profession. Showing what was to become a habitual ingenuity, he soon found another way. On 19 July 1763, in St Augustine's Church, Watling Street, around the corner from the street where he had been born, aged twenty-four, he married Charlott Denison. Mrs Phillip had been born Margaret Charlott Tybott, the daughter of a farming family in the northern Wales county of Montgomery, in 1722. In August 1759 she had married John Denison, a prosperous cloth and wine merchant of King Street, Cheapside, who also owned property in Lambeth, and farming lands in Dorset. On her husband's death early in the next year, she inherited his considerable estate, which included £120 000 placed in trust for her at the Bank of England, and thus became a widow rich enough to attract a young man more interested in prosperity than in passion. What may have attracted Charlott Denison to Arthur Phillip is a matter only for speculation, for it is one of the mysteries of Phillip's life that not one letter between them, or between him and members of her family, seems to have survived. Contemporary portraits of the pair show a pudgy and rather dour young man, and a handsome woman of simple yet elegant taste. At forty-one, she was probably past conceiving. In any case, the couple seem not to have had children. She was not naive where money and property were concerned. In a rather unusual step for the time, before she married she concluded an indenture of release and settlement with Phillip, whereby he gave up any claim to the farming lands in Dorset, and any control of the trust fund.[3]

Where the Phillips lived, and in what manner, is uncertain. If they remained in London for any time, they presumably did the fashionable things, such as frequent the theatre or stroll in St James's Park. Bordered by the striking avenues of Pall Mall and the Birdcage Walk, this park was then a favourite resort for society, where the brilliant might display themselves, the less brilliant gawk or bristle with envy, and the thirsty refresh themselves with mugs of warm milk taken immediately from the cows that, grazing quietly, provided a note of 'rural simplicity'. At some time early in their marriage, though, the Phillips seem to have set themselves up at Hampton Court, on the banks of the Thames about 24 kilometres southwest of the city, where Henry VIII's palace stands. Then noted for its parks and gardens, the area attracted the rich; and the Phillips seem to have lived there in some style, creating a household which exhibited such trappings of wealth as silver plate and carriages. What Arthur Phillip worked at—if anything—in these years is uncertain. Given John Denison's connection with the wine and linen trades, and Phillip's own later interest in them, it is reasonable to think that he may now have begun to participate in the trade to Portugal and Spain, either as a minor entrepreneur using some of his wife's money, or as the master of a ship sailing on behalf of his wife or of his friends the Lanes, merchants exporting to and importing from North America,[4] or others.

After two years of living near London, the Phillips were eager for change. Charlott, according to one source, was a lover of country life;[5] and the idea of becoming a country gentleman no doubt held its attraction for Arthur. For personal or business reasons, he may also have found it convenient to locate himself closer to Portsmouth, where Michael Everitt had his home. Whatever the cause, the Phillips went to live at Lyndhurst in the New Forest. The time of their arrival and the duration of their stay are both uncertain. Phillip was appointed one of the parish's Overseers of the Poor on 5 April 1766, but in April 1768 he obtained permission to pay another to do his duty; and he was replaced permanently by the end of July. These and the circumstances described hereafter suggest that they arrived some time prior to 1766, perhaps in the autumn of 1765, and that he, at least, had left by the spring of 1768.[6]

The farm which the couple took up, still known as 'Vernals', lies on the southern edge of the town. No contemporary description is easily to be found, but as there is unlikely to have been much change to its boundaries in the intervening time, one can assume that the mid-nineteenth-century tithe survey offers some authentic details. In the early 1840s, Vernals consisted of a house, farm offices, garden, and shrubbery on one and three-quarter acres, with 22 acres of pasture adjoining.[7] An eighteenth-century report says that Phillip spent £2000 of his wife's money 'principally in domestic disbursements'.[8] Presumably a part at least of this sum went towards the augmenting of the farm. About a year after he took up Vernals, by purchase or lease he acquired Glass Hayes, the area on which the Lyndhurst Park Hotel now stands, and which in the 1840s consisted of a house, offices, garden, and pleasure ground on 6 acres, and 4 acres of adjoining fields, 3 of which were pasture. He also acquired Black Acres, which cannot now be identified, but which may have composed the fields between the two farms. And, as befitted a country gentleman, he 'discharged assiduously those provincial offices, which, however unimportant, occupy respectably the owners of land'[9]—that is, he was an overseer of the parish charity from 1766 into 1768.

Whether the Phillips were committed to serious farming is uncertain. Lying at the western edge of southeast England's chalk deposits, the New Forest land is not rich. Consisting of sand, clay, and marl, it has a high acid content, and is therefore unsuitable for the extensive raising of crops. The forest itself is open, with growths of beech, birch, ash, oak, and holly. The holdings scattered through it exhibit beech, oak, and a few ash, with hedgerows of hawthorn. Then, as now, these were predominantly dairy farms, with some small scale crop production to provide fodder for the cattle; and with some keeping of sheep, poultry, and pigs, to contribute towards self-sufficiency. To augment the limited fertility of their holdings, farmers obtained dung, and sometimes seaweed, from Gosport and Portsmouth; and exercised commons' rights in the forest.

It seems probable that the Phillips were as interested in enjoying a life of country leisure as they were in farming seriously. With their 'shrubbery', 'pleasure ground', and surrounding 'pastures' their properties were not highly productive farms. What is likely is that the couple oversaw a small-scale production, kept horses, and enjoyed fruits from orchards and vegetables from gardens. Still, these circumstances would have offered Phillip knowledge that would later prove more than useful—of the yearly surge of flowers, and the cycle of the seasons and the farmer's year; of the ways to prepare ground for plantings, of how grains might yield, vegetables flourish, fruit trees bear, cows produce, milk thicken to cream and cheese.

There was also experience of country people. If those about him conformed to the general pattern, they would likely have been unmarried adults and youths, who may have come from other localities in search of more desirable positions in the small hierarchies of farm and household service. But if they might be distinguished from their equivalents in other pursuits by this mobility, other attributes would have linked them strongly with their class. Most would have had little, if any, formal education. Many might have been apathetic or indifferent to organized religion, and one or two perhaps entirely ignorant of its tenets. They would rather have exhibited the beliefs then prevalent among labouring and country folk in the efficacy of magic and the potency of herbal medicine and of the 'wise' or 'cunning' man's advice. In this, they would perhaps have been little different from numbers of the sailors whom Phillip had encountered in his service; but then diverse experience and naval discipline would have constrained such primitive belief. In a forest community, however, such belief would have been a factor daily to be taken into account. The forest might have influenced the lives of those with whom Phillip dealt in other ways, too. At this time, forest-based communities were commonly held to be the unruliest of the country, since, providing opportunities for easy evasion of law and for escape from the reach of authority, the forest acted to prevent the establishment of respectable order and permanence. The Lyndhurst community might not perhaps have been so marked by this attribute as some others, for it had a developed centre, and church and gentry did have some domain. But popular unrest and disrespect for the decorums of polite society were likely never far from the surface, in a condition to rise in time of stress.

The middle years of the 1760s were such a time. In March 1766, snow blanketed England, with the falls being particularly heavy in the West Country. In June, heavy rains and the floods which followed ruined the grain crops. Through August into October, across the country the poor rioted in protest at the resultant prohibitive prices of wheat and barley, potatoes, butter, cheese, and bacon. While there seems to have been no rioting at Lyndhurst itself, there were disturbances at centres in neighbouring counties—at Exeter, Ottery St Mary, Barnstaple and Wincanton in Devon, at Bath in Somerset, at Sidbury in Wiltshire. At Salisbury in Wiltshire the risings were 'very serious'; and at Alton, farther to the east, in Hampshire, one writer threatened to burn the whole town if merchants and authorities did not lower prices. In January 1767, the heaviest snows in living memory covered England. When they melted the next month, there was again widespread flooding. Though the government took some steps to alleviate the famine, there could be little help, as grain production was down throughout Europe, and when the most severe weather in a generation once more ruined crops in 1768, rioting again erupted.

The life of a country gentleman in the mid-1760s, then, was potentially a troubled one. In any case, we may suppose that its pursuits could not be such as to satisfy entirely one ambitious to make his mark at sea, in battle or in discovery. And all about Phillip in these years were irons to stoke the embers of his dreaming. The road running past the door of Vernals led on to the Channel port of Lymington. From the forest, contractors took timbers for the Royal Navy, and carried them by water to Portsmouth. At this great base, the hub of the Navy's operations in the Channel, about the coasts of Europe, and in the vast world beyond, Michael Everitt commanded a guardship. In strange atmospheric conditions, the Arctic phantasmagoria that Phillip had once viewed at close hand lit the night sky. The winds that wuthered through the forest were those that loosened sails, carried ships to distant waters, and bore them home again.

Before Phillip's innate yearning might impel him forth, however, another cause intervened to do so. In the words of the eighteenth-century commentator, 'some circumstances occurred which induced [him] to wish for a separation'.[10] Precisely when Arthur and Charlott Phillip abandoned their marriage is again unclear. Phillip's engaging another to fulfil his office of Overseer of the Poor in April 1768, and his being superseded in this office by William Lake in July 1768, suggest that he may have left Vernals in the spring of that year. The formal 'indenture of Separation' which the couple concluded on 22 April 1769 points also to a break about this time, stating as it did that they had 'lately lived separate and apart'.[11] By this agreement, Arthur Phillip 'bargained sold and delivered' to Charlott's guarantor 'all and every the Household Goods Plate, Chair, Horses Furniture fixtures and things whatsoever then in the possession or Use of the said Margaret Charlotte Phillip or in or about her Dwelling House or Place of abode at Hampton Court in the County of Middlesex and also all her Wearing Apparel, Jewels, Diamonds, Watches Rings and Ornaments of her person'. Nowhere in anything he is known to have written subsequently did Phillip refer either to the circumstances that lay behind the separation, or to his feelings about it. Involving as it did the loss of his wife's resources, it must have been a considerable disappointment.

By mid-1769, then, Phillip was once more in the necessity of making a way in the world with his own resources only; but before he might begin to do so he had once more to restore his body. In September, he sought and obtained from the Admiralty permission to go to St Omers, in northern France, for six months 'for the benefit of his health'.[12] Though it is not recorded, it is likely that he subsequently obtained a six months' extension of this leave, for he next appears in England in November 1770, when he joined the *Egmont*, a 74-gun line-of-battle ship, as fourth lieutenant.

The *Egmont* was then being fitted out as part of the activation of the Navy consequent upon the quarrel with Spain over the Falkland Islands, which reached crisis point when a force from Buenos Aires expelled British colonists from Port Egmont in June 1770. Indeed, it might well have been the prospect of war which brought Phillip back from France, but if so he was to be disappointed, for his service in the next seven months was routine. In November, December, and January he joined in the general recruiting campaign, when he led a press gang in London; but, reaching an accord with the Spanish, the British discontinued their preparations in late January. Phillip rejoined his ship at the mouth of the Medway on 23 February. The *Egmont* was at the Nore until early March, when she began to work in light winds out of the Thames estuary. She was off the Gunfleet light on the Essex coast on 11 March, and six days later was proceeding down the Channel. She moored at Spithead on 18 March, where she was to remain for several years. Phillip left her on 8 July,[13] with the only unusual circumstance having been Lord Sandwich's first official visit to Portsmouth yard in April. His name was entered in the Half Pay register the next day, and there it stayed without interruption until January 1775.[14]

It seems that Phillip's reason for giving up his post was again illness, for in August he asked for, and obtained, permission to go for twelve months to 'Lille in Flanders for the benefit of his health'.[15] What he did between September 1772, when this leave expired, and the middle of 1773, is unknown; but in July 1773, he sought permission to spend another twelve months in France 'for the recovery of his health', this time at St Amand les Eaux in Hainault.[16]

Repeated references confirm that Phillip's health was precarious throughout his life; but these sojourns in France may have involved a good deal more than its simple recovery. For one thing, if we are to believe the eighteenth-century commentator, in these years Phillip made enough money to repay his estranged wife what he had spent of her fortune.[17] John Denison had had an interest in the cloth trade, and Phillip later showed that he too was acquainted with it. The Low Country towns he lived in or near were centres of the renowned continental manufactory; and it is therefore not impossible that Phillip traded in Flanders cloths, either on his own behalf, or on that of English merchants, such as his friends the Lanes and the Duncombes. The 'Brazil diamond ring' that the merchant Charles Duncombe gave to Phillip may have been simply a gift of friendship. Equally, though, it may have been a reward for good service.

For another thing, Phillip may have pursued engineering and military studies in these years. By his own and others' testimony, by the mid-1770s he possessed an unusual 'theoretical' knowledge of his profession,[18] and was also 'well up in fortification and every other branch of the military profession'.[19] The mines of the Low Countries offered lessons applicable to military engineering; and if Phillip did not reside exclusively in the towns he cited in his applications for leave, then there are other possibilities. Later, he was to be identified as 'the oldest and most intimate friend' of Isaac Landmann, a German who was in the early 1770s Professor of Artillery and Fortification at the Ecole Militaire in Paris, and from November 1777 the holder of the equivalent post at Woolwich Arsenal. If Phillip did reside in Paris for a time, he may well have attended Landmann's lectures in a private capacity.[20]

There is another tantalizing thread trailing from these years. In a later remark, Phillip indicated that sometime before 1778 he had viewed the French navy's dockyards and arsenal at Toulon with a professional eye. In the spring of 1773, the British were greatly alarmed by reports that the French were arming their fleet there.[21] At the end of April, the North ministry announced that as a counter to the French threat it would fit out 'fifteen ships of the line', and a 'proportionable number of frigates'.[22] In July, the Secretary of State requested the Chargé d'affaires in Paris 'constantly [to] attend to what is passing in the French ports, and [to] lose no time in transmitting the earliest intelligence of what comes to your knowledge'.[23] The details which the British received in these months presented conflicting pictures of French activity. Who better to send after authentic information than a naval officer possessed of good theoretical knowledge and fluent in French? And if the Admiralty did employ Phillip to spy on the French at this time, this would have led to his renewing contact with Augustus Hervey, who was one of the Lord Commissioners dealing with the alarm.

Whatever the details of all this may have been, by the summer of 1774 Arthur Phillip had returned to England, richer in experience, perhaps richer in pocket too, perhaps also in better health, and in any case eager for active service again.

Pilar

2

Beyond Western Stars

South America, 1774–78

… my purpose holds
To sail beyond the sunset, and the baths
Of all the western stars

Tennyson, 'Ulysses'

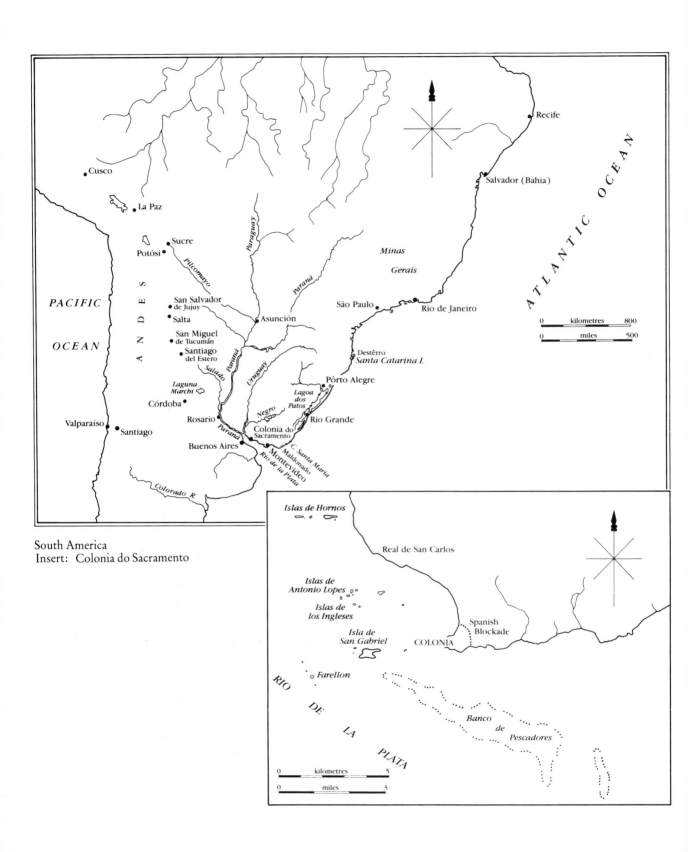

South America
Insert: Colonia do Sacramento

South America, 1774–78

At thirty-six Arthur Phillip had acted a good many parts, even if some of them but briefly. He had known the rigours of a poor childhood, and of the northern whale fishery. He had seen the ports of England, Germany, France, Spain, Portugal, and Italy; and active service in the Mediterranean and amongst the West Indian islands. He had been a husband and a country gentleman, and afterwards someone with an interest in the cloth trades, a student of artillery and fortification, and, if not precisely a spy, certainly someone who travelled sharp-eyed while on 'private affairs'.

By mid-1774, Phillip had emerged as a person of considerable intelligence, experience, and resourcefulness. But considering what must have been his central ambition, to advance himself in the Royal Navy, he was also clearly at something of an impasse. He had been a lieutenant for thirteen years, and, whatever the reason, his eight months' stint in home waters in 1770–71 had not led to a permanent posting in the Royal Navy, for which he might have needed better health, and perhaps more wealth or friends with more telling social or political influence than he had. Lacking these resources, and given the peace, he was at this time, like so many of his colleagues, a capable junior officer without definite prospects. Essentially, his situation was that which Sandwich described to Augustus Hervey a couple of years later, of one who had 'served well and long but your Lordship well knows there are too many in that situation who can never be promoted'.[1] Late in the summer of 1774, however, three distinct circumstances came together to offer Phillip a new and more promising avenue. These were the conflict between Portugal and Spain; Portugal's attendant need of persons with such skills as Phillip's; and the emergence of a patron interested in advancing Phillip's cause.

The conflict between the Iberian nations arose from their long-standing disagreement about which had the right to what Dauril Alden has termed the 'Debatable Lands' in South America—that is, the area between the Portuguese settlements in Southern Brazil, and the Spanish ones above the River Plate estuary: what is now the Brazilian state of Rio Grande do Sul, and Uruguay.[2] After their initial explorations of this area at the turn of the sixteenth century, both nations had neglected it for 150 years. Then, Spanish Jesuits established missions there, only to be expelled by the legendary, lawless *bandeirantes* or roaming gangs of the São Paulo captaincy. In 1680, in order to strengthen their claim, the Portuguese founded a settlement, Colonia do Sacramento, on the peninsula on the northern shore of the Plate estuary, adjacent to San Gabriel Island. This soon became a conduit for a considerable trade, with the Portuguese smuggling European manufactures to the Spanish colonists beyond, and taking hides and silver in return.

The illicit trade greatly annoyed the Spanish authorities, who responded by capturing and destroying the Portuguese fort. The site was scarcely defensible. The roadstead did not offer a good anchorage; the soil was infertile; there were no trees about; and there was higher ground to the east and north, so that the Spanish from Buenos Aires were able to dominate the fort by both land and sea as they chose. However, anxious to continue to reap the benefits of the trade, the Portuguese rebuilt the fort three years later; and in the next decades they tried to make it more secure by sending there, first, convicts sentenced to exile (*degredados*), and later, a few settler families. Though the colony quickly became notorious for the dissoluteness of its inhabitants, these did succeed in establishing some agriculture, and they extended the clandestine trade with their Spanish neighbours. Further annoyed by these developments, Spain retook Colonia in 1705, when she and Portugal were arguing in Europe, but was forced to restore it in the Peace of Utrecht of 1713. Portugal re-occupied the site in 1716, and, recognizing the need to strengthen its lines of support, began to augment the settlements that the restless Paulistas had made about Santa Catarina Island in the second half of the seventeenth century. Now, too, with the support of British merchants, the Portuguese extended their clandestine trade with the Creole Spanish into the vast regions beyond the Plate estuary, bringing in large quantities of British manufactures via Lisbon and Rio de Janeiro. As a counter-measure, the Spanish authorities fortified Montevideo harbour in 1724. The conflict over possession of the Debatable Lands then widened, to continue at varying levels of intensity for the next four decades. In August 1762, when the nations were at war in Europe, the Spanish general Cevallos placed a large force from Buenos Aires around Colonia, which surrendered at the end of October. Greatly outnumbered in men, ships, and other resources, Portugal sought the help of her traditional ally Britain. In January 1763, a joint force sailing from Rio de Janeiro failed to retake the outpost. Cevallos then marched 1000 men to the Portuguese forts south of the Lagoa Mirim, which surrendered quickly in April. He moved on to the town of Rio Grande, which he also took immediately, but before he could advance further, he heard that the Courts had agreed to end hostilities.

This agreement was part of the general one reached to end the Seven Years War in 1763. But the Peace of Paris left unresolved the question of possession of the Debatable Lands, with Portugal insisting that it meant she should regain the Rio Grande area, and Spain that she had agreed to restore only Colonia. In this troubling circumstance, Portugal continued to seek Britain's help. In June 1763, the British Admiralty gave permission for a number of its now-unemployed lieutenants, among them one Robert M'Douall, to enter the Portuguese navy.[3] Simultaneously, the Portuguese Court recruited others skilled in warfare, such as the Austrian general Böhm, and the Swedish engineer Funck, who had served with the British at the capture of Havana.[4] The Marquis of Pombal pressed the British for more help in the next years, but being unhappy with Pombal's new commercial regulations, and arguing with the Spanish over possession of the Falkland Islands, the British refrained from giving it.

Although they did try to negotiate a settlement of the long-standing dispute in the late 1760s, Portugal and Spain did not succeed in reaching one. The situation was particularly uneasy in the Plate estuary, with the Spanish maintaining a constant blockade of the Portuguese outpost. The Spanish also continued to occupy the area they had captured in Rio Grande, from which the local Portuguese governor tried unsuccessfully to drive them in May 1767. Further negotiations failing, the Crowns relapsed into their familiar squabbling. By 1773, when Portugal had repaired her alliance with Britain, and when Spain and Britain had settled their dispute over the Falklands, Portugal and Spain had cleared their political decks to do battle again for the Debatable Lands.

The Spanish were as intent as the Portuguese on settling the protracted dispute, and Britain's gathering troubles in North America were to their advantage. The Iberian nations did not wait long to engage each other. In 1773–74, Vertiz, the new and enthusiastic governor of Buenos Aires, attempted to drive the Portuguese entirely from Rio Grande. After some initial success he was badly beaten by Portuguese forces using guerilla tactics. Sensing that the tide had turned in their favour, the Portuguese responded quickly. Immediately, the Marquis of Lavradio, who had become Viceroy of Brazil in 1769, sent reinforcements to Rio Grande, and pleaded with home for additional forces and materials. Then, during 1774, the home government marshalled the country's resources for a decisive war.

Only two of the preparations in Portugal need concern us here. First, responding to Lavradio's request for much-needed naval forces, the Court set about organizing a squadron of four small line-of-battle ships (*Santo Antonio* (66), *Ajuda* (64), *Prazeres* (62), *Belém* (55)), six frigates (*Graça* (42), *Nazareth* (42), *Príncipe do Brazil* (34), *Princeza do Brazil* (28), *Gloria* (26) and *Assumpção* (24)), to be despatched unobtrusively and to assemble under Robert M'Douall's command at Rio de Janeiro. The first of these ships sailed from Lisbon in July 1774, the last in February 1775.[5]

Second, the Portuguese once more sought help from Britain. In mid-1774, Pombal asked the North administration to threaten Spain with naval squadrons, which the British, again not wishing to be drawn into a general war, declined to do. Simultaneously, Mello e Castro, the Secretary of State for the Marine and the Colonies, had Pinto de Souza, the nation's ambassador in London, ask the reluctant ally to release some of its navy's half-pay officers to run the ships which his nation was then fitting out.[6] Souza accordingly approached Augustus Hervey at the Admiralty. Hervey knew Mello e Castro personally and responded helpfully.[7] It is impossible that he should have done so without at least the tacit approval of the Admiralty Board and of the administration. No doubt, too, the favourable response he offered was not disinterested. One of Britain's oldest and deepest-seated dreams was to open the resources and markets of South America to her merchants, manufacturers, and Treasury.[8] The trade via Colonia had constituted a substantial beginning at realizing this dream. Indeed, informed opinion had it that, had the Seven Years War lasted a little longer, 'we should by this inlet have supplied with English goods the greater part of the Spanish settlements in America'.[9] In the mid-1760s, when regulations established by both Iberian nations had threatened to disrupt this very profitable trade, the British government had instructed its ambassador to Spain 'to procure the most exact information concerning the strength and weakness of the Spanish dominions in South America, the truth and amount of the discontent which are supposed to prevail there, the nature and degree of the dependence of those provinces on Old Spain, the state of the military and fortifications, the points which may be supposed to be most open to attack, and the inclinations which may be expected to be found in such provinces in such cases'. He was likewise to 'procure any maps or charts of those provinces, either manuscript or printed, together with plans of their towns and fortifications'. The ambassador to Portugal received similar instructions concerning Brazil. There were rumours that the British even sent surveying parties to the Spanish Main.[10] And in May 1771, Hervey himself suggested that Britain might very usefully obtain naval timber from Brazil.[11] While nothing substantial seems to have come of these moves, they serve to indicate what would have been the drift of the British responses to Mello e Castro's request. By providing officers to help Portugal defeat Spain in South America, Britain would place Portugal in her future debt, she would contribute to the weakening of Spain's hold over her colonies, and her officers would return with valuable intelligence. By helping Portugal at the moment, Britain would put herself in a position the better to obtain later the place she wanted in South America.

Augustus Hervey told Pinto de Souza that while in general the officers who might be interested in serving Portugal were not such as he could approve of, he could unhesitatingly recommend one who had served under him at the siege of Havana. Arthur Phillip, he said, possessed theoretical knowledge as well as much practical experience; he spoke good French; and, while he was only a lieutenant, he well deserved promotion.[12] The terms of this recommendation only obliquely convey Hervey's and his government's profound motives for meeting the Portuguese request. To say that Phillip was worthy of a command was not after all very distinctive—as Sandwich was to tell Hervey a little later, there were many of whom this was true. To say that he combined theoretical knowledge with practical experience was to hint at some larger resource in him, perhaps, but was still not very illuminating. To say that he spoke French well was, in the context, rather strange, and it is this characterization which directs us to what Hervey left unsaid regarding why he recommended Phillip. For what Hervey thereby alluded to was Phillip's character of a 'discreet' officer, one of those whom the Admiralty, and also the state departments from time to time, employed either to travel observantly in Europe, or sent to distant waters on specific missions.

What Hervey did not say about Phillip, together with subsequent events, tells us why the British authorities were willing that he should serve Portugal: that he was an intelligent man, whose knowledge of languages permitted him to move freely about the European world and its extensions; that his naval and military expertise enabled him to assess accurately the utility of harbours and the effectiveness of fortifications as he did so; that he was an officer who could be relied upon to report his observations discreetly; that, in effect, he was one from whom in time might come most useful information concerning 2500 kilometres of South American coastline, concerning the Spanish fortifications and forces about the River Plate estuary, concerning the geography, products, and economies of the Spanish and Portuguese colonies in America.

All this, together with his financial need of employment, his ambition to advance himself in his profession, and his passion for active service, meant that, bearing Hervey's letter of recommendation, on one of the last days of August 1774 Lieutenant Arthur Phillip attended on Pinto de Souza to state his conditions. These were three: 'that, in consideration of what he gives up here, and the superior advantages which it is the custom for English officers to enjoy when they are on the Retired List, he be allowed, in the Portuguese Service, the same pay as foreign officers receive when on active service at sea'; that 'when on the Retired List he be allowed half of that pay'; and that 'a promise be made to him that, immediately upon his arrival in Portugal, a Commission of Captain of the Fleet will be issued to him'.[13]

The ambassador referred Phillip's requests to his Court, together with one of his own concerning the possibility of Phillip's receiving an allowance to cover the cost of travel to Lisbon. Mello e Castro was tardy in replying, but by early November it was clear to all parties that the business might go forward. The Portuguese Court was pleased to be obtaining the services of someone whom Hervey could recommend so strongly. Phillip should have a captain's commission, and receive, on shore as well as at sea, double the pay given to Portuguese officers—that is, 40 000 réis per month on land, and 80 000 per month at sea. As 1000 réis then equalled approximately 5 shillings and 6 pence, this was an adequate reward. If he were appointed to a frigate, he would in addition receive 4880 réis per day table money; and if to a ship of the line, 6400 réis per day. As it was 'not usual for deserving officers to retire so long as they [were] able to serve', there was no provision for half pay, but if Phillip performed well, then the Court would reward him when he left its service.[14] This information left some points to settle still. Showing clearly that, in addition to his other motives, he had decided to be Phillip's patron, Hervey responded that while Phillip could not wish for better terms so far as money was concerned, his ambition was to be post captain of a ship of the line; and he (Hervey) wished to know whether in the Portuguese navy officers of such rank also sailed in frigates. The ambassador wrote to his Court again.[15]

The parties continued their preparations as they waited for a reply. On 1 December, the Admiralty formally gave Phillip permission to enter the service of Portugal,[16] and he then made final arrangements. Mello e Castro's reply reached Pinto de Souza on 22 December. This was that in the Portuguese navy a first and second captain frequently sailed on the same ship, whether of the line or a frigate, and that length of commission determined seniority.[17] The ambassador immediately communicated this information to Hervey and Phillip, who was on the eve of setting out. Phillip agreed to accept the appointment in these terms, though he thought the practice of two captains serving in the same ship a 'hard' one.[18] Ten years later, this situation, and this perception, were to give him much trouble.

Lieutenant Arthur Phillip left London for Lisbon on or soon after 22 December 1774, accompanied both by the Portuguese ambassador's renewed commendation that 'everyone' spoke highly of his intelligence and merit, and by Hervey's personal one to Mello e Castro that Phillip would vindicate this reputation.[19] Phillip would have travelled by the King's 'packet' service that ran between Falmouth on the Cornish coast and Lisbon. The length of the trip varied with conditions in the Bay of Biscay, but seldom took more than fourteen days, and sometimes as few as five. Accordingly, Phillip would have reached Lisbon in the first days of 1775. On 14 January, the Portuguese king, Dom José, signed a warrant providing for him to be commissioned a captain in the Portuguese navy. The Council of War issued this commission two days later; and on 17 January, Phillip was appointed second captain of the *Nossa Senhora de Belém*, then fitting out in the Tagus River under the command of Captain António de Sales e Noronha.[20]

Phillip came to a disarrayed city, one between a cluttered and ravaged past, and an enlarged future. On the one hand, with whole streets still in ruins, Lisbon showed many signs of the devastation wrought by the great earthquake that had struck suddenly in the morning of 1 November 1755. On the other, under the guidance of the Marquis of Pombal, a striking new city was rising from the ruins. The central focus of the new age was to be the majestic Square of the Palace, with three sides formed by extensive state buildings, and the fourth by the Tagus. In the middle was to be a massive bronze equestrian statue of Dom José. At the beginning of 1775, the western side of the square had been completed, and work was proceeding on the India House, the Exchange, and the statue. Almost 200 new houses of uniform design, of four or five stories in striking white stone, had been built behind the square to the north; as had, to the west, the capacious Naval Arsenal. For the convenience of those who walked about their business, the broad streets had raised and flag-stoned footpaths.

In the last weeks of January, Phillip oversaw the multitudinous business of readying a large warship for sea—the loading of food, water, and stores for the voyage, and a great quantity of munitions for Brazil; the checking of masts,

An artist's impression of Lisbon's new square as it was being built. (*c.* 1775)

Tower of the Navigators, Belém

spars, planks, rigging, and sails, and the replacing of faulty items; the completing of the ship's crew; the finding of accommodation for the troop reinforcements to be carried out. As he attended to all such necessary things, he must have moved repeatedly among the presentiments of the enlightenment city's impending splendour, and at the same time entered an ethos of distant voyaging and empire, one haunted by the presences of the great age of Portuguese discovery.

Since Phillip was an enquiring man, with an eye for the picturesque, he may also have found time to inspect some of the city's features. The hallowed Tower of the Navigators, and the monastery of the Jerónimos with its striking cloisters, being built above the solid rock of Belém, had survived the earthquake intact. Also at Belém was the king's winter palace, notable not so much for its style as for its garden filled with exotics from the reaches of the Portuguese empire; for the animals in its menagerie—elephants, tigers, polecats, weasels, lions, leopards, panthers, bears, and zebras—and for its 'five hundred' singing birds. The church of São Roque was famous for its rich decorations of marble, jasper, greenstone, granite, lapis lazuli, and other stones. There were plays and operas to be seen, and ensembles playing Brazilian music to be heard; and there was the acquaintance of the members of the English Factory to be cultivated. Perhaps Phillip may have climbed to Sintra, the 'agreeable' and 'romantic' village nestling in the mountains above Lisbon, where the rich kept summer houses with elegant gardens, and from where the Atlantic could be seen curving towards new worlds.

On 25 January, Sales e Noronha and Phillip received permission to travel to Salvaterra de Magos, to take formal leave of the king.[21] Located some 50 kilometres up the Tagus, this country seat of the Portuguese monarchs consisted of a palace and the houses of the nobles who attended the Court, and buildings reflecting the leisure activities of the inhabitants: a bull ring, a falconry, and an opera house. The captains would have travelled by water, perhaps with the day cold, with lowering, rain-laden clouds sweeping in from the Atlantic and the river surging before the wind. They would have left the river for the canal that ran the last distance to the town, landing near the royal chapel alight with baroque gilding, and proceeded through the houses to the palace, where, for the brief period of their stay, they would have experienced the productions of the great medieval kitchens.

But a life of such indulgence was not a naval captain's lot. Sales e Noronha and Phillip were soon back at their ship. On 6 February, having completed her equipping, and with hundreds of crew and soldiers aboard, they loosened her sails. Proceeding downstream towards the mouth of the Tagus, they passed the

Tower of Belém, whence the old sailors had left for their Indias. But the wind dropped, and they were forced to anchor in the broad estuary. The need to replace a rotten topgallant mast delayed them further. On 9 February, with a fresh breeze from the north, the *Belém* at last crossed the bar of the Tagus, and headed into the Atlantic Ocean.[22] As the mouth of the river receded into the distance, as the hills of Lisbon diminished and then disappeared, as the stars shifted along the ship's southwest route towards the fourth part of the world, Phillip was Odysseus again.

The *Belém's* passage across the Atlantic was quick and evidently uneventful, and she reached Rio de Janeiro on 5 April.[23] In the 1770s, a ship ran to this port through an array of fortification. She had first to pass by the Purple Beach with its initial battery at larboard, then by the ominous Sugar Loaf, then between the headlands with the matched batteries of São João and Santa Cruz, and past the battery on Laje Island. But this gauntlet run, those aboard, like emergent Jonahs, found the world transformed. Before them extended a harbour then without parallel, and still, in its magnitude and shelter, one of the three or four finest in the world. As their ship moved up Guanabara Bay for the city of São Sebastião they glimpsed the rows of white-sand beaches that edged their goal, and on the hills beyond, its churches, and the villas and gardens of its wealthy inhabitants. When the ship reached the anchorage formed by the city's harbourside and the Ilha das Cobras, with its naval yard and arsenal, those she carried had endured the ocean.

The Portuguese had chosen the site and developed the city according to the criteria considered appropriate to a colonial settlement at the end of a long sea route.[24] The area offered an abundance of land for agriculture and grazing, of timber for building and fuel, and of water; its anchorage was sheltered, and access to it convenient; and there were elevations from which the settlement might be defended. The commercial section was laid out on a grid system, with its centre piece the required square fronting the harbour. The Viceroy's palace formed the eastern side of this square, the Carmelite convent its southern, and an imposing row of shops its western one. In the middle of its harbourside was a fountain from which ships and the populace drew water brought from the mountains behind via a striking aqueduct. The Viceroy's palace was a long, rectangular building. Though not lavish in comparison with European counterparts, it had the distinction of being the only building in the city with glass in its windows.

Behind the square ran the principal street, Rua Direita, containing, as decreed by the ordinances promulgated by both Portuguese and Spanish authorities, the Customs House and other government buildings and the Council

Jean Massé, 'Plan of São Sebastião [Rio de Janeiro]' (1713)

Leandro Joaquim, 'The square before the Viceroy's palace, Rio de Janeiro' (1780s?)

The fountain at the quay was fed by water brought along an aqueduct from the mountains behind the city.

Jean Baptiste Réville, 'The Aqueduct and part of the city, Rio de Janeiro' (mid-eighteenth century?)

Leandro Joaquim, 'An English squadron, Rio de Janeiro' (1780s?)

Chambers; and a large number of 'handsome' shops and merchants' offices besides, and churches. Along other of the more important streets were stone buildings of two or three stories, with shops below, and above apartments with latticed balconies where residents sheltered from the summer heat; and more churches. The intersecting streets were narrower, and dank, their footpaths only wide enough for two persons to walk abreast. Beyond the city centre were the slave and other markets, and the cluttered and flimsy dwellings of the poor and the slaves. On the hills buttressing the city were churches and hospitals—on the eastern side the Military and Misericórdia hospitals and the church of Nossa Senhora da Glória; on the western, the Franciscan monastery, and its companion of São Bento, casting baroque benedictions towards the water. The placing of these institutions on the hills was not accidental. Not only were their elevated situations healthier, but also, again in accordance with received principles of town planning, they were fortified, and together with the arsenal on the Ilha das Cobras formed a second line of defence for the city. On the coolness of farther hills, the wealthy raised elegant villas and kept elaborate gardens. Viewed from the harbour, the whole presented 'a rich and magnificent appearance'.[25]

By the time the *Belém* arrived, Robert M'Douall had taken the other ships of the squadron to their southern base at Santa Catarina Island; but before he had done so, the tensions that were to plague the naval operations of the Portuguese for the next three years had become only too evident. The problem was in essence the commodore. M'Douall was a blustering, bombastic man, but also, as events were to show repeatedly, one most reluctant to accept the responsibility of decisive action. Already by April 1775, by his autocratic behaviour, and by his public declarations that those whom the Portuguese Court had commissioned were good for nothing, he had succeeded in thoroughly alienating the majority of his officers; and he had offended the Viceroy with his bumptiousness and his reluctance either to accept advice or to defer to superior authority.[26]

As quickly as he had developed an intense and enduring dislike of M'Douall, Lavradio took a liking to Phillip. Since he too had his masters, the Viceroy was no doubt encouraged to do so by the recommendation from Mello e Castro which Phillip brought with him. They had had from London, the Minister for Colonies and the Marine announced, conspicuous information concerning Phillip's intelligence, ability, and character, in which together he excelled all other of his countrymen recruited. He was an ideal person to have in the nation's service, and an officer in whom Lavradio might confide; and it would perhaps be most to the point to keep him at Rio de Janeiro, so as to have the constant benefit of his advice.[27] The Viceroy took the none-too-subtle hint, soon reporting back that not only was Phillip most proficient in his naval business, he also showed himself to be a man of honour, one willing to conform to Portuguese custom and to respect authority. To the harassed Lavradio, the contrast between M'Douall and Phillip must have been as stark as that between chalk and cheese. Seeing an opportunity not to be passed up, Phillip in his turn was not slow to cultivate the Viceroy's regard, telling Lavradio within days of his arrival how impressed he was by the enthusiasm and discipline of the city's volunteer guard, and giving the distinct impression of being interested in continuing permanently in the service of Portugal.[28]

His dislike of the commodore foisted on him by a Court so distant as not to feel the hardship, and the appearance of another officer in whom he might have confidence, led Lavradio to develop a distinctive scheme the better to defend the southern edges of the empire he governed, and to minimize M'Douall's role in the defence of the whole. Early in May, Lavradio removed Phillip from the *Belém*, preparatory to appointing him to one of the two merchant vessels he was then fitting out as frigates, and to giving him overall charge of a small squadron to patrol the Plate estuary out of Colonia and protect Portuguese fishing and trading vessels from the depredations of Spanish *guardacostas*.[29]

The Viceroy's scheme meant that Phillip remained in Rio de Janeiro for four months, while he waited for the *Nossa Senhora do Pilar* to be converted and armed. How he spent this time we may surmise in a general way, and in one or two particular ones. As he had served in the West Indies, Phillip would not have found the tropical lushness of Rio de Janeiro's environs entirely strange. Still, numbers of the aromatic shrubs and flowers, and of the gaudy birds and insects were such as to command the attention of one interested in natural history. There was the opera to attend; the city's famous churches to be inspected; and the customs of the inhabitants, as exotic as the birds, fruits, flowers, and overgilded churches, to be comprehended.

Among the attitudes strange to a northern European of Protestant culture was the Brazilians' religiosity. In the manner of a colonial people determined to impress the metropolis, and aided by the heady superstition of the blacks, these had brought their observance to an intensity such as to beggar even that for which the Iberians were renowned. At each intersection in the city stood a 3-metre-high pole on which hung a crucifix or saint's image, before which bypassers genuflected. The bells of the churches sounded morning, noon, and night. On feast days, the inhabitants dressed in their finest clothes and in carriages, on horseback, or on foot, formed processions that ended at night with candles and fireworks. These festivals served more than a religious purpose. Charlatans

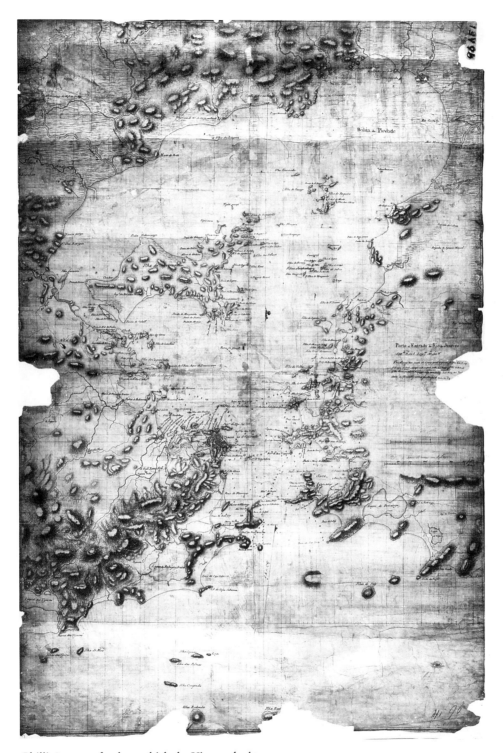

Phillip's copy of a chart which the Viceroy had
had prepared of the harbour at Rio de Janeiro.
Phillip checked the details carefully. (*c.* 1776)

hawked articles proclaimed as relics, and musicians performed for the crowd. Brazilian women, who were in the habit of casting nosegays at those in whom they were interested, mingled with the throng to achieve their assignations. Phillip's personal thoughts about all this have not survived. The Viceroy's comment that he 'respects our laws' indicates that, if they were unfavourable, he kept them to himself.[30]

Equally colourful were the festivities of the blacks, enslaved and free, whose fandangoes and general exuberance added to the lush ambience of the city. But those, particularly foreigners, who wandered through the poorer sections of the city did so at some hazard. It was notorious that there was 'no Place in the World where People will commit Murder at so cheap a rate' as at Rio de Janeiro.[31] A decade later, one of Phillip's seamen was to disobey orders, and sleep on shore. Though his cap carried the Portuguese coat of arms, he was beaten and robbed; and on his return to the *Sirius*, Phillip told him sternly that he was lucky to be alive. It was advice deriving from close experience of the city.[32]

Phillip did not, however, neglect serious concerns in the face of these distractions. There was the language to be better learned; and within twelve months he spoke and wrote Portuguese fluently. And, given his friendship with Lavradio, and the interest in the country's products which he subsequently

The Portuguese squadron (1776)

manifested, he may have attended the meetings of the Scientific Society that the Viceroy hosted in his chambers. There was also the largest reason for his having come to South America to attend to; and this he diligently began to do. He obtained a chart of the harbour and its surrounds which Lavradio had had surveyed at 'a very great expense', and checked the details carefully. This was information to reserve against the Admiralty's need, should it mount a South American expedition in the future.[33]

As Lavradio and Phillip waited for the artificers to finish their work on the *Pilar*, there were dramatic oscillations in the Portuguese Court's view of the desirability of retaining Colonia. In April, fearful that the large expedition that the Spanish were mounting at Cádiz, ostensibly to send against the Dey of Algiers, was in fact destined for South America, Mello e Castro instructed the Viceroy to strengthen the squadron,[34] which Lavradio was in the process of doing anyway. A month later, evidently hoping to create a pretext by which to enlist Britain's active support, Pombal ordered Lavradio to withdraw the troops from the outpost.[35] In mid-August, her conversion to a frigate mounting 26 guns and with a crew of 218 having been completed, Lavradio gave Phillip the command of the *Pilar*.[36] Having had to give up his scheme to defend Colonia in the face of Pombal's orders, he now directed Phillip, and Stevens in the *Nazareth*, to transport three companies of infantry and artillery to Santa Catar-

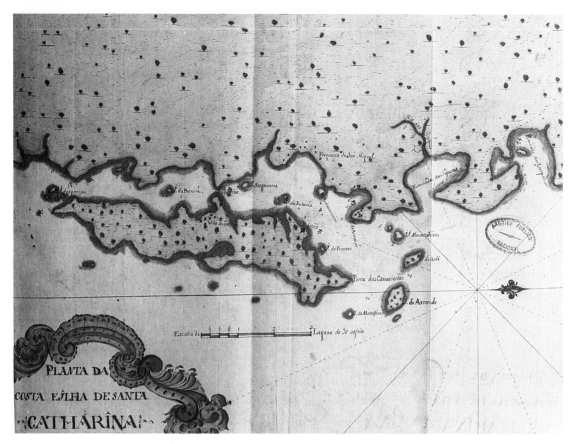

Santa Catarina Island and environs (1776)

ina, enclosing orders to M'Douall to send the ships on to Colonia.[37]

Aided by the prevailing northwest winds, the captains had a quick passage to Destêrro, which they reached on 28 September. The last section of the route took them down the narrow strait that divides the island from the mainland, a passage which the high, wooded mountains on either side made spectacular. At Destêrro, they found the necks of land which jut from either coast to form a good anchorage; and a pretty town. Located among green fields and orange groves 500 metres uphill from the landing, Destêrro's houses were of two or three stories, and well built, with boarded floors. There were neat gardens, in which myrtles, rosemary, and passion flowers abounded; roses and jasmine bloomed year-round; fruits and vegetables grew in profusion; and domestic animals thrived.

Santa Catarina is 57 kilometres long, and between 6 and 16 kilometres in breadth, with a variegated surface of swamps, fertile plains, and mountains. Its climate is subtropical, moist but healthy, with afternoon breezes keeping the days pleasant. Among its native fauna are opossums, monkeys, armadillos, snakes, cranes, hawks, parrots, humming birds, and toucans. In Phillip's time, in addition to fruits and vegetables, it produced rice, maize, coffee, sugar, in-

digo, flax, timber for building, shipbuilding, and fuel, and some meat. There
was a budding cochineal production, and a whaling station at Tijucas Bay on the
adjacent mainland, with an average catch of 300 to 400 animals in the season
between December and June.

Phillip did not have the opportunity to take all this in on his first visit, for
he sailed for Colonia only two days after he reached Destêrro.[38] Proceeding
south with Stevens, he passed Cape Santa Maria, and, swinging west, the Spanish fort at Maldonado, to reach the broad expanse of the estuary. Running past
Montevideo and the fishing banks, he reached Colonia on 12 October. Two
days later, the outpost's governor, Francisco José da Rocha, suddenly marshalled the regiment and sent it aboard the frigates, which arrived at Rio de
Janeiro on 10 November. Only ten days later, these troops were on the frigates
again, heading back for Colonia. Behind this about-face was yet another abrupt
shift in the Portuguese Court's instructions to its Viceroy. In mid-July, news
had reached Europe of the Spanish expedition's having been very badly beaten
at Algiers. Seeing that this offered an opening to act over the Debatable Lands,
Pombal quickly changed his ploy, ordering Lavradio to retain Colonia, and to
move against the Spanish in the Rio Grande. Hence Lavradio's returning the
regiment, which reached its outpost again in mid-December.[39]

While there were no declared hostilities between the Courts at this time,
the Spanish about the Plate estuary had taken to harassing the Portuguese
in various ways. The troops which encircled it were a constant reminder to
Colonia of its likely fate. Rocha maintained a network of spies amongst them,
and at Buenos Aires and Montevideo, from whom he had repeated rumours that
the Spanish were moving towards attack.[40] The activities of the cluster of small
merchantmen that Vertiz, the Governor of Buenos Aires, commissioned as
guardacostas gave substance to these rumours. Treating the estuary as solely a
Spanish water, the commanders swooped on Portuguese fishing and trading
vessels, seizing any goods that might conceivably be contraband, and considering all slaves on board as escaped Spanish ones. Adding to these trials, the Portuguese often received no succour from Santa Catarina or Rio de Janeiro for
months at a time. In this extremity, the defenders burnt the dung of their beasts
for fuel in the winter, and when this proved inadequate turned to cutting their
orchard trees, thus further diminishing their fragile resources. In these wastes of
distance and unyielding environment, surrounded by the forces of an inveterate
enemy, Colonia do Sacramento was, as its governor bitterly observed, not a
fortified refuge but 'a prison, and the ruin of its inhabitants'.[41]

When Phillip and Stevens reached it again in mid-December, the outpost
was in desperate straits. The Portuguese held the fort and township, and a small

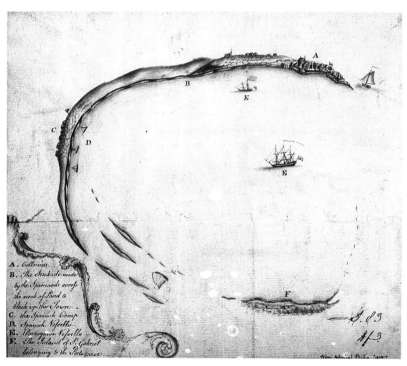

Phillip, Charts of Colonia (1775)

band of orchards and farms behind. They also had batteries on two of the adjacent islands, San Gabriel and San Antonio. But even this description represents Colonia's situation as better than it was. Earlier in the year, Rocha had told the Viceroy that the fort's walls were narrow and crumbling, and were incapable of withstanding siege fire and that the batteries were poorly laid.[42] For reasons of age, illness, and disability, the garrison was also incapable of defending the settlement adequately. Rocha reported plaintively on 1 December that in the absence of the regiment he had had to form another company of blacks, for the sentries remaining were so old and sick that they sat while on duty, and there were not enough of them for him to be able to form different guards. The storehouses were empty of food and munitions. The settlement lacked fuel. And beyond the palisade they had built across the isthmus to hem in the Portuguese, the Spanish camped troops in superior numbers.[43]

On his arrival, Phillip took up the question of what to do about the activities of the Spanish *guardacostas*, which on their route to and from Montevideo and the Spanish camp at Real de San Carlos were sailing provocatively between the batteries at Colonia and San Gabriel Island without flying their flags or otherwise identifying themselves and stating their purpose. Taking a legalistic view, Phillip thought that the Portuguese should force the Spanish to conform to the naval conventions practised elsewhere, and offered to show the way. Conscious that the promised supply ships had not arrived, and of how any assertion of authority might provoke the neighbours into retaliation, Rocha asked Phillip explicitly not to try. In return, Phillip made Rocha aware that the authority as land commander did not extend over the commodore of a naval squadron; and that, as commodore at Colonia, he had the right to inspect all vessels using his port.[44]

Phillip soon found an occasion to assert his perceived prerogative. On 16 December, two Spanish *guardacostas* entered the Colonia roadstead for San Carlos. As usual, their masters declined either to display their flags, or to send a boat to announce their presence and purpose. Deciding he would bear the indignity no longer, Phillip fired a blank across the bows of the leading ship. When this did not produce the desired effect, he fired four balls over it. The master still not obliging, Phillip fired two balls at the ship (which seem to have missed). This ship passing beyond range, Phillip fired at the second one, and damaged it. An alarmed Rocha immediately sent an officer to explain the incident to Orduy, the Spanish commander of San Carlos. He took pains to point out that he had orders to act defensively only; that Phillip had acted against his wishes; and that, to avoid further such incidents, it would be best if the Spanish ships refrained from using the route past Colonia while the English captains remained there. Independently, Phillip also sent an emissary to Orduy, to explain that while he was not out to provoke hostilities, he was determined to extract good manners from the masters of the Spanish vessels. Orduy reported the incident immediately to Vertiz at Montevideo, and developments as they occurred. Knowing that the cover which the shore batteries offered the Portuguese frigates made it dangerous to attempt any retaliation, Vertiz told Orduy to instruct the masters of the *guardacostas* not to use their customary route. However, Orduy was also to insist to Rocha that the Spanish had a right to sail freely in the area, and that, if they did not do so, it would only be from a desire to maintain good relations.

In December, before Orduy could convey these sentiments, another *guardacosta* whose master was unaware of the altered situation ventured into Phillip's domain. When he did not oblige either by flying his flag or answering signals, Phillip fired two shots, causing the intruder to flee. Orduy reported this fresh incident to Vertiz, and protested to Rocha at the continued efforts to restrict Spanish navigation in a manner quite contrary to established usage. His resolve now strengthened by the arrival of a storeship, and presumably also by the Spaniards' obvious reluctance to retaliate, Rocha stated that the Portuguese wished only to have the Spanish conform to the naval conventions obtaining among all civilized nations. He also asserted that the Spanish had only navigated the area without any restraint in recent years, when the Portuguese forces had been too weak to exercise their right to be acknowledged. A week later, Rocha enlarged vigorously on this last point, and counterclaimed that whereas previously the Portuguese had enjoyed a free navigation all about the estuary, recently the Spanish had sought to confine them to the bay formed by the cordon of islands about Colonia. Finding this less-subservient Portuguese attitude a dangerous development, Vertiz reported fully to his Court.

Given Colonia's inherent weakness, Phillip's was a rather impulsive attitude. However, it was one that turned out well, for by making the *guardacostas* more circumspect in their operations, he loosened the noose about the beleaguered outpost; and, though it showed Lavradio that he was perhaps 'a little headstrong', it showed also that he was not afraid to act. As this was a quality so singularly lacking in M'Douall, its presence in Phillip counted much with the Viceroy.[45] Rocha seems to have been rather less impressed, for he subsequently complained that Phillip had appropriated to his squadron much of the wood the supply ship brought from Santa Catarina.[46] In any competition for inadequate resources, it was inevitable that land and sea commanders should have different perspectives. Warships that could not fight efficiently might serve no effective purpose. Colonia depended for its existence on Phillip's squadron keeping its lines of supply open; and this it could not do if the crews were unhealthy: therefore, Phillip needed fuel. But a settlement without adequate fuel was a forlorn place, especially when the ships to succour it were gone; and through the next twelve months Rocha and his miserable band were to measure time according to the unpredictable arrival of storeships. Theirs was an unenviable lot.

In accordance with Pombal's new orders, Lavradio sought to improve the Portuguese position in Rio Grande, ordering Böhm and M'Douall to prepare a decisive move against the Spanish about the Lagoa dos Patos. By the end of January 1776, M'Douall had the squadron almost ready; but now came the first of a number of surprising actions. Considering that her shallow draught made the *Pilar* well suited to operating in the coastal lake, the Viceroy had ordered Phillip to join the squadron at Santa Catarina after he had unloaded the regiment at Colonia.[47] Leaving the outpost on 30 December, Phillip had done this on 18 January.[48] But then, instead of using the *Pilar* in the combined operation at the lake, on 27 January M'Douall sent Phillip to hunt for Spanish prizes off the Plate estuary.[49] When, through bad management and mischance, the Portuguese offensive failed on 19 February, M'Douall abandoned the area, and took most of the squadron back to Santa Catarina. Phillip rejoined it there on 28 March, after a fruitless cruise of sixty days in an often stormy south Atlantic Ocean.[50]

The Viceroy was furious with M'Douall for these actions. 'You commenced by not allowing the frigate *Pilar* to be one of those appointed to enter the river, alleging that it was impossible for [her] to do so; whereas, when the vessels entered, it was evident that the river was quite deep enough for her to have entered just as the others did. ... the frigate *Graça Divina*, the frigate *Pilar*, the frigate from Pernambuco, and the corvette *Nossa Senhora da Victoria* would have been more than a match [for the Spanish vessels in the lagoon]. All of these, with the exception of the corvette, were much stronger than the Spanish vessels ... if [my] orders had been carried out to the letter, the result would have been vastly different to what it was ... The vessels [you sent] were manned by the worst sailors of the Fleet. [You used inexperienced officers while those] who had been in battle, and under fire, such as Arthur Phillip ... and other officers of great value on account of their honour and energy, were left out, and sent to do that which the others could have done equally well.'[51]

Lavradio might have saved himself some of this rage. On 1 April, with help from the motley collection of craft which M'Douall had left under Captain Hardcastle's command, Böhm succeeded in capturing the Spanish forts about the lake; and on this day, Lavradio received Pombal's orders to cease hostilities immediately, for the Courts had turned to negotiation again. The truce offered the squadron a welcome respite, for the service in the south Atlantic through the summer of 1775–76 had been arduous, with frequent storms straining the ships and exhausting the crews, so much so that the captains were moved to observe that the seas were indescribably rough, and that European seas even at their worst were not to be compared with them.[52]

As negotiations proceeded in Europe the parties in South America observed the truce only uneasily. Tension remained high, particularly in the Plate estuary, where Spanish authorities continued to try to suppress the trade which they found so annoying between their countrymen and the Portuguese at Colonia. They kept their troops encamped about the Portuguese settlement, and the attentions of the *guardacostas* were particularly close: as Lavradio complained, 'the moment [these] discover on board [our merchant vessels] any hides or other merchandise which they could allege have been obtained by contraband, and, as regards the fishermen, even without that excuse, they capture them and seize the slaves which they find on board'.[53] In this atmosphere, the Portuguese at Colonia remained alert, with Rocha seeking intelligence from his spies, and reporting it to the Viceroy.[54]

Annoyed in turn by the depredations of the *guardacostas*, Lavradio returned to his scheme of stationing a small squadron of frigates permanently at Colonia.[55] In April, he sent there the *Pilar*, the *Nazareth*, and the *Gloria*, once more giving Phillip overall command. The captains had some good success in the winter months, making the masters of the *guardacosta* much more circumspect in their operations, and capturing two Spanish vessels: as Lavradio reported with satisfaction, 'the presence of [the frigates] effectually put a stop to all the acts of daring which [the Spanish] practised upon our merchant vessels and upon the fishermen'.[56] But this deployment of frigates at Colonia did not fit well with the truce, and after Spain complained, the Portuguese Court instructed Lavradio to give way. Rather than abandon his scheme completely, the Viceroy scaled it down. In August, he ordered the *Nazareth* and the *Gloria* to withdraw, the one to Santa Catarina, the other to Rio de Janeiro. His new idea was to have one frigate permanently at Colonia, another at Santa Catarina; and a third in reserve at Rio de Janeiro, ready to relieve one of the others at need. Such a system, he wrote home, was 'the only way to make ourselves respected and ensure quiet'.[57] What he did not say was that this was also a way of obtaining greater personal control of naval matters, and thereby reducing his necessary dealings with M'Douall, in whose ability and reliability he had by this time quite lost confidence, and who gave him 'constant pain' by expressing such views as that the King should cut off the heads of his generals, who were all 'ignorant traitors'.[58]

It was no accident that Lavradio should have first given Phillip charge of the small squadron at Colonia, and then kept him there, rather than one of the other captains, until the end of 1776. Between September 1775 and March 1776, Phillip had confirmed the good impression that the Viceroy had formed of him at the outset of their acquaintance. While Phillip's health was 'delicate', he reported to his Court, he never complained 'except when he had nothing special to do for the Royal Service'.[59] In sharp contrast with M'Douall, Phillip was a distinct asset, as he again showed at Colonia, where he oversaw the supplying of cattle and wood, and dealt with the *guardacostas*. Swooping on the small Portuguese fishing boats in search of contraband, seizing the fishermen and their catches, and immediately selling any slaves to Spanish planters, these vessels continued to be the bugbears of the outpost's existence. As he had done the previous year, Phillip beat them back, and, reversing the roles, captured two small Spanish vessels. Though not glamorous, it was very necessary work; and it must have given him a certain satisfaction.[60]

Despite Phillip's best efforts, though, Colonia's situation worsened steadily during 1776. It continued to receive supplies only intermittently; and in September one of the supply ships ran aground in a storm. In November, it was very short of provisions; showing the effects of her unrelieved service, the *Pilar* needed extensive repairs; and a single frigate was proving no longer enough to keep the *guardacostas* in check. In the midst of these trials, the Spanish discovered Rocha's spy in Montevideo; and others reported that the Spanish were building up for an attack. When Rocha relayed these reports, Lavradio gave them sufficient credence to send them on to Lisbon; and he asked Rocha and Phillip to consider how the settlement's defences might be strengthened.[61]

In the midst of all this, Phillip again pursued his private interests quietly. As he sailed between Rio de Janeiro and Colonia, he charted the coast, and noted the unfrequented harbours that offered wood and water.[62] At Colonia, he charted the adjacent shores and islands. From his own observations, and from conversation with others, he gathered details of the Spanish settlements. Maldonade, he found, was not a strong base. The harbour provided no shelter in southeast gales, and in any case, it was too shallow for large ships, being only 3 to 6 fathoms deep. The battery consisted of only a half-dozen 4-pounders, and there were only about fifty ill-trained soldiers to man it. The more substantial base at Montevideo was the key to the control of the estuary. Here, the harbour did provide good shelter to large ships, and 'a fleet at anchor in the Road entirely commands the Navigation of the River'. One ship of the line and three frigates were permanently stationed here. Between May and August, to protect them from the winter gales, they were run into the mud. Batteries of 9-, 12-, and

18-pounders covered the anchorage. There were usually about 300 poorly-trained and ill-equipped European troops stationed there; and the township of 4000 persons was surrounded by a metre-high mud wall topped by stakes. There was rising ground behind the town, from whence its fortifications might be commanded.

Buenos Aires was a city of 10 000 persons. It was poorly fortified, there were only one regiment of about 500 men, and a company of artillery, to defend it. From a Brazilian who had been raised in Buenos Aires, Phillip learned that, by the post which covered 25 'leagues' (approximately 120 kilometres) a day, it was six days' journey to Córdoba, then another four to Santiago, another one and a half to San Miguel, five more to Salta, one and a half to Jujuy, and then ten to Potosí with its fabled mines. To these centres and their hinterlands the Spanish carried European goods by flat-bottomed boats and by mule train. From them they brought grain, wax, and hides, and, escorted by cavalry, the production of the silver mines. They gathered these goods at Buenos Aires, and sent them overland to the small port of Barragana, and then across the water to Montevideo, from which they went by regular convoy to Spain. The trade through Montevideo was extensive, with as many as a hundred ships, some of them large ones of 800 or 900 tons, sailing annually between the Old World and the New. While Montevideo harbour was reasonably well defended, frigates might easily enter that of Barragana, which had very weak defences. The Spanish about Montevideo and Buenos Aires lived in constant fear of attack by bands of Indians; and the daring Paulistas often drove their cattle off. Scattered about the region, too, were persons of Portuguese origin, who might prove very useful allies in any campaign.[63]

Reflecting his connections with the English cloth trade, Phillip also developed an interest in cochineal production. This reddish-purple dye is derived from the body of a small insect that lives on a variety of prickly pear. The Spanish had first found the Aztecs using it, and, keeping its source secret, had gained a monopoly of the supply. By the mid-eighteenth century, it was in great demand throughout Europe, selling for more than fourteen shillings per pound; and from 1759 onwards, the British Society of Arts, Commerce, and Manufactures offered a prize of £100 to whoever might produce 25 pounds in a single year in Jamaica. At the beginning of the 1770s, Rocha found colonies of the insect on Santa Catarina Island; and Lavradio then established a large plantation there, from which he had the plants and their inhabitants dispensed freely to calling ships and to other parts of Brazil.[64] It was from this source that Phillip obtained the specimens that, observing their cycle closely, he bred for some months in his cabin; but 'the Cold Weather setting in, when I was in the

River of Plate they all died'. The experiment was promising enough to convince him that the insect might be 'carried into our west India Islands and there bred to the great advantage of the Nation, as well as to the very great profit of the Planter'.[65]

In November and December 1776, responding to Rocha's urgent request, Lavradio sent food, wood, coal, and bricks, and emphasized that the outpost must be held.[66] At the same time, though, he ordered Phillip to rendezvous with the squadron at Santa Catarina. Repairing his ship as best he could, Phillip sailed in December.[67] He had done good work at Colonia, and the Viceroy was very pleased with him. 'The merchant vessel *Nossa Senhora do Pilar*', Lavradio reported to Pombal, 'which also serves as a frigate, has been staying at Colonia, for the purpose of restraining the continual attacks which the Spanish corsairs have been making upon the inhabitants of that place, and which have only been prevented by the presence of that small vessel'. Phillip was 'intelligent and active, and shews that he has been reared as a soldier'; and with only his own frigate, he made the Spanish respect the fortress 'as they ought to'.[68]

The new orders followed on the Viceroy's having received ominous news from Europe. Outraged by Pombal's failure to inform Brazil of the truce at the same time as they had informed their settlements about the Plate, and at the subsequent Portuguese victory at the Lagoa dos Patos, the Spanish determined to send a massive force to South America to settle the business. This they gathered during the middle of the year, and selected Cevallos to command it. Underlying the seriousness of their purpose, they created the new viceroyalty of La Plata for Cevallos to administer. When it sailed from Cádiz in the middle of November, the expedition consisted of twenty warships and ninety-six transport, manned by 8500 sailors and carrying 10 000 troops. The size of the expedition was such that the Spanish could not well conceal either its existence or its destination, and Lisbon was soon aware of the threat to Santa Catarina, Rio Grande, and Colonia. Pombal and Mello e Castro accordingly sent Lavradio fulsome instructions on how he should look to his empire's defences.[69] It was in accordance with these instructions that, at the beginning of 1777, M'Douall once more assembled his squadron at Santa Catarina.

The Viceroy's scheme for defending the island involved having the squadron lie in wait in Garoupas Bay, but M'Douall subsequently obtained Lavradio's agreement to basing patrols on Arvoredo Island instead. The watching Portuguese frigates first sighted the leading ships of the Spanish expedition at noon on 17 February. Three hours later, they had so many enemy ships in sight that 'it was impossible to count them'. At this point, Phillip made 'every effort' to persuade M'Douall to engage the Spanish; and for the next two days, the commodore did make rather desultory attempts to cut out individual enemy ships. Failing in this, he withdrew the squadron northwards, whereupon Phillip wrote to him privately, 'imploring him, for the sake of his own honour and that of the [English] Nation, not to refrain from attacking'.[70]

On 20 February, when the concentration of the Spanish fleet in the Santa Catarina roadstead made it impossible that the Portuguese squadron should succeed in an attack, M'Douall called his captains to a council of war, to consider what they might now do, and—it seems—to create grounds with which to counter Phillip's criticism. The royal orders to the Viceroy did provide for an attack on the Spanish settlements about the Plate estuary, but M'Douall appears to have wanted to set definite limits to the squadron's future activities, as well as to justify its present inertia. He achieved this by reading passages from both the royal orders and the Viceroy's instructions. He evidently read very selectively, choosing paragraphs from older despatches that best served his purposes, and ignoring those from more recent ones that would have shown up his indecision. At least, it seems this is what we should conclude from the subsequent fury of the Viceroy, who told Pombal that though M'Douall denied having ever seen his most recent instructions, he 'mixes up things in such a way that he confesses some and denies others'; and that 'this lack of sincerity is the spirit in which this Officer has always sought, sometimes to deny, and at others to misinterpret the orders given to him, to avoid the carrying out of which he refrained from mentioning them when he called the Council of the Captains'.[71]

After hearing passages which stressed the ultimate need to preserve the squadron, five of the eight captains jointly signed a statement approving of M'Douall's actions, and supporting his idea that they return to Rio de Janeiro to obtain fresh orders from the Viceroy.[72] A sixth offered a separate statement to the same effect.[73] One, José de Mello of the *Prazeres*, dissented strongly, arguing instead that they had 'no course to pursue other than to attack' the Spanish, for if the Portuguese Court had known the coastline 'as we know it', it would have given 'the clearest and most precise orders' to this effect.[74] Phillip stood between these opposites. Obviously influenced against his private inclinations by the royal injunctions cited by M'Douall, he said that his opinion 'always has been that our Fleet ought to remain at Santa Catarina to assist the fortresses in defending this island; or, if we left it, that we ought to attack the Spanish Fleet at all risk'. After pointing to the difficulty of attacking a far superior squadron at anchor, and to the impossibility of succeeding in an attack on Maldonado, Montevideo, or Buenos Aires without suitable ships and supporting troops, Phillip concluded that he saw, 'at this moment, no advantage to be gained by disobeying His Majesty's orders'.[75] At this distance, it is difficult

'A View of the Works of Inhahij in the District of Serra do Frio dos Diamantes'

'A Diamond Smugler who having emptied the bed of a brook in the unfrequented part of the Countrey & procurd some gravel is washing it in hopes of finding diamonds, when these smuglers are taken they are Transported to Angola for Life.'

Augustus Earle, 'Negro fandango' (1821–24)

Augustus Earle, 'A catamaran, Madras Roads' (1829)

Though of later dates, these paintings show what Phillip would have seen

to determine the relative merits of these conflicting views. Given the sheer size of the Spanish expedition, M'Douall clearly had a point. Yet, had he acted immediately on the appearance of the first Spanish ships, as Phillip had urged, presumably he might have achieved something. And behind the lines of Phillip's considered opinion we may sense both his zeal for battle and his passionate indignation at his compatriot's readiness to take refuge behind the royal orders so as to avoid this.

Having obtained from most of his captains the gesture he wanted, M'Douall turned the squadron for Rio de Janeiro—one Portuguese official wrote that he fled 'like a Chinaman'.[76] As it proceeded north, the land commanders surrendered Santa Catarina with as little resistance. When the squadron neared Rio de Janeiro on 6 March, M'Douall sent Phillip ahead to give the Viceroy the distressing news.[77] Lavradio was predictably furious, and his first impulse was to order the captains to sea again immediately, to cut the Spanish expedition's supply line to Montevideo and Buenos Aires. When the commodore represented the damage the ships had suffered in recent storms, Lavradio relented, and allowed them to refit.[78]

The squadron sailed from Rio de Janeiro again on 1 April, to patrol off the Debatable Lands; and at last Phillip was able to satisfy his desire for stirring action.[79] On 14 April, they captured a small Spanish guardship, whose papers showed that two large battleships from Europe had reached Montevideo on their way to Santa Catarina. The Portuguese sighted one of these ships on 19 April, and gave chase. Having the fastest sailers, and being besides clearly the most actively inclined of the captains, José de Mello and Phillip led the pursuit, and soon outdistanced their colleagues. The next day, Mello fired as soon as he came within range, but Phillip pressed on quietly. 'Unable to convince themselves that a vessel so small and so weak in artillery would venture to attack a 70-gun ship', the Spanish assumed that the *Pilar* was one of their ships, and allowed her to close, for Phillip to shatter their illusion with a broadside. His idea was to retard the enemy sufficiently to allow Mello to come up, but the ploy failed. Phillip and Mello lost their prey in the night, when the wind dropped; but dawn showed her close to the rest of the Portuguese squadron, and after a brief engagement, her captain surrendered.[80]

The *San Agustin* was a considerable prize. A 70-gun ship of the line carrying 550 men, she was 'a new vessel, built of excellent wood', with 'first-rate artillery' and 'all munitions and accessories of the first class'. Finally in a position to show the Viceroy some positive result, M'Douall headed back to Rio de Janeiro, arriving on 26 April. Lavradio gladly added the *San Agustin* to his outmatched squadron, in which she became distinctly the most powerful ship.

He showed his appreciation of Phillip's service by appointing him to command her.[81] Refitted and refreshed, the enlarged squadron sailed for another patrol in southern waters at the end of May.[82] Unlike the previous one, this ended in a comically disastrous fashion, when one evening, each taking the other for the enemy, the captains of the *Prazeres* and the *Ajuda* poured broadsides into each other, with Mello also firing on the *Santo Antonio* when M'Douall intervened. The imbroglio caused M'Douall to cut short this patrol too, and the squadron reached Rio de Janeiro again at the end of June, when Lavradio learned that Colonia had also surrendered. He ordered the captains to sea again on 7 July. The next month he learned that the European courts had reached yet another truce, and ordered all his forces to cease hostilities.[83]

The new lull followed, on the one hand, the death of the Portuguese monarch José, the accession of Maria I, and the attendant eclipse of Pombal as chief minister; and on the other, Florida Blanca's replacing Grimaldi as the chief minister of the Spanish Court. Being therefore in a position to get beyond old attitudes, on 1 October 1777 the Courts converted the truce into the Treaty of San Ildefonso, whereby Spain returned Santa Catarina to Portugal and recognized Portugal's possession of Rio Grande; and Portugal relinquished Colonia, and her claim to the lands about the northern shore of the Plate estuary. Both governments quickly sent details of the accord to their officials in South America. One minor consequence of this peace was that Lavradio was finally able to satisfy his long-held desire to remove M'Douall from the command of the squadron. In December 1777, Mello e Castro ordered that the commodore should be sent on the first ship to Lisbon to be court-martialled for his part in the loss of Santa Catarina; and the Viceroy accordingly despatched him in February 1778.[84] Another minor consequence was that Phillip lost the command of the *San Agustin*, which Lavradio returned to the Spanish in April.[85]

Phillip presumably spent the nine months between August 1777 and April 1778 in much the same way as he had his earlier sojourn at Rio de Janeiro—that is, in keeping his ship in good order, discussing affairs of state with the Viceroy, discussing scientific matters with others interested in them, enjoying the pleasures of the city, and gathering more useful information. If he had not previously done so, he now acquainted himself with the gold and diamond production in the interior of the country. These products were mined in the Minas Gerais, the mountainous area some 500 kilometres north of Rio de Janeiro.[86] The gold was distributed more widely than the diamonds, but where the two were found together only the gems were extracted. The diamond-producing area was an elliptical one of about 56 by 32 kilometres in the Serro do Frio. In the 1770s, this area was under the control of officials appointed by the Crown, who were responsible for overseeing the mining by contractors, the collecting of a fifth (*quinto*) of the production for the Crown, the conveying of this production safely to Rio de Janeiro, and the prevention of illicit mining. Provisions reached the area, and the diamonds left it by tedious mule train; and access to it was strictly regulated. 'No person of any state, quality, or condition, might enter the Forbidden District, without previously transmitting a petition to the Intendant, accompanied with a certificate from the local authorities of the place which he was about to leave, and stating the business upon which he was going, and the place to which he was bound. The Intendant and the Administrators should then give or withhold permission, as might to them seem best; fix the term of his stay; and, upon just cause, grant a prolongation of that term, but for once only. All persons, whether Whites, Mulattos, or free Negroes, who had no lawful calling, known establishment, or ostensible means of life, were consequently to be suspected of living by some secret practices, and therefore to be expelled.'[87] Penalties for illegal presence were harsh: for a first offence, a fine and six months' imprisonment; for a second, a larger fine, and transportation to Angola for ten years.

Historical tradition has it that John Mawe, who went with the Prince Regent's express permission in 1809, was the first Englishman to penetrate to the Forbidden District. This tradition was never entirely right, for some Britishers who had embraced Catholicism and married Portuguese had resided in the Minas Gerais in the mid-eighteenth century. However, entry to the area was so closely regulated as to make Mawe's royally-sanctioned tour a striking event. It is therefore a matter of considerable interest that Phillip may have anticipated him by forty years. The question of whether Phillip did so is a vexed one. There is extant a five-page extract from what was clearly a comprehensive journal of his Brazilian years, dealing with diamond and gold production.[88] These pages show that, as well as written descriptions, the journal also contained 'Views of the Diamond works ... taken on the Spot'. These views are evidently the three watercolours and five pencil drawings that accompany Sir Joseph Banks's notes on Brazilian diamond mining, which also seem to summarize Phillip's missing journal.[89] If these watercolours and sketches are Phillip's own work, he must have visited the site. If he obtained them from another, then he may still have gone in person, for his notes show a precise knowledge of the diamond works, including some details not present in contemporary sources. If Phillip did not go in person, he certainly obtained his information from persons who had.

After describing the changes made in the early 1770s to the arrangements by which the mines were worked, Phillip recorded the business of mining itself. Five thousand African slaves owned by contractors and supervised by overseers did the work. The deposits lay in the third stratum, and to reach these the miners either turned rivers entirely from their natural courses, or diverted them for a distance via wooden aqueducts. The turning of the rivers and the clearing of their beds required 'immense' labour, for the miners 'have often immense Rocks to split or support that they may dig under them... They split those Rocks by making fires on them, till they are violently heated and then a run of water is turn'd on them, which splits them and they are carried away ... when those Rocks in the bottom of the Rivers are too large to be split or removed, they shoar them up, tho' not without great trouble and risk, and then dig under them.'

When the diamond-bearing gravels had been gathered, they were searched to recover their treasure. This took place in an open shed 20 or 30 metres long, where slaves worked a series of troughs, sorting among the stones as water sluiced the dirt away. Each slave was watched over by an overseer armed with a whip, whose seat, to keep him alert, lacked both back and arms. Given the constant bending and raking, the work was very arduous; and was relieved only by the prospects of small or large reward it offered. As Phillip noted, 'any Slave [who] finds a Diamond that weighs a Oitava [17½ carats] he is free, that is the Crown purchases his freedom, and he is paid his daily labour the same as the Master receiv'd for him, he that finds a Diamond of three Quarters of a Oitava is Cloathd; of one half a Oitava receives a Hat, or something of equal Value, and if of less weight a Knife or Handkerchief, and always on finding the smallest spark, which is call'd Olho de Musquita, he has a few pinches of snuff, or piece of Tobacco.'

All diamonds found were placed in a bowl of water hanging from the middle of the shed. To prevent deceits, the slaves were unpredictably rotated from trough to trough, and searched at the end of the day. All diamonds were collected by the Intendant and his officials, weighed, and, at intervals amid tight security, transported to Rio de Janeiro to be shipped to Lisbon. Despite these precautions, clandestine extraction and smuggling of diamonds were rife. Phillip observed that 'the Negroes are very dexterous in concealing a Diamond, and from their Infancy, practise the tossing grains of Indian Corn into their Mouths without raising the hand, & that they do in a manner that would do credit to yᵉ best slight of hand Juglers'. The residents of Minas Gerais encouraged their slaves to conceal finds; and often these residents followed occupations only so as to have a legitimate front to conceal their smuggling. Interlopers also ventured into the Forbidden District, to search secretly for the gems. 'There are many of these People,' Phillip observed, 'who hiding themselves in the Woods, and where they find a convenient place in the River, make a Dam & digging

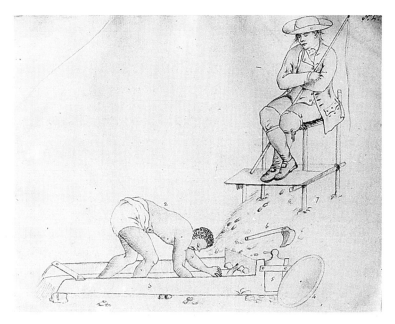

'An Overseer of the Diamond Contract super-
intending a negroe'

'A View of the Shed Calld a Cavage in which
the Diamond Gravel is washd'

down to the Strata in which they suppose Diamonds are contain'd, throw it on the side of the River and marsh, or search for the Diamonds by throwing water on the heap of sand and Gravel, scraping it down with the other hand, and the Eye fix'd on what they rake down, the smallest spark does not escape them'.

Those who were apprehended in these illegal activities were harshly dealt with, but the potential rewards far outweighed the deterrents. In collusion with officials of the district and naval officers, merchants operated elaborate rings to get the stones to Europe. In 1778, for example, Lisbon officials seized a packet of diamonds totalling 2700 carats; and this was only to scratch the surface of the clandestine commerce. Phillip estimated that more than a third of all diamonds found were smuggled. Neither were the inhabitants of Minas Gerais behindhand in dealing illegally in gold. Phillip again commented that the central administration had had to forbid the circulation of coins in the area, for the locals had taken to counterfeiting coins 'equal in weight, and as good Gold as what was Coined by the Government', so that the Crown once more lost its revenue. Consequently, the inhabitants had to deal in gold bars and gold dust; and the losses occasioned in weighing made 'the sweeping of the Houses … a considerable article'.

In mid-1778, Phillip's Portuguese service drew to a close. Learning that France had taken the part of the rebellious American colonies in their war with Britain, he determined to rejoin the Royal Navy. Giving him the command of M'Douall's *Santo Antonio*, the Viceroy employed him and José de Mello in the *Prazeres* to escort a convoy to Lisbon. On the warships went the regular shipment of diamonds, with five chests 'the size of the small Childrens trunks in England … lin'd with Velvet, Lock'd and Seal'd up at the Mines' being put on board Phillip's.[90] After an uneventful voyage, Phillip reached Lisbon on 20 August, his ship was paid off four days later, and he resigned his commission.[91]

Phillip had served well in these four years, and the Portuguese authorities knew it. Lavradio reported that he was 'one of the officers of the most distinct merit that the Queen … has in her service in the Navy, and I think that it will be a most important acquisition to [retain him] in the Royal Service. … As regards his disposition, he is somewhat [distrustful]; but, as he is an Officer of education and principle, he gives way to reason, and does not, before doing so, fall into those exaggerated and unbearable excesses of temper which the majority of his fellow-countrymen do, more especially those who have been brought up at sea. He is very clean-handed [*sic*]; is an Officer of great truth and very brave; and is no flatterer, saying what he thinks, but without temper or want of respect. The length of my Report upon this Officer implies that I regret [his departure] very much, and I confess that I do. It is the consequence of my having noted the great difference in the way he served, as compared with the greater part of the others.'[92]

Metropolitan officials shared the Viceroy's opinion of Phillip. The Portuguese Court, the British ambassador reported home, 'is extremely satisfied with the conduct of this Gentleman, & ... he has served in the Brasils with great Zeal & Honour'.[93] When Phillip sailed for England on 20 September, he carried a letter from Mello e Castro to the Portuguese ambassador, praising his service, stating that the queen had found herself unable to refuse his patriotic request to rejoin the Royal Navy, and conveying Her Majesty's wish that he be promoted in that service.[94] It took some time for Phillip to have his reward, but on 2 September 1779, partly in response to the request of Maria I, the Lords Commissioners of the Admiralty promoted him to master and commander.[95]

In both public and personal ways, Phillip's years in the service of Portugal marked a distinct turning point in his life. He had gone to Brazil a capable junior officer without real prospects. He returned to Europe after distinguished service in coastal patrol, battle, and the command of a line-of-battle ship. He returned also with knowledge of the coasts and harbours of the Portuguese and Spanish colonies in South America, of the larger settlements and their defences, of the geography of the interior and its products. These were things to bring him to the notice of his naval superiors in England. These years had also shown Phillip how European colonization might proceed, on a small scale or a large one. At Colonia do Sacramento, he had experienced the difficulties of sustaining an outpost with few local resources; with distant sources of supply, and uncertain lines to them; and with a populace with little enthusiasm for the venture. At Rio de Janeiro, in the careful planning of the port to meet the needs of ships arriving from long voyages, and in the defence of these facilities, in the Viceroy's authority and the signs of this authority, he had perceived what might be the sweep of empire. And, showing how imperial resources might be used, the splendid city rising from the rubble of old Lisbon had reinforced this sense. These were perceptions to employ when selecting the site of a future colony, archetypes with which to humanize a future wilderness.

Across these years, too, Phillip had come to certain abiding perceptions about human society and his own circumstance. When he left Brazil, he must have been confirmed in his belief that there was no place for slavery in a free land. He had also found that, whatever he might do in future, he likely would do it against persistent ill-health. Though he had still one or two experiences to add to the total that, ten years hence, would set him on a unique course, he had now largely laid its basis.

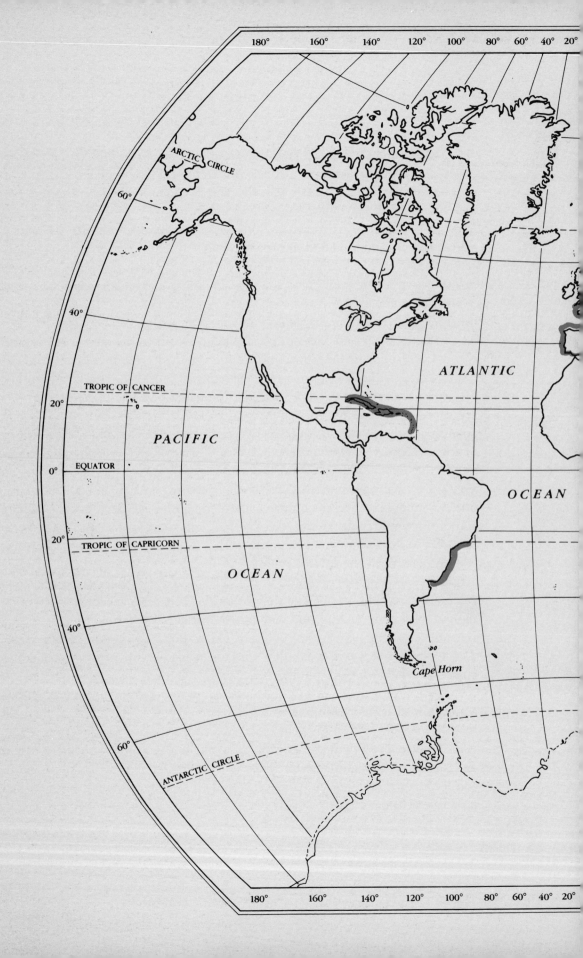

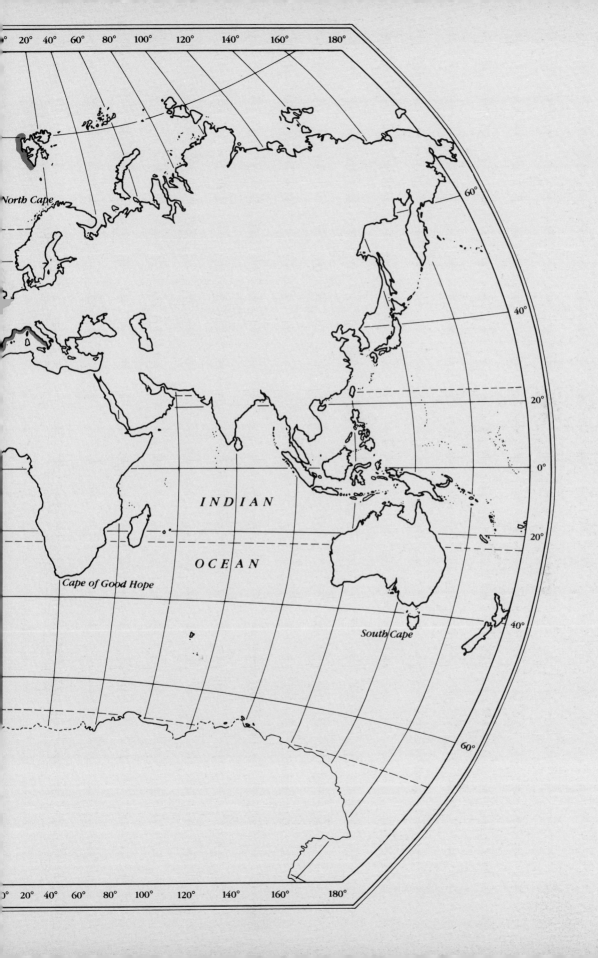

AWAITING OPPORTUNITY: HOME WATERS, 1778–82

I know nothing that could hurt me so much as remaining unemploy'd in times like the present, & though your Lordship has been pleas'd to say, that when an occasion offer'd, you would give me an opportunity of getting what is due to me at Lisbon; yet I beg leave to say that to whatever part of the World Service be first offer'd to me, will be most agreable.

Arthur Phillip to Lord Sandwich, 19 July 1780

As Arthur Phillip proceeded homeward in September 1778 the first task before him was the difficult business of again taking up his way in the Royal Navy. For someone as ambitious as he was, the need to renew this task must have had distasteful aspects. He who had in the Portuguese navy held the rank of post captain and commanded the best ship, had once more to accept a lieutenant's obscurity; and, with his old patron Augustus Hervey retired, from this junior position to importune men who knew little of him for service and preferment.

Phillip began to bring his merits to the attention of a new group of superiors as soon as he reached England. On the way from Lisbon, the packet boat had passed the French fleet of more than thirty ships sailing southwards from Brest. Phillip gave this information to Philip Stephens, the Secretary of the Admiralty, immediately he reached London on 5 October, adding that he had 'now return'd to His Majesty's Service (which I had done much sooner but was in the Brazil till 20.th of Augt when I arriv'd at Lisbon with the *St Antonio* under my Command)'.[1] His presenting this information and himself had some effect. Four days later, he took up duty as first lieutenant of the *Alexander*, a 74-gun line-of-battle ship carrying a crew of 600, under the command of Captain Richard Kempenfelt. This was a distinctly more senior position than his last in the Royal Navy, and his being given it is a clear sign that the Admiralty now valued his service. He joined the ship at Deptford, where she was fitting for service. On 31 January 1779, she shifted to the Nore, from where she sailed into the Channel, passing the Downs on 23 February and reaching Spithead on 4 March.[2]

The middle months of 1779 were most anxious ones for the British. Spain joined with France in the war and the combined French and Spanish fleet cruised within sight of Plymouth. The presence of these ships and the massing of French troops across the Channel gave rise to fears of invasion, creating great 'affright and terror in every part of the kingdom'.[3] In mid-June, so as to place the well-tried wooden wall between England and her enemies, Sir Charles Hardy took the Channel fleet out from Spithead, with the *Alexander* joining on 29 June. She cruised about the western approaches to the Channel through July. From 28 July to 1 September, the '52 Sail of the French & Spaniards' were repeatedly in sight'; but though both fleets manoeuvred for action several times, they did not engage. Hardy brought his ships back to Spithead on 2 September.

While the cruise did not provide Phillip with any opportunity to distinguish himself, his career in the Royal Navy now continued to advance. On 2 September, responding at last to his claims and to the Portuguese queen's request, the Lords Commissioners promoted him to the rank of master and commander, the Navy's first position of independent command, and appointed him to the *Basilisk*, which they simultaneously ordered to be fitted for Channel service as a fireship carrying eight guns and a crew of forty-five.[4] Fireships were old vessels loaded with combustibles and fitted with special ventilation to help these burn, which were driven against enemy ships and set alight. Service on a fireship was accordingly dangerous work, for which there were special rewards. If they succeeded in burning an enemy ship of 40 guns or more, the commander received either £100, or a gold chain and medal, and the crew £10 each. They received double these rewards if they destroyed a flagship.

The *Basilisk* was 'very Old, weak & consequently unfitt to Cruise with a fleet';[5] and in early September, it was clear that it would take the artificers some considerable time to make her seaworthy. Showing again his desire for active service and the opportunity to distinguish himself in battle, Phillip asked Lord Sandwich, the First Lord of the Admiralty, for permission 'to go the Cruise as a Volunteer in the *Victory*'.[6] No doubt he named this ship deliberately. Of 2162 tons and carrying 100 guns, she was the flagship of the Channel fleet. Twenty-five years later, she was also Nelson's flagship at Trafalgar; and now preserved at Portsmouth, she remains an impressive monument to the greatness of the eighteenth-century Royal Navy. The musterbooks do not confirm that Philip

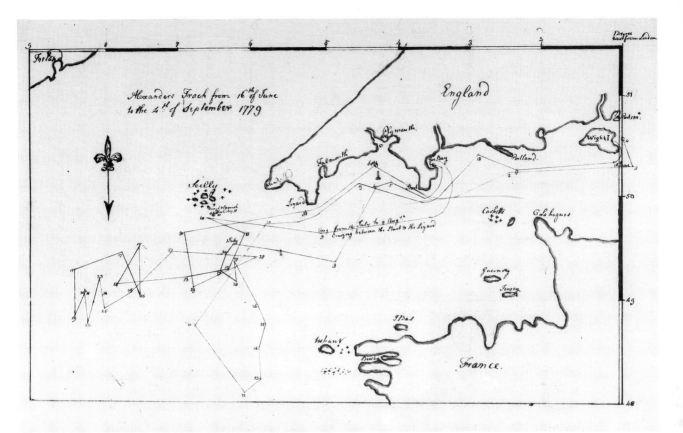

Thomas Pakenham, Chart of the *Alexander*'s cruise, 1779

sailed on her at this time. If he did so, he would have seen only mundane Channel service, but the cruise would have been otherwise important, for putting him in contact with Evan Nepean and John Blankett, who were then aboard the ship, and who were in the next decades to become significant figures in his life.

Early in 1780 dockyard officials decided that the *Basilisk* was not worth repairing; and while she stayed in commission for some months, the crew was finally paid off on 4 July.[7] During this period, 'private affairs' took Phillip to London for four weeks, in March and April.[8] Whether his business there was entirely private is a matter of doubt, since captains and Admiralty officials frequently used the term as a euphemism to cover secret consultations. As Phillip seems to have talked with Lord Sandwich in the spring of 1780, it may well be that such was the case. If so, it is safe to assume that he went to London to tell the Admiralty about South America.

With the *Basilisk* out of commission, by early July Phillip was again unemployed. Immediately, he wrote to the Admiralty to say that he was ready to serve elsewhere. This approach not leading at once to a posting, nine days later he took his request directly to Sandwich. Announcing that nothing could 'hurt me so much as remaining unemploy'd in times like the present', he reminded the First Lord of an earlier promise 'that when an occasion offer'd, you would

give me an opportunity of getting what is due to me at Lisbon'. Perhaps knowing that there was no vacant command in the small squadron based there he
added that service in any part of the world whatsoever would be agreeable to
him.[9] He had to wait a considerable time before he received another command.
Late in 1780 he briefly relieved the captains of the *St Albans* and the *Magnanime*
while these ships were fitting in the Thames, but both officers returned to duty
when the work was finished. Galling as Phillip must have found this inactivity,
at least it gave him some time with the Lanes, from whose address in December
he wrote to Stephens asking for his name to be entered in the Half Pay list for
the periods of unemployment since he returned from Portugal, and to be paid
for the time he had acted as relieving captain.[10]

January 1781 found Phillip offering Lord Sandwich further advice; and
then, in one of those mysterious silences that perplex the biographer exceedingly, he disappears from view for nine months, suddenly to reappear as relieving
captain of the *Ariadne* in mid-October. His name appears in the Half Pay list
without a break during this time;[11] and, contrary to what might be expected,
there are no letters in the Admiralty correspondence from him offering his services or discussing any other matters. The only discernible mention of him
comes in an 'appointment' book kept by Lord Sandwich, in which he is entered
as having been recommended for promotion and active service by Pinto de
Souza and a 'Mr Shafto'.[12]

On 10 October 1781, the Admiralty appointed Phillip acting captain of the
Ariadne, a 24-gun frigate then fitting in the Thames, which he joined five days
later.[13] In November, he completed the ship's fitting, and joined squadrons
patrolling home waters, but to no particular purpose.[14] Then, on 30 November,
the Admiralty promoted him to the rank of post captain, confirmed him in the
command of the *Ariadne*, and ordered him to proceed immediately to the Elbe,
to escort a transport that was to bring to England a detachment of Hanoverian
soldiers destined for India.[15] We may presume that his knowledge of German
recommended him for this task.

As Phillip learned to his chagrin, it was very late in the season to be navigating the Elbe.[16] On reaching Cuxhaven on 18 December, he found that the
harbour master had ordered the master of the transport to run her ashore, out
of reach of the ice that was daily expected. He found also that some of the
troops had mutinied, so that their officers had been forced to withdraw them to
Otterdorf, 20 kilometres away. Phillip immediately arranged for the colonel
in charge of the troops to embark them in the *Ariadne* within forty-eight hours;
but even as he did so the estuary filled with ice; and in order to save her, he had
to run his frigate into the mud at the harbourside. As he reported to Stephens, 'I

have Sir consulted with the Pilots and acted for the best, the running of the Ship into the Mud was the only means of saving her, and that was not done untill many hours after the Pilots who were on board declared it to be absolutely necessary, and refused either to carry her to Sea or to take any further charge of her if she remained at Anchor'.[17] In the next days, Phillip hired fishing boats to take off the *Ariadne*'s guns and equipment, and with the harbour master's help, he drove her further up the mud, out of danger. Equally marooned, he and the master of the transport then waited for the ice to recede. In an unusually severe winter, the Elbe was not sufficiently clear for them to be able to leave for several months. The transport sailed on 7 March, and *Ariadne* followed fifteen days later, reaching the Nore on 25 March.[18]

Back in England, Phillip once more busied himself with the refitting of the ship. Showing his knowledge of artillery, and presumably also his friendship with Isaac Landmann, on 12 June he asked for 'twelve pound Fire Balls' and 'Quill Tubes'. This was an unusual request for, as Stephens told him, Navy ships had not previously carried these items. Phillip replied that they were available at Woolwich, and that he had elsewhere used them with good effect—a remark which most likely refers to some acquaintance with Sir Charles Douglas.[19] A gunnery enthusiast, Douglas replaced loose powder-and-fuse ignition with goosequills filled with powder, which allowed much more controlled firing, perfecting the procedure while captain of the *Duke* from 1779 to 1781. This innovation, together with another by which Douglas swivelled guns forward, was the basis of the British victory of the Saints in April 1782, when Douglas was Rodney's flag captain. After the battle, Douglas reported to Sandwich that 'of 2600 goosequill tubes not a single one failed'.[20] Phillip's request shows his habit of keeping abreast of developments in his profession, and his ceaseless enthusiasm to distinguish himself in battle.

Work on her completed, the *Ariadne* sailed from Sheerness on 24 June, but whether she carried the armaments Phillip wanted is unknown. She patrolled around the Channel until mid-August. On 19 August she was involved in a collision with the *Princess Royal*, as she worked out of the Downs. A week later, Phillip put into Sheerness to have the damage repaired.[21] The four weeks this took gave him the opportunity to offer more private advice in London, after which he sailed down the Channel to Spithead, which he reached on 6 November. He then cruised across the Atlantic entrance of the Channel until 19 December, when he returned to Spithead. Four days later, the Admiralty appointed him captain of the *Europe*, a fourth-rate of 64 guns, and at last he found fulfilled his ambition to command a large warship in the Royal Navy.

Though Phillip's active service from October 1778 through to the end of

1782 was confined to the English Channel and along adjacent European coasts, this period was for a number of reasons of considerable significance in his career. Even though he did not serve continuously, he advanced steadily in rank, from first lieutenant to master and commander to post captain in charge of a small battleship. While it was not at all unusual for officers with influence to progress in this manner, especially in wartime, Phillip did not possess influence, neither does he seem to have had any patron at this time who might have compensated for this lack. Certainly it was possible for men to rise in the eighteenth-century Royal Navy entirely as a consequence of the merit they displayed; and numbers did so. But possessing merit was one thing; finding situations in which to display it, or having superiors who would perceive it, was another. There was many a capable junior officer whom fate decreed should remain undistinguished and unpromoted.

This was not Phillip's lot; and we can only conclude that it was not because he had the kinds of expertise needed for unusual tasks. The Admiralty's employing him to bring the Hanoverian troops to England is a small example of this. The officials who arranged the despatch of the troops could not have known that they would mutiny, or that the ice would arrive with such finality; but in sending an officer who had a German background, a flexible outlook, and who was given to improvization, they provided for the meeting of such contingencies. And conversely, Phillip was also able to turn the situation to his advantage. While ice-bound at Cuxhaven, he looked about him in his characteristically interested way, and was struck by the great numbers of Elbe seamen whom the Dutch enlisted. This led him to investigate the possibility of the British doing likewise. Consulting one of George III's German Privy Councillors, he learned that as Elector of Hanover the King exercised some authority in Hamburg; and he accordingly told the Admiralty on his return that they might profitably station an officer at Stade, to recruit among the seamen of Hamburg and Hanover.[22] Such thoughtful advice could only further the already-established impression that Phillip was an officer whose views were worthy of attention.

It was in these years, too, that Phillip first discernibly made the acquaintance of a number of persons who would henceforth be significant in his life. Foremost among them was Evan Nepean, in 1779–80 the purser of the *Victory*. Like Phillip, Nepean rose from poverty and obscurity on his merits. The son of a Plymouth shipwright, in the early 1780s he became Secretary to the Port Admiral there, and Lord Shelburne then made him Undersecretary at the Southern Department, which soon afterwards became the Home Office. Later, he was Secretary of the Admiralty. Another such was John Blankett, with whom he was to join to offer strategic advice to a succession of administrations, and to spy in France. A third was Philip Gidley King, whom Phillip took into the *Ariadne* and the *Europe*, and then also to New South Wales. Phillip had extensive dealings with these men in the most important years of his life. While the nature of his relationship with Blankett is unclear, Nepean and King proved his enduring friends; and with them he shared confidences and the secret or isolated moments of his life over twenty years.

In terms of the rhythm which his extensive periods at sea give to Phillip's life, his home service in the years 1779–82 constitutes an interlude; but it is important as a fulcrum between one phase of his voyaging and another and very different one. Up to 1778, no matter how well he had performed his work in the Royal Navy, nor how good an impression he had made in the Portuguese one, he was only a capable junior officer among many others, with small claims on the attention of posterity. After 1782, he was one whom fate impelled to a unique endeavour, and the remembrance of nations. As now appears, his secret advice and service were the key to his passing from the one phase to the other.

3

To Indias of Mine and Spice

The Secret Expeditions, 1780–84

*There is not one place from California to
Cape Horn, capable of resisting such an
Equipment, if properly provided and properly
conducted. Some advantageous Posts
should be fortified, and terms of
independence offered to the Native
Mexicans, Peruvians, and Chilians.*

*If these Settlements were effected it is
evident that the Trade of South America
would be opened to our East-Indian
Territories; if these Settlements were not effected,
still the Blow to Spain must be fatal, because
her richest possessions would be alarmed,
their Commerce and Remittances
interrupted, their Ships destroyed, their
Towns plundered, and the Inhabitants incited
to revolt.*

*William Fullarton, Memorandum to
Lord North, 3 June 1780*

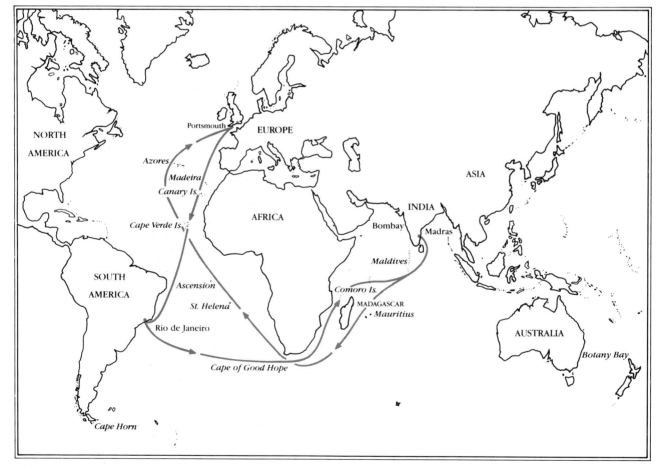

NORTH
AMERICA

Portsmouth

EUROPE

Azores

Madeira

Canary Is.

AFRICA

ASIA

INDIA

Bombay

Madras

Cape Verde Is.

Maldives

SOUTH
AMERICA

Ascension

St. Helena

Comoro Is.

MADAGASCAR

Mauritius

Rio de Janeiro

AUSTRALIA

Botany Bay

Cape of Good Hope

Cape Horn

The *Europe*'s voyage, 1783–84

The Secret Expeditions, 1780–84

However mundane Arthur Phillip's life from the time he left the Portuguese navy until the end of 1782 may seem from the immediate records, it was in reality a good deal more complex and interesting. All the while he edged the northern European coasts, currents were gathering to sweep him far beyond those now familiar shores. In his Portuguese service Phillip had earlier felt eddies off these currents: by the end of 1782, they had caught him up.

What was to impel Phillip beyond Europe again, and this time farther than before, was Britain's renewed pursuit of her long-held dream of American wealth. From the first decades of their colonizations, the British had envied the Spanish the riches of bullion and production they obtained from the New World. Drake's and Hawkins's raids were early and brutal manifestations of this envy. Narborough's 1671 venture to the South Seas would have been too, had it succeeded. There was a second purpose to Narborough's expedition—the establishing of political and commercial contacts with the Creole Spanish and Indian inhabitants of Chile and Peru—and it was this subtler course that the British tried to follow in the early eighteenth century, when the directors of the South Sea Company gave much attention to the possibility of developing an extensive trade with South America.[1] The *asiento*, or annual contract to supply the colonies with slaves and some manufactures, which Britain won from Spain in the Treaty of Utrecht (1713) raised immense hopes, which deflated with the bursting of the South Sea Bubble in 1720–21. Anson's expedition of 1740–44 marked a return to the earlier, more immediately effective, approach of decisive plundering; but it too had the broader dimension of subversion and future trade.

As well as with the treasure of the annual Manila galleon, Anson returned with developed ideas of how to open a trade along the Pacific coasts of America; and he sought to implement his scheme when he joined the Board of Admiralty in 1748. From this time until well into the nineteenth century, whenever Britain was at war with Spain, administrations received proposals for expeditions against Spanish America. These show a remarkable consistency. Inevitably, the proposers' immediate view was the capture and plundering of strategic points about the coasts. But they always had a longer term object, which was also the much more profound. By helping the Creoles and Indians to throw off the 'Spanish Yoke', Britain would enable her merchants to gain that access to vast markets that the liberated peoples would offer in grateful return; and this would quickly lead to an enormous augmentation of the nation's wealth. Through almost one hundred years, administrations of very different casts showed a persistent interest in these ideas, and mounted a number of the expeditions proposed. The details of some of these—those against Havana and Manila in 1762, that against Buenos Aires in 1806—are well known. Much less familiar are those of the war of 1778–83, which are of particular interest, since they mark the first attempt to turn Cook's discoveries to strategic advantage, and since Phillip had a leading hand in them.

From the moment Spain joined France and the rebellious American colonies in the war in mid-1779, merchants, patriots, and adventurers bombarded the North administration with proposals for damaging the Spanish in their American colonies. In England, Robert White and John Call suggested the general fomenting of revolution. Call, who was to propose colonization of New South Wales or New Zealand in 1784, suggested 'an Expedition to the South Seas, to give countenance and Support to the Inhabitants of Chili and Peru, by Assistance of Arms, ammunition, and Troops from India; that these Provinces or Kingdoms might be enabled to fulfil their disposition and throw off the Spanish Yoke'. From Rome, John Hippisley, in contact with disaffected Jesuits, urged that a force be sent from India against the ports on the west coast of Mexico.[2] In the event, the North administration became interested in Sir John Dalrymple's scheme. In June 1779, Dalrymple suggested to Lord Germain, the Secretary of State for America, that a privateering expedition, sailing either from

Britain by the Cape of Good Hope and New Zealand or from India 'by the Philippines to hold north, or by New Holland to hold south', should raid the Spanish settlements on the west coasts of the New World. If initially successful, the adventurers might sell their spoils in China and India, re-equip their ships, and make another sally.[3]

Soon, though, the ministers were preferring another version by William Fullarton. Taken up at the beginning of 1780, this suffered a number of vicissitudes, until Fullarton presented it again in the middle of the year, when he suggested that the expedition be mounted in the main from India. If a force of 1500 British troops and 2000 Sepoys, escorted by some of Sir Edward Hughes's squadron, were to sail the following May, it might 'secure one of the small Luconian [Philippine] Islands, and then ... proceed to some healthy spot in New Zealand, in order to establish means of refreshment, communication, and retreat'. From here, it might sail directly to South America. There was not one settlement between California and Cape Horn, Fullarton asserted, that was 'capable of resisting such an Equipment, if properly provided and properly conducted'. The British might take and fortify some 'advantageous' spots, and offer 'terms of independence ... to the native Mexicans, Peruvians and Chilians'. Even if the venture were not to succeed in these great objects, Spain's war effort would be crippled 'because her richest possessions would be alarmed, their Commerce and Remittances interrupted, their Ships destroyed, their Towns plundered, and the Inhabitants incited to revolt'. But if it were to succeed, then 'the Trade of South America would be opened to our East-Indian Territories'.[4]

The North ministry negotiated with the East India Company for support, but by the time arrangements were settled at the end of September, new circumstances had arisen to cause the ministers to change direction again. Late in the month, a privateer brought the Spanish frigate *Carona* into Glasgow. Aboard her were despatches describing risings in Spanish America, and giving details of the treasure fleet due to sail from Montevideo in December. Aboard her also was a Spanish Jesuit, Don Francisco Gorman, whom the Secretaries of State soon interviewed with much interest, for they shared the common British belief that all Jesuits bore an 'implacable animosity to the Court of Spain', and might therefore 'prove *essential instruments* in effecting a reduction of New Spain'.[5]

Their ears once more caught by the siren songs of great treasure and general insurrection, the ministers asked Commodore George Johnstone to develop a plan to ravage the Spanish settlements about the River Plate estuary, and to encourage rebellion there and elsewhere. For advice, Johnstone turned to Phillip's old commander Robert M'Douall, who drew up a number of memoranda.

M'Douall began the first of these in his usual prolix way, by asserting that 'the provability of distressing Spain by a small squadron cruising in the mouth of the River Plate and seas to the southward of the line is evidently clear'. He saw that such an operation might, variously, disrupt the trade between Spain and Buenos Aires, capture the treasure ships coming from Peru and Chile round the Horn to Buenos Aires, and capture the ships carrying bullion from Buenos Aires to Rio de Janeiro for transshipment in Portuguese vessels to Spain. It might also occupy Trinidada, the island one thousand kilometres off the coast of Brazil that lay directly across the route between Buenos Aires and Europe, and use it as a base from which to raid the small Spanish settlements off the African coast when the weather made cruising about the Plate estuary impossible. All this, M'Douall saw, would 'put Spain in greater difficulties how to guard against such a flying squadron than any other [scheme] yet proposed, and consequently must weaken their force in Europe to guard against [it]'. Subsequently, M'Douall gave details of the navigation of the Plate estuary, and of the Spanish forces in Buenos Aires, Maldonado, and Montevideo, which he estimated at one battleship and three frigates, and 5000 troops.[6]

On the basis of this information, Johnstone proposed three variants of the scheme to Sandwich. The first was that a force of one 64, two 50s, two 40s, three frigates, two sloops, two cutters, two fireships, and armed transports with 2500 troops might sail by 1 January, and attack the Spanish towns, holding and fortifying at least one. The second was that if only 1000 troops could be spared, then a naval force of one 64, one 50, one 40, two frigates, one sloop, two fireships, two cutters, and two victuallers, sailing either by 1 January or 1 June, might 'push and surprise the ships in the River Plate'. If they found these to be superior, they 'might cruise on the coast of the Brazils towards the island of Ascension or Fernando Noronha to intercept the enemy's trade from the South Seas, Buenos Ayres, and Manilla', and return to Europe in the track of the enemy's ships. If they did not find a large naval force in the Plate, they might capture either Buenos Aires or Maldonado, and 'by this means assist the insurgents, if any of the inhabitants are disposed to rise'. The third was for a small squadron of one 64, one 50, one 40, two frigates, and one cutter to sail immediately 'to try what can be done and return to Europe before the bad weather sets in on the coast of South America in June'. Some privateers, which might rendezvous with this squadron at Ascension Island, might assist in the venture. M'Douall favoured this idea most, but Johnstone doubted that its small size would allow much success.[7] On 2 November, Cabinet agreed to mount the second of these schemes, with the proviso that a 50-gun ship should replace the 64-gun one, which could not be 'spared'. Late in the month, the ministers decided that the best way to succeed in the venture was to add to Johnstone's expedition 'the Ships and Forces going to the East Indies'. These were to assist 'only in the *first* operations', and then, no matter what the outcome, 'to proceed on their intended Service'.[8] The ministers authorized the raising of additional troops; the Admiralty and Navy Boards proceeded to fit out a squadron; and Johnstone sought out persons either fluent in Spanish, or experienced in the navigation of the Plate estuary.[9]

The ministers had no sooner combined the schemes to attack both the west and east coasts of Spanish America than other events arose to give the force yet another direction. On 20 December, taking a move they had been contemplating from the middle of the year, the British declared war on the United Provinces over the issue of the Netherlanders' supplying France, Spain, and the American colonies with munitions and naval stores. This development made Britain's hold on her Indian establishments precarious, for it meant that between them her enemies would control the Cape of Good Hope, Mauritius, Trincomalee, Negapatam, and Batavia. The Chairmen of the East India Company now insisted that they could not risk their ships in the proposed attack on Buenos Aires;[10] and, clearly understanding the urgency of the need to strengthen the line of communication with India, the ministers decided on 29 December that the whole force should be 'employed in an attack upon the Cape of Good Hope'; and that if this failed, 'the two thousand Men originally intended for the East Indies [should] pursue their voyage thither, and the additional thousand with the Artillery Stores & c. originally allotted to them [should] go to the West Indies'.[11]

What this minute does not indicate is that the ministers did not abandon all their hopes over South America, for latent in the new determination was the proviso that Johnstone's force might swing across the Atlantic to the Plate after the attempt on the Cape. In January 1781, Sandwich asked Arthur Phillip for information about the east coast of South America. Phillip provided copies of his charts, with their details of the coastline and 'three good harbours, where Ships that wanted to wood & water, would find only a few settlers'.[12] Indeed, the administration may even now have broadened the scope of Johnstone's venture, to include a sortie up the west coast, and the supporting of the large scale rebellion of Tupac Amaru in Peru. The historical waters are murky at this point, but in early February, the Portuguese envoy in London reported that the Jesuit was aboard Johnstone's ship, and that the commodore was seeking not only charts of the Brazilian coast from Rio de Janeiro to the Plate, but also 'of the South Sea and the coast of Chile'.[13] Again intriguing is a later report that Johnstone's squadron carried munitions for the insurgents in Peru.[14]

The expedition sailed on 13 March. Two weeks later, when at the Azores, Johnstone sent M'Douall off with orders to land Gorman 'on some part of South America', and to gather information about the states of the Spanish colonies and their forces.[15] Gorman's preference was for Rio de Janeiro, and this suited M'Douall, who was as usual not over-eager to venture into more dangerous waters. Capturing some Spanish fishermen on the way, M'Douall reached his old stamping ground on 4 May. Suspicious, the new Viceroy, Luis de Vasconcelos, allowed him to replenish his wood and water, but did not permit him or his crew to land. None the less, M'Douall managed to get Gorman ashore; and from William Roberts, one of his former captains still in the Portuguese service, he learned that the Spanish had few forces in the Plate estuary, and that revolt was said to be general in the interior of the Spanish provinces. He also obtained some information concerning the movement of bullion between Buenos Aires and Rio de Janeiro. On 7 May, he sailed again to rendezvous with Johnstone at St Helena.[16]

While M'Douall scouted, Johnstone took the squadron down to the Cape Verde Islands, where it was attacked by one under Suffren which the French had sent after it. The delay caused by the need to repair the damage to the ships meant that by the time the expedition reached the Cape, Suffren had alerted and reinforced the Dutch there; and Johnstone quickly gave up any lingering hope of attacking the colony. Instead, he sent the Company ships and the troops on to India, and took his squadron to St Helena, whence he wrote to Sandwich that he had 'many objects in contemplation'.[17] What these added up to was an implementation of M'Douall's idea of making Trinidada a base for cruising operations about the Plate estuary and across the route to Europe. Late in September, he sent three of his captains to occupy the island, and cruise (to no real purpose, as it turned out) off the Plate.

On his arrival home in February 1782, Johnstone pressed the advantages of Trinidada on the new Rockingham administration, arguing that from its situation and fertility it might be 'an invaluable Jewell in His Majesty's Crown'. Shelburne appointed a committee of Admiralty and East India Company officials to examine Johnstone's flight of fancy, who decided that they were 'not competent at present to decide'.[18] This unenthusiastic response was as well for the British, on two counts: the bleak Trinidada was not nearly as fertile as the commodore claimed; and the Portuguese protested bitterly at the occupation of the island, which they saw to lie squarely within their South American orbit. Such was the fury of the Portuguese that they threatened to send three warships to throw off the English party, and to colonize it themselves. Faced with this resentment and its considerable threat to an old and much-needed alliance, the

Shelburne administration agreed to give up the island. The Admiralty issued the appropriate orders in August; and a warship took off D'Auvergne's party in December.[19]

Though the details remain obscure, Phillip had an intimate connection with Johnstone's expedition, which may have included more than simply offering advice. He ended his 17 January 1781 letter to Sandwich on an expectant note: 'As it is probable that I may be call'd forth by your Lordship at a very short notice, I have Seal'd up a Copy of each Chart, & which, with your Lordships approbation, I mean to deliver to Mr John Lane, a Merchant near Lombard Street. He, My Lord, will be an intire stranger to any thing more, than that they are Charts which the Board may wish to have, when I am at Sea.'[20] This clearly suggests that he was expecting imminent service; but, as mentioned, the records are entirely silent about his whereabouts and doings from this time until mid-October, when he became acting captain of the *Ariadne*. How is this gap to be filled?

The *St James Chronicle* of 2 February 1787 offered the following anecdote:

Capt. Phillip, the Commander in Chief of the Expedition to Botany-Bay, was several Years in the Portuguese Service, and obtained no small Degree of Reputation from the following Incident: Being employed about five Years since to carry out with him near 400 Criminals from Lisbon to the Brasils, during the Course of the Voyage an epidemical Disorder broke out on board his Ship, which made such Havock, that he had not Hands sufficient to navigate her; in this Dilemma he called up the most spirited of the Transports, and told them, in a few Words, his situation, and that if they would assist in conducting the Vessel, and keep their Companions in Order, he would represent their Behaviour to the Court of Lisbon, and, in short, do all in his Power to get their sentence mitigated. This Speech had the desired Effect; the Prisoners acted with Fidelity, and brought the Ship safe to Buenos Ayres, where they were delivered into the Custody of the Garrison; and on Capt. Phillip's Return to Lisbon, and representing the meritorious Conduct of the Transports, they were not only emancipated from their servitude, but had small Portions of Land alloted them in that delightful Country.[21]

On the face of things, this story makes little sense. Five years prior to February 1787, Phillip was not in the Portuguese navy; and neither the Portuguese nor the British were then transporting convicts to the River Plate area. To suppose that the journalist got the number of years wrong, and that the voyage occurred during Phillip's period of service in the Portuguese navy from 1775 to 1778 does not help resolve the puzzle. There is no evidence extant of Phillip's having transported convicts in these years; and the extent of the available records—especially the Viceroy of Brazil's regular reports concerning the behaviour and merits of the naval officers—makes it unlikely that such a voyage then should not be recorded. But suppose that, even if other details are incorrect, the *number* of years is approximately right? This would mean that in 1782, or 1781, Phillip sailed from Lisbon with 400 convicts to South America. That is, does this report offer an oblique insight into Phillip's activities in 1781: did he sail to South America under some cover to assist in Johnstone's coming raid?

There are some pieces of circumstantial evidence which might be part of such an indeterminate puzzle. First, there is Phillip's expectation that Sandwich would imminently require his services. Conversely, his promotion to post captain in November suggests that he was rewarded for something. Second, there is the idea of both M'Douall and Johnstone that privateers might aid in the Plate venture. Third, there is the tradition recorded by Phillip's relatives that John Lane fitted out a 'frigate' in which Phillip sailed 'to the other side of the world'.[22] Fourth, there is the report from the Spanish fisherman that M'Douall was interested in information about a 'Regiment of Fusiliers said to be being sent from Lisbon via Rio de Janeiro to Buenos Aires'.[23] Fifth, there is the fact that the Portuguese were sending large numbers of recruits, including many convicts, to India via Brazil in the early 1780s.[24] Does all this add up to Phillip's sailing in a privately fitted-out ship to South America in mid-1781, under a blind of transporting Portuguese convicts, but with the real purpose of reconnoitring the Plate estuary ahead of Johnstone's squadron? It is an intriguing possibility; and it is much to be regretted that no Portuguese records relating to transportation at this time seem to survive.

There is another hypothesis to be advanced, almost equally intriguing in its possibilities. Bearing in mind Phillip's friendship with Charles Duncombe, the 'Mr. Shafto' who recommended him to Sandwich for promotion about this time[25] was almost certainly Robert Shafto, who was married to Anne, the daughter of Charles's brother Thomas Duncombe. From 1778, Shafto was Comptroller of Fines and Forfeitures for the Outports; and he entered parliament in 1784 in the Duncombe family interest, when he and Henry Duncombe became supporters of Pitt. This Duncombe–Shafto connection may have provided Phillip with some not inconsiderable political patronage, but more significant from the present point of view is the fact that Shafto had earlier been a successful spy. His career in espionage is obscure, but in 1765 the Rockingham administration granted him a pension of £200 per year in recognition of his services. Was it Shafto who recruited Phillip into the British secret service? Do Shafto's commendations of Phillip to Sandwich in 1780 and 1781, the silence concerning Phillip's whereabouts in 1781, and Sandwich's promotion of him to post captain at the end of this year, indicate that Phillip was engaged in secret service? Regrettably, the relevant records, such as they are, are silent on these points too.

The failure of Fullarton's and Johnstone's proposals for expeditions against Spanish America did not deter others from advancing new ones. About July 1781, Richard Oswald proposed a version whereby Britain would join with Russia in a grand move across the Pacific Ocean. In mid-1782, when negotiating for Britain in Paris, and with Spain making great difficulties over terms of peace, Oswald revised his earlier memoranda, and sent them to Shelburne. The new Prime Minister was interested, and had the Foreign Secretary put the idea to the ambassador at St Petersburg, who replied that there was no prospect of the empress's agreeing to it.[26]

Visionary as Oswald's scheme now seems, Shelburne had some solid reason to be interested in a move against Spanish America. For twelve months and more, the British had received a multiplicity of reports of rebellion there. First had come news of massive insurrection and the breakdown of metropolitan authority in Peru. Then, there was information that Spanish authority did not extend more than 150 kilometres inland from Buenos Aires. Then, that the insurgent army was marching from Peru against the Plate province, so as to overthrow Spanish rule throughout the continent.[27] By August 1782, so pervasive was this report that it was figuring in newspapers, and even in diplomatic correspondence. On 30 July, the *St James Chronicle* told readers that 'the Insurrection in South America has arisen to a Height that [leaves] not the smallest Prospect of the Tumult being quelled by the Power of the Spaniards, from whose tyrannous Yoke the Natives [have] irrevocably determined to rescue themselves'.[28] On 6 August, the Portuguese ambassador informed his government that the British were receiving such information.[29] On 13 August, Shelburne sought the ambassador out, to tell him that Britain might try to capture the Plate settlements, and to offer some general help to the rebellious Creoles and Indians. The Prime Minister pointed out that Britain's view of the treaty which Portugal and Spain had concluded in 1778 was that it required Portugal to help Spain only in an offensive war; and he asked for information about Spanish forces in South America.[30]

After this extraordinary signalling of its intention—occasioned by Portugal's announced anxiety at the general idea and profound resentment over Trinidada[31]—the Shelburne administration proceeded to plan the venture. As was customary, a Secretary of State rather than the Admiralty assumed responsibility for it, in this instance Thomas Townshend, the Secretary for Home Affairs. Given Townshend's habitual inattention, this meant that it was Evan Nepean who sought advice and co-ordinated measures. In late August, Captain John Blankett drew up a sketch of a 'Force proposed for an Expedition to Buenos Aires; & to the S° Sea conditionally'. He proposed 'One Ship of 64

Guns, 4 of 50, 2 Frigates, 2 Sloops & 2 Cutters. 10 Ships Coppered, (North Country Barks recommended), for the Transporting of 2000 Soldiers, including one Company of Artillery, Provisions, Stores & all necessaries for the Expedition. The Ships of War to take on board 300 Soldiers, in order to give good room in the Transports, The Artillery Stores of every kind such as cannot be taken in the Ships of War to be equally divided in the Transports for fear of accidents from parting Company. The Artillery to be all for the field, some travelling Carriages for the Ships Guns in case of their being wanted. The Expedition might proceed to the Isle of S! Catherine's or Rio Negro for intelligence or Water, & failing of success at the River of Plate to proceed immediately round to Callao. On success at the River of Plate, such force as could be spared might be sent as a Reinforcement to India, or to the South Seas, as the circumstances of the Case should make most prudent.'[32] In late August and most of September, Phillip was also in London, ostensibly on 'private affairs', but in reality to advise the administration, especially concerning the strength of the Spanish forces about the River Plate. 'If you have nothing further for Captain Phillip,' Keppel, the new First Lord of the Admiralty, told Townshend on 25 September in discussing the venture, 'we shall send him to his Ship.'[33] When Phillip sailed downriver a few days later, the Portuguese ambassador reported that there was good reason to suppose he was going 'to investigate the situation in the River Plate'.[34]

The Shelburne administration's interest in the idea of attacking the Spanish settlements was directly related to the progress of the peace negotiations. Spain wanted Gibraltar, but was offering what the British considered to be inadequate exchanges. What the British wanted in return for the fortress rock was significant territory in the West Indies and/or the right to trade 'with Spain & its Colonies on the same terms as France'. But Spain was reluctant to give up any of her fertile West Indian islands; and the idea of opening her colonial markets to British merchants ran quite counter to her long-established policy of tightly controlling their trade. In the autumn of 1782, the Shelburne administration saw the capturing of some of the American settlements as the most effective means of breaking the impasse in the peace negotiations, and the encouragement of the rebellion that of gaining the desired access to markets. As Townshend reinstructed Oswald, if there were no quick progress in the talks, they would 'incline to listen to the Proposal of attacking the Spanish Possessions'.[35]

In this atmosphere, the administration pressed ahead with the scheme. With the ministers having firmly decided upon it on or about 25 September, Shelburne turned to Sir Charles Middleton, the head of the Navy Board, for help in mounting it. On 26 September, Middleton outlined the arrangements to be made. They would need warships, transports for 1000 to 1500 troops, victuallers, storeships, and flat-bottomed boats for landing the troops and navigating the coastal rivers. They would have to obtain artillery and ordnance, provisions for twelve months, arms for the Chileans and presents for the Indians.[36] Shelburne then asked what force might be quickly mounted, 'so as to save the Season, for rounding Cape Horn, if what has been propos'd [i.e., the attack on the Plate settlements] should be found impossible'; and also about how they might increase both their ships and troops in the East Indies.[37] Middleton replied on 3 October that 'Ships sailing from England the latter end of November may get round Cape Horn provided they are not diverted on their way by any intervening Service, & 1800 Men may be embarked in the King's Ships & Coppered Transports by that time. This number will give great alarm & probably do great Mischief in support of the Rebellion. They ought to carry 18 Months provisions & the Victuallers to be coppered as well as the Transports.' He added, 'unless the Superiority at Sea [in the East Indies] is decidedly one in our favour the Country powers assisted by the Dutch & French will prove too powerful for us & the Consequences are fatal'.[38] Late in November, disturbed at the lack of tangible progress, Middleton told Shelburne that the ships of the 'Southern' expedition might sail without their reserves of stores and provisions, which might follow 'with great Security'; and he again emphasized the need to increase the naval force in the east.[39]

The administration now determined to meet the two contingencies by sending a small squadron out via South America to India. In November, Nepean drafted a request to the Admiralty to prepare three ships of the line and a frigate 'with all possible expedition'.[40] In response, the Admiralty had the Navy Board fit out the *Elizabeth* (74), *Grafton* (70), *Europe* (64), and *Iphigenia* (32). On 17 December, the Admiralty Lords ordered the other captains to put themselves under Robert Kingsmill's command, and told Kingsmill 'to hold yourself & them in constant readiness for sailing; for which you may daily expect to receive our orders'.[41] On 21 December, the Home Office issued a despatch to the admiral commanding the India squadron explaining that the enemy had lately sent some more 'Ships of the Line' to the East, and that therefore Kingsmill's squadron was sailing 'with all Possible Expedition'.[42] On this day too, the Lords ordered Phillip to hold himself ready for foreign service.[43] Then, reflecting the secret purpose of the expedition, on 23 December they commissioned him captain of the *Europe*. He took up the command four days later.[44] On 1 January 1783, Kingsmill acknowledged the receipt of the Lords' 'several Orders & Packets';[45] and the squadron sailed on 16 January, three days before Spain suddenly gave up her demand for Gibraltar, and agreed to peace.

A fierce winter storm ravaged the ships in the Bay of Biscay. For three days, 'violent Gales' and 'great seas' swept them, until three were so crippled that their captains put back.[46] Only Phillip continued the voyage.[47] Having lost sight of his companions, on 29 January he opened his first rendezvous, to find he was directed to Madeira. He worked down towards it for the next two weeks, with the weather continuing 'extremely bad'. There were only two days when he could open the lower deck ports to air the ship. When in the latitude of Madeira, with scurvy rife among the crew, he found that a malfunctioning of the compasses had placed them 320 kilometres to the west. With both winds and currents against him, he thought it best not to try to work back. Opening the second rendezvous when off the Canaries, he decided to run down to Port Praia in the Cape Verde Islands. When he reached this port on 1 March, he repaired the ship as best he could, and took on wood, water, and some food and animals. Finding no news of Kingsmill, he rightly assumed that the rest of the squadron had returned to England; and decided to follow his contingent orders to proceed on to India. But when, a few days out of Praia Bay, it became apparent that the ship was not in a condition 'to weather a Gale of Wind', he headed for Rio de Janeiro, where he knew he could unload her in safety, and therefore repair her better.[48]

The *Europe* reached Rio de Janeiro on 15 April. As Phillip waited outside the heads for a favourable wind, the Viceroy sent a party to learn his business.[49] Much to his surprise, as he proceeded towards São Sebastião, the fort at Santa Cruz fired several shots to bring him to. He knew that this was the standard treatment by the Portuguese of all ships that had not announced their presence and purpose, but this was not his situation. He also knew that 'their own Ships of war never [bring] to'. Therefore, he reported to the Admiralty, 'I paid no attention, nor did I return the forts fire; but after the Ship was anchored, I waited on the Vice King and informed him, that unless I received ample satisfaction for the insult offered to His Majesty's Colours I should be obliged to fire on the fort'. Phillip asked that the fort's commandant apologize in person—'which was done'. With national and personal honour satisfied, Phillip saluted the fort with fifteen guns, and was answered with nineteen. Thereafter, matters went smoothly, with the Viceroy offering 'every possible mark of respect & attention ... & every assistance'.[50]

As he repaired his ship, Phillip picked up information about the state of the Plate settlements. Much to his chagrin, he learned that this was 'such as I always thought them. Of five Companies of Regulars, sent out from Cordova only Seven Men returned, the rest were either killed or deserted to the Indians ... All the Regulars in Buenos Ayres Monte Video, and the different Guards in the

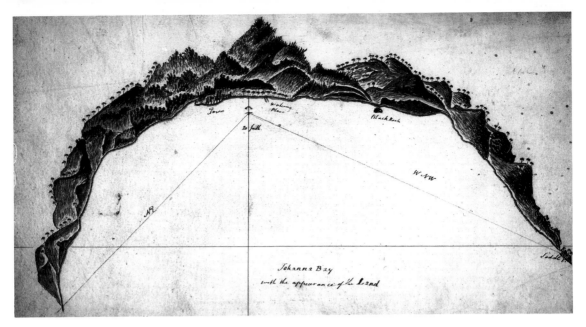

Captain Scott, 'Johanna Bay' (1785)

River of Plate do not amount to five hundred Men. No ship of the Line and only two frigates in the River'.[51] Years later, he was to continue to see that a grand opportunity had been lost. When at Rio de Janeiro again in September 1787, on his way to New South Wales, he wrote back to Nepean: 'You know how much I was interested in the intended expedition against Monte Video, and that it was said that the Spaniards had more troops than I supposed. The following account I have from a person who was there all the war, and I am certain that the account is exact: One Regiment under 700; Four Companies of Artillery 400; Dragoons 400; Two Batallions of Infantry 700. These were divided on the north and south shores, and in different towns. Monte Video would not have been defended, as half these troops could not have been drawn together. Of this you will be so good as to inform the Lords Sydney and [Shelburne]; it will corroborate what I mentioned before I left town.'[52]

Phillip sailed from Rio de Janeiro again on 5 May, after having taken on board twenty bulls and other supplies. Ten days later they sighted a number of large ships, and he ordered the *Europe*'s decks cleared for action, but these proved to be Indiamen from England, who gave him news of the peace. Even so, he continued wary as he proceeded towards India, stopping and identifying a number of vessels as he rounded the Cape of Good Hope at the end of the month. Having pleasant breezes and clear weather, the *Europe* reached the southern tip of Madagascar on 13 June, and four days later she entered the harbour at Johanna [Anjouan] in the Comoro Islands. Though small, Johanna was 'a very beautiful and fertile spot'. Game birds roamed its mountains, and monkeys and mongooses its woods, streams cascaded to the sea, and ducks abounded on the waters. Coconuts, plantains, oranges, limes, guavas, plums, bananas, and pineapples grew 'promiscuously'. The Johannans added to the natural profusion of their 'terrestrial paradise' by raising cattle, sheep, goats, pigs, and poultry, and masses of vegetables, and by catching parrot-fish, flat-head, and mullet. In the early 1780s, there were some 30 000 people on the island, of mixed Negro and Arab descent. The town consisted of 200 houses, 'very low' and built of stone, and the king's 'lofty and spacious' palace.[53]

The island's position and fertility made it a favoured port of call for ships using the inner passage (between the mainland and Madagascar); and the islanders had quickly understood how they might gain from the contacts. Whenever a ship appeared in the road, they swarmed about it in outriggers filled with produce and small animals, in desperate competition to make the first sales. Earlier, they had been satisfied with the Europeans' usual baubles of trade, but by Phillip's time they had learned the value of gold and silver, and insisted on payment in specie, or in arms and ammunition. They also routinely asked European captains, who were in no position to refuse the request, for subsidies to support their trade with the mainland. On his arrival, Phillip set up a tent on shore, and began gathering in the island's largesse. Every day the Johannans came with 'Eggs, fowls, Plantains, and Bananas'. When, as was customary, a member of the ruling family came on board with his retinue, Phillip presented him with some muskets and ammunition and a brass box compass. In return, the prince gave 'half a dozen of their small Bullocks'.[54] Having completed the ship's wood and water, Phillip sailed again on 26 June, to the cheers of the crew of the *Fox* Indiaman.

As he traversed the Indian Ocean, Phillip continued to be worried by the state of the *Europe*, and to ease the strain on her frame he decided to stow some of her guns in the hold. On 6 June, when the ship was 2400 kilometres from Johanna and 1100 kilometres from the Maldive Islands and therefore far beyond help, disaster threatened briefly, when a fire broke out in the slop room. Luckily, the crew put this out with negligible damage, and the voyage continued. Passing by the Maldives, the *Europe* rounded Ceylon a week later, and the wind being off the land, the crew experienced 'the Aromatic smell of the Cinnamon with which this island abounds'.[55] Phillip then ran up the Coromandel coast for Madras, which he reached on 18 July, and where he found Sir Edward Hughes and the India squadron.

Having no harbour, Madras could offer ships only an uncertain anchorage a mile and more offshore. European boats did not attempt the intervening surf. Rather, native watermen, almost naked, with stores of energizing betel in their distinctive caps, plied from shore to ship in 'masoula' boats (ones with planks tied by coir ropes) or in trimarans. The city exhibited all the ambience of the East. The British, numbering only approximately 500, inhabited Fort St George

Fort St George, Madras (1780)

or the 'White' town, a walled rectangular area about 2 kilometres long which had some handsome streets and houses. The Portuguese, Moorish, and Armenian merchants, and richer Indians, lived in the 'Black' town, which was also fortified, and which was a place of great bustle and activity. In the suburbs beyond lived the poorer Indians. To Madras came the products of Mocha, Persia, Sarat, the Malabar coast, Bengal, and China. From it went, to Europe especially, diamonds and calicoes.

On Phillip's arrival, Hughes drew on the *Europe*'s stores to replenish the squadron's generally; and Phillip gave the admiral personally some of the Johanna bullocks. After a survey showed the *Europe* to be badly strained, Hughes ordered essential repairs. In the next weeks, carpenters stripped and fished the mainmast, the crew overhauled the rigging and stored more guns, and took on water and provisions for the return voyage, for the *Europe* was one of the twelve ships the admiral was sending home under Sir Richard King's command, with an instruction to send one ahead from the Cape of Good Hope with his despatches.[56] The ships sailed on 2 October. The northeast monsoon at their backs gave them a quick passage across the Indian Ocean, and they were near the Cape at the end of November; but fierce gales and seas then damaged them greatly, and they were unable to make the port until 9 December. By the time they did, about 1800 of the crews were afflicted with scurvy, and there had been many deaths.

Immediately upon reaching Table Bay, King sent Phillip to the Dutch governor to request permission to land the sick. The squadron's arrival, and the commodore's request, placed the governor in a considerable quandary, for he had received no advice from Europe that the rumoured truce between his country and Britain had actually come into effect. He accordingly refused the request. Astonished and enraged, King gave Phillip a copy of the order he had from Sir Edward Hughes to cease hostilities with the Dutch, and sent him back 'to reason with the Governor'. This second approach brought a reluctant approval from the governor and his council for the British to land their sick at Robben Island, and to buy provisions.[57] At the same time, the council agreed that the British should repair their ships, which were similarly unfit. The *Hero*, for example, was very leaky; the *Sceptre* needed all her masts replaced; the *Exeter* proved beyond help, and was burnt. Unseasonably rough weather prevailed in December and January, delaying and increasing the work necessary to get the squadron in a condition to sail again. One day, a sudden gale drove the rudderless *Cumberland* towards a reef, and only a desperate towing action by the ships' boats saved her.[58]

During this time, King shifted his broad pennant to the *Europe*; and he and Phillip moved ashore. There was much for them to do. They had first to organize the supplies needed to restore the sick—fresh meats, cabbages, peas, and 'fruit of all kinds'. As Robben Island was 9 kilometres up the bay from the dock, it was a quite complicated business to get supplies there, with the boats having to ply backwards and forwards in the mornings before the winds blew up. There were other provisions to obtain, too. On 19 January 1784, King asked the governor for large quantities of bread and flour, wine, raisins, peas, sugar, and vinegar, without which 'it will be impossible ... to prosecute [the] Voyage to England'. The Dutch offered to supply all but the items which the squadron was most in need of, so that King was forced to ask again. In doing so, he alluded darkly to 'the astonishment it must occasion in England ... [if] the greater part of the Squadron otherwise ready to proceed, was detained in the Port of a State at Peace and in friendship with great Britain by want of Bread and Flour for Sea Stores, at a time when there is no apparent scarsity of grain'.[59]

Because Phillip lived ashore and was involved in resupplying the squadron, he had the opportunity to learn of the Cape colony's resources and society. The Dutch East India Company had founded the settlement in 1652, so as to have a way station for their ships plying the route to and from the East Indies. The township which had developed by the 1780s exhibited in a general way those principles which the Spanish and Portuguese had followed in their colonial ports. On the northern side was the fort, within which was the arsenal and the governor's offices, and beside which projected a pier so fitted that a number of boats might fill their water barrels simultaneously.[60] Between the fort and the hospital and principal church was a broad open area,[61] to the south and east of which the town extended along a regular grid system, with one and two storey houses whitewashed or painted green, fronted by courtyards and rows of oaks.

The centre piece of the settlement was the garden which the Company had laid out to succour 'worn-out and scorbutic sailors'.[62] It was surrounded by a 12-foot-high wall reinforced by lines of poplars and hedges of myrtle and alder, and the only entrance to it was via 'a Very Handsome Stone Gate where two Sentrys always attend'.[63] Covering 60 acres, it was divided into symmetrical plots, in which gardeners and slaves raised a multitude of fruits and vegetables, and as well 'all kinds of fragrant trees, which both please[d] the eye and re-fresh[ed] and divert[ed] the senses'. Reinforcing this effect were the gravel walks between the plots—five avenues planted with oaks, bay-trees, and myrtles, with borders of roses, and twelve crosswalks. By the 1780s, the oaks had so grown as to form arches over the paths. A bricked canal carried water to the garden, where a mill dispersed it through a series of aqueducts to the various plots. This resource, then, was also a pleasure ground providing 'beautiful and pleasant' surrounds, where people might spare themselves the 'burning heat of the sun and the tiring wind'. Adding further to its interest was the menagerie located on its upper perimeter, in which were kept such 'rare and uncommon' animals as lions, elephants, rhinoceros, gazelles, oryx, zebras, and 'great numbers of birds'. Not surprisingly, the governors found it convenient to maintain a 'handsome summerhouse' within it, from which they were able to view 'the entire harbour with the ships in it, and tell from the colours to what nationality a ship belongs'.

Yet if this garden was a place of great beauty and repose, it also exhibited the colony's dark underside. The garden flourished only on the labour of slaves, whose habit of spying on those who frequented it was one manifestation of the suspicion and fear that permeated the colony's whole life. The garden reflected the colony's dualism in other ways, too. On its east side, amid its fruits and flowers, and with its commanding view, was the governor's residence. On its perimeter adjacent to the township was the company's slave house. In 1783, this was the sleeping place for some 470 male and 170 female slaves. It was also notorious as a place of prostitution, where the black women satisfied the sexual needs not only of the white colonists, but also of visiting ships' crews. Nor was prostitution confined to the slave house. Slave women wandered the streets

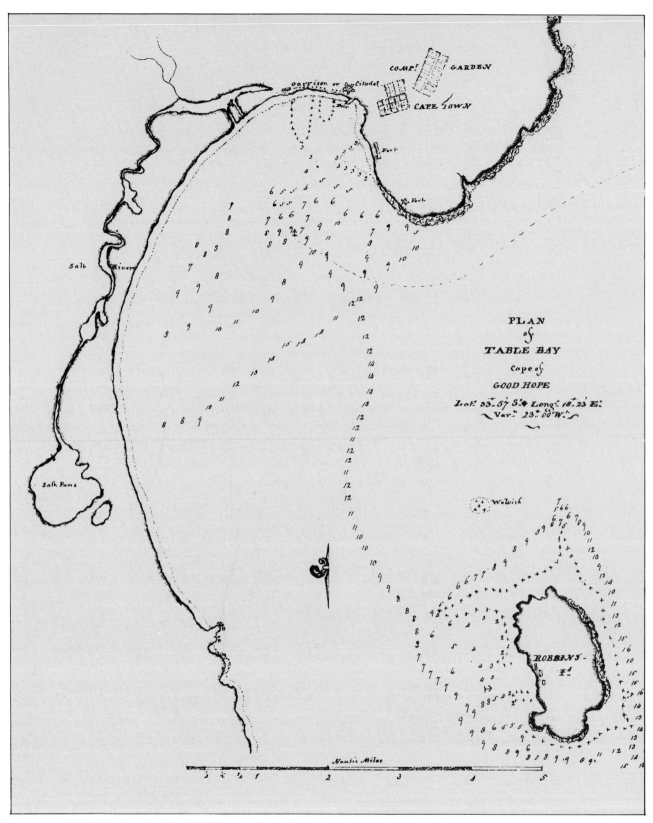

George Raper, 'Plan of Table Bay, Cape of
Good Hope' (1787)

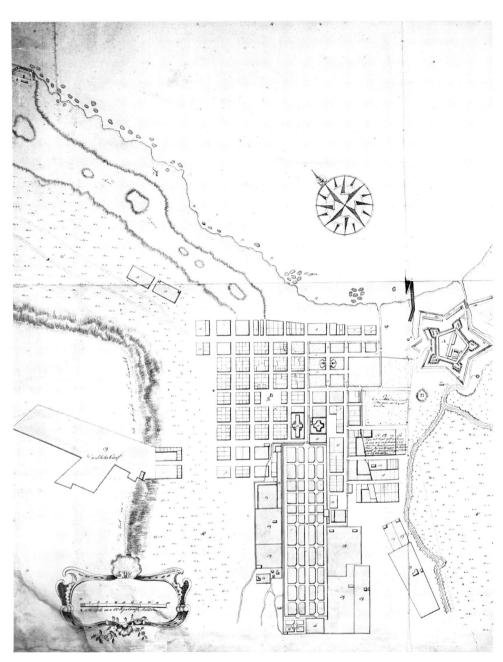

The Cape of Good Hope (1767)
Key:
A   Fort   29   Hospital
24 Gardens 30   Church
25 Menagerie

seeking customers to provide the money that their masters expected from them each week. It was sailors' lore that at Cape Town 'you will be able to have a good time with the black women, if you have the money'.[64]

The scene was not entirely one of deprivation and exploitation. Sometimes, slaves were able to live in stable relationships for long periods, and to maintain families; and sometimes, the female children married into white families. Such accommodations were necessary to obtain some social cohesion, for men much predominated over women in the colony throughout the eighteenth century, and slaves outnumbered citizens—there were approximately 17 000 whites in the colony in the early 1780s, and 30 000 slaves, with more than three men to each woman.[65] Still, the lot of the slaves was generally an unenviable one. To them fell the heavy work of building, of cutting timber and hauling water, of preparing the farms in the outlying districts for their grain crops, of tending vines and harvesting and pressing grapes. Those who were domestic servants in the township had a less arduous time; but all were subject to the rigours of a terrible criminal law, whose standard punishments included breaking on the cross and the wheel.

We have no record of Phillip's private perceptions of the colony; but considering his view of slavery, these can scarcely have been favourable. None the less, his time at the Cape was important. Three years later, he was to show himself strikingly aware of how its resources would be central to the success of an expedition to the edge of the world, and how, in colonial circumstances involving much sexual imbalance, it might be necessary to permit prostitution in order to obtain a minimal necessary social harmony.

Such perceptions could scarcely have dominated his thinking in January 1784, though, when the succouring of the sick and the refitting and resupplying of the squadron were his paramount concerns. So great were the obstructions that he and Sir Richard King encountered as they tried to ready the ships for sea again that King decided to send him on ahead to deliver Hughes's despatches, and to represent personally to the Lords Commissioners of the Admiralty 'the difficulties which have attended the Refitting His Majesty's Squadron at the Cape of Good Hope'.[66] This mission was another mark of the sense of merit that Phillip now increasingly conveyed to his commanders. He sailed on 20 February. Passing by St Helena and Ascension, the *Europe* had a quick passage, and reached Spithead on 22 April.[67] Following his orders, Phillip went immediately to London, where he reported to the Admiralty. His crew was paid off on 15 May.

If Phillip were asked what he thought of his life in these years, he would most probably point to frustrations and disappointments. He had rejoined the

Royal Navy in 1778 anxious to make a mark; but the schemes that would have best allowed him to do so—those for Anson-like raids on the Spanish settlements in South America—came to nothing in the end. 'You will Sir,' he wrote to Thomas Townshend from Rio de Janeiro in April 1783, 'easily suppose how much I must be mortifyed in being so near & not at liberty to Act.'[68] Adding to the mortification was the fact that his participation in the planning of these ventures, and the officials' holding him ready to sail on them, meant that he missed service elsewhere that might have led to prize money and promotion. 'You [will] recollect,' he afterwards remarked to Nepean, perhaps with a little bitterness, 'that in the late War I was depriv'd of the chance of those advantages every other Officer enjoy'd, & put to no small expence.'[69]

Still, there were some benefits. In July 1780, Phillip had told Sandwich that he was ready to serve in any part of the world, no matter how distant; and by 1784 he had certainly had his wish. South America was no new experience, but the voyage from there to India and the one home again were; and the experience of such places as Johanna, Madras, and the Cape of Good Hope would later stand him in very good stead—as would, if indeed he did make it in these years, that of the convict voyage to Brazil. Equally important, in this period Phillip gained the confidence of those who were soon to fix his destiny. As a consequence of his good service for Portugal, he had come to the attention of the British Admiralty, and Lord Sandwich had drawn on his expertise. This and his friendship with Nepean had led him into contact with the members of the Shelburne administration, so that he had become acquainted with Shelburne himself, and with Thomas Townshend, soon to be Lord Sydney. He may also have met William Pitt, who as Chancellor of the Exchequer was a member of Shelburne's cabinet, and who took a keen interest in naval affairs.

In his confidential advice to naval superiors and politicians, in the precise ways in which he concealed his real purposes and followed his orders, in his success in negotiations with foreign authorities, and in his grasp of the geographical realities of the world beyond Europe, Phillip showed in these years that he was such a 'discreet' officer as the nation would need to begin a colony of convicts in the southwest Pacific, one intended to increase Britain's strategic capacity in the East and on the way to Spanish America. In mid-1784, it was to be two years before Phillip would take up this task; and before he would do so, there would be more secret service. Still, by the time he returned to England, though he could not have known it, he was on his way to New South Wales, with all that this would mean for him personally, and for history.

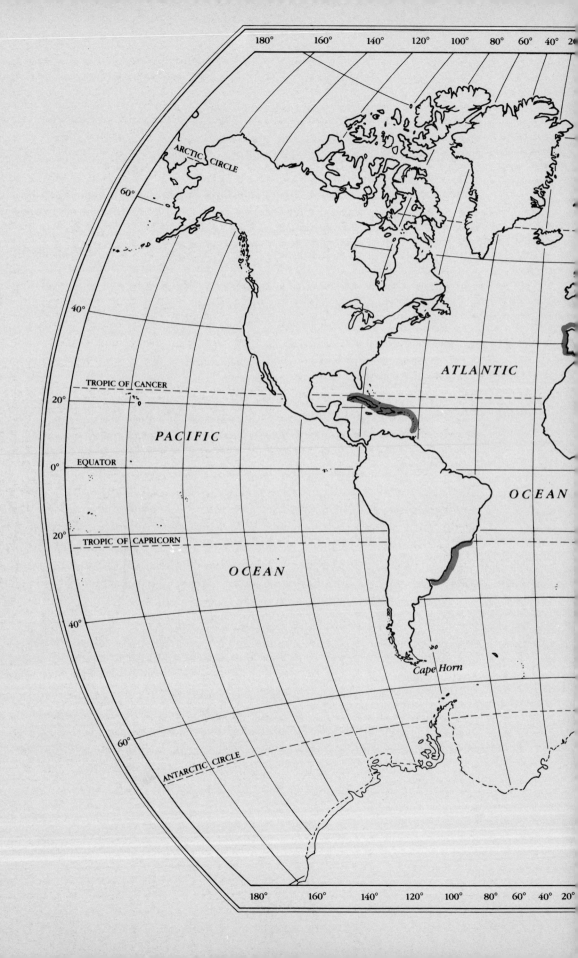

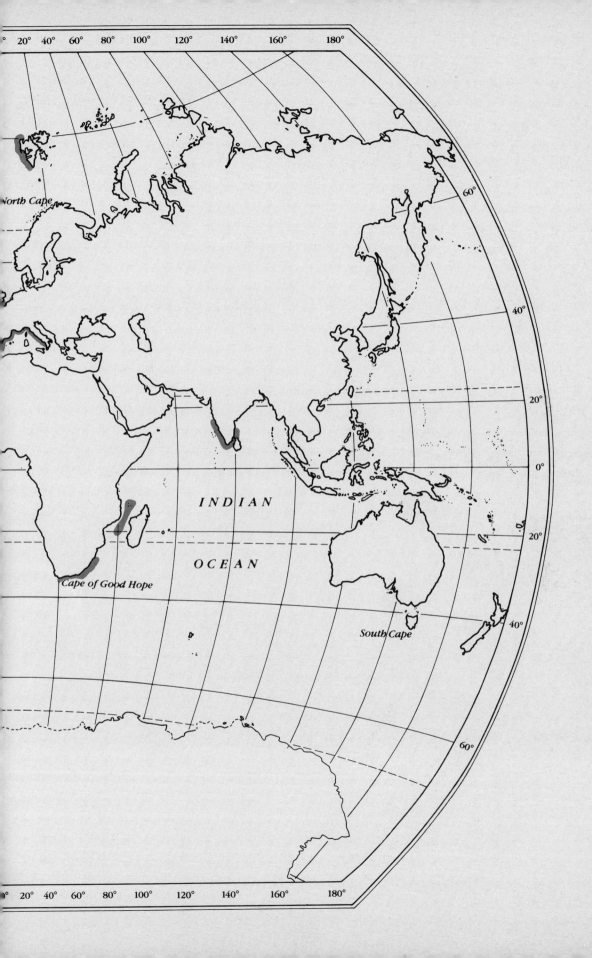

North Cape

INDIAN

OCEAN

Cape of Good Hope

South Cape

20° 40° 60° 80° 100° 120° 140° 160° 180°

60°

40°

20°

0°

20°

40°

60°

20° 40° 60° 80° 100° 120° 140° 160° 180°

PRIVATE AFFAIRS: FRANCE, 1784–86

I mean chiefly to shew the necessity of our having both land and Sea officers, well acquainted with the neighbouring Nations, with the fort and foible of the country, with the people, their Government and their Coasts, and particularly with their Ports and Arsenals, both on the Sea and land sides, with the nature and resources of the adjacent Country.

Anonymous advice to the North administration, *c.* 1779[1]

In the eighteenth century, as in the twentieth, Britain minded her neighbours' business via an extensive espionage system. Though she might cast her net a good deal more broadly, inevitably she tended to concentrate her intelligence-gathering efforts on the military and naval preparations of France and Spain, her inveterate enemies. Some of these efforts were more casual than others. Administrations received some information gratuitously from sea captains and travellers who noticed unusual things and reported them in bursts of patriotic fervour. Other information arrived as part of routine observation. It was the duty of consuls to report the movement of shipping to and from their ports; and when these reports gave rise to suspicion, the State departments passed them on to the Admiralty for evaluation. Similarly, ambassadors were expected to report pertinent titbits of diplomatic gossip; sometimes, they were requested to investigate specific points.

Though it might have its distinct uses, the gathering of military and naval information in these ways can hardly be termed espionage in the modern sense, but there was also much of this too, then as now paid for by grants hidden in the annual expropriations and conducted by professional spies. The Treasury and the State departments maintained surreptitious links with merchants and smugglers whose business put them in a way to know of warlike preparations in European ports, and who could report unobtrusively. These spies might be paid for occasional work, or on a regular basis. Sometimes, as with Richard Oakes in the early 1780s, the departments paid a principal to organize his fellows into a loose network.[2] At other times, the departments employed individuals to undertake specific missions, such as that of Richard Cadman Etches to free Sidney Smith from his Paris prison in 1798.[3]

More organized still was the Admiralty's formal espionage. In this period, though it was controlled by the secretary, it was based on Holland; and it spread its tentacles throughout Europe. The business was the brainchild of a Dutch couple in Rotterdam named Wolters. During the Seven Years War, Mijnheer Wolters built on earlier contacts to establish a network of spies in Paris and the principal French ports; and at the war's end he extended his organization to Spain. On his death soon after, Mevrow Wolters took the work over. She enlarged and systematized the network, creating centres in Paris, where she had agents in the departments of Marine, War, and Foreign Affairs, and in Madrid and Vienna, and added to the branches. By the early 1780s, she was receiving weekly reports from Paris, Madrid, and Vienna, and regular ones from Dunkirk, Nantes, Brest, Rochefort, Ferrol, La Coruña, Cádiz, Cartagena, and Toulon. She sent summaries of these across the Channel by packet-boat.[4] It was a most efficient system. In 1778 the British knew the terms of the alliance between France and Spain within forty-eight hours of its signing.[5] And in 1790, at the time of Nootka Sound crisis, they received detailed reports on the strength of the Spanish navy at regular intervals.[6] In an age when only those women who ruled usually participated in affairs of state, Mevrow Wolters was clearly a person of very considerable abilities; and she retained the confidence of Philip Stephens and his superiors at the Admiralty for more than twenty years.

The Northern and Southern Departments of State, which were reorganized into the Foreign and Home Offices in 1782, and the Treasury mounted smaller spying operations, of which the most important feature was the employment of individuals to investigate particular circumstances abroad. Those who undertook these missions were carefully chosen for their expertise, their knowledge of European languages, and their discretion. In 1765, the Southern Department sent a spy (possibly Robert Shafto) to report on French preparations.[7] Throughout the 1770s, North and Robinson at the Treasury similarly employed a Lieutenant Mante; and the Southern Department continued to use him in the early 1780s.[8] The reorganization of the State departments left some untidy ends, including that of the Home Office's remaining responsible for espionage in

France and Spain. This meant that, from 1782 into the 1790s, Evan Nepean employed spies and received their reports. Arthur Phillip was one such spy.

Nepean turned to Phillip in late 1784 because of news from France. In April, the administration began to receive reports from Mevrow Wolters that the French were arming their fleet.[9] From September, information from other sources centred this activity on the Mediterranean base of Toulon. The commodore of the Mediterranean squadron passed on a report, which reached the Admiralty on 7 October, that the French were building up their timber supplies there.[10] A few days later, the Foreign Office passed on another from the consul at Nice that the French were working 'Day and Night in arming'.[11] A week later came one from the consul at Genoa that the French had ordered 'all the Caulkers and Carpenters' in Marseilles to go to Toulon, where 'orders were gone to lay Six Line of Battle Ships on the Stocks'.[12] Then came another from Nice that there were sixteen battleships and between sixteen and twenty frigates at Toulon, and that the French had brought 'a great deal of Timber, and many Masts and large Spars ... into the Dock Yard, since March last'.[13] Simultaneously, Mevrow Wolters wrote that that yard had orders to fit all the battleships and frigates for sea, and that the officials expected to have thirty battleships ready by January.[14]

Though they had just concluded treaties of peace with the French and the Dutch, the British continued extemely anxious about French ambitions to drive them from India. They must take it for granted, Henry Dundas told Sydney on 2 November, that 'India is the quarter to be first attacked'.[15] Coming amid others that the Dutch were sending ships and troops to the East,[16] the reports of preparations at Toulon could only fuel British anxiety; and the Pitt administration quickly took steps to determine their accuracy. On 19 October, Carmarthen, the Foreign Secretary, asked the British ambassador in Paris for 'the fullest & most accurate intelligence of the present state of the French Marine, of the particular Force now fit for, or preparations for service both at Brest and Toulon, as well as what Ships of War may have sailed from either of those Ports, since June last, & as far as possible the respective destination of such ships'.[17] Simultaneously, Nepean engaged Phillip to 'undertake a Journey to Toulon & other ports of France for the purpose of ascertaining the Naval Force, and Stores in the Arsenals'.[18]

As an officer on half pay, Phillip had to obtain formal leave from the Admiralty to travel abroad. On 14 October, giving the blind of needing to go to Grenoble 'on Account of my private Affairs', he asked for permission to be absent for twelve months, which the Admiralty granted.[19] On 11 November, Nepean paid him £150 for salary and expenses.[20] Precisely when Phillip left on his mission and the route he took to Toulon are unknown. He may have travelled by packet-boat or naval vessel to Gibraltar, and gone on by merchant vessel to Marseilles. Or he may have crossed from Dover to Calais or Boulogne, and gone by coach to Paris. From the capital, he would have proceeded by coach to Lyons, where he might have taken the *diligence d'eau*, a large boat drawn by horses and designed to accommodate travellers on the grand tour. Traversing the deep Rhône valley, he would have passed through a romantic countryside cluttered with villages, farms, castles and country houses, and an oppressed peasantry, into the Languedoc, pleasant with ripening olive trees, figs, and vines. After Avignon and its Roman ruins, he would have skirted the Camargue, that region of horses, marshes, and waterfowl, on his way to Marseilles.

Whichever route he took, Phillip would have found the Mediterranean coast of France a world away from winter-bound northern Europe. Marseilles was a flourishing commercial centre, its harbour filled with vessels plying the Mediterranean and West Indian trades, its wide and tree-lined streets flanked with substantial dwellings and artisans' shops. The intervening country to Toulon was well-watered, lush with vineyards, cornfields, orchards, and meadows which provided good grazing for cattle: as a contemporary described it, 'When you are within a few miles of *Toulon*, the whole face of the country wears a most joyful appearance, though [the] lofty hills still continue; but then they are cloathed with ever-greens, such as oranges, lemons, olives, and fig-trees, which are so delightfully interspers'd with country seats and vineyards, &c on the one hand; and a most extensive view of the *Mediterranean* on the other, then the whole forms the most beautiful prospect imaginable'.[21]

The land traveller entered the town over a drawbridge and through an imposing gate, to find a town of narrow but regularly-formed and clean streets flanked by white stone houses. There was a spacious central square, where the guard exercised daily. It was commonly said that 'the king of France ... is greater at Toulon than at Versailles',[22] for the base was the heart of French naval power. The harbour was capacious and well defended. The basin could accommodate up to twenty battleships at a time; and the adjacent quay, docks, and magazines were carefully laid out so as to permit efficient refitting, with water piped to the harbourside.

When Phillip reached Toulon early in January 1785, he found a firm basis for the reports that the British had been receiving. The French were importing timber from Albania, and recruiting shipwrights from neighbouring ports. There were fourteen battleships refitting in the basin, twelve of which had their lower masts in and rigging up; and eleven frigates and storeships, nine with their lower masts stepped. The dockyard officials had orders to fit seven battleships for sea immediately, and then another five. 'The French,' he reported, 'certainly pay the greatest attention to their Navy.' Later, he added that, while the orders to fit the squadron for sea had not been pursued, there were ten battleships and several frigates that could 'be ready for Sea in a short time', and that the arsenal was 'in very good Order and very superior to what it was when I saw it before the War'.[23]

From Toulon, Phillip went along the coast to Nice. As he went, he found the smaller arsenals closed to visitors, not, he thought, 'in consequence of any thing now going on, but from the Yards in England being shut to French Officers'.[24] Nice, which was then part of the King of Sardinia's domain, was another garden of delights. The city constituted the stage of a natural amphitheatre. From it, one might see both the rugged peaks of the Alpes Maritimes and, across the clear Mediterranean, the gentler ones of Corsica. The winter that froze the Alps scarcely touched this spot of perpetual spring, whose countryside presented a patchwork of whitewashed farmhouses, cultivations, groves of oranges, lemons, and citrons, gardens of vegetables and salad greens, and plots of roses, carnations, anemonies, and daffodils, garlands of which were sent as far as Paris, and even London.

There is no information about which other ports Phillip inspected during 1785, but Admiralty records indicate he remained abroad the full period, returning only at the end of October.[25] It was a brief return, for on 1 December he asked for another twelve months' leave, to go 'on his private affairs' to Hyères in Provence.[26] There are no reports extant to indicate that Phillip was again off spying, but it is impossible that he was not so engaged, for Hyères is only 15 kilometres east of Toulon; and at the beginning of November Nepean paid him another £160 of secret service money.[27]

There is again no record of precisely when in 1786 Phillip returned to England. Perhaps he rested on the French shores of the Mediterranean until he received Lord Sydney's invitation to found a convict settlement at the extremity of the world. It was to be his life's loneliest and most demanding work—and his most significant.

Sirius

4

Out of the World
New South Wales, 1786–92

*Having nothing new to communicate I
should hardly have troubled you with a
letter was it not customary for Men to take
leave of their friends before they go out of
the World, for I can hardly think my self in
it so long as I am deprived from having any
Connections with the civilized part of it,
and this will soon be my case for two years
at least.*

*Captain James Cook, from the Cape
of Good Hope, November 1772*

*. . . for tho' I am out of the World, still
there are those in it, in whom I feel my self
Interested.*

*Arthur Phillip, from New South Wales,
September 1788*

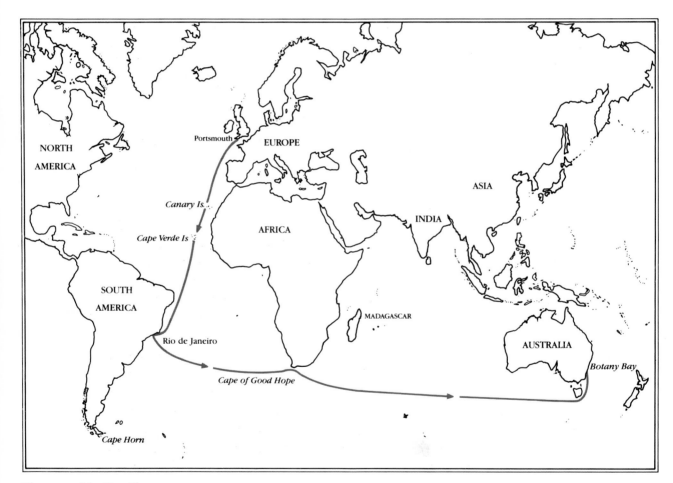

The route of the First Fleet

The Decision to Colonize

It might perhaps be practicable to direct the strict employment of a limited number of convicted felons in each of the dock-yards, in the stanneries, saltworks, mines, and public buildings of the kingdom. The more enormous offenders might be sent to Tunis, Algiers, and other Mahometan ports, for the redemption of Christian slaves: others might be compelled to dangerous expeditions; or be sent to establish new colonies, factories, and settlements on the coasts of Africa, and on small islands for the benefit of navigation.

William Eden, *The Principles of Penal Law* (1771)[1]

A number of reasons combined to take Arthur Phillip to New South Wales: members of the Pitt administration decided to use convicts to build a naval base to increase Britain's strategic capacity in the East and to provide a way station to China and the west coasts of America; certain of the officials saw Phillip as a person competent to oversee such a venture, and wished to reward him for past services; Phillip needed employment of some kind, and he saw a challenge in this one.

The presence of a large number of convicts posed a domestic problem in the mid-1780s. Before 1776, the British had transported some 1000 convicts a year across the Atlantic, with contractors selling their labour to planters, mostly in Virginia and Maryland. This was a quite efficient practice. It ridded the mother country of undesirables, and provided a cheap labour force for the colonies, which in turn enabled the colonists to produce materials for sale to the mother country and to buy her manufactures. Via a change in environment, it offered the miscreants a chance to reform. As a contemporary put it, it frequently happened that, 'during the period of their legal servitude, [the convicts] became reconciled to a life of honest industry, were altogether reformed in their manners, and rising gradually by laudable efforts, to situations of advantage, independence, and estimation, contributed honourably to the population and prosperity of their new country'.[2]

Transportation to America stopped abruptly when the colonies rebelled. Thinking that the need would be temporary, the North administration decided to keep transportees on hulks moored in the Thames, and to employ them in dredging and dockyard work. These hulks were never, as is popularly believed, grossly overcrowded. Rather, the contractor Duncan Campbell regulated the numbers on them carefully, and accepted new inmates only when death or the expiration of sentences created space.[3] But as Campbell's accommodation was limited, and as magistrates continued to sentence miscreants to transportation at the same rate as before the war, those institutions which became overcrowded were the county and local gaols. This meant that the local authorities were responsible for feeding and clothing many more prisoners than usual, and it was this fact, rather than simple overcrowding, that occasioned the loud volume of criticism which sheriffs and gaolers directed at successive administrations concerning the failure of central government to meet its legal duty and remove the transportees to regions beyond the seas.

Between 1778 and 1784, the North, Shelburne, and Pitt administrations investigated the various possibilities of transporting convicts to Africa, to Brazil, to Honduras, even to the newly independent American states. None of these moves bore any fruit; and by mid-1784 it had become clear to Pitt and his advisers that they would have either to find some new mode of transportation, or legislate a different punishment. Progressively they took up the idea suggested earlier by William Eden, that those who had forfeited their freeborn right to the benefits of society might be 'compelled to dangerous expeditions; or be sent to establish new colonies, factories, and settlements on the coasts of Africa, and on small islands for the benefit of navigation'.

In 1784 and 1785, officials received a series of proposals for settlements which would satisfy the intertwined requirements of punishing as the law prescribed, of removing the criminals to such a distance as to make their return difficult, and of bringing the state an advantage in return for the inevitable cost. The areas suggested were the Das Voltas Bay region, on the southwest coast of Africa; the one about the Krome River, on the southeast coast of Africa; and Botany Bay, on the east coast of New South Wales.[4] The proposers saw that each colonization would have a 'naval' or strategic dimension. A settlement at Das Voltas Bay would be a place 'for our Indiamen to call at & refit & come up with [the] SE trade in War to avoid the Enemy'.[5] One at Krome River Bay would similarly enable 'Our Ships [to] run the less risque ... and call there to recruit our Troops as well as Seamen when going to India'.[6] One at Botany Bay would give Britain access to the potentially rich sources of naval materials constituted by the Norfolk Island pine and the New Zealand flax; create a base from which squadrons might sail to attack the French at Mauritius, the Dutch in the East Indies, or the Spanish in the Philippines and on the west coasts of America; and prevent the French taking possession of a territory from which they might plunder Britain's eastern trade, and expand their own.[7]

While it is likely that they always had *two* schemes of convict colonization in mind—one for hardened criminals in Africa, another for young offenders in New South Wales—from mid-1785 into mid-1786 the officials of the Pitt administration were clearly more immediately interested in placing a colony at Das Voltas Bay, so as to obtain a direct equivalent to the Cape of Good Hope. When a survey showed this site to be quite barren, officials turned to Botany Bay, about which they had Cook's and Banks's detailed reports, and James Matra's, Sir George Young's, and Sir John Call's elaborate proposals. Early in August 1786, working from these proposals and from information supplied by Duncan Campbell, Evan Nepean and the Treasury secretaries made detailed estimates of costs, which appeared acceptable. Nepean then drew up the Heads of a Plan, and the ministers formally approved the venture on 19 August.[8]

By arriving at the Settlement three or
three Months before the Transports, many &
very great advantages would be gained —
Huts would be ready to receive those Convicts
who were Sick, & they would find Vegitables,
of which it may naturally be suppos'd
they will stand in great need, as the Scurvy
must make a great ravage amongst people
naturally Indolent, & not cleanly.

Huts would be ready for the Women — the
Stores would be properly lodg'd, & defended
from the Convicts, in such a manner as to
prevent their making any attempt on them.
The Cattle & Stock would be likewise
properly Secured ——— And the Ground
mark'd out for the Convicts. — A list of
those intended to be sent being) given to
the Commanding Officer, mentioning their Age,
Crimes, Trades & Characters. — they might
be so divided as to render few changes
necessary — & the Provisions would be read

The First Fleet

I was honored with your obliging letter of the 11th of April by the hand of Governor Phillip. I need not tell you that it gave me great satisfaction, for I was almost out of hopes of hearing from my friends any more. We had for some months ago the news of this extraordinary expedition to the Antarctic regions, but I always doubted the truth of it.

Francis Masson, from the Cape of Good Hope, November 1787

On 21 August, Evan Nepean and Lord Sydney officially informed the Treasury of the decision to colonize New South Wales, and asked for funds to set the venture in train.[1] On 31 August, the Home Office informed the Admiralty of it, and asked for ships to carry the convicts out and marines to guard them in New South Wales. On 15 September, the Home Office informed the East India Company, whose approval the administration needed to obtain, and which it wanted to help lessen the cost by giving the transports homeward cargoes of tea.

The various departments then proceeded with arrangements. On 1 September, the Navy Board advertised for tenders of transports.[2] In September, it accepted William Richards's proposed terms, and it and the East India Company inspected the ships he offered.[3] Simultaneously, the Navy Board fitted out the *Berwick*, of 540 tons, renaming it the *Sirius* after 'the bright star in ye Southern constellation of the Great Dog',[4] and the *Supply*, of 175 tons. By late October, what would become known to Australian history as the First Fleet consisted of the *Sirius, Supply, Alexander, Charlotte, Scarborough, Friendship, Lady Penrhyn, Fishburn, Golden Grove*, and *Borrowdale*.

As the Navy Board attended to logistics, the Home Office chose a gov-

The first page of Phillip's memorandum
concerning the colonization

ernor. When Sydney told Howe at the end of August of his intention to appoint Arthur Phillip, the First Lord of the Admiralty replied rather waspishly that 'the little knowledge I have of Captain Phillip would [not] have led me to select him for a service of this complicated nature'.[5] John Blankett, Phillip's fellow naval captain and spy, seems rather to have been Howe's choice.[6] Whether Blankett was not interested, or whether Sydney, whose department was responsible for the convicts, overruled Howe, is unclear. What is clear is that by 3 September 1786 Arthur Phillip was on his way to New South Wales.

Despite Howe's unenthusiastic appraisal, Phillip was well qualified for the task. He had sailed beyond Europe several times, to the West Indies, Brazil, and India, so that he knew the routes and their hazards, and the inevitable difficulties of keeping ships' companies healthy on long voyages. He was familiar with the resources of the Canaries, Rio de Janeiro and Cape Town, on which he would need to draw extensively, both for the voyage and the colonization; and at these places he was known to the authorities, with whom he could negotiate in common languages. His time in the New Forest had given him some experience of farming, a knowledge indispensable to the successful planting of a colony in an uncultivated land. He enjoyed the confidence of politicians and officials—if not of Howe, who may indeed have been ignorant of his secret service, then certainly of Sydney and Nepean, perhaps even of Pitt himself. He had spied for Nepean and had helped the Shelburne and North administrations plan expeditions against Spanish America. He may well have given the Shelburne and Pitt administrations advice about the disposal of the convicts, for it seems more than coincidence that the two occasions in 1782 and 1784 when Nepean discussed the question of transporting British convicts to Brazil with Portuguese officials were exactly the times when he was discussing other matters with Phillip.[7] And if Phillip had indeed ferried Portuguese convicts to South America, then he knew the difficulties which a party of intractable persons added to a long voyage. In any case, his humble origins and his wide experience of diverse cultures, which had given him something of an egalitarian outlook and a tolerance of people's failings, made him well suited for the task. As two persons who knew him observed, he was 'a Man who [had] seen much of the Service, and much of the World; and [had] studied it. He [was] possess'd of g^t. good Sence, well inform'd, indefatigable upon Service, [was] humane and at the same time spirited and resolute.' He was, in short, 'made on purpose for such a Trial of Abilities' as the Botany Bay venture would prove.[8]

Soon after he accepted the appointment, Phillip set forth in considerable detail his views on how the venture should be mounted and the colony developed. In certain ways, this is the most considered and extended discussion by him that exists. It shows clearly how he conceived of this unique business; and, if various of his statements are related to his previous experience and one reads between some lines, it also provides insights into his imagination and personality.[9] Concerning practical matters, Phillip thought that the ships should carry not only seeds from England, but also 'such Fruit Trees, & Cuttings, that will bear removing ... as likewise Roots that will bear keeping that length of time out of the Ground'. They should take on other items, particularly live-stock, at the Cape of Good Hope; and these supplies, together with trading goods, should be distributed amongst the ships, so that the loss of one would not deprive the party entirely of any single item. He thought that no convict with venereal infection should be embarked; and that the relatively uncorrupted women should be segregated from the others during the voyage, and they should not be 'abused and Insulted' by the sailors. The 'greatest Villains' among the men should be transported together in the one ship, and specially guarded. During calm spells, he would go about the ships to see that hygienic conditions prevailed and the convicts were properly fed. On these visits he would make the convicts 'Sensible of their Situation', tell them 'that their Happiness or Misery is in their own Hands', and exhort them to reform and develop industrious habits.

When Phillip drew up this memorandum, he and the officials were con-templating sending the expedition directly from England to the Cape of Good Hope, and from there to Botany Bay.[10] They must allow six months, he observed; and he knew only too well that 'Sickness must be the Consequence in so long a Voyage'. While exercise in fresh air would retard the onset of scurvy, he was apprehensive about allowing the convicts on deck. When in port, however, he would seek to land the sick, to speed their recovery. Despite what-ever precautions he and his surgeons might take during the voyage, though, he knew that inevitably there would be significant numbers of sick by the time they reached their destination, for 'Scurvy must make a great ravage amongst people naturally Indolent, & and not cleanly'. To meet this eventuality, he thought that he should proceed ahead from the Cape with a group of artificers. He might gain 'many & very great advantages' by arriving two or more months sooner: 'Huts would be ready to receive the Convicts who were Sick, & they would find Vegetables, of which it may naturally be suppos'd they will stand in great need.'

This move might also lead to more general benefits. Arriving ahead, he would have more time to choose the best site in the vicinity. 'Huts would be ready for the Women—the Stores would be properly lodg'd, & defended from the Convicts in such manner as to prevent their makeing any attempt on them. The Cattle & Stock would be likewise properly Secured. And the Ground mark'd out for the Convicts. [From] Lists of those intended to be sent being given to the Commanding Officer, mentioning their Age, Crimes, Trades & Character, they might be so divided as to render few changes necessary, & the Provisions would be ready for Issuing without any Waste.' All this would facilitate the immediate disembarkation of the convicts, which was a crucial consideration, for to keep them '*more than a few days*, on board, after they get into a Port, considering the length of time, which they must inevitably be Confined, may be attended with consequences easier to conceive, than to point out in a letter'.

Once the stores and party had been landed, the real tasks of colonization would begin. Phillip hoped to find a site where rivers would form natural barriers between the Europeans and the Aborigines, and between the garrison and the convicts; but in any case he would need to construct a small fort to protect the settlement. His 'great object' would then be to build up herds and flocks, and to establish agriculture, without which the colony could not become self-sufficient. In order to preserve for breeding the animals initially carried out, he would control the slaughter of the privately-owned as well as of the government's. After they had worked for the government, convicts might cultivate small plots for themselves. So too might the marines. It would prove advantageous to have some prefabricated houses. The country might most easily be explored by horsemen, therefore he would need horses and saddles.

Relations with the Aborigines were another large concern. Interestingly, Phillip was 'not of the general opinion that there are very few Inhabitants in this Country'; and he thought it would be 'a great point gained if I can proceed in this Business without haveing any dispute with the Natives, a few of which I shall endeavour to persuade to settle near us, & who I mean to furnish with every thing that can tend to Civilize them, & to give them a high Opinion of their New Guests—for which purpose it will be necessary to prevent the Transports Crews from haveing any intercourse with the Natives if possible. The Convicts must have none, for if they have, the Arms of the Natives will be very formidable in their hands, the Women abused, & the Natives disgusted.' If any of the convicts took Aboriginal women for wives, they must treat them well. Phillip said nothing concerning negotiating with the Aborigines for land, but as the British considered New South Wales to be *terra nullius* this is not surprising.[11] On the other hand, the annexation of New South Wales technically made the Aborigines subjects of the King, and provided them with his formal protection. No explicit statement of this legal position by an administration official seems to have survived; but that it was so is confirmed by Phillip's subsequent comment that 'Any Man who takes the life of a Native, will be put on his Trial the same as if he had kill'd one of the Garrison. This appears to me not only just, but good policy'.[12]

To establish order, and to enable the colony to find its feet, Phillip thought that there should be martial law, which would give the governor discretionary powers. During this time, it would be necessary to keep the convicts apart, with perhaps segregation of sexes. But he also thought that it might prove wise to condone a certain amount of prostitution, in order to reduce tension. In any case, convicts should not have any contact with visiting ships. He thought that the governor should retain wide powers even after the settlement was established, especially to punish and reward. The secondary punishments he envisaged were, for the ill-treatment of the Aborigines, exile to isolated spots where the miscreants would have to survive entirely by their own efforts; and, for murder or sodomy, exile to New Zealand, where the cannibal Maoris would make the culprits regret their crimes. He hoped to avoid putting persons to death. The rewards he envisaged were emancipation for good behaviour, and the granting of land, so that he needed to know what promises of land he might hold out to convicts whom he would encourage to marry and settle, and to marines, who might wish to take Polynesian wives and establish themselves as yeomen farmers after their tour of duty.

Though in this memorandum he was concerned mostly to consider the getting of the party to Botany Bay and the colony's immediate future, Phillip also took a longer view. Displaying an uncharacteristic severity, as he did 'not wish Convicts to lay the foundation of an Empire', he thought 'they should ever remain separated from the Garrison, and other settlers that may come from Europe, & not be allowed to mix w.th them', even after they had served their sentences. And, as the colony would ultimately be governed under English laws, there was 'one' that he wished to prevail from the outset: 'That there can be no Slavery in a Free Land—& consequently no Slaves.'

These observations together show Phillip to have been a person of unusually thorough and precise imagination, with a touch of the visionary. Both attributes were to serve him well, not only in New South Wales, but also during the preparations for the venture, in which he immediately joined. Since the group of officials responsible for mounting the First Fleet—Evan Nepean at the Home Office, George Rose and Thomas Steele at the Treasury, Philip Stephens at the Admiralty, Sir Charles Middleton at the Navy Board, and Phillip—had no real precedent for undertaking a colonization of a virgin land 19 000 kilometres distant from Europe with a party of 750 convicts, 200 marines, and a handful of officials, the need of many of these arrangements only appeared as preparations proceeded.

There were the ships to gather and fit; and stores and provisions to order and load. There were clothing and shoes, tents, tools and medicines to obtain. There were marines to recruit; and the colony's officers to appoint. There were the convicts to bring from the hulks and gaols, and place aboard the ships; and the ships to be brought together. There was the arrangement to conclude with the East India Company; and the detailed route to plan. The colony's legal basis had to be established, and Phillip's instructions drawn up. Altogether, the preparations took nine months, and required the writing of about 800 letters.

This perplexing, this 'disagreeable and troublesome business',[13] caused the officials many headaches and some strained relationships. In the middle of it, at Middleton's suggestion, Nepean and Phillip adopted the procedure that had served Cook so well, of Phillip's calling personally at the various departments, telling the Heads what he needed, and waiting while they issued the necessary requests. This meant that from early December onwards the preparations moved more smoothly. Even then, there were still major and unexpected difficulties. In December, for example, so as to reduce the sexual imbalance a little, the Home Office decided to increase to 180 the number of women to be transported. The Navy Board could not find room for the extra persons on the ships it was fitting out; nor could it stow part of the marines' baggage and stores. The Home Office and Treasury responded by hiring the *Prince of Wales*; but this ship could only be months behind the others in its fitting out. Then, the security of the convicts' quarters on the *Alexander* proved inadequate; and at Portsmouth typhus fever broke out amongst the inmates of this ship. There were deficiencies in some stores and medicines; it took the administration months to settle the legal arrangements.

In all of this, Phillip played a leading part. He personally chose his officers and men; and he showed his concern for those in his charge, and for the future of the colony, by his zealous attention to the needs of the ships, the surgeons, and the crews, marines and convicts. Indeed, such were the frequency and magnitude of these requests that he exasperated the Navy Board officials used to simpler tasks and less concerned commanders. Captain George Teer complained in December that 'Capt Phillip has from time to time so increased the Orders for Stores, implements for Botany bay, and Increased the Number of Marines from seventy four up to One Hundred & Sixty, ... [that] they will occupy ... upwards of Three Hund^d Tons space, each day, & week, continuing to add more, that I was Obliged to put a stop to his wishes still to add.'[14] Phillip persevered, however, and he generally had his way. He saw the ships were altered and repaired as required; he had the Navy Board purchase extra supplies of medicines; he persuaded officials to victual the companies in unusually generous ways; and he saw that these companies were fed 'indiscriminately' with fresh foods while they waited to sail.[15] Phillip took this care for the general good, but he was also anxious to protect his reputation. As he told Sydney, 'I have only one fear … that it may be said hereafter the officer who took charge of the expedition should have known that it was more than probable he lost half the garrison and convicts, crowded and victualled in such a manner for so long a voyage.'[16] In the end, his efforts bore good fruit. According to Teer, the transports were '*Completely fitted*', with their 'Provisions and accommodations' being 'better than any [other] Set of Transports I have ever had any directions in'.[17]

There was one matter in which Phillip's pride was particularly involved. So as to leave him free to remain at the settlement, where his supervision would be constantly required, when the *Sirius* was away, the administration decided to appoint a second captain to the ship. There was no precedent for two post captains serving on the same sixth-rate, and the arrangement therefore required a special order from the Privy Council. It also raised the question of whether Phillip might fly the broad or distinguishing pennant allowed a commodore in charge of a detached squadron sailing on a particular purpose. Phillip thought that he should have it, not—to be fair to him—simply as evidence of his superior status and as a matter of personal satisfaction, but because he foresaw there might be difficulties if he did not. While he would remain senior captain of the *Sirius* in all circumstances, if she were away and he needed to sail on the *Supply* or another naval vessel, he might have no superior authority unless he held the rank of commodore. Disliking any innovations in naval protocol, Lord Howe refused the request.[18]

Phillip persisted. However flattering he found the offer of the governorship, he told Sydney, the task was not without its 'désagrémens', for which the pennant would compensate. The granting of it was of small consequence to the nation, but of 'considerable' consequence to him.[19] But the point was a delicate one. Though he was a most difficult man, Howe's attitude here was not unreasonable. The broad pennant was flown in naval service; and it brought the recipient additional pay. Though Phillip would exercise a naval command while the *Sirius* escorted the convict transports to Botany Bay, once there he would direct the colony on behalf of the Home Office, to which he would be answerable, and which would pay his salary. In the end, naval precedent prevailed and Phillip sailed with the compromise that naval commanders junior to him arriving at New South Wales would have to submit to his authority, and with John Hunter as second captain.

As the officials busied themselves with the practical arrangements, so too did they with the necessary legal ones. On 12 October, when they expected that the colony would initially be under a 'military' form of government,[20] administration officials commissioned Phillip to be governor of New South Wales, 'extending from the northern cape or extremity of the coast called Cape York, in the latitude of 10°37' south, to the southern extremity of the ... South Cape, in the latitude of 43°39' south, and of all the country inland to the westward as far as the one hundred and thirty-fifth degree of longitude, ... including all the islands adjacent in the Pacific Ocean'; and enjoined him to obey instructions 'according to the rules and discipline of war'.[21] Two weeks later, with similar injunctions to act 'according to the rules and discipline of war', officials commissioned Major Robert Ross, the commander of the marine detachment, to be lieutenant-governor; Captain David Collins to be deputy judge-advocate; Richard Johnson to be chaplain; and John White to be surgeon.[22]

Immediately, the Law Officers pointed out that persons sentenced under civil law in Britain were not amenable to military justice elsewhere.[23] This made it necessary for the administration to create a basis of civil law for the colony. Knowing that the composition of the initial population precluded the implementation of the common law in its fullness—'the Component Parts of it are not of the proper Stuff to Make Jurys in Capital cases especially'[24]—on the analogies of Gibraltar and Senegal the officials established military-like machinery to administer a truncated civil law.[25]

The first requirement was to change Phillip's status as governor from that of a military to that of a civil one. This the officials did by recourse to North American precedents, specifically to that of Lord Dorchester's appointment in 1786 as governor-general of the Canadian provinces.[26] It was, however, necessary to depart from this model in one notable way. Whereas Dorchester's commission enjoined him to frame regulations for the provinces in concert with a nominated council and an elected assembly, as there would be initially no substantial group of free men in New South Wales to provide members for such bodies, Phillip's civil commission was silent concerning them.

Apart from this, it followed Dorchester's article for article.[27] Like his Canadian counterpart, Phillip was enjoined to swear allegiance to, and maintain, the Protestant succession; to administer civil justice impartially; to enforce the laws relating to trade and plantations; to appoint 'justices of the peace coroners constables and other necessary officers and ministers in our said territory and its dependencies for the better administration of justice and putting the law in execution'; to care for idiots and lunatics, and administer their estates. He might pardon (absolutely or conditionally, according to the seriousness of the crime); he had 'full power and authority to levy arm muster and command and

Claude-Joseph Vernet, 'The Port of Toulon' (1756)

Claude-Joseph Vernet, 'Toulon: City and Harbour' (1756)

Knud Bull, 'Aboard the *John Calvin* in the northeast trades near Madeira' (1848)

Curiously, the First Fleet artists seem not to have considered convicts an appropriate subject. This considerably later painting is almost unique

William Bradley, 'Santa Cruz on the SE side of Teneriffe; *Sirius* & Convoy in the Roads. June 1787'

employ all persons whatsoever residing within our said territory and its dependencies under your government and as occasion shall serve to march from one place to another or to embark them for the resisting and withstanding of all enemies pirates and rebels both at sea and land'. He might proclaim martial law in war or other emergencies; he might 'erect raise and build ... such and so many forts and platforms castles cities boroughs towns and fortifications' as he should judge necessary; in wartime, he might appoint and promote naval officers, and exercise his powers as vice-admiral through the court of that office; he might assign lands, establish 'fairs marts and markets'; his subordinates were to obey him, or those to whom he delegated his authority; he was to pass all formal instruments under the colony's Great Seal.

Phillip's civil commission conveyed a number of distinct jurisdictions, the basis of which the administration laid in the opening months of 1787. Considering that the delegation of the King's civil authority lay within his prerogative, by Letters-Patent dated 2 April 1787 the administration provided for the governor of New South Wales to constitute a Court of Civil Judicature. The members of this court were initially to be the judge-advocate, and 'two fit and proper persons' to be appointed by the governor or lieutenant-governor. This court was 'to hold plea of and to hear and determine in a summary way all pleas concerning lands, houses, tenements, and hereditaments, and all manner of interests therein, and all pleas of debt, account, or other contracts, trespasses, and all manner of other personal pleas whatsoever'. The justices had the power to 'grant probate of wills and administration of the personal estates of intestates dying within the place or settlement'; and to issue summonses, and to imprison, in civil causes. There was to be appeal from the decision of this court to the governor; and when there was a sum of more than £300 in question, from the governor's decision to the Privy Council.[28]

Next, there was a Court of Criminal Jurisdiction, the members of which were to be the judge-advocate of the colony, together with 'six officers of his Majesty's forces by sea or land'. Proceeding in 'a more summary way than is used within this realm according to the known and established laws thereof', this court was empowered to try and punish for 'all such outrages and misbehaviours as if committed within this realm, would be deemed to be treason or misprison thereof, felony or misdemeanor'. It was to proceed by deposition and examination under oath, and its judgments for capital or corporal punishment were to be issued under the 'hand and seal' of the governor or lieutenant-governor. Five members of the court would need to agree before it could issue a capital sentence; and the colonial authorities could not effect such a sentence 'until the proceedings shall have been transmitted to his Majesty and by him approved'. (This very impractical provision seems never to have been followed.) The court was to be a 'Court of Record', and to have 'all such powers as by the laws of England are incident and belonging to a Court of Record'. A summary procedure—one in which 'there is no intervention of a jury, but the party accused is acquitted or condemned by the suffrage of such person only, as the statute has appointed for his judge'—was not unknown in criminal law in England, but, since 'the common law [was] a stranger to it',[29] it required the explicit sanction of Parliament. Accordingly, in February 1787, the administration enacted legislation providing for the criminal court in New South Wales to proceed in this manner.[30]

The third judicial commission was for a Vice-Admiralty Court in New South Wales, so that Phillip might be able to try pirates who might operate in adjacent seas. At the Admiralty's request, the Privy Council approved of Phillip's appointment as vice-admiral on 4 April. Simultaneously, Sydney requested the Privy Council to give Phillip the power to move against pirates. The Council referred this request to its Committee of Trade and Plantations on 12 April, and Nepean gave in a list of names for insertion in the commission the next day. The Committee reported in favour the same day; and the Privy Council gave its approval a week later, ordering that 'his Majesty's Advocate-General, with the Advocate of the Admiralty, do forthwith prepare and lay before his Majesty at this Board the draught of a commission, in order to be passed under the seal of his Majesty's High Court of Admiralty'. By Letters-Patent of 5 May 1787, the King then empowered Phillip to convene a Vice-Admiralty Court.[31]

Later, the administration added a fourth jurisdiction, to enable Phillip to remit convicts' sentences. Because the remitting authority would not be the same as the conferring one, the Law Officers found some difficulty in providing for this.[32] They put together an expedient which they thought (mistakenly) would answer, which the administration legislated, and then issued Letters-Patent based upon the legislation.[33]

In the end, then, Phillip received such powers as he thought the founding governor should have. Allowing him to govern without a council, and giving him domain over half a continent, these legal arrangements gave him an authority such as was given to few other royal representatives in British history. In theory, Phillip was as much Viceroy as those who governed Brazil or Mexico. What prevented him fully from enjoying the exalted status was the absence of a rich and populous empire. Still, as befitted his position, he had an interview with his sovereign before he sailed—on 3 January 1787, at St James's Palace.[34] Regrettably, history does not record what passed between the monarch with a passion for farming and the naval captain who would begin the planting of a continent.

As these preparations went forward, Phillip, Nepean, and Middleton attended to the details of the voyage. By early January they had settled on a route that clearly reflected Phillip's previous experience of the Canaries, Rio de Janeiro, and Cape Town:

In case of no unforeseen accident it is expected that the Instructions will be ready, the Convicts be embarked, and the Convoy prepared in all respects for their departure by the first or second week in March.

The Convoy will probably arrive at Teneriffe in three weeks, which will bring it to the last week in March or the first in April.

The passage from thence to the Cape of Good Hope direct may be about Seven weeks at most. But it is imagined that it may be of advantage to touch at Rio de Janeiro, where there is a certainty of obtaining Supplies, and which is not to be depended upon at the Cape. The passage will of course be lengthened and will most likely delay their arrival at the Cape 'till the latter end of July or the beginning of August.

The passage from the Cape of Good Hope to Botany Bay will most likely be effected in two Months which will bring it up to the latter end of Octor or beginning of November, the Spring of that Country.

It will be a Winters passage from the Cape to Botany Bay, but if the favorable Season was to be preferred, it would occasion a considerable delay and the Convoy would arrive at a time when the Settlers ought to be employed in gathering their Crop.[35]

In the next weeks and months, Phillip sought clarification on a number of points relating specifically to the voyage. His queries, and the determination of them, again show the care with which the administration approached the business. Were the marines' wives to be provided for in the same way as the others who sailed?–Yes. Was he to obtain fresh foods for all the groups on the ships while in the ports en route?–Yes. Could he buy wine (thought to have medicinal value) en route?–Yes. Could he replace items consumed en route, especially bread and beef?–Yes; for the whole party?–Yes. Was he at liberty to land the sick at these ports, so as the better to recover their health?–Yes. During the voyage, if need arose, might he make one of the transports into a hospital ship?–Yes.[36]

Just as they consulted Phillip concerning the voyage, so too did the administration officials consult him concerning his general intructions, and adjust these to meet his requirements. Drafted in March, and finalized in April and May,[37] these provided, first, for his sailing via the Canaries, Rio de Janeiro, and Cape Town, refreshing at each port and taking in new supplies; for his sailing ahead from the Cape; and for his being able to select a site other than Botany

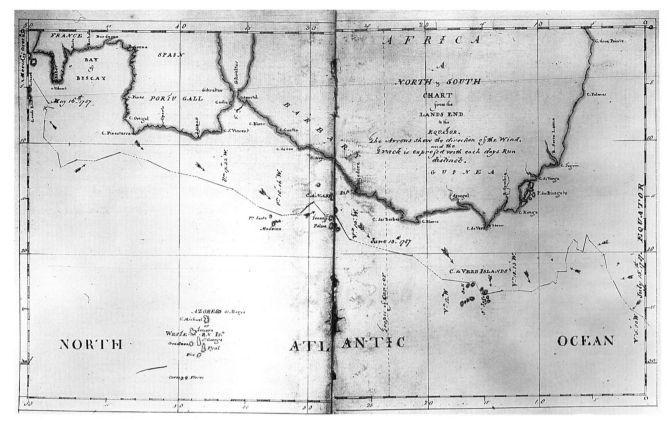

George Raper, 'The route of the First Fleet
down the Atlantic' (1787)

Bay if he considered one more suitable. He was to decide on the site quickly,
though, so as to unload the transports and speed them on their way to China,
where the East India Company had agreed to give them homeward cargoes. The
instructions also offered guidelines concerning the manner in which he was to
form the colony. After landing and securing the stores, he was to put the convicts to work under 'inspectors or overseers', at clearing, building, and cultivating. His immediate tasks were to provide shelter for the group, establish grain
and vegetable crops, and breed herds and flocks. To add to the animals landed
from the First Fleet, he was to send the *Sirius* and the *Supply* to such islands as
Savu and Tahiti for others. And he was very carefully to control the slaughter of
animals, until a 'competent stock' had built up.

He was initially to have all the convicts labour for the common good. In
time, though, he might permit those emancipated or those who had served their
term to cultivate small allotments for themselves and their families. Similarly, he
might make small grants of land to marines and sailors who wished to settle in
the colony. He might give settlers initial help with tools, animals, and seeds, and
victual them off the government store for the first twelve months. To diminish

the imbalance of the sexes, he might bring in Polynesian women, but he was not to do this by force or false pretences. In all of this, he was to pay strict attention to economy. He was to see the colonists made 'due' religious observance. He was to prevent 'every sort of intercourse' between the colonists and the European settlements in Asia. He was to establish friendly relations with the Aborigines, and to see that the Europeans treated them well. Concerning larger purposes, he was to occupy Norfolk Island 'as soon as circumstances will admit of it', so as to reserve its naval materials. He was to set up a flax manufacture, for clothing and 'maritime' purposes. He was to survey the adjacent coasts and explore the seas. One point on which he seemingly did not receive written instructions was how he was to act 'in case of being opposed by any European Ships when I arrive on the Coast'.[38] Presumably, he had Lapérouse most immediately in mind, and in the event, his fear was to prove groundless.

As recompense for all the labour and trials, Phillip was to receive, in addition to his pay as captain of the *Sirius*, £1000 a year, £90 for a secretary, and £20 for stationery. The officials supposed it would take him three years to establish the colony. He himself expected to be absent for between three and five years, and he hoped that when he returned the colony would be not only well-ordered and self-sufficient, but also 'of the greatest consequence' to Britain.[39]

All the necessary arrangements were not completed until the beginning of May. Having received his commission and instructions, and the various Letters-Patent, and bearing also the chronometer and sextant he was to use, Phillip then went from London to Portsmouth where the convoy had gathered, arriving on 7 May. He gave the chronometer, which was one Cook had used on his second and third voyages, to William Bayley, the astronomer who had sailed with Cook and who was now head master of the Portsmouth Naval Academy, to determine its accuracy precisely;[40] and made final preparations.

On 10 May, with the convoy gathered at the Motherbank, Phillip signalled the ships to prepare to put to sea. He paid the crews of the *Sirius* and *Supply* two months' advance on 12 May, and the *Hyena* arrived, to help guard against any mutiny by the convicts while the transports were within reach of England. Several new difficulties appeared. Quantities of clothes ordered for the women convicts did not arrive; nor did the musket balls. And, protesting that their ships' masters had not advanced them wages to purchase goods for the voyage, the crews of the transports declined to put to sea. The lack of the clothing and musket balls did not bother Phillip greatly, for he knew that he might either obtain them at a port en route, or that they might follow in the *Bounty*. But the difficulty with the sailors was another matter, and he spent the day rectifying it. On 13 May, at day break, with the wind from the southeast, the *Sirius* weighed

anchor '& made sail to the W¦ward within the Isle of Wight, in C⁰ His Maj
Ship *Hyaena*, Armed Tender *Supply* w⦂6 Transports & 3 Storeships under
Convoy'.[41] At 9 a.m. they passed through the Needles into the English Channel. Forty-eight years old, and traveller of goodly states and kingdoms and wide
oceans, Arthur Phillip was on his way out of the world.

The voyage began auspiciously. Whereas on the last occasion Phillip had
sailed from Europe, winter storms had shattered his squadron in the Bay of
Biscay and he had had to proceed alone, now he sailed in 'fine' weather with a
'good breeze' at east southeast.[42] Five hundred kilometres out from Portsmouth, he farewelled the *Hyena*, and headed his ships southwest into the Atlantic. Sailing down the route that thousands of voyages had made second nature to
European navigators, the First Fleet reached for the Canaries. The weather continued good. Preparing for the tasks of colonization, Phillip gathered details of
the convicts' 'different trades and occupations';[43] and with him and his surgeons
paying particular attention to diet and hygiene, the general level of health far
exceeded expectation. Especially was this true of the convicts. After three
weeks, not only were these 'not so sickly as when we sailed', but the 'whole
fleet' was 'remarkably healthy'.[44] And already, in their behaviour, they showed
the benefit of change of circumstance. There was a brief worry with some
rogues on the *Scarborough*, but the officers quickly put paid to their intended
mutiny. Indeed, Phillip found so little cause for concern that he gave permission
for the males to be unfettered, and for all to be allowed above deck at intervals.
He reported from Teneriffe, 'in general, the convicts have behaved well ... They
are quiet and contented'.[45]

The Fleet was among the Canaries in the first days of June. The position of
these islands across southerly winds and currents meant that they were ideally
situated to be a place of refreshment for ships sailing to the West Indies, South
America, Africa, and India; and after settling them in the fifteenth century, the
Spanish colonists had quickly provided for the demand, raising animals and
poultry, vegetables and fruit. In time, they also produced goods for the European mainland—first sugar, then wines. By the 1780s, Santa Cruz, the chief
town on Teneriffe, had become the group's central port, and had a population of
more than 6000. To it came a great variety of European goods—beef, pork,
butter, fish, candles, wheat, maize, rice, timber, cloths. From it went wines, silk,
and orchilla.[46]

Having sighted the famous Peak of Teneriffe the previous day, the ships
reached Santa Cruz on 3 June, where the governor received Phillip helpfully. In
the next week, Phillip provided for the party's present and future well-being,
giving the marines and convicts one pound of fresh beef per day, which he

considered 'absolutely necessary', together with rice, wine, and what vegetables and fruit were available, and taking on fresh water. He also met some of friendship's obligations, and bought quantities of wine for Sydney and Nepean. During these days, the officers inspected Santa Cruz and its surrounding districts. They found the town to be 'very irregular and illbuilt', but none the less to have some 'spacious' and 'convenient' houses; and they were shocked at the 'restless importunity' of the beggars and the brazen behaviour of the prostitutes. Beyond the port and Laguna, the island's capital, they found 'fertile' valleys and 'highly romantic' rises.[47] Nevertheless, the pioneers did not see the Canaries at their best. Vegetables were scarce, and fruits not in season. Still, in the substantiality of Santa Cruz, the underlying fertility of the environs, the production of wines, dye, cotton and silk, and the establishment of a regular government over the mixed population, they saw enough to gain a sense of how a small-scale European colonization might succeed. Teneriffe was the first in a series of such experiences during the voyage to render more familiar to them the business they were about.

Phillip took the ships to sea again on 10 June. A week later, when at the Cape Verde Islands, he decided the voyage was going well enough for him to be able not to stop again, so he pressed on for Brazil. Despite some tropical heat and storms, the weather continued favourable, and the party's health good. The waters swarmed with fish, with which the people supplemented their diet. When they reached Brazil early in August, they had lost only fifteen convicts and one marine's child; and most of these had been on embarkation 'such objects as could not have been supposed would have lived, had they remained in England'.[48]

The arrival at Rio de Janeiro was something of a homecoming for Phillip, who brought his convoy through the heads with flags flying and cannon sounding. His friend the Marquis of Lavradio was no longer Viceroy; but the new ruler, Luis de Vasconcelos e Souza, greeted him as an equal, returning his salute, providing him with accommodation on shore, and ordering the palace guard to receive him formally whenever he landed. Phillip found the soldiers' attention a hindrance to the efficient conduct of his business, and sought to avoid it by landing where they were not expecting him—which led to the comical sight of desperate soldiers running to meet him and hastily drawing themselves up on parade.[49] Inconvenient as this attention was, Phillip had for the most part to accept it, for he needed the help which accompanied it. The Viceroy made the country's resources freely available; and, in a rare gesture, he permitted the British officers to move without military escort about the city and its environs. This was in sharp contrast to the obstacles that Lavradio had placed in Cook's way in 1769, and Vasconcelos himself in M'Douall's in 1782; and it reflected Vasconcelos's awareness of his nation's debt to Phillip.

Phillip's greatest concern was the health of the party. Immediately on arrival, he obtained 'great plenty' of vegetables, fruits, and fresh beef; and he saw that all persons continued to have supplies throughout their stay. These foods were cheap, and Phillip ordered very generous allowances—more than a pound of beef per adult per day; a pound of rice; yams, plantains, radishes, cabbages, lettuce, and endive; and oranges, limes, guavas, and bananas. He landed the sick at the Ilha das Cobras; and the fresh air and fresh foods 'soon removed every symptom of the scurvy prevalent among them'. By the time the Fleet sailed from Rio de Janeiro, the convicts were 'much healthier than when we left England'. As he attended to immediate needs, Phillip also looked further, purchasing items that they would need either during the rest of the voyage, or in the colonization: 115 pipes of rum and 15 of wine; 100 sacks of the bread substitute casada; 10 000 musket balls. He gathered plants and seeds, too—for Sir Joseph Banks, some rare varieties; for the Fleet, those that he expected would flourish in New South Wales, such as fruits, vines, coffee, cocoa, indigo, cotton, and some cochineal.[50]

While Phillip forwent the pleasures of the city, the officers, to whom it was unfamiliar, spread about it. Some, like John White and William Dawes, discussed professional matters with their Portuguese counterparts. Others were simply tourists, and wandered to admire the imposing civic square, the towering aqueduct, and the churches. Many joined the throngs at the colourful festivals, enjoyed the displays of fireworks, and sought out 'tender' attachments. As those who have travelled since to this romantic city have found, while it offered great contrasts of wealth and poverty, it also offered an abundant sense of life. To the officers, it was a welcome interlude amid tedious wastes of ocean; and it showed them how European colonization might succeed on a grand scale.[51] They might have enjoyed it less had they shared more Phillip's sense of the difficulties that lay ahead.

The company refreshed, the ships reprovisioned and bearing more of what the party would need in New South Wales, Phillip sailed for the Cape of Good Hope on 4 September. The good fortune continued. Despite the weather being rougher than before, there were no serious incidents; and while some were sick with scurvy and dysentery, by the time they sighted the Cape on 13 October, in general the expedition remained unusually healthy.

At Cape Town, Phillip followed a similar procedure to that at Rio de Janeiro. He saluted the fort as the ships entered Table Bay; and after the port master had ascertained that the ships carried no contagious illnesses, he paid his compliments to the governor, requesting permission to purchase food and live-stock. At first, the Dutch authorities restricted the amounts of bread and flour, giving as their reason the failure of crops two years before. After repeated applications and explanations, Phillip's 'judicious perseverance' paid dividends; he received permission to buy most of what he wanted, and the expedition once more enjoyed fresh food.[52] He must have found the situation all too familiar; and the difficulties entirely justified his and Nepean's earlier perception that he should first touch at Rio de Janeiro, and also not sail ahead of the Fleet until leaving Cape Town. The Dutch merchants' charging double or treble their usual prices was another annoyance, but as he could not manage without their supplies, there was little Phillip could do about this. He saw that all the ships' companies received soft bread, fresh meat, and vegetables daily, with the convicts, 'men, women, and children', having 'the same allowance as the troops, except wine'. In this circumstance he found it unnecessary to land the few sick, who were 'perfectly re-established in three or four days'.[53] On the face of things, there was little reason for the party not to be confident. The voyage was going well, far better than might reasonably have been expected.

Phillip and some of the officers lodged ashore. As always, he was more concerned with business than pleasure—John White, for example, was moved to speak of his 'sagacity and industrious zeal for the service'; but his juniors again looked interestedly about a locality that was strange to most of them. They noticed the township's regularity and neatness, and its avenues of oak. Predictably, they were most struck by the company's garden, by its fertility, its cool passages, and its menagerie, which put a number in mind of St James's Park; and Governor Graaf added to their pleasure by entertaining them at his residence. And as it had done in Brazil, analogy suggested a happy outcome to the British venture. 'The Cape is situated in a fine Climate,' one wrote, '& Yields most of the necessarys of Life, and some of its Luxuries—We have good hopes of B.ỵ Bay—it being In nearly the same Latitude.'[54]

But a distinct sobering of outlook also attended arrival at the Cape; and the records show a loss of optimism, the growth of a sense of menace. The Cape colony itself occasioned the first manifestations of this sense. Though prosperous enough, Cape Town was no Rio de Janeiro; and however much they enjoyed it, the officers found that it 'certainly suffer[ed]' in comparison. Here there were no 'picturesque and beautiful' environs 'abounding with the most luxuriant flowers and aromatic shrubs', but rather the forbidding Table Mountain, on whose bleak rocks renegade slaves took refuge.[55] Here there were no taverns for the officers to lodge at, provisions were dear, and the governor was uncertain about allowing the British access to them. The regularity with which the township was laid out, and the regulation of its inhabitants' lives bespoke the Calvinism of the Dutch. Here were no exuberant festivals. Here ladies did not let passion slip past enticing veils, throw nosegays from balconies or gather at the gates of convents to encourage assignations, or mingle with the festival crowds to achieve them. Rather, they sat demurely in the middle of austere churches, with the men about the walls to surround them. Wearing black, couples married only on Sundays. Slaves moved about the streets in fear, not in celebration.

And constantly the British felt death's presence. A few weeks before their arrival, an unhappy Malay had run amok, murdering fourteen men and desperately wounding another thirty, before being broken alive on the wheel.[56] His fate, the British quickly gathered, was the criminal's typical one. The principal law officer had 'People under his directions, who constantly patrole the streets armed, for the apprehending all disorderly persons; Every 14 days Offences are tried'. The punishments inflicted were: 'Breaking upon the Cross, upon the Wheel impalements, flogging to that degree that Death is frequently the effects of the severity'. Over the door of 'a small Wooden House, wherein are kept the Instruments of Execution' was inscribed: 'Happy is the Man whom other Mens misfortunes make wary.' Neither did the Dutch confine their admonition to this. Along shore and in front of the town were 'many Gallows & other impliments of punishment ... There were also Wheels for breaking Felons upon, several of wh. were at this time occupied by the mangled Bodies of the unhappy wretches who suffer'd upon them.'[57]

The change in their mood resulted in some part directly from what the British saw at the Cape; but there were other causes, one quite practical. Knowing that they were destined for a region 'that does not furnish any of the necessarys of Life',[58] Phillip acted to take on as many of these as he possibly could. He shifted persons from one ship to another, crowding them together to make room for the stalls which he filled with animals: 'Bulls, Cows, Horses Mares, Colts, Sheep, Hogs, Goats Fowls and other living Creatures by Pairs'. He likewise gathered 'a vast Number of Plants, Seeds & other Garden articles, such, as Orange, Lime, Lemon, Quince Apple, Pear Trees, in a Word, every Vegetable Production that the Cape afforded'.[59] And the company at large now felt the urgency of the need. 'This is the last port we touch at in our Way to the New Settlement,' a junior officer wrote, '[and it] has been a Time of constant Bustle —indeed it is right to take every advantage of it, for the leaving behind of any of the many Articles that are requisite, and necessary, would be now irreparable.'[60]

There was a larger, less tangible cause. Instinctively, the British knew that to leave the Cape of Good Hope for the southern Indian Ocean was to leave the world. As Cook had written from there to his old master and friend John Walker in November 1772, 'having nothing new to communicate I should hardly have troubled you with a letter was it not customary for Men to take leave of their friends before they go out of the World, for I can hardly think my self in it so long as I am deprived from having any Connections with the civilized part of it, and this will soon be my case for two years at least'. Now, those on the First Fleet faced this reality. 'The land behind us was the abode of a civilized people,' David Collins observed as they prepared to sail, 'that before us was the residence of savages. When, if ever, we might again enjoy the commerce of the world, was doubtful and uncertain'.[61]

In this atmosphere, the voyagers clutched at the intangibles of their world. Some of them had received letters just before they sailed, and as the ships moved away from the Cape, they encountered the *Kent* whaler: 'On our first discovering her, as she seemed desirous of joining or speaking to the fleet, we were in hopes of her being from England, probably to us, or at least that we might get letters by her; but our suspense on these points, a suspense only to be conceived by persons on long voyages, was soon put an end to by hearing she had been so many months out.'[62] The disappointment gave finality to the move from the Cape. 'We weighed anchor,' Tench wrote, 'and soon left far behind every scene of civilization and humanized manners.'[63]

With each ship like 'another Noah's Ark', crowded with cattle, sheep, pigs, horses, and poultry, and loaded deep with food and extra water for these beasts and the plants, with his own cabin 'like a Small Green house', Phillip sailed again on 11 November. He did so without the gardener Francis Masson, who was then engaged in collecting at the Cape and whom Banks had intended should go with the expedition, but who was unwilling to do so. Unfortunately, Banks did not learn of this reluctance until after the First Fleet had left England, when it was too late to engage another. It was an absence the colonists were to feel deeply.[64] Phillip now decided finally to go on ahead. Shifting into the *Supply*, and taking trusted junior officers and some convict artificers with him, he set off with three of the faster sailers. This advance party lost sight of the body of the convoy on 27 November, and proceeded eastward through 'a great number of black & Blue Petrells' and a 'prodigious quantity of Whales', as well as frequent squalls and high seas, when the wind was 'seldom more than twenty-four hours in one quarter, veering regularly from the Northward to the Westward where it seldom stood more than a few hours,... [and was] seldom to the Eastward & then for a few hours only'. Interspersed were days of 'very pleasant & serene Weather'. The *Supply* sighted the South Cape of Van Diemen's Land (Tasmania) on 3 January, and entered Botany Bay in the afternoon of 18 January 1788,[65] to be followed by the three transports the next day.

Meanwhile, Phillip's departure had increased the psychic dislocation

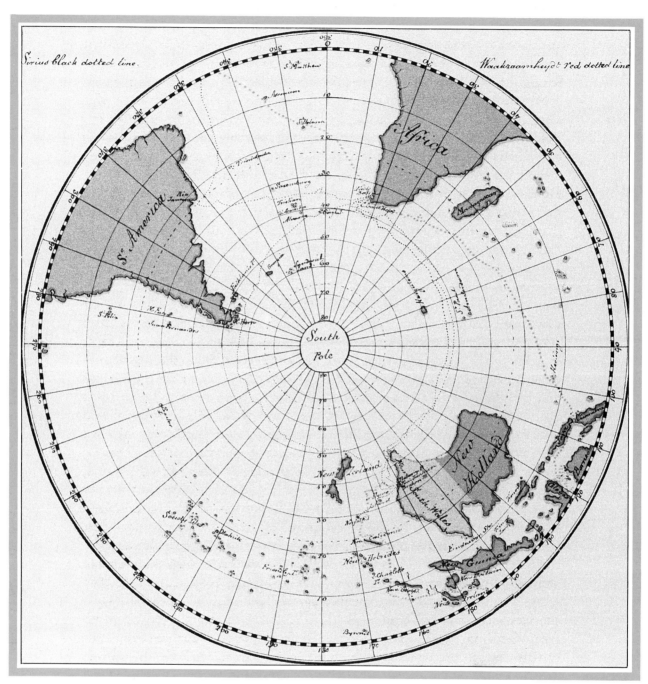

William Bradley, 'Tracks of the *Sirius* & *Waak-zaamheydt* in the Southern Hemisphere, 1787–1792'

amongst the main party. Hunter, now responsible for seven ships and about 1000 persons, became excessively cautious. Put out by Phillip's not consulting him about his decision to sail ahead, Major Ross grew bitter. The convicts fell back into old patterns of behavior, and became fractious. In December, the passage grew distinctly worse. The ships wallowed constantly in the great swell, and encountered fogs and gales. Disease and cold caused great mortality amongst the animals, whose food began to grow short. So as to preserve the water for them and the plants, Hunter put the company on a litre and a half a day. Illness increased, and there were frequent injuries from the ships' equipment shifting in the gales and seas. As they entered the longitudes of New Holland, the officers pored over the charts deriving from Cook's voyages, so as to know when theirs would end. At Christmas, nostalgia for country and friends half a world away engulfed them.[66] Then came those portents they were longing for. Some of the plants from Rio began to bloom; and on 6 January 1788 they sighted the southern coast of Van Diemen's Land. Cook's charts allowed them to identify their position, and the captains distributed wine. They swung away from land again, but more briefly now they knew, to have a clear run up to their destination. On 19 January, they came upon the coast of New South Wales just south of Botany Bay. The wind was 'fair', the sky 'serene, though a little hazy', the temperature 'delightfully pleasant', the coastline as Cook and Banks had described it. The next day, they entered Botany Bay, to find the ships which had gone ahead.[67]

As the ships of the second division arrived so quickly, Phillip was not able to prepare beforehand as he had intended. However, this was the only blemish in an achievement remarkable on a number of counts. To have eleven indifferent sailers traverse a route that only Cook had previously come, through 'a long Track of Ocean ... Totaly Unknown' to their masters,[68] and arrive within two days of each other, was a remarkable feat of navigation, which says much for Phillip's and Hunter's technical competence. To pass such a long voyage without any serious incidents on the ships, too, reflects the alert care with which the commanders supervised the venture. While there were several plots laid on the *Scarborough* and *Alexander*, these were quickly discovered, and the shells of rebellion easily broken. It might have been otherwise. In 1783, for example, convicts being transported to Nova Scotia rose as their ship was passing down the Channel, and forty escaped into Sussex. The next year, a hundred of another consignment destined for Maryland similarly mutinied and escaped into Devon.

Yet it is in its health record that the voyage is most remarkable. Despite its length, and despite numbers of the convicts having begun it ill, Phillip and his captains and surgeons lost only forty-eight persons from embarkation—thirty-six male and four female convicts and five children of convicts, and one marine, one marine's wife, and one marine's child.[69] What is especially noteworthy is that perhaps as few as a third of these forty-eight died of scurvy.[70] Consider these comparisons: in 1740–44, 626 of the 961 men who proceeded into the Pacific with Anson died of scurvy (he lost only four in battle); in 1783, after a voyage of only eight weeks from Madras, Sir Richard King's squadron reached the Cape of Good Hope with some 1800 sick from scurvy; in 1789, when the *Sirius* reached the Cape after a three months' voyage from Port Jackson (where, admittedly, scurvy had been rife) 'Even those that were doing there duty when Biteing an Aple, pare or Peach, the Blod would run out of our Mouth, from our gums';[71] and in 1790, after burying 267 of its 1017 convicts at sea, the Second Fleet reached Sydney with another 450 officially classified as sick, and scores more so debilitated that they could scarcely stand.[72]

From the time of his appointment to head it, Phillip showed himself aware that scurvy would be the great hazard of the voyage. He opened his September 1786 memorandum with the observation that one of the principal benefits of his arriving early at Botany Bay would be to have huts 'ready to receive those Convicts who are Sick, & they would find Vegitables, of which it may naturally be suppos'd they will stand in great need, as the Scurvey must make a great ravage amongst people naturally Indolent, & not cleanly'.[73] And he complained repeatedly to the Navy Board officials and to Sydney and Nepean about the fitting out of the transports and the victualling of those they were to carry. In March 1787, for example, he pointed out that 'the men's being crowded on board such small ships, and from victualling the marines according to the contract, which allows no flour, as is customary in the Navy ... must be fatal to many, and the more so as no anti-scorbutics are allowed on board the transports for either marine or convict'.[74] Simultaneously, he persuaded officialdom to give the convicts then embarked at Portsmouth fresh provisions.[75]

In all of this, Phillip showed no unusual perception. By the 1780s, it was common knowledge that the sailor's habitual diet, with its absence of fruits and salad greens and its concentration of salt, encouraged the onset of scurvy; and the measures followed by Cook to prevent it had received wide publicity. These measures, which adhered in a general way to the regimen earlier proposed by James Lind, included: serving fresh meats, salad greens, and fresh vegetables at every possible opportunity; attention to personal hygiene, including wearing dry clothes; keeping living quarters clean and dry, by ventilation, by the lighting of fires between decks, and by the airing of bedding above deck; a plentiful consumption of water; and regular exercise.[76]

By his comments and actions, on other voyages as well as on that of the

First Fleet, Phillip showed himself to be quite aware of Cook's procedure. He ordered that the First Fleet ships should be cleaned and ventilated regularly, and when masters or surgeons failed to do so, or failed in other duties, he acted swiftly. He replaced the incapacitated Altree as surgeon of the *Lady Penrhyn* as early as 2 June, for example.[77] Then, six weeks later, John White reported that the illness which had appeared on the *Alexander* 'was wholly occasioned by the bilge water, which had by some means or other risen to so great a height that the pannels of the cabin, and the buttons on the clothes of the officers, were turned nearly black by the noxious effluvia. When the hatches were taken off, the stench was so powerful that it was scarcely possible to stand over them,' Phillip again acted decisively. White records: 'Captain Phillip, who upon every occasion showed great humanity and attention to the people, with the most obliging readiness sent Mr King, one of his lieutenants, on board the *Alexander* with me, in order to examine into the state of the ship, charging him, at the same time, with the most positive and pointed intructions to the master of the ship instantly to set about sweetening and purifying her. This commission Mr King executed with great propriety and expedition; and, by the directions he gave, such effectual means were made use of, that the evil was soon corrected.'[78] Phillip's ordering the convicts to be unshackled and allowed on deck was another one of his measures to prevent scurvy, as was his assiduity in procuring fresh provisions at Teneriffe, Rio de Janeiro, and Cape Town.

Still, such attention to details was perhaps not more that any competent officer or surgeon conscious of what Cook had achieved would have shown. Yet there is among Phillip's measures an unexpected one. Cook had succeeded in controlling scurvy without properly understanding what brought the disease on, and what prevented it. Rather than in Lind's correct remedy of orange and lemon juice, which he deprecated, Cook had placed his faith in essence ('wort') of malt, and sauerkraut, the one entirely deficient in vitamin C, the other possessing only very small quantities, and in such attendant measures as copious quantities of water and air, and exercise.[79] The great explorer's reputation ensured the predominance of these views in the 1780s; and it was not until 1795 that the Royal Navy finally accepted what Lind's by then fifty-year-old experiment had indicated, and ordered the general issue of lemon juice.[80]

In 1787, however, eight years in advance of his profession, Phillip followed Lind rather than Cook. At Teneriffe, most fruits were out of season, but at Rio de Janeiro he obtained great quantities of oranges. Nagle reports how 'the Prisoners ware Supplied with Boat Loads of Oranges'. Smyth records how 'the Canoes alongside brot. prodigeous quantities of Oranges of 2 Sorts, one very small of a dark red colour [perhaps tangerines]; very sweet & rich flavour'd

& the other remarkable large—The Officer of the Guard Boat brot. a Bucketful as a present of the largest I ever saw wh. measured a foot in circumference'. Easty described serving a daily ration of ten oranges 'per man to all the Convicts and marines'. White noted that 'the commissionary supplied the troops and convicts with rice ..., with fresh beef, vegetables, and oranges, which soon removed every symptom of the scurvy prevalent among them'.[81] The other measures Phillip followed did play a part in retarding the onset of the disease, but modern knowledge indicates that it was the addition of Brazilian oranges to the diet that enabled him to bring the First Fleet to New South Wales without great mortality. As White adhered strongly to Cook's belief in the efficacy of wort of malt and water, one can assume that the emphasis on citrus fruit was Phillip's own.[82]

The management of a group of transports was less glamorous than the discovery of islands and the charting of unknown coasts, but it was not less demanding. If Cook had overseen the voyage of the First Fleet, we would find in the results yet other signs of his greatness. It is much against the historians of Australian settlement that Phillip has not had due recognition of the magnitude of his achievement, which David Collins perhaps evoked best:

Thus, under the blessing of God, was happily completed, in eight months and one week, a voyage which, before it was undertaken, the mind hardly dared venture to contemplate, and on which it was impossible to reflect without some apprehensions as to its termination ... in the above space of time we had sailed five thousand and twenty-one leagues; had touched at the American and African Continents; and had at last rested within a few days sail of the antipodes of our native country, without meeting any accident in a fleet of eleven sail, nine of which were merchantmen that had never before sailed in that distant and imperfectly explored ocean: and when it is considered, that there was on board a large body of convicts, many of whom were embarked in a very sickly state, we might be deemed peculiarly fortunate, that of the whole number of all descriptions of persons coming to form the new settlement, only thirty-two had died since their leaving England.[83]

George Raper, 'Entrance of Rio de Janeiro (Brasil) from the Anchorage without the Sugar Loaf bearing N.W.½N. off Shore 2 miles'

George Raper, 'View of the Table-Land from the Anchorage in the Bay Cape Good-hope. (1) Devil's Mount S. b W. (2) Sugar-loaf W.S.W. (3) Green Point W.N.W.'

William Bradley, 'Botany Bay. *Sirius* & Convoy going in: *Supply* & Agent's Division in the Bay 21 Jan.ʸ 1788'

[Port Jackson Painter], 'A View of the Entrance Into Port Jackson Harbour the South head bearing NNW dis.ᵗ 3 or 4 Miles' (*c.* February 1791)

This shows the lookout erected by Phillip and Hunter to announce the arrival of ships

Planting New South Wales: Difficulties

if any of my letters have been written in a doubtfull stile, it would not be wondered at could it be known how I have been harassed for full thirty months; with the loss of these Ships & a hundred more désagrémens than you would conceive possible to exist.

Arthur Phillip, July 1790

Immediately on his arrival on 18 January, Phillip had landed on the north shore of Botany Bay, to find the landscape to be as Cook and Banks had described it, with 'a great deal of very good grass & some small timber trees'. Finding no water, he had proceeded around the bay, to his first encounter with Aborigines, who had pointed him to a small stream. The next day, after the arrival of the *Alexander*, *Scarborough*, and *Friendship*, Phillip began to inspect the area in earnest. But a whole day's tour produced no cheering information, for the party found only 'low & boggy' country, with little running water.[1] After the *Sirius* arrived with the rest of the convoy on 20 January, Phillip took parties to explore the southern shore of the bay. While these did find areas of dark soil and grasslands, they found very little fresh water, and 'not any spot very inviting for our purpose'. It became clear that there was no site really suitable for a large settlement, which needed an adequate and permanent supply of water, and fertile surrounding areas. Simultaneously, the naval officers surveyed the bay, to find that while it offered anchorage in 4 to 7 fathoms, it was 'wholly exposed' to easterly winds, and that there was 'no possibility of finding shelter from those winds' in any part of it.[2]

The exposed nature of the anchorage, and the absence of any attractive site, determined Phillip to investigate Port Jackson, 16 kilometres to the north, noticed but not entered by Cook. He had suspected before he had sailed that this might be a better location, partly because the harbour was likely to be superior, partly because it seemed to offer islands where livestock might be 'secured' from the depredations of the Aborigines.[3] Conscious of his orders that he was not to use the 'pretence' of searching for a better location to delay disembarking the convicts,[4] he took three boats north so as to survey more quickly. And in case the probe did not have a good result, he ordered the officers he left at Botany Bay to land all the artificers, who were to begin clearing ground at Point Sutherland, and to dig sawpits. This caution turned out to be unnecessary. Passing through the 'high, rugged, and perpendicular' heads of Port Jackson in the early afternoon of 21 January, he had 'the satisfaction of finding the finest harbour in the world, in which a thousand sail of the line may ride in the most perfect security'. For two days, he and Hunter surveyed the arms of the harbour, inspected the shores closely, and found that the land was 'greatly superior in every respect' to that at Botany Bay. Phillip selected the area at the head of the indentation he called Sydney Cove, which had 'the best spring of water', and 'in which the ships can anchor so close to the shore that at a very small expence quays may be made at which the largest ships may unload'.[5]

Returning to Botany Bay, Phillip ordered the convoy to shift north. On 25 January, he proceeded ahead in the *Supply*, with some of the marines and convicts, leaving Hunter to bring up the transports. As the convoy was moving out of Botany Bay the next day, two strange sail appeared off the entrance. These were the ships under Lapérouse, who had sailed from France in August 1785, ostensibly on a voyage of scientific exploration, but with political purposes. The Frenchman had left with a personal instruction to investigate any British settlement in the south Pacific; and he had been informed of the New South Wales one in a despatch he received at Kamchatka in September 1787. The Pitt administration had told Phillip to take possession of Norfolk Island before Lapérouse did so; and Phillip had been apprehensive that there might be trouble, but his fears were not realized. Hunter helped the visitors bring their ships through the heads before he left, and contact between the two groups of Europeans remained cordial until the French departed six weeks later. There was, however, a good deal of reserve concerning whereabouts and intentions. Phillip did not wish the French to perceive the excellence of Port Jackson; and his failure to invite the French commander there may reflect some fear that he might be known as a spy. For their part, the French were reluctant to give the British details of their voyage.[6]

Landing at Sydney Cove in the early morning of 26 January 1788, Phillip

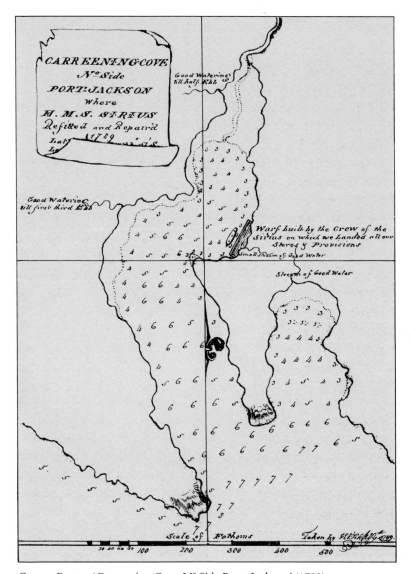

George Raper, 'Carreening Cove N° Side Port-Jackson' (1789)

set his convicts to clearing a space. Lieutenant William Collins of the marines ran up British colours in the middle of it, and Phillip took formal possession of the site, with the officers toasting the health of the sovereign and the success of the venture. The marine guard fired a 'feu de joie'; and all those on shore gave three cheers, which were returned by the crew of the *Supply*. The marines and convicts then began to lay out the camp. In the evening, when Hunter had brought the convoy into the cove, Phillip repeated the flag-raising ceremony.[7] The next day, 27 January, the pioneering work began in earnest. Phillip landed carpenters, marines and most of the male convicts, whom he set to clearing ground. While they cut many of the trees, others they simply blasted out with gunpowder and rolled into the harbour. Phillip decided to locate the marines, the male convicts, and the hospital on the western side of the cove; and himself, the civil officers, and the majority of the women convicts on the eastern. By dark, the first tents were up, and some of the colonists spent their first night on shore.

This work continued on 28 January, in hot weather, with more marines and male convicts coming ashore, and stock being landed; and Hunter began a detailed survey of the harbour. On 29 January, more of the stock was landed, and the carpenters began to erect the timber-framed canvas house that Phillip had brought from England. On 30 January, his private stock of twenty-three sheep, five lambs, one horse, and greyhounds, rabbits, turkeys, geese, ducks, and fowls were landed, the plants he had brought from Rio de Janeiro were put into the ground, and convicts began work on storehouses.[8] On 1 February, a party of convicts under the direction of Phillip's old farm servant Henry Dodd began clearing ground at Farm Cove, and planting it with vegetables and salad greens. On 3 February, the Reverend Richard Johnson held the first European religious service on Australian soil.

It was inevitable that there be much confusion at first. As David Collins described the scene, 'Parties of people were every where heard and seen variously employed; some in clearing ground for the different encampments; others in pitching tents, or bringing up such stores as were more immediately wanted; and the spot which had so lately been the abode of silence and tranquillity was now changed to that of noise, clamour, and confusion.'[9] Yet after a week some progress could be seen: 'all the Tents of the Battallion, the Labaratory, and Hospital, and several of the Civil Officers Tents have been pitched,—likewise those for yᵉ Men and Women Convicts, the Governors House got up, a Spot of Ground enclosed, and some culinary Seeds put in. The Plants that we brought from *Rio de Janeiro*, and the *Cape of Good Hope* all landed and put in the Ground. a few Beans, Peas, small sallad, that were sown on our arrival here, have come up and appear at present very luxuriant.'[10]

On 6 February, progress had been such as to enable Phillip to land the women convicts. These went ashore through the day, and there followed a 'Scene of Debauchery & Riot ... beyond ... abilities to give a just discription of'. The male convicts were among the women first, closely followed by marines and seamen with alcohol. Surprising as this scene may now seem, return voyages to England usually ended in this way; and Phillip's experience told him it was wiser not to interfere, but rather to let the pent-up passion of the eight months' voyage run its course through a night of swearing, quarrelling, drinking, singing, and debauchery. Appropriately, this orgiastic release went forward to the accompaniment of the most violent electrical storm, with its ship-shaking thunder and cascades of rain, that the officers had ever experienced.[11]

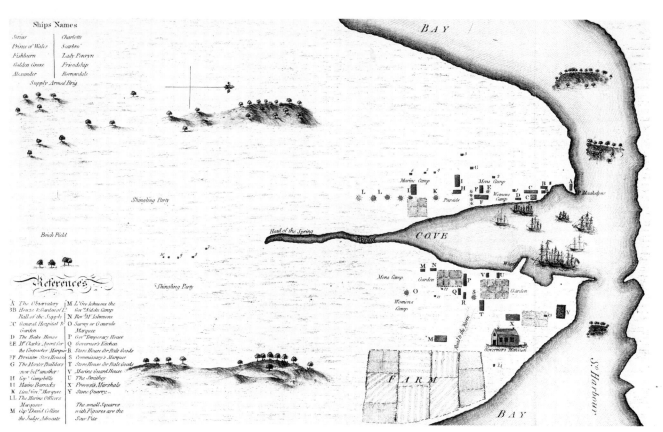

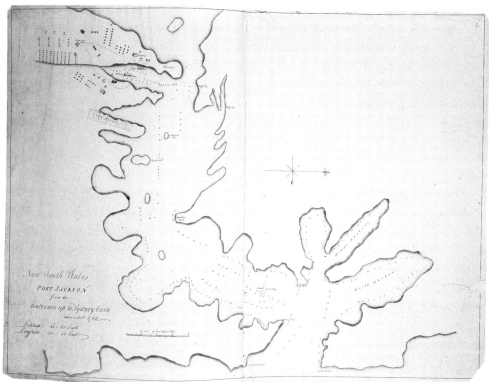

Francis Fowkes, 'The Settlement at Sydney, 16 April 1788'

[Port Jackson Painter], 'New South Wales. Port Jackson from the Entrance up to Sydney Cove taken in Oct.ʳ 1788'

The next day Phillip moved to re-establish order.[12] At 10 in the morning he had the whole party assemble at the marines' parade ground on the west side of the cove. When the convicts had been gathered together and ordered to sit, the marines entered, led by their band and with their colours flying, to form an encircling guard. Phillip stood bare-headed in the centre, in company with his principal officers; and all heard the deputy judge-advocate read the governor's commission and the letters-patent establishing the colony's courts. At intervals, the marines marked the occasion with volleys of muskets and the band played bars of 'God Save the King'.

Empowered as the giver of law and dispenser of mercy, Phillip addressed the convicts—in a 'short speech, extremely well adapted to the people he had to govern', according to one who heard it; in a 'mild and humane manner', said another; in an 'excellently adapted Speech, accompanied with many judicious Exhortations', said a third. From the records of such observers, we can reconstruct a good deal of what Phillip said at this, the colony's formal beginning. He praised those who had behaved well during the voyage, and pointed out how he had been lenient towards those who had not. He was convinced, he said, that there were many fundamentally good persons amongst them, who had succumbed to vice in moments of misfortune, or drunkenness, or under the influence of bad companions. But he also feared that 'there were some Men & Women among them, so thoroughly abandoned in their Wickedness, as to have lost every good Principle'. He urged all 'to forget the habits of vice and indolence in which [they] ... had hitherto lived; and exhorted them to be honest amongst themselves, obedient to their overseers, and attentive to the several works in which they were about to be employed'. He pointed out that only 200 of the 600 men had done the work in the past days, while the others had 'skulked' in the woods. Henceforth, those who would not work would not eat, for the '*good* Men ... should not be slaves for the *Bad*'. He forbade the theft and slaughter of the colony's livestock; and assured his audience that all transgressions would be punished with the utmost severity, no matter how 'it might distress his Feelings'. He said the sentries would fire on any men trying to enter the women's tents at night; and he urged the convicts to form regular relationships by marrying. He told the convicts that it was 'intirely in their power to atone to their country for the wrongs done at home, that nothing but a new repetition of their former demerits could draw down upon them the severity of those laws of which he was invested with the dispensation'. He would ever be ready, he said, 'to shew approbation and encouragement to those who proved themselves worthy of them by good conduct and attention to orders; while on the other hand, such as were determined to act in opposition to propriety, and observe a contrary conduct, would inevitably meet with the punishment which they deserved'. He extolled the humanity of the law which they had transgressed; and, citing the absence of temptation in their new situation, pointed out how this offered the opportunity, not only 'to expiate their offences', but also 'to become good, and even opulent men, as many of the first settlers in the western world had been convicts like themselves.' 'Nor,' said he, 'could shame be imputed to such as reformed and became useful members of society.' He concluded by wishing them 'reformation, happiness, and prosperity, in this new country'—and established an Australian tradition by giving them the day free from labour. The officers then accompanied him to a 'cold collation', to which he curiously did not invite the officers of the transports, whose chagrin was presumably mitigated by the knowledge that the mutton had been 'full of maggots'.[13]

Inevitably, the colonists' first tasks were the interrelated ones of erecting shelters, obtaining supplies of fresh foods, and establishing breeding herds and flocks. As one witness summarized after the first months, 'the principal Business has been the clearing of Land, cutting, Grubbing and burning down Trees, sawing up Timber & Plank for Building, making Bricks, hewing Stone, Erecting temporary Store-houses, a Building for an Hospital, another for an Observatory, Enclosing Farms & Gardens, making temporary Huts, and many other Conveniences'.[14] The clearing the ground for building and agriculture proved much more difficult than anticipated. The English axes blunted and broke against the eucalypts. The removal of the felled trees, and the extraction of their large and widespreading roots required a great deal of labour—'of which it [is] hardly possible to give your Lordship a just idea', Phillip told Sydney.[15] While there were pockets of good soil, the ground in general was rocky, and in places the topsoil did not cover the sandstone against which the shovels broke. Gradually, exploration led to the discovery of areas of better soil and fewer large trees, but Phillip had to conclude that the effort that would be involved in relocating the camp and moving the stores was too great to be borne. For better or for worse, the site he chose first had to remain the permanent one.

Nor did the colonists derive much benefit from the trees they cleared with such labour. The cutting of the eucalypts into frame timber and planks again took great effort, blunting saws and wearing out the sharpening files; and the sawn pieces warped and split as they dried. By May 1788, this cause had rendered one early building 'useless', and others were deteriorating rapidly.[16] And as the reeds with which the colonists thatched these timber buildings dried, the spectre of irreparable loss through fire also appeared. The colonists had little better success from their first attempts at building in brick. While they quickly found clay to fire, they found no lime for mortar, so that they were obliged to use a puddle of clay, which resulted in walls 'of an extraordinary thickness', and which was liable to wash out in wet weather.[17] Phillip was not helped in this general endeavour by his failure to hire more than a handful of artificers from the ships' crews, many of whom seem quickly to have decided that the prospective work was not to their taste.

Success in cultivation proved as difficult to obtain. Immediately on locating the party about Sydney Cove, Phillip and White planted vegetables for the sick. 'On first appearing above ground, [the plants] looked promising and well, but soon after withered away.' As they knew they had planted in the wrong season, this did not entirely surprise the governor and surgeon, but in the next weeks and months others had little better success—'all the culinary Plants that have come up, degenerate exceedingly, Peas, Beans, Cabbage Plants &c do not thrive, & many of them have withered', Worgan reported in June. Having been heated on the voyage and infested with weevil, much of the seed grain put into the ground in the first spring failed to germinate; and mice ravaged that which did. And lacking animals, the colonists could not encourage growth by manuring.[18]

The want of animals presented a very considerable obstacle to progress. Numbers of those loaded at the Cape of Good Hope had died on the passage; and various causes removed others in the first months of settlement. A large limb of a tree rent by lightning during the storm of 6 February fell on Major Ross's animals, killing five sheep, some lambs, and a pig. Other sheep ate grass that did not agree with them, and died. Pigs did not thrive, and poultry did not multiply at the usual rate. At the end of April, dingoes killed another six sheep. Officers killed their stock without much thought for the future; and hungry convicts and Aborigines added surreptitiously to the slaughter. In June, the convict in charge of the government's two bulls and four cows neglected his duty, and the beasts wandered off, not to be found again. Such mischance dogged every facet of the colonists' efforts to establish a food supply. One of the attractions of Botany Bay had been the large stocks of fish Cook had found there. Immediately on his arrival, Phillip set parties to gather this sea-harvest, designating different coves of Port Jackson as the provinces of different ships' crews. Initially, the fishing parties made some good hauls, but then catches became increasingly erratic, and were much diminished in the winter months when the fish migrated northwards. Nor did those who ranged the countryside for kangaroos and game-birds have more consistent success.

In these circumstances, the colonists were forced to consume a much higher proportion of their stores than was either good for their health or prudent for their future. While they had arrived in general much healthier than might have been expected after such a long voyage, their subsequent diet and their cooking in copper pots soon gave rise to scurvy and dysentery. By the end of March, there were more than 200 on the sick list.[19] Phillip had to speed the construction of a hospital to shelter them and to do his best to establish a permanent garden beside it, but neither was a task easily achieved. Widespread illness also placed a sudden strain on the party's supplies of medicines, which White attempted to counter by seeking out native plants with beneficial properties.[20]

And as the party made greater than expected inroads into their stores, Phillip had to ration these so as to stretch them further. He began to do so quietly, by having quartermasters give six persons the amounts specified for four, but after eight months he could no longer conceal the seriousness of the situation. In October, he formally reduced the weekly allowance of flour by a seventh. Later, he squeezed it more. The absence of fresh foods and the progressive reduction of the ration further weakened the party and led to general debility, which in turn delayed further the moment of their succouring, for Phillip could not work the weak and sick as hard as was necessary quickly to establish agriculture.

Persuading the convicts to work in any case was another of Phillip's considerable problems. In the first days, fewer than a third of the men showed themselves ready to labour in the heat; and the attitude of the marine officers scarcely helped. These had been fully aware when they had volunteered for the service that they were to form the guard in a convict colony, and that their tasks would be 'entirely unconnected with maritime affairs'.[21] Phillip's idea was that part of the officers' duty would consist of supervising the convicts at their labour; and soon after settling at Sydney, he asked them to 'occasionally encourage such [convicts] as they observed diligent, and point out for punishment such as they saw idle or straggling in the woods'. But once in New South Wales, not conceiving that 'any interference with the convicts' might legitimately be expected of them, the officers declined to take on this role, except—significantly—with those 'employed for their own particular service'. The officers' 'want of Temper', as Phillip dryly termed it, caused him much difficulty.[22]

Rather than work, either for the common good, or, in the time which Phillip allowed for the purpose, for their own benefit, many of the convicts preferred to steal. A lifetime of stealing had made these impervious to notions of honesty or decency; and the colony's progress was soon impeded by a myriad minor, and some major, thefts. Improvident or lazy convicts stole provisions and clothes from their more prudent fellows, and from the marines. They raided gardens for vegetables and salad; they took poultry, and fish and game brought in by the hunters. Where they could, they stole from the government store. Some even had the effrontery to use the occasion of the celebration of the King's birthday in June to rob tents. Others stole the sheep that Phillip was fattening for the celebration of the Prince of Wales's birthday. And inevitably, male convicts, and marines and seamen as well, were caught in the women's tents, or trying to persuade them to 'goe up in the woods'.[23]

To make matters even more difficult, those in authority were riven with various dissensions and jealousies. Some of these surfaced even before the party had reached New South Wales, when Major Ross found himself 'much hurt' at Phillip's not consulting him about the plan to sail ahead after the Cape of Good Hope. Others too found fault with Phillip for making this sensible move—a 'Don Quixote Scheme', one called it; a 'mere abortion of the Brain, a whim which struck him at the time', said another.[24] These people continued disgruntled at Sydney. Captain Campbell quickly came to consider Phillip the worst possible person for the task, being aloof, capricious, and unwilling to delegate authority. 'This Man,' he said, 'will be everything himself never, that I have heard of, communicates any part of his Plan for establishing the Colony or carrying on his work, to any one—much less, consult[s] them.' Major Ross developed this line of criticism. He knew nothing, he wrote to Nepean, of the government's intentions with the settlement, 'for the Governor has never told me, neither has he ever advised or consulted with me on the subject, and I believe every body else are in the dark as well as myself'. Some muttered too about the governor's meeting his own convenience by pressing on with the building of his permanent house, the only one with windows. One or two of the sea officers joined in the chorus of private complaint, with Daniel Southwell becoming incensed by Phillip's failure to promote him.[25]

Nor did the marine officers vent their spleen only on the governor. Quickly, they also fell to quarrelling amongst themselves. When a court martial sentenced a private either to make a public apology or to receive a hundred lashes, Major Ross took great exception to the determination, for, leaving it 'in the breast of the prisoner to receive or not receive the punishment', it removed from him as commandant the 'most essential and necessary power … of mitigating or inflicting the punishment'. When the officers who comprised the court declined to alter it, Ross arrested them, and asked Phillip to try them for insubordination. Knowing the impossibility of preserving any order in the settlement with almost half of the marine officers in prison, Phillip postponed convening a general court-martial until such time as there were 'a sufficient number of officers' to constitute it and also 'for the necessary duty of the camp'. Instead, he referred the dispute to the authorities in England, thus obtaining a respite of at least two years. But other problems involving questions of authority followed, some of them nearly as divisive. The dissensions caused Major Ross to grow even more cantankerous, and to write home darkly about young officers being led astray and showing a 'shameful inattention' to their duties. All of this could only confirm Phillip's view of the officers' lamentable 'want of Temper'.[26]

We may see much of this dissension, so petty and unnecessary, as the result of the profound psychic dislocation inherent in the move to New South Wales and of the stresses arising from the isolation of life there. For more than thirty months, from the time they left the Cape of Good Hope in November 1787, until the arrival of the Second Fleet in June 1790, the colonists were literally out of the world as they knew it, with only the brief presence of Lapérouse's ships and the foray of the *Sirius* to the Cape in 1788–89 to break the alien silence. Cast adrift from all they knew, beset by difficulties, they struggled to establish a new life, and numbers of them could not emerge from the struggle untouched. Some of the convicts wandered aimlessly off into the bush, to die of hunger or from an Aboriginal spear. Others gave themselves over to dreams of gold. Others again nurtured unlikely plans to steal boats and escape by sea. Still, the directions they received did give a daily purpose to their lives, so that as a group they were somewhat better off than the civil and military officers. Left without a civilized—and a civilizing—cultural matrix, one by which to locate themselves in time and space, many of these latter wilted as sadly as the first plantings. Some stood excessively on their honour. Others drank heavily, or lapsed into an ennui of body as well as mind only to be relieved by return to Europe. One or two became quite insane, such as Lieutenant George Maxwell, who buried seventy guineas singly in the hospital garden, saying he would have a 'good Crop' next year.[27]

The stresses led many of the officers to view the endeavour in aberrant ways. John White, for example, quickly came to find the country a 'place so forbidding and so hateful as only to merit execration and curses';[28] and though he succeeded strikingly in his care of the sick, he omitted almost all reference to his work in his journal. Others found the whole business crazy. It would be cheaper, said Ross, 'to feed the convicts on turtle and venison at the London Tavern than be at the expence of sending them here'. And the long period between their arrival and that of the Second Fleet persuaded many that 'Government' had indeed forgotten them, and abandoned them to a lingering death in a country that was 'the outcast of God's works'.[29] In all these troubles, only Phillip seems consistently to have viewed the venture dispassionately, maintained a sense of purpose, and remained optimistic. It is a singular mark of his character, and of his fitness for the task, that when he did complain to his superiors and friends in England, he did so with much restraint. In July 1790, for example, he told Banks, 'if any of my letters have been written in a doubtful stile, it would not be wondered at could it be known how I have been harassed for full thirty months; with the loss of these ships & a hundred more désagrémens than you would possibly conceive to exist'.[30]

This sense of abandonment flourished in the absence of succouring ships. On receiving Phillip's first reports, the Pitt administration acted to remedy the colony's deficiencies in personnel, food, and equipment, by despatching £70000 worth of supplies, seven agricultural supervisors, and twenty-five convicts selected for their experience in building or agriculture and gardening, in the *Guardian* in September 1789. The *Guardian* loaded wine at Santa Cruz, and livestock at the Cape of Good Hope, then struck an iceberg in 41° East longitude on 13 December. After heroic struggle, her commander Edward Riou brought her back to the Cape, where a storm wrecked her. Riou had departed the Cape with horses, cattle, sheep, pigs, and poultry, and 'upwards of one hundred & fifty different sorts of Trees Plants and Shrubs in the highest State of perfection'; and with 'a pleasing idea of the Consequence we should be of to Governor Phillip and his Infant Colony'.[31] When he learned of the accident, Phillip commented, 'it has been a fatal one to this Colony by its consequences, for it has thrown us back almost to where we were a few months after landing'. Three months later came news of the wreck of the *Sirius* at Norfolk Island, which caused a 'general despondency' amongst the colonists.[32]

Planting New South Wales: Solutions

tho' this Colony is not exactly in the state in which I would have wished to have left it, another year may do much, & it is at present so fully established, that I think there cannot any longer be a doubt but that it will, if Settlers are sent out, answer in every respect the end proposed by Government in making the Settlement.

Arthur Phillip, March 1791

The period between settling the colonists at Sydney and the arrival of the Second Fleet in June 1790 may be seen as the time when Phillip tried to overcome, or at least to mitigate, the initial difficulties principally by drawing on whatever local resources he could find or create. This inevitably involved a good deal of improvization, but in his actions in this period we may discern the thread of a consistent method, which did give rise to permanent as well as temporary solutions, and which laid the basis of a distinctive social organization.

Some of the problems were much more tractable than others. To reduce the labour of clearing the land, Phillip adopted the expedients of rolling those trees felled about the harbourside into the water; of blowing stumps and roots out of the ground with gunpowder; and of having convict women carry stones from the centre of the clearings and pile them against the rough picket fences which the men raised. As they felled and cleared, the colonists began to learn the properties of the different species of tree. The frames and planks they cut from the eucalypts soon proved defective, but they found the cabbage palm made adequate walls, and the she-oak good shingles. The local clay also made good bricks, and by May James Bloodworth and his band of convict helpers had prepared more than 20 000 for firing. Once between brick walls and under timber shingles, the colony's precious stores were much less liable to vanish in sudden fire. And even if the work of building seemed to proceed slowly, it did proceed. By the end of the first year, the settlement had, as well as storehouses, a hospital measuring 25 by 7 metres, all the officers had huts, most of the troops had barracks, and the first Government House was well advanced. There were even two streets—'if four rows of the most miserable huts ... deserve that name'.[1]

By this time, there was some progress at agriculture too. After the first-planted vegetables and salad greens had withered, Phillip hit upon an expedient that led to good results. This involved making particular groups of the colonists, as well as individuals, responsible for meeting their own needs. He set up a large garden at the hospital, and another of 6 acres at Government House. The crew of the *Sirius* planted at Garden Island, that of the *Supply* at a site near the hospital. Phillip set aside 2 acres for each of the civil and marine officers, and commons for the body of the marines, and for the convicts. By September, he could report that 'those who have Gardens have Vegitables in plenty & exceeding good in kind'. Results with the plants carried to New South Wales were even better. By September, Phillip could report that 'all the plants and fruit-trees brought from the Brazil and the Cape that did not die in the passage thrive exceeding well'.[2] There was a little progress with grain crops too, with Dodd having 6 acres under wheat at Farm Cove, 8 under barley, and 6 under other grains. Some of the officers also had promising germinations.

Because they might only breed on an extensive scale from imported animals, the colonists found the raising of herds and flocks a much more difficult task, and real success in this had to await the more regular arrival of beasts, particularly from India. Nor did hunting and fishing prove dependable substitutes. In order to increase the catch about Sydney, Phillip appointed certain colonists as hunters. He also systematized fishing, designating particular coves as the provinces of individual ships and groups, and giving the duty to individuals, whose numbers he augmented at times of particular need by others, including the civil and military officers. The boat parties would fish through the nights, the hunters range sometimes for days on end, but the sporadic nature of their takes soon showed that these activities could not offer a permanent solution to the colony's difficulty. Nor was Phillip able to convert such windfalls as the turtles and fowls that the crew of the *Supply* found at Lord Howe Island in March 1788 into regular supplies. As another expedient, Phillip decided to send the *Sirius* to Cape Town for additional stores, especially flour and medicines. Hunter left in October, sailing east, and the prevailing winds gave him a very rapid passage. Eight months later he was back, with a much-needed cargo which included 120 000 pounds of flour, seed wheat and barley, and medicines. The safe arrival of this cargo was a welcome relief to the colony; but given the risks and uncertainties that such a voyage necessarily involved, it was a means of relief not to be relied upon permanently.

Always aware that the true solution to the colony's difficulties lay in the creation of extensive agriculture, Phillip moved to achieve this even as he pursued his expedients. In November 1788, he took Henry Dodd, 100 convicts, and a detachment of marines to the head of the harbour, to begin cultivating an area of good soil that was relatively free of timber. Phillip considered the country about what became known as Parramatta to be 'as fine as any I have seen in England', and the progress of the colonists there soon vindicated his optimism. By the end of 1789, the party had erected huts, a barn and a granary, and had 77 acres under grain. Their first harvest yielded 'about two hundred bushels of wheat and sixty of barley, with a small quantity of flax, Indian corn, and oats', all of which Phillip reserved for the next sowing.[3]

As the settlement at Parramatta developed, Phillip elsewhere pursued the same policy of making sections of his party responsible for their sustenance. The small group that he had sent to Norfolk Island in February had found the soil to be exceedingly rich. By the first spring, they had 'vegetables in great abundance' and promising germinations of grain. He accordingly sent another forty colonists there in October. By the end of 1789, despite the failure of some seed to germinate, thefts, and the ravages of caterpillars, rats, and parrots, they had harvested sufficient grain for 'six months' bread for everyone on the island', and had raised 'vast quantitys' of vegetables.[4] At the beginning of 1790, fresh supplies having still not arrived from Europe, Phillip decided to transfer a substantial part of the colony there, in the knowledge that they would more easily be able to support themselves. On 6 March, Major Ross sailed in the *Sirius* with 280 men, women, and children.

In order to counter the ill effects arising from the lack of fresh foods and the shortage of medicines, John White and his fellow surgeons sought out local plants with beneficial properties. They found that 'wild celery, spinach and parsley' grew 'in abundance about the settlement', and that 'those who were in health, as well as the sick … found them a pleasant as well as wholesome addition to the ration'. The doctors also found that red eucalyptus gum was efficacious in treating dysentery, and yellow gum in treating lung infections.[5] So as not to weaken the convicts further, Phillip reduced their hours of labour while the settlement was on short rations. The situation was far from ideal, but by the end of the year the combination of the local greens and the vegetables that the colonists could raise had led to a distinct improvement in their health. The medicines which the *Sirius* brought in May 1789 assisted this progress, as did the climate—'a finer or more healthy [one] is not to be found in any part of the world', the governor wrote.[6] Under the circumstances, Phillip and White and their colleagues did an extraordinary job. As Phillip reported at the beginning of 1790, 'Of 1,030 people who landed, many of whom were worn out by old age, the scurvy, and various disorders, only seventy-two have died in one-and-twenty months; and by the surgeon's returns it appears that twenty-six of those died from disorders of long standing ... which it is more than probable would have carried them off much sooner in England.'[7] In the same period, there were fifty-nine births, so that the group showed a net loss through illness of only slightly more than 1 per cent, a very much better record than those of other colonizations in their first years.

No matter how small they were, no matter how slowly they appeared, these gains were essential ones if the colony were to take root and prosper; and Phillip could not possibly have obtained them without bringing his incipient society to some order. Of all his first tasks, this one was perhaps the most difficult, inhibited as its progress was by the officers' churlishness and the convicts' recalcitrance, indolence, and ignorance. Phillip soon discovered that the convicts were 'in general so very Indolent that if left to themselves they would Starve';[8] and when the officers declined to take any hand in the supervision of them, he met the difficulty by appointing as supervisors such free persons as Henry Dodd and Henry Brewer, and a number of the more promising convicts. As many of the convict superintendents were afraid 'to exert any authority',[9] this solution was a distinctly limited one. Dodd, however, seems to have had a commanding presence; and the convict James Bloodworth also led well. Some such system was needed; and in the circumstances this one was probably the best Phillip could have adopted.

Just as it was difficult to persuade the convicts to work, either for their own or for the common good, so too was it difficult to stop them from stealing. The punishments which the courts meted out to offenders were severe ones, and while Phillip sometimes showed leniency in the hope of obtaining reform, more often he thought he had to proceed with the full sentences in the hope that these would deter others. Initially, at least, there were distressingly few signs of re-generation, to the obtaining of which thefts and other disorderly behaviour by marines and sailors did not contribute. To counter the thefts, Phillip initiated a watch of twelve trustworthy convicts who patrolled through the night and thereby prevented many robberies.[10] Though Phillip was repeatedly driven to distraction by the depredations of the recidivists, the situation was essentially no different from that which obtained in England in times of dearth, and there was a slow improvement in the convicts' behaviour. After six months, Tench commented that, since their arrival, this had 'been much better than could ...

have been expected'.[11] And for all his frustration, anger, and despair, Phillip himself knew this to be so.

Many factors that operated quietly shaped the colonists into an embryonic society. In the weeks following Phillip's speech at the establishing of the colony, twenty convict couples came forward to be married. While some of these were soon back asking to be unmarried, their first gesture was the more important one, for it established a precedent for others, many of whom had in England led lives entirely untouched by respectable precepts. Marriage and family gave some of the convict men a sense of responsibility previously unknown to them, and caused them to live more providently. These states gave the women roles previously denied them, which allowed them to satisfy some of their most profound instincts. And as Phillip rewarded those who behaved well and worked hard, persons emerged who were satisfied with their lot, who developed a keen interest in seeing that the settlement succeeded, and who became examples to others.

As he sought to create more socially productive patterns of behaviour in convicts, so too did Phillip seek to reduce dissension amongst those who ruled them. When Ross first complained about lack of consultation, Phillip both read his instructions to the crusty major and explained the administration's 'intentions' as fully as he could. Ross professed himself satisfied at the time, but continued to complain privately to his officers, and to Nepean and Stephens. Because an open rupture would have harmed the cause of the settlement, Phillip tolerated his deputy's bad temper and excessively developed sense of honour for as long as he possibly could; and he mediated between Ross and the dissident junior officers. Increasingly, though, the major's 'warmth of temper' prevented Phillip from, 'as far as the service permits, calling on [him] otherwise than as the commandant of the detachment'. Ross's peremptory refusal in January 1790 to agree to the night watchmen exercising any authority over straying marines came as the last straw. In March, Phillip resolved the situation by sending Ross to Norfolk Island, where he continued as difficult as ever, but where his obstinacy did less harm.[12] This move is the major example of Phillip's acting to isolate a difficult individual so that the colony might get on better, but it is not the only one. Earlier, he had sent Ross's favourite, Captain Campbell, who was equally antagonistic, to superintend the settlement at Parramatta; and he also assigned some of the malcontent junior officers to duty at the lookout he established at South Head. While these moves increased the resentment of the officers 'exiled', at least they meant that those persons were less able to involve others in their recalcitrance, so that they did, as Phillip would have put it, 'tend to the good of his Majesty's service'.

It proved as difficult to diminish the sense of the isolation of life in New

South Wales as it did to obtain social cohesion there. Such activities as reading books, writing letters or journals, and socializing in the evenings certainly helped to ease private desolation, but a good deal of this still remained afterwards. As Elizabeth Macarthur said in explaining why she had asked Dawes to instruct her in astronomy, 'I wanted something to fill up a certain vacancy in my time which could neither be done by writing, reading or conversation'.[13] In their loneliness, many of the officers formed liaisons with convict women. These unions seem not to have been promiscuous ones begun for transient pleasure. Rather, in their emotional stability and their continuing and domestic comfort, they constituted the recovery of an element essential to the officers' lives, which the tedium of the new world now made doubly important. Phillip seems to have held himself entirely aloof from this solution. None of the surviving records offers the slightest hint that he took any sexual interest in the women convicts; and given the animosity that the marine officers held towards him, it is unlikely that they would not have uttered this charge if he had given them any opportunity of doing so. In a lesser way, the exploring expeditions along the coasts and towards the distant blue mountains also gave the officers a welcome respite from the loneliness of Sydney. Tench, for example, is almost joyous in describing these; and they are also a major focus in John White's journal. But while such activities might have brought their own interest and comfort, in the end they could go only some of the way towards assuaging the settlement's general isolation. To lose their pervasive sense of this, the colonists needed contact with the world they had left; and in the first two years only the *Sirius*'s voyage to the Cape of Good Hope provided it. This voyage was as important for the colonists psychologically as it was materially, for Hunter returned both with letters from England and news of Europe generally; and his arrival aroused sustaining expectations of more.

At the beginning of 1790, thinking that these must surely soon occur, Phillip and Hunter established a lookout at South Head, with a flagpole from which those staffing it might signal the appearance of a ship.[14] For months, the people at Sydney daily fixed their sight upon a bare staff, whose absence was broken only by the false alarm in April, when the *Supply* appeared from Norfolk Island with the cruel news of the wreck of the *Sirius*. But then, in the evening of 3 June, the 'joyful cry of "the flag's up", resounded in every direction'.

Tench conveys the quality of the moment best:

I was sitting in my hut, musing on our fate, when a confused clamour in the street drew my attention. I opened my door, and saw several women with children in their arms running to and fro with distracted looks, congratulating each other, and kissing their infants with the most passionate and extravagant marks of fondness. I needed no more; but instantly started out, and ran to a hill, where, by the assistance of a pocket glass, my hopes were realized. My next door neighbour, a brother-officer, was with me; but we could not speak; we wrung each other by the hand, with eyes and hearts overflowing.

Finding that the governor intended to go immediately in his boat down the harbour, I begged to be of his party.

As we proceeded, the object of our hopes soon appeared:—a large ship, with English colours flying, working in, between the heads which form the entrance of the harbour. The tumultuous state of our minds represented her in danger; and we were in agony. Soon after, the governor, having ascertained what she was, left us, and stept into a fishing boat to return to Sydney. The weather was wet and tempestuous; but the body is delicate only when the soul is at ease. We pushed through wind and rain, the anxiety of our sensations every moment redoubling. At last we read the word *London* on her stern. 'Pull away, my lads! she is from Old England! a few strokes more, and we shall be aboard! hurrah for a belly-full, and news from our friends!'—Such were our exhortations to the boat's crew.

A few minutes completed our wishes, and we found ourselves on board the *Lady Juliana* transport, with two hundred and twenty-five of our countrywomen, whom crime or misfortune had condemned to exile. We learned that they had been almost eleven months on their passage, having left Plymouth, into which port they had put in July, 1789. We continued to ask a thousand questions on a breath. Stimulated by curiosity, they inquired in turn; but the right of being first answered, we thought, lay on our side. 'Letters! letters!' was the cry. They were produced, and torn open in trembling agitation. News burst upon us like meridian splendor on a blind man. We were overwhelmed with it; public, private, general, and particular. Nor was it until some days had elapsed, that we were able to methodize it, or reduce it into form. We now heard for the first time of our sovereign's illness, and his happy restoration to health. The French revolution of 1789, with all the attendant circumstances of that wonderful and unexpected event, succeeded to amaze us. Now, too, the disaster which had befallen the *Guardian*, and the liberal and enlarged plan on which she had been stored and fitted out by government for our use, was promulged. It served also, in some measure, to account why we had not sooner heard from England. For had not the *Guardian* struck on an island of ice, she would probably have reached us three months before, and in this case have prevented the loss of the *Sirius*, although she had sailed from England three months after the *Lady Juliana*.[15]

This arrival, and those of the *Justinian* storeship on 20 June and of the transports of the Second Fleet a week later, came as a monsoon after years of drought; and the colony was never again to be in quite the same desperate psychic or physical straits.

As Phillip struggled to establish the colony physically and socially, he also struggled to establish good relations with the Aborigines. He had sailed with what were for his time surprisingly realistic expectations of their circumstances and of the difficulties likely to arise from the arrival of a large group of European settlers. He thought, for example, that there might be many more Aborigines than Cook's and Banks's reports indicated; that the European men would inevitably seek to use the black women; and that the men might well strike back, whether in open aggression, or by covert means such as setting fire to the grasslands where the colonists grazed their animals. He therefore thought it would be a 'great point gained' if he might 'proceed in this Business without haveing any dispute with the Natives'. To prevent conflict, he would punish any person who wantonly harmed Aborigines, in the same way as if the victims were European; and he would 'endeavor to persuade [a few of the Natives] to settle near us'. These he would furnish 'with everything that can tend to Civilize them, & to give them a high Opinion of their New Guests'.[16]

It is difficult to relate these expectations and attitudes to much in Phillip's past, as it now appears. Certainly in the West Indies and Brazil he came in contact with blacks, but he has left no record of his attitudes to them. He was opposed to slavery, so that there may be a connection between his experiences at these times, and his attitudes concerning the Aborigines. Again, his view of slavery might indicate an evangelical bent; but there is also no explicit indication of his religious views. Indeed, if his lack of sympathy for the Reverend Richard Johnson in his predicaments in New South Wales is a true guide, Phillip was rather less than more religious—a view perhaps given substance by his July 1788 comment that 'Miracles have ceased, or I would pray, to have all the Convicts changed into fifty good farmers.'[17]

Still, it is possible to find Cook an important referent for Phillip in dealings with the Aborigines. Just as Cook's charts offered the only navigational guide to Botany Bay, just as Cook's and Banks's descriptions, whatever their flaws, offered the only extended account of the geography, fauna and flora, and inhabitants of New South Wales, so too did Cook's procedure on his voyages offer the only immediate precedent for Phillip and his companions in their dealings with the Aborigines. Based on enlightenment and evangelical precepts, this procedure provided a general model for contact with non-European peoples, but it was not necessarily equally appropriate to each one.[18] Initially, Phillip and his officers showed little awareness that there might be important differences between Polynesian, Melanesian, and Aboriginal cultures. Since the perceptions which would in the nineteenth century give rise to the discipline of ethnology were only then forming, this is hardly surprising; and it is therefore even more a mark of Phillip's flexible discernment that he quickly came to appraise the Aborigines only in European and their own terms, and not in those of a third people as well.

Phillip had his first encounter with Aborigines on his first day in New South Wales. Looking for water on the north shore of Botany Bay, he and his party observed 'a group of the Natives'. On his making to land near where they had left their canoes, the Aborigines 'got up & called ... in a Menacing tone, &

at the same time brandish[ed] their spears or lances'. The Europeans indicated by dipping a hat into the sea and making to drink that they needed water, and the Aborigines directed them around a nearby point to a stream. On landing, Phillip followed in Cook's footsteps. He advanced towards the Aborigines 'alone & unarmed, on which one of them advanced towards him, but would not come near enough to receive the beads which the Governor held out for him, but seemed very desirous of having them & made signs for them to be lain on ye ground, which was done, he (ye Native) came on with fear & trembling & took them up, & by degrees came so near as to receive Looking Glasses & c'.[19]

Phillip and the officers behaved in similar fashion at their next meeting with the Aborigines, even when some of the blacks hurled spears. And Phillip extended his precautions, permitting his colonists to gather water and grass for the stock, but maintaining a guard at the landing-place 'to prevent the seamen from straggling, or having any improper intercourse with the natives'.[20] Within two days, the Europeans and the Aborigines were on reasonably familiar terms, with the Aborigines eagerly accepting European baubles, and permitting the sailors 'to dress them with different coloured Papers, and Fools-Caps'.[21] Nor was the amusement confined to the one side. The Aborigines were very curious to know the nature of the strange beings who had arrived on their shore, and pulled at the Europeans' clothing. The discovery, when one of the officers removed his hat, that they covered their hair, caused much Aboriginal mirth, and led naturally to interest in the sex of the now obviously humans. King removed this doubt by having one of the sailors reveal his genitals. Obligingly, the Aborigines then offered some of their women. As an English officer should, King decorously applied a handkerchief to one woman where 'Eve did ye Fig leaf'— whereupon one of the male Aborigines 'went into the Wood, and presently came forth again, jumping & laughing with a Bunch of broad Leaves tied before Him'.[22]

Phillip continued these procedures as he settled his party permanently about Sydney Cove. He issued strict instructions that colonists were not to molest the Aborigines;[23] and by sending patrols about the woods to find malingerers[24] and not allowing the fishing parties to carry muskets,[25] as much as he conceivably could he made it impossible for the ignorant to disregard these instructions. It was his personal determination 'never to fire on the natives but in a case of absolute necessity',[26] and he kept this resolution for more than six difficult months, through a series of encounters that the records note but give few details of. Whenever Phillip examined the reaches of the harbour of the adjacent country, he 'Endeavoured to Naturelize [the Aborigines],... giving them Clothing and Trinkets and would not permit them to be [misused] by any Means, though he Run many risks of his Life by them'.[27]

In return, Phillip required from the Aborigines an equal attention to the principles of honesty and open dealing. One anecdote of his exploration of the Broken Bay area at the beginning of March 1788 makes this point well. 'Another curious Circumstance happened to them, while they were on the Business of exploring this Bay; They had landed, where there was a great many of the Natives; and in one of their Huts, the Governor, saw a large Crawfish, which, He Bartered for, giving the Owners of the Fish a Hatchet, and distributing Bawbles among many of Them whom, he thought might have a share of it, The Governor, now took the Fish, and was walking down towards the Boat with it, when, one of the Natives meeting Him, snatched it out of his Hand, and ran up with it to the Hut, where he had bought it, The Governor took no Notice then, but got into the Boat; soon after, they saw the same Fellow running down to the Boats hollowing and holding out the Fish, his Comrades, having told him, as they imagined that they had given something for it, however, the Governor, & the Gentlemen went on shore again, would not accept of the Fish but went up to the Huts where he got it, and took back all the Presents he had given them, this Conduct, was a great matter of Surprise & Mortification to them'.[28]

Despite the absence of initial clashes, and despite all Phillip's subsequent precautions and accommodations, it was inevitable that there be trouble, as educated Europeans bearing assumptions of racial and cultural superiority, and as uneducated ones bearing age-old fears of blackness and the forest, began to move more freely about their new environment; as the Aborigines began to understand that these beings whom they could scarcely comprehend were more than visitors; and as both parties began to compete for food resources that progressively diminished. The first untoward incident was not of British doing, though. In an ugly episode, Lapérouse's men fired on some of the Botany Bay Aborigines.[29] Immediately, those about Port Jackson distanced themselves from the British.[30] Then, some of the convicts pillaged Aboriginal camps for artifacts to sell to the crews of the ships returning to England.[31] And it seems some of those who hunted in the bush fired on or otherwise mistreated Aborigines.[32] On 21 May 1788, one convict who had been 'gathering greens' staggered back to camp with a spear in his hip, and reported a companion murdered. A week later, Aborigines killed and mutilated two convicts who were cutting rushes for the thatching of huts.[33]

Suspecting that the first convicts had done something to provoke the attack, and knowing that the second ones had stolen a canoe, Phillip searched for the Aborigines responsible but did not attempt any general revenge.[34] Nor did these and other incidents deter him from seeking further contact with the

Aborigines, and from gathering ethnographic information. By July, encounters with groups of up to 200 had convinced him that the Aborigines were indeed much more populous than supposed, and that they were not confined to the coast. He had come to think that there might be as many as 1500 in the Botany Bay–Port Jackson–Broken Bay area. He had noted that the women were 'constantly employ'd in fishery', at times on the open sea; that 'almost all the Men want the right front tooth in the upper Jaw ... & most of the Women [want] the two first joints of the little finger on the left hand'; that there seemed to be a good deal of violence between individual Aborigines and amongst tribes; and that they cremated their dead, and 'cover the Ashes over without disturbing them, with Earth, ferns a few Stones & bark'. He had also noticed many figures of men, shields, and fish 'roughly cut' into rocks. Curiously, Phillip also lacked the upper right incisor. This point of identity, as well as his obviously friendly intentions, led the Aborigines to view him with respect and to offer him some attention; and as he became better acquainted with them he left behind the low opinion with which he had arrived. The Aborigines did not, he came to see, 'want Courage, they very readily place a confidence ... [and] are strictly honest amongst themselves'.[35]

By mid-1788, the situations of both groups were more difficult than at the beginning of the year. Fish had become scarce, and Phillip remarked that the Aborigines were consequently 'very much distressed for food, several have been seen dying in the Woods, & visibly for want of food'. They would gather where the Europeans fished, 'anxious to get the small fish, of which they made no account in the Summer'. Once, a group of twenty holding their spears poised seized most of a catch. Phillip ordered that the Aborigines should receive a portion of each catch. He saw such help as a matter of common humanity, and also a means of gaining the Aborigines' confidence.[36]

Things continued much in a state 'of petty warfare and endless uncertainty'[37] until the end of 1788, with some of the colonists molesting the Aborigines, and with the Aborigines killing several more of the colonists. The Aborigines continued willing enough to meet Phillip on his expeditions about the harbour and in the surrounding countryside, but declined to become more familiar and enter the European settlement. Phillip was thus unable to learn more than a few words of their language, or to gain their attention by showing them the superiority of civilization. To attain both ends, he now resorted to the rather desperate expedient of capturing and forcibly detaining one by the use of fetters. Arabanoo was seized on 31 December, and it took some weeks for him to lose his not unnatural resentment at his treatment, but he slowly became more confident, and the Europeans were able to learn something of his language, and to offer him something of theirs. Quite how well they came to understand each other is uncertain, though Newton Fowell said that Arabanoo 'gave much information concerning their manners'. Hunter published a vocabulary gathered by Phillip and Collins, but this must contain later additions. Nonetheless, it seems that Phillip learned enough to be able to convey his friendly intentions. In March 1789, he had Arabanoo witness the punishment of a group of convicts who had gone to attack some Aborigines. And when 'smallpox' began to ravage the Aboriginal population in April, he used Arabanoo to help convince some of the sick to accept European treatment, including a girl called Abaroo whom the Johnsons took in after her recovery. So impressed was Phillip by Arabanoo's solicitous behaviour that he ordered the fetters struck off. Phillip himself had from the first been, and he was to remain, uneasy at this mode of obtaining a desirable end; and it was good that he freed Arabanoo when he did, for Arabanoo himself died of the disease on 18 May. With considerable grief, Phillip buried him in the garden of Government House.[38]

In the last four weeks of his life, Arabanoo had stayed with the Europeans through choice. His sudden death defeated Phillip's plan to bring the races together, and meant that the Aborigines generally continued to view the Europeans with the 'same suspicious dread', and that 'the same scenes of vengeance acted on unfortunate stragglers, continued to prevail'.[39] The material circumstances of both groups also continued to worsen, with disease still ravaging the Aborigines, and with no supplies from Europe reaching the colonists. Competition for available resources increased further, and with it conflict. In November 1789, Phillip returned to his earlier expedient, and captured two more Aborigines, Bennelong and Colbee. While Colbee soon escaped, the Europeans retained Bennelong for six months, only to have him then escape too. 'I think that Mans leaving us proves that nothing will make these people amends for the loss of their liberty', Phillip wistfully recorded.[40]

There were no dramatic changes in the colony's circumstances until the arrival of the Second Fleet in June 1790. Immediately, this increased difficulties, for the ships carried many old or decrepit convicts, who could not possibly labour for the colony's good. The hundreds who landed sick also put an enormous strain on medical resources. There was a succession of further material difficulties to be overcome—the consequences of the losses of the *Guardian* and the *Sirius*; the drought that parched the region from July 1790 to October 1791; further shortages of rations. To these troubles were added the absence of any sense of community amongst the new arrivals, and further setbacks in relations with the Aborigines.

In the longer term, however, these were rather surface difficulties, contrary waves beneath which the tide set differently, for the arrival of the Second Fleet marked the real turning point in the colony's progress. With increased supplies, and with the arrival of some of the skilled supervisors and convicts first embarked on the *Guardian*, Phillip was able to work the healthy convicts harder, and to offer more support to those who wished to settle. He was thus finally able to begin laying a firm agricultural basis, a process which the subsequent arrival of stores at more regular intervals permitted him to continue. In October, the *Supply* returned from Batavia, to be followed two months later by the transport that her commander had hired there. Together, the ships brought 20 000 pounds of flour, 200 000 pounds of rice, 80 000 pounds of beef, 60 000 pounds of pork, and smaller quantities of sugar, sago, vinegar, and medicines. These provisions and the limited autumn 1791 harvest nurtured the colonists until the arrival of the *Gorgon* and the ships of the Third Fleet in August, September, and October, and allowed them to continue their work. When the long drought finally broke in the spring of 1791, Phillip had the mainland colony in a position to obtain substantial agricultural returns. By the end of the year, there were 350 government acres under maize at Parramatta, 44 under wheat, 6 under barley, 1 under oats, 2 under potatoes, a garden of 6 acres about Government House there, and 150 acres cleared for turnips, while civil and military officers and settlers there had another 200 acres under various cultivations.[41] There had also been similar progress on Norfolk Island. Despite continuing problems with caterpillars, rats, and birds, and unreliable subordinates, Major Ross was able to report at the end of 1790 that he had flour, corn, and potatoes for the next twelve months, and 600 grape vines which promised well.[42] His colonists continued this progress during 1791, so that Phillip was able to increase their number to 1800 with arrivals from the Second and Third Fleets.

The combination of more regular supplies and expanding agricultural production led to a dramatic improvement in the colony's circumstances in 1792. First came the copious autumn harvest. Then, the *Atlantic*, which Phillip had despatched to Calcutta for supplies the previous October, arrived back in June. The next month, the *Britannia* came in from England loaded with supplies, to be followed by the *Royal Admiral* in October and the *Kitty* in November. Progressively, Phillip brought more government land under cultivation, and officers and settlers enlarged their holdings. The colonists now succeeded in increasing the numbers of their animals, too. The *Gorgon* brought some, and the *Atlantic* more; and, being better cared for and enjoying better pastures, those already in the colony began to multiply at faster rates. By the time Phillip left the colony at the end of the year, he could report that at Sydney and Parra-

THE SETTLEMENT in NEW SOUTH WALES
of
NEW HOLLAND

Phillip, The Sydney Settlement, December 1792

Phillip prepared this survey as he was leaving the colony. In time, the inner boundary defined the Sydney Domain and Botanic Gardens

I   Workshops
K   Government House
L   Palmer's Farm
M   Officers' Quarters
N   Magazine
O   Gallows
P   Brick-kilns
Q   Brickfields

SYDNEY COVE

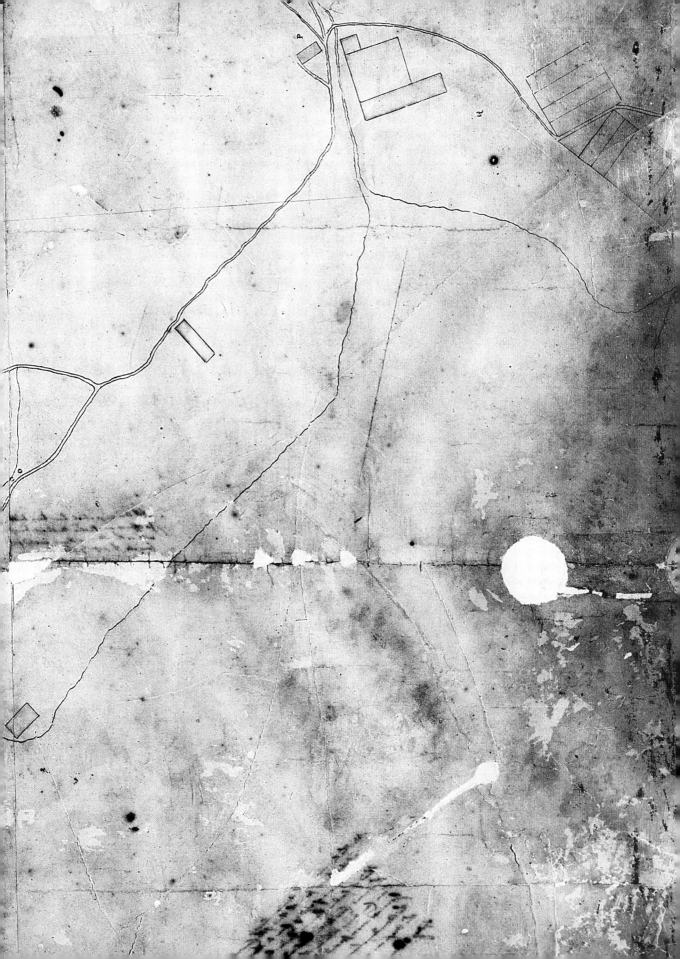

matta there were 208 government acres under wheat, 24 under barley, 1186 under maize, 121 of gardens, 23 cattle, 11 horses, 105 sheep, and 43 pigs. There was similar progress on private farms and at Norfolk Island.[43]

By 1792, it was apparent that the colony's material difficulties were indeed diminishing. After his arrival with the New South Wales Corps in February 1792, Major Grose reported to Nepean, 'to my great astonishment, instead of the rock I expected to see I find myself surrounded with gardens that flourish and produce fruit of every description. Vegetables are here in great abundance, and I live in as good a house as I wish for. I am given the farm of my predecessor, which produces a sufficiency to supply my family with everything I have occasion for. In short, all that is wanting to put this colony in an independent state is one ship freighted with corn and black cattle. Was that but done, all difficulties would be over.'[44]

With more rations, and progressively greater quantities of fresh foods, the general health and strength of the colonists improved. One hundred and forty-three persons died of illness in 1790, 171 in 1791, 473 in 1792.[45] These numbers may seem high, but they most reflect the desperate state of the convicts on the Second and Third Fleets, hundreds of whom landed so emaciated as to be mere skeletons, with little or no hope of recovery. John White's return for 5 November 1791 listed 626 colonists 'under medical treatment and incapable of labour—576 of whom are those landed from the last ships [i.e., the Third Fleet]'.[46] On learning how badly the ships' agents had treated the convicts during the voyages, the Pitt administration took steps to prevent any repetition. And in New South Wales, White and his fellow surgeons slowly nursed those capable of recovering back to health. By the end of 1792, there were more than 4000 colonists at Sydney, Parramatta, and on Norfolk Island, the great majority of whom were in good health, with many 'much better and fatter'[47] than when they had left England.

At the end of Phillip's term, something like a stable society had also emerged. The sentences of many of the first arrivals were expiring, and numbers of these desired to settle. So too did numbers of the marines. Phillip gave land, and help from the government store, to those whom he considered worthy and likely to succeed. While some of the newer arrivals behaved as they had done in England, there was a distinct improvement in the behaviour of those who had been longer in the colony. David Collins had begun to notice this feature in mid-1790. By the beginning of 1792, he could say of some particularly vicious incidents at Parramatta that 'to the credit of the convicts who came out in the first fleet it must be remarked, that none of them were concerned in these offences'. Nor did this escape Phillip's notice. In urging that the administration send out a 'few honest, intelligent settlers', he told Grenville in November 1791 that he could say 'with great truth and equal satisfaction that the convicts in general behave better than ever could be expected', and that 'their crimes, with very few exceptions, have been confined to the procuring for themselves the common necessaries of life, crimes which it may be presumed will not be committed when a more plentiful ration renders those little robberies unnecessary'. By the end of 1792, Collins could see that this general improvement had begun to appear.[48] Dissension amongst those in authority in the colony had also lessened. This cause was much helped by the replacement of the marines by the specially recruited New South Wales Corps under Major Grose. Though when they arrived Phillip had left only a limited time in which he needed their commander's co-operation, and though some awkward questions arose, his relations with Grose were certainly much easier than those with Ross had been. An enlarging population made for a greater range of social intercourse, too, and less unavoidable contact with persons of opposing temperaments; and the presence of a small number of middle-class women, which led the new officers to be more conscious of propriety than the first ones had been, provided a civility previously lacking in the infant society.

As the colony's circumstances eased, Phillip found more time to pursue some private interests which also satisfied obligations of friendship. Banks had become fascinated by the strange fauna and flora of New South Wales during the *Endeavour*'s voyage, and the specimens which he, his fellow naturalist Daniel Solander, and Cook had brought back had aroused widespread interest in Europe. From the first, the colonists acted to satisfy this interest, capturing and taming kangaroos, shooting and examining dingoes and marsupial animals and a great variety of birds, including the surprising emu and black swan. In 1792, Phillip had four kangaroos, which slept beside the fire in his kitchen; he sent specimens and seeds, and sometimes living examples, mostly to Banks but also to other friends, at every opportunity; and he obtained drawings 'of all the flowering Shrubs in this Country', and of animals and Aborigines.[49] Other officers did likewise, most notably John White, who took greater pleasure from collecting than from his official duties. By 1792, scientists such as Banks, Hunter, and Hooker had begun to sort these riches, identifying new species and establishing new genera. Phillip was on one occasion startled by the interest New South Wales artifacts engendered. When he learned from Banks that one kangaroo had been valued at £500, he replied indignantly, 'surely it is not supposed in England that I am in partnership with a Show man'.[50]

With the improvement in the colony's circumstances, and the more frequent arrival of ships, the sense of desolation and isolation that had pervaded it in its first years diminished. But the distance from Europe remained too great for this sense ever to disappear entirely. In its swings between depression and elation the colony's collective emotional life continued to mirror the presence and absence of shipping. Increasingly, however, colonists found satisfactions to alleviate the tedium of times without ships. In March 1791 Mrs Macarthur found that the impending loss of 'some valuable members of our small society and some very good friends' made her spirits 'low, very low'. Six months later, after the arrival of the Patersons, the Kings, and the Parkers, she reported that 'our little circle has been of late quite brilliant. We are constantly making little parties in boats up and down the various inlets of the Harbour, taking refreshments with us and dining out under an awning upon some pleasant point of land or in some of the creeks or coves, in which for twenty miles together, these waters abound. There are so many ladies in the Regiment that I am not likely to feel the want of female society as I at first did.'[51]

And at last Phillip succeeded in making substantial contact with the Aborigines. This was a success born out of potential disaster. On 7 September 1790, learning that Bennelong and Colbee were among a large group who had gathered at Manly to feast on a beached whale, he went to seek them out. In an awkward encounter, one Aborigine speared him in the right shoulder. Amid an exchange of musket-fire and spears, Phillip made for the boat, but was hindered by the 3-metre long spear striking the ground as he went. A desperate Waterhouse succeeded in breaking the shaft; and the Europeans headed for Sydney. Phillip was bleeding profusely, so much so that he and his companions did not expect him to live; and he swore a rough will as the sailors rowed. At the settlement, the surgeons succeeded in removing the spear, and found the wound not so serious as feared, and he recovered quickly.[52]

Though he recalled exploring parties, and warned the colonists at Rose Hill to be on their guard, Phillip did not seek any general revenge, for he continued to believe that the Aborigines' distrust arose either from 'having received injury, or from misapprehension'.[53] Mercifully, he then began to obtain the results he had long desired. A week after the Manly incident, Bennelong and some other Aborigines sought a meeting with the Europeans, there was an exchange of presents, and with the help of Abaroo, the parties arranged another meeting, so that the Europeans might return fishing equipment that the Aborigines said had been stolen. With this done, a third meeting, between Phillip and Bennelong, was arranged. After several more meetings, Bennelong and some of his friends came to see Phillip at the European settlement. This visit went well; and in the next weeks Aborigines began to frequent Sydney, 'so that every gentleman's house was now become a resting or sleeping place for some of them every night;

[and] whenever they were pressed for hunger, they had immediate recourse to our quarters, where they generally got their bellies filled'.[54]

Seeking to encourage this intercourse, Phillip had a 4-metre square hut built for Bennelong. But this favour, and others such as coffee and wine at Government House, led to the Aborigine's developing an exalted view of his status; and Phillip had to prevent him from murdering a young Aboriginal woman, and bar him from the hospital while she was treated for her wounds.[55] Then, in December, Phillip's gamekeeper McIntyre was speared while on a hunting expedition near Botany Bay. Though McIntyre bore a bad character with Europeans as well as with Aborigines, this attack seems to have been un-provoked by any immediate circumstance. As this was one in a series, and 'well convinced that nothing but a severe example, and the fear of having all the tribes who resided near the settlement destroyed ... [would] ... put a stop to the natives throwing spears',[56] Phillip decided on a punitive expedition against the male Aborigines in the area. At first, his orders were to kill ten, capture two, and destroy 'all weapons of war'. At the same time, he 'strictly [forbade], under penalty of the severest punishment, any soldier, or other person, not expressly ordered out for that purpose, ever to fire on any native except in his own defence; or to molest him in any shape, or to bring away any spears, or other articles, which they may find belonging to these people'. Tench persuaded Phillip to modify his views, and order instead the capture or death of six. When the first attempt failed dismally, Phillip ordered a second, which also failed.[57]

This was the nadir of relations between the groups, but even with it the colonists' contact with the Aborigines was never entirely lost, and this gradually grew more cordial again. In March 1791, Phillip wrote quite cheerfully of the Aborigines' being 'as much at home at Sydney as they are in their woods', observing without rancour that 'in bringing this about they treated me rather roughly, however I don't find any inconvenience from the hurt that I received'.[58] Others viewed this situation with less equanimity. John Harris, for example, wrote that 'the Whole Tribe with their Visitors have plagued us ever since [Phillip's wounding] nor can we get rid of them they come and go at pleasure They are very Fond of our Bread, Beef, etc'.[59] By the middle of the year, some of the Aborigines had developed a trade in fish with the Parramatta colonists. Convicts again disrupted this contact, when they destroyed a canoe belonging to Balloderry, one of the principal traders. Phillip punished those responsible, having one hanged, but Balloderry took his own revenge when later he speared a wandering convict who had had no part in the theft. On this, Phillip forbade Balloderry to enter the settlements, which led to the loss of almost all contact with Aborigines. Two months later, when Balloderry disregarded this edict, Phillip sent armed parties to arrest him. When these did not succeed, he ordered that Balloderry 'was to be taken whenever an opportunity offered; and that any native attempting to throw a spear in his defence, as it was well known among them why vengeance was denounced against him, was, if possible, to be prevented from escaping with impunity'.[60]

These vicissitudes continued through 1792, with threats and counter-threats, depredations and occasional deaths on both sides. Still, the situation slowly improved, at least about Sydney, and something akin to friendship sometimes developed between individuals of either race. When Phillip left in December 1792, he took with him Bennelong and Yemmerrawannie, whom Collins characterized as 'much attached to his person', who went 'voluntarily and cheerfully', and who 'withstood at the moment of their departure the united distress of their wives, and the dismal lamentations of their friends, to accompany him to England, a place that they knew was at a great distance from them'.[61]

By this time, the two races had become much more at ease with each other in the Sydney area. There, the Aborigines admitted the Europeans to their corroborees;[62] and the Europeans received the Aborigines into their homes. The Spanish explorer Malaspina, who called at the colony in March 1793, recorded how his party saw 'both Boys and Girls received and cared for with great attention in the houses of the principal persons of the colony. Both men and women ... have been admitted to the dining room in our presence, and have enjoyed delicacies from the same table. At times we heard entire families salute us in English. Sometimes we saw Aborigines dancing and singing in the principal streets about a fire the whole night, without anyone disturbing them.'[63] The situation was rather different on the fringes of European settlement beyond Parramatta, where colonists over whom Phillip and his officers had less immediate control were intruding on the territories of tribes to whom they were much less familiar; but, all things considered, the Sydney situation was quite remarkable, and Phillip has received far too little credit for his part in bringing it about.

Phillip's sense of what he accomplished materially in his five years in New South Wales was always overshadowed by what he knew he might have done had he been 'more fortunate in receiving the necessary supplies and a few intelligent men' in better time. But, as he told Grenville in June 1790, when he considered how, 'from the day of our landing to the present hour, [the colony] has laboured under every possible disadvantage, and many obstacles have been met with which could not have been guarded against, as they never could have been expected', it was rather 'a matter of surprize that a regular settlement exists than that it is not in a more flourishing state'.[64] And even given all this, in another year, he could see that if they 'go on but slowly', they did 'go on', and that they did so much better than, really, anyone could have expected. At this time, Phillip was able to inform Grenville that he thought 'every doubt respecting its future independency as to the necessaries of life' had disappeared. Another year on, and he was able to tell Dundas that 'the time now approaches in which this country will be able to supply its inhabitants with grain'.[65] When he left the colony at the end of 1792, he did so in the knowledge that he had effectively won the struggle to establish it.

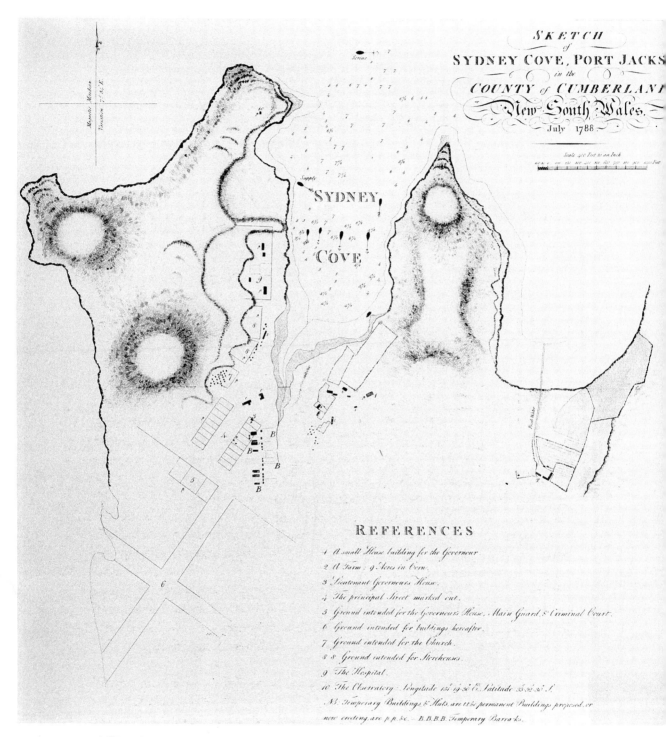

Phillip/John Hunter/William Dawes, Plan of
Sydney (present and projected), July 1788

Founding Australia

I do think God Almighty made Phillip on purpose for the Place; for never did man better know what to do, or with more determination to see it done; and yet, if they'll let him, he will make them all very happy.

Captain John Fortescue, 1789

The Port Jackson area was an appropriate site for the founding of a branch of a European maritime nation, offering as it did 'the finest harbour in the world, in which a thousand sail of the line may ride in the most perfect security'.[1] Phillip may have had a touch of the visionary about him, but this comment is not necessarily—as it has often been taken to be—a sign of this quality. Others, some of them certainly of prosaic outlook, described the harbour in similar terms;[2] and before anything else, Phillip was a person of wide naval experience, for whom the practicalities of manoeuvring ships into harbours after long voyages, of anchoring them safely, and of refitting and refreshing them were paramount considerations. Without success in these practicalities, there might be no success in the whole voyage: what might have been the fate of Sir Richard King's squadron in 1783–84, for example, if it had not had the use of Cape Town's facilities? More than evincing a visionary gleam, Phillip's characterization of Port Jackson bespoke his naval experience, and his practical outlook.

Phillip judged carefully and well. Port Jackson conformed almost exactly to the model of the perfect harbour. Its tall, narrow-set heads concealed and sheltered extensive waterways behind, and offered the prospect of effective fortification. Breaking the expanse of the harbour into smaller sections, the various arms increased its shelter, and in this it was clearly superior to the renowned Rio de Janeiro. There were deep-water paths to these arms and their coves, with only a few isolated rocks to threaten danger. A number of the coves offered anchorage very close to shore, and their solid bottoms meant that anchors did not drag easily. Some of the coves offered streams of water, and trees that might be cut for naval timbers grew on the slopes beyond. In its natural attributes, Port Jackson was indeed one of the four or five finest harbours in the world.[3]

In 1788 these attributes needed to be embellished before the site could become an effective naval base. The colonists needed to make quays, raise a town, establish agriculture, raise herds and flocks, and create supplies of naval materials. The town to be built needed to conform to the principles that hundreds of years of voyaging had shown necessary to the success of ventures at sea. As already discussed, these principles included the main square or plaza lying adjacent to the harbourside; the plaza being of extensive dimensions, with the main streets running outwards from it; the placing of the church, hospital, viceregal palace, council chambers, customs house, and naval arsenal about the plaza, not only for convenience of access, but also to form part of the defences; the site being healthy, and partly elevated; and there being land about for farming and grazing, with timber for building and fuel, and fresh water.[4]

Phillip's wide experience offered many good models, including the Greenwich he had known as a boy, the Royal Navy's yards at Portsmouth and the French navy's at Toulon, Pombal's Lisbon and the imperial capital at Rio de Janeiro, and Cape Town.[5] He chose the cove he named Sydney as the site of first settlement because it 'had the best spring of water', and because it offered anchorage 'so close to the shore that at a very small expence quays may be made at which the largest ships may unload'.[6] Just as he chose the site, so did he draw the lines of the future township with a naval eye. He located the hospital on the western side of the cove, immediately adjacent to the area of the proposed quays, but in a 'healthy' situation clear of the town site.[7] On this site, he allowed for a large square, one corner of which intersected the entrance of the Tank Stream to the cove. The town's main avenue, which was to be 200 feet wide,[8] was to run up the elevation behind this square, which commanded 'a capital view of Long Cove, and other parts of the harbour'.[9] On this hill, Phillip intended to place the permanent Government House, the guard house, and the court houses. Behind the hill, to the south and southeast, lay 'nearly level' ground offering a 'very good situation' for future expansion.[10]

After six months, it was possible for the colonists to say that 'the Town now begins to cut a figure'.[11] It would take some years before the colonists would establish agriculture and raise the herds and flocks from which to supply visiting ships; and they would be disappointed in their attempt to create a source of naval supplies. Indeed, in this last endeavour appears the one real failure of Phillip's years in New South Wales, although it is one for which neither he nor any of his colleagues was personally responsible. He sent King and a small party including flax-dressers to Norfolk Island two weeks after he settled on Sydney Cove as the site of the main settlement; and this group cut the pines and harvested the flax. Early, they had high hopes for the business. Phillip reported to Sydney in September 1788 that 'the island will, in a very short time, be able to furnish a considerable quantity of flax', and that it 'affords excellent timber for ship-building, as well as for masts and yards, with which I make no doubt but His Majesty's ships in the East Indies may be supplied, as likewise with pitch and tar'.[12] But these hopes progressively diminished as the timber proved generally unsound, and the flax resisted European techniques.

Phillip's general intentions as he began the colonization were overwhelmingly practical ones: he had to ensure simple survival, by housing the people and by creating food supplies—the 'great object' they had to attain, he told Ross in 1788, was 'the rendering the settlement independent with respect to the necessaries of life';[13] and he had to raise a maritime town, for, whatever else it might in time become, he knew that the settlement would primarily be a port at the end of a very long sea route, and occasionally a place of refreshment and supply for ships proceeding into the Pacific Ocean. Yet the realization of such practical purposes could not but create other meanings. Take, for example, the matter of the governor's accommodation. Phillip had sailed from England with a pre-fabricated timber and canvas house '45 feet long 17 f⸱ 6 ins Wide 8 under the Halls ... with five windows of a Side 3 f⸱ 9 by 3 f⸱',[14] and had had this erected on the eastern side of Sydney Cove in the last days of January 1788.[15] Though this provided him with more handsome accommodation than that enjoyed by anybody else in the settlement, the violent late summer and autumn thunderstorms soon revealed its inadequacies: in May, he asked Sydney to excuse 'the confused manner in which I have in this letter given an account of what has past since I left the Cape of Good Hope. It has been written at different times, and my situation at present does not permit me to begin so long a letter again, the canvas house I am under being neither wind nor water proof.'[16] Clearly, he could not conduct his governor's business efficiently in such circumstances, and he set James Bloodworth and his convict band to building a more substantial structure on the slope adjacent. By the next April, these had created a two-storey structure with glass windows, around which other convicts had laid out gardens. Even then, Phillip did not intend that this should be the governor's permanent residence, but, a striking form among the cluster of tents and huts and the surrounding wilderness, it was none the less a potent sign of his presence and of the authority he exercised.

The colony was from the first marked by the operation of this central authority. Providing for him to govern without a council, Phillip's commission seemed to those under him 'a more unlimited one than was ever before granted to any Governor under the British Crown'.[17] It and his instructions gave him immediate supervision of the activities of such subordinate officers as the deputy judge-advocate who administered the law; of the commissary, who fed the party; of the surgeon, who kept them healthy; and of the commandant of marines, who guarded them. It also allowed him to take direct responsibility for town planning, for agriculture, for land-granting, and for policing and penal policies. Phillip's long training as a naval officer, and his experience in captaining large warships led him naturally into exercising this authority, which he did insistently. He chose the site, and he planned the town to rise about it. He oversaw the physical operation of the colony in all its details. He directed groups of colonists to other sites, and sent ships out into the world to obtain supplies. He mediated in the bitter quarrels between the officers. He supervised the administration of justice, and he dispensed the King's mercy.

A generation later, in considering what changes had become necessary because of the colony's development, Chief Justice Forbes eloquently described Phillip's role: 'In a new country such as this was at the landing of the expedition under Governor Phillip, the second object, after providing for the care and correction of the prisoners, was that of procuring sustenance; every thing necessarily centred in the governor as the primum mobile of the machine; the police, the roads, the market, the importation of supplies, the cultivation of provisions, and even the prices of every article of daily consumption, were regulated by the orders of the governor; these phirmans entered into some of the minutest matters of domestic life, and gradually became so familiar to the inhabitants, that instances are to be found of domestic quarrels being referred to the fountain head of authority, and there settled with all the form and sanction of legal supremacy. This was a very natural order of things; a government, situated like that of New South Wales, necessarily became patriarchal'.[18]

Phillip's decisive fulfilment of his role meant that the infant society developed two features which 200 years now show to be characteristic Australian ones. The first of these is only what one should expect, perhaps. The dominance of central authority, and the population's reliance on it for such things as food, health, and social order meant that the New South Wales venture was always different from, for example, a number of seventeenth-century American counterparts, which were marked by the separateness of their communities and the individualism of their inhabitants. The second, though, is rather surprising. Bearing in mind the extent of Phillip's powers and his efficient exercising of them, taking into account the presence of a small and discrete group of civil and military officers, and given the general temper of the age, one might expect a rigid social distinction to have been to the fore in the first years—that is, one might expect the colony to have exhibited a system of apartheid which divided the few free from the majority of transgressors. Yet the very opposite is in fact true, and its being true provides us with an intriguing glimpse into Phillip's private self.

The simple fact is that a surprising egalitarianism quickly came to prevail in the colony. 'Could I possibly have imagined,' Major Ross complained to Philip Stephens in July 1788, 'that I was to be served with, for instance, no more butter than any of the convicts ... I most certainly would not have left England without supplying myself with that article.' Disgruntled officers also resented the huts of the convicts being 'equal in magnificence' to their own. In April 1790, Phillip reduced the weekly ration 'for every person in the settlement without distinction'. In July, Captain Hill commented that 'all here, the officer, soldier, sailor, and convict have the same ration allowed by the Governor'. In October 1792, Phillip replied to Grose's complaint about the quality of the food with 'I cannot acquiesce with you in thinking that the ration served from the public stores is unwholesome; I see it daily at my own table.' This attitude was in sharp contrast to Grose's, who altered the proportions in favour of the marines immediately Phillip left. And Phillip's invitations to dinner bore the proviso, 'Bring your own roll.'[19] In time of dearth, in Phillip's New South Wales even the governor would not have more than the meanest of those he governed. It is doubtful that what now appears as egalitarian was ideological, so much as it was practical; but to those used to the hierarchies with which officers and gentlemen enveloped themselves, Phillip's attitudes must have appeared as singular as the rising Government House.

Nor was this merely a matter of *noblesse oblige*, for the convicts by no means had the status of chattel slaves only.[20] In the first weeks, Phillip tried to work them throughout the day, but he quickly found that this was not feasible. He therefore began a system of 'task' work such as had been established in the English dockyards, whereby he allotted 'a certain quantity of ground to be cleared by a certain number of persons in a given time, and allowing them to employ what time they might gain, till called on again for public service, in bringing in materials and erecting huts for themselves'. By October 1788, he was allowing the convicts to have Saturdays free from public labour, 'for the purpose of collecting vegetables and attending to their huts and gardens'.[21] In April 1790, he reduced the convicts' hours of labour, so that they worked from sunrise to 1 p.m. only, with a short break for breakfast. In June, after the arrival of the *Justinian*, he restored the afternoon work period; but two years later he was forced to adjust the hours again, ordering that the convicts should work 'from five in the morning until nine; rest until four in the afternoon, and then labour until sun-set'.[22]

Recognizing that the aged, infirm, and ill could not be expected to work even the relaxed regimens he set, Phillip exempted them entirely. The women he also generally exempted from manual labour. He relieved those who became pregnant from all burdensome tasks, and provided for the newly-born children from the government store. In these unusual circumstances, the convicts also asserted themselves, negotiating in the fashion then spreading amongst the working classes in England for reductions in the amounts of work set, or in the hours of labour. They worked harder for themselves or for others who paid them than they did for the government. Women found advantages in pregnancy and motherhood—a situation quite the reverse of that which they had all too often known in England.[23] Nor did Phillip exclude the Aborigines from this general treatment. He shared the catches of fish with his black neighbours from the first; he offered them medical help; and when at last he had established a substantial connection with them, he opened the settlement to them, accepting that they should come and go freely as they chose.

Phillip exempted no-one, not even himself as governor, from the general constraints which the colony's early circumstances necessitated. He ate the rations that were issued to officers, marines, and convicts alike. In the early days of Parramatta, he slept on the floor of his former servant Dodd's hut.[24] He did not spare himself the labours of exploration, even when these labours aggravated the pain from which he was seldom free; and when exploring, he dined in company with those accompanying him.[25] Nor, in distinct contrast to the marine officers, was he too haughty or honour-bound to take a hand in the supervision of the convicts in their work. He allowed Bennelong and other Aborigines to enter his house at will, and shared his meals with them without formality.[26]

Numbers of those who sailed with Phillip to New South Wales praised him for his humane regard for all under his care; but his general procedure in the colony was based on more than a simple humanitarianism, no matter how unusual in a hard-bred naval captain of the time. Nor, most interestingly, did it arise only in reaction to the peculiar circumstances that emerged there, even though this would have indicated a remarkable man. Though we now cannot recover the origins of Phillip's egalitarianism, a cluster of circumstances and events makes clear that it was well developed before he reached New South Wales. The first glimpse we now have of it comes during his training under Michael Everitt. Although naval regulations allowed midshipmen to command sailors to perform the task, Phillip and his fellow cadets carried their own hammocks above deck each day to air them.[27] While much more must have gone into the making of Phillip's outlook, this is a discernible basis for what thirty years later had become a pervasive habit. In February 1783, when water began to run low as the *Europe* proceeded down the Atlantic, Phillip put himself and his officers on two quarts a day, but he did not ration the crew.[28] His actions at the Cape of Good Hope later that year provide another insight. Among his crew was one William Sutton, who was in charge of manoeuvring the watering boat between ship and shore. The labour of loading the boat was not for Billy, who would absent himself to the nearest tavern while the rest of the crew filled the casks. By the time the boat was ready for the return of the ship, Billy would be drunk, but he would nonetheless take charge. On one such return, seeing his inebriation, the second lieutenant insisted on taking the helm, whereupon the indignant sailor struck him. While the striking of an officer was an offence punishable by death, the lieutenant showed forebearance by confining Sutton to the ship. Phillip was at this time living on shore, so he did not learn of the incident until the next day, when he missed Billy from the watering party, and went out to the ship to enquire. Learning the story, he insisted on restoring Sutton to duty, saying 'I know he gets drunk ... but does he ever come off without bringing what he went for?'[29]

Phillip showed this same tolerant and egalitarian disposition also on the way to New South Wales. Soon after departure, the third lieutenant of the *Sirius* began to follow the accustomed course of 'starting' the seamen to make them work harder. This was an ugly practice, in which the men were struck with a cane or knotted rope, and which could have serious consequences if the blow fell on the base of the neck. The lieutenant's actions led to a tumult amongst the crew, and on hearing it, Phillip ordered every officer, 'even to a Boatswain's Mate', to his cabin. There, he told them that 'if he new any Officer, to Strike a Man on Board, he would Brake him Amediately, he said, those men, are all we have to depend Upon, & if we abuse those Men, that we have to Trust to, the Convicts will Rise & Massure us all, those Men are our Support, we have a Long and Severe Station to go through, in Settling this Collona, at Least we Cannot Expect to Return in Less than Five years, This Ship and her Crew is to Protect and Support the Country and if the[y] are Ill treated by their own

The following Regulations to be observed by the
Night Watch, appointed for the more effectual Preservation
of Public and Private property, and for preventing, or
detecting the Commission of Nightly Depredations.

A Night watch, consisting of twelve persons, divided into four
parties, is appointed, & fully Authorised to patrol at all hours in the Night,
and to Visit such places as may be deemed Necessary for the discovery of any
Felony, Trespass, or Misdemeanor, and for the Apprehending, and Securing for
Examination, any Person or Persons that may appear to them Concerned therein, either by
Entrance into any Suspected Hut, or dwelling, or by such other Manner as may
appear expedient.

2.d

Those parts in which the Convicts reside, are to be divided, and
Numbered in the following Manner.
The Convict Huts, of the Public Farm on the East side of the Cove, to be the
First Division.
Those at the Brick kilns, & the Detached parties at the different Farms
in that district, the Second Division.
Those on the Eastern Side, as far as the line that separates the District
of the Women from the Men, the Third Division.
The Huts occupied from that line to the Hospital, & from thence to the
Observatory, to be the Fourth Division.

3.

These Districts, or Divisions to be each of them under the particular
inspection of One Person, who shall be judged qualified to inform himself
of the Actual Residence of each Individual in his District, as well as of his
Business, Connections & Acquaintance.

4.th

Cognisance is to be taken of such Convicts as may sell, or barter
their Slops, or Provisions, as also of such as game for either of the aforesaid
Articles, & report is to be made of them to the Judge Advocate.

5.th

Any Soldier or Seaman found Stragling after the Tap too has beat,
or who may be found in the Convicts Huts, is to be detained & information to be
immediately given to the nearest Guardhouse.

6.th

On any person's being robbed during the Night, he is to give immediate
information thereof to the Watch of his District, who on the instant of Application
being made, shall use the most effectual Means to trace out the Offender.

A page of Phillip's Regulations for the Night Watch

Officers what Support Can you Expect of them, the[y] Will be all Dead, before the Voige is half out, and who Is to bring us back again'.[30]

It took two more incidents for the officers and men to understand Phillip's determination on this point. A few days after his first admonishment, a midshipman ordered the armourer's mate to carry his hammock on deck. When the sailor said that he could not do so immediately, because he had 'a job for the Captⁿ', the midshipman struck him, knocking out one of his teeth. The sailor complained to Hunter and Phillip. Nagle relates that 'the Govenor was very angry, after giving Such Puncktual Orders for any Officer not to Strike a Man, Mr Hornsby [the midshipman] was Call'd upon the Quarter Deck, the Govenor repremanded him Severly and told him he would break him if he ever atempted to give Such another Offince, he ordered all hands to be Turned up on the Quarter Deck, he spoke to the Midshipmen one & all and told them when he was Midshipman the[y] had to carry their own hammocks up on Deck, and in Lew of having a Barber, the[y] had to, tie and Dress one anothers hair themselves, and he thought that they were no batter than he was. He then Turned to the Ships Company & told them if he found any Man to Carry up a Midshipmans hammock, or Cot, he would Amediately flog him.' Much to his astonishment and anger, a few days later Phillip discovered a seaman carrying up another midshipman's hammock. Phillip asked the man 'whose hammock that was nowing it was not his Own being made of fine Canvis, the Man told him it belonged to a Midshipman, he Call^d the Boatswain & ordered the hands to be turned up for Punishment, he had him tied up, and told the Ships Company that he was Determened to flog every Man that disobayed his Orders, but as the Captⁿ and Mr Bradley, first Lieutenant, plead hard for him and being the first Offence, he forgave him, but desired him not to be guilty of Such another Offence as he was determined not to Look over it any more, & dismist them.'[31]

As this outlook pervaded Phillip's governance, it was a major influence on the emerging society. It was reinforced by another, which was not immediately of Phillip's doing, but which he encouraged. One of his greatest needs was to create a social order, a need made the more difficult of realization not only by the recalcitrance of the officers, but also by the lawlessness of some of the marines. At this time, those who served as common soldiers were not generally noted for their character. Illiterate or at best only minimally educated, they came from the same social groups as the convicts, so that it was often a matter of chance on which side of the law they lived. Sometimes, indeed, these soldiers were ex-convicts, released from prison on their agreeing to enter His Majesty's service. In any case, they were scarcely of such character as to resist temptation to crime, particularly when their personal circumstances grew difficult.

This was the situation in the first years of New South Wales. Some of the marines exchanged spirits for the sexual services of convict women. One severely beat a woman who 'would not goe up in the woods with him'.[32] Another raped a child.[33] Others fought viciously. For eight months across 1788 into 1789, seven systematically plundered the government store they were assigned to guard, to be caught out only when their forged key broke in the lock. This last one was potentially the most dangerous crime, for it threatened not only the colony's precious resources, but also the order that Phillip was so slowly and painfully establishing. As Collins noted, 'a crime of such magnitude called for a severe example'. Upon conviction by court-martial, the marines were sentenced to death, and executed. That one of their officers could describe them as 'the flower of our battalion' indicates how close to anarchy Phillip and those in his charge lived in the first years.[34]

The ever-present sign of this anarchy was the nightly robbing of gardens, huts, and stores, which was mostly the doing of convicts, but in which (it was strongly suspected) marines and seamen were also involved. As the marine officers refused to accept the policing of the settlement as part of their duty, Phillip had to adopt the expedient of a nightwatch of twelve worthy convicts.[35] This was one of his most successful moves. Indeed, Collins described it as being 'of infinite utility. The commission of crimes, since [its] institution, had been evidently less frequent, and [the watchmen] were instrumental in bringing forward for punishment several offenders who would otherwise have escaped. The fear and detestation in which they were held by their fellow-prisoners was one proof of their assiduity in searching for offences and in bringing them to light; and it possibly might have been asserted with truth, that many streets in the metropolis of London were not so well guarded and watched as the small, but rising town of Sydney, in New South Wales.'[36]

In the infant colony, those sent to maintain order and uphold the law might transgress, and those who had previously transgressed might become the guardians of society. Being one of great reversal, this situation offered the potential for individual redemption and improvement. A man who had served his sentence or who had had part of it remitted, and who desired to settle, could expect a basic grant of 30 acres, with 20 more if he were married, and 10 for each child. He could expect the government to provide him with tools, seeds, and a few domestic animals, and that he and his family would be fed from the government store for the first year of their endeavour, with perhaps some additional help in subsequent years.[37] While numbers squandered these opportunities, others made good use of them. As they did so they advanced in a way inconceivable in England; and as their fellows saw how hard work and honesty might give access to society's benefits, they also came to see these benefits as rights to follow reformation. Ideas of equality, justice, reform, and social acceptance quickly came to dominate the infant society as massively as did the heads of Port Jackson the entrance to the new world.

The story of James Ruse shows this development better than any other.[38] Ruse was born at Launceston, Cornwall, in 1760, and in that country of stone, ruins, green ridges and abiding seascapes was bred up to a farmer's trade. On 29 July 1782, he was convicted at the Bodmin Assizes of 'burglariously breaking and entering the dwelling house of Thomas Olive about 1 in the Night and stealing thereout 2 silver watches value 5£ and other goods value 10s.' He was sentenced to death, which was then commuted to transportation 'to one of his Majesty's settlements on the coast of Africa for the term of 7 years'. The commuted sentence was never effected. Instead, Ruse spent the next five years in local gaols, and on the *Dunkirk* hulk at Plymouth.

In May 1787, he sailed on the *Scarborough* for New South Wales. In August 1789, having 'shewn a strong inclination to be industrious, and to return to honest habits and pursuits', he pointed out to Phillip that his sentence had expired, and asked for a grant of land. Not having details of the convicts' sentences, Phillip could not be certain of Ruse's claim, and so put off a firm decision. But wishing to encourage Ruse in his private endeavour and to make his attitude more general amongst the colonists, as an interim measure Phillip 'caused two acres of ground [at Parramatta] to be cleared of the timber which stood on them'. Phillip had a third, very pragmatic, motive for favouring Ruse in his requests. He was anxious to discover 'in what time an industrious active man, with certain assistance, would be enabled to support himself in this country as a settler; and for that purpose, in addition to what he caused to be done for him at first, he furnished him with the tools and implements of husbandry necessary for cultivating his ground, with a proportion of grain to sow it, and a small quantity of live stock to begin with'.[39]

Ruse began working his plot in November 1789. Across the first half of 1790, the farmer prepared methodically for grain plantings. He burned the felled trees, dug in the ashes, then turned the ground. He dug in grass and weeds, and turned the soil again. In May, he planted his first wheat, and more in June—3 bushels in all, over 1½ acres. At the end of August, he planted a half-acre of maize. At the end of the year, he harvested about 12 bushels of wheat, and in April 1791 a proportionately much greater amount of maize. On this success, Phillip gave Ruse possession of 30 acres, and built him a house. By the end of 1791, he had 11½ acres under cultivation, mostly of maize, and more cleared. He had four sows, and thirty fowls.[40]

Making progress in his farming, Ruse began to fulfil Phillip's and the Pitt administration's expectations of the whole venture. On 5 September 1790 he married Elizabeth Perry, who had been sentenced to seven years' transportation at the Old Bailey in October 1787, and who had come out to New South Wales in the Second Fleet. In February 1791, Ruse asked that he be taken off the government store, and at the end of the year, he assumed full responsibility for feeding his wife and the daughter who had been born in August. At the same time, he took on a convict labourer, whose ration he also met from his own resources. In 1792, he took on a second labourer.[41] This gathering of independence was a matter of fierce pride for Ruse. In May 1791, on hearing rumours that he was starving, Phillip went to him and offered to put him back on the store. Ruse denied he was in want, and 'absolutely begged permission to *decline* the offer'.[42] As he achieved independence, he regained integrity. In November 1790, he told Tench that the 'greatest check' to his progress was 'the dishonesty of the convicts, who, in spite of all my vigilance, rob me almost every night'.[43] In Phillip's time, neither Ruse nor his wife gave any cause for complaint, and the governor rewarded them accordingly. In February 1792, giving him title over his 30 acres at Experiment Farm, Phillip made James the recipient of the colony's first formal grant of land. In July, Phillip granted Elizabeth an absolute remission of her sentence. In a real sense, this convict pair were Australia's first European settlers; and their story stood as a striking example of what industry and honesty might make of life in the new land.

That life had a number of other distinct benefits, too. January and February were hot and humid months, with temperatures ranging from 20°–30° Celsius and beyond, and violent thunderstorms.[44] Some days were hazy or filled with cloud, or windswept, but others showed the harbour 'as smooth as a Mill-pond', its surface like 'a sheet of molten lead'.[45] In March, April and May, the southeast trades brought in cooler air (15°–21°), days were often hazy or foggy, and there was a good deal of rain, sometimes gales and great rolling seas. By May the heathlands about the settlement were overspread 'with a variety of the most beautiful flowering shrubs',[46] among them the tea-tree, 'bearing an elegant white flower, which smells like English May'.[47] In June and July, the temperature dropped further (10°–20°), there was more rain, and blustery weather, but also 'fair and pleasant' days, and some early spring flowers, such as the parrot pea, appeared. From August onwards, spring gathered force. The temperature began to rise, there were clear days of the most delicate yet intense blue, and the heath- and swamp-lands filled with flowers. By October, when the temperature might rise to 27°, acacias filled the air with scent and sunlight, waratahs and bottlebrushes set witches' fires in the dawns and dusks. The hot weather returned in November and December (15°–38°), with days again growing hazy and cloudy, and with more storms. The hardy banksias and bottlebrushes endured, and there were more flowers with the colours of the religious season—the Christmas bush and the Christmas bell. It was soon clear that the New South Wales environment was conducive to good health. The climate was 'a very fine one', Phillip commented in July 1788, 'equal to any I ever was in', he added in September. In February 1790, when the evidence was all about him, he wrote 'I believe a finer or more healthy climate is not to be found in any part of the world.'[48]

The evidence was the general good health of the colonists. As the voyage was to begin, Hunter compared their situation favourably with those of English country towns of equivalent populations;[49] and, once established, the New South Wales colony continued, despite all the impediments encountered, to gain in the comparison. Without severe winters, and in any case with abundant supplies of fuel available; without epidemics; and with competent medical care for the normal exigencies of life, the colonists did not die in anything like the numbers that the circumstances of other colonizations[50] or of contemporary English towns might have led a percipient observer to expect.

Indeed, not only did they not die, but they bred at a quite unexpected rate. Tench commented in some amazement on the 'great number of births which happened, considering the age, and other circumstances, of many of the mothers. Women, who certainly would never have bred in any other climate, here produced as fine children as ever were born.'[51] Though there were a number of factors involved in this remarkable burgeoning, the more significant one is likely to have been that, despite the long periods of rationing, the basic food intake was sufficient to increase the women's general health to a level where many became fertile again after years of barrenness.[52]

Equally as important, because they were at least adequately fed, and because they were not ravaged by such childhood banes as measles, scarlet fever, whooping cough, and smallpox, the children did not die at the rates then usual in England. While there is uncertainty about exact numbers, it seems that thirty-six or forty-one children landed in January 1788, and that their number had increased (from arrivals on the Second and Third Fleets as well as by births in the colony) to 250 by the end of 1791. In the same period, perhaps thirty-seven had died; so that the infant mortality rate was about 1 in 8, or 125 in 1000. Again, while comparisons can be only approximate, the rate of infant death in New South Wales was distinctly better than that of London then, and rather better than that of England generally (where an infant mortality rate of 160 per 1000 seems to have prevailed until the end of the nineteenth century[53]). By the end of 1792, there were more than 300 children at Sydney, at Parramatta and its environs, and on Norfolk Island;[54] and, in distinct contrast to their counterparts in England, these did not have to enter the labour force at the earliest opportunity, for they were fed from the government store.[55] The question of how they should be prepared for life therefore inevitably arose; and giving great point to the answer was the perception that it was upon these children's avoidance of the evil ways of their or their friends' convict parents that the colony's future well-being ultimately depended.

The common way of inculcating individuals with right values was by giving them an education with a heavy religious component; and the colony's 'rising generation',[56] being free of the need to labour arduously, had the time in which they might be so educated. Phillip's additional instructions provided for his reserving 'a particular spot in or as near each town as possible ... for the building of a church, and four hundred acres adjacent thereto allotted for the maintenance of a minister, and two hundred for a schoolmaster';[57] but by the time he received these in 1790, he had already begun to meet the need. By 1789, Isabella Rosson (later Richardson) was operating a dame school at Sydney under the Reverend Richard Johnson's supervision. Another convict woman, Mary Johnson, opened one at Parramatta in late 1791; and in November 1791 Thomas MacQueen became the first schoolmaster on Norfolk Island. These schools were free to the children of convicts, while officers and marines made a small contribution for their children's attendance. Unfortunately, details of how many children attended are lacking, but those who did were taught to read and write; and these schools clearly met a distinct need. The next year, Phillip told Richard Johnson that if the Society for the Propagation of the Gospel in Foreign Parts would send out additional teachers, he would 'allow them a certain allotment of ground and some assistance to cultivate it'. Alternatively, if the Society would employ Richardson, Johnson, and MacQueen and a fourth person at £10 per annum he would 'continue them in their places'; and further, if the Society wished to expend the £40 rather 'in articles the most useful as wearing apparel, a little soap, tea, sugar &c and direct them to him or the principal commanding officer for the schoolmasters, he will see that they be properly and equally distributed amongst them'.[58]

By the end of 1792, there was no doubt but that the colonization would endure, and shortly prosper. The centre of the Sydney settlement occupied more than 3 acres. In and about it were the brick cottages of the officers roofed with shingles or tiles, a Government House windowed with glass, brick storehouses and a brick hospital, and numbers of convict huts. These buildings were placed with some regularity, so that there was an embryonic township, shaped by roads and streets, delimited by fences. The officers each had 2 acres for cultivation, the hospital had a large garden, and there were over 6 acres of gardens about Government House. At Government Farm, there were stables and storehouses, and convicts grew vegetables, fruits, and maize. Parramatta contained a Government House, about which were 6 acres under maize and other grains, 4 acres under vines, and 2 planted with potatoes. There was a village, with officers' cottages and convicts' huts, the barracks, hospital, hall, and storehouses. Spread about were government cultivations of 1000 acres, and private ones of 400; and a track joined this satellite with Sydney. At Norfolk Island, there was also an embryonic township, with brick as well as timber buildings, and 250 acres of public cultivations. The population of Sydney and Parramatta districts exceeded 3000, and there were more than 1100 persons on Norfolk Island. And though the total was still small in terms of the whole population, the number of these who wished to settle was growing rapidly— 124 in all. A few of these had come out to the colony as officials, more were marines or sailors who had decided to stay. Most, however, were former convicts, who now saw their future lying in the colony. At Parramatta, there were fifty-four persons of this last description; at Norfolk Island three, with another forty-five desirous of joining.[59]

So, under Arthur Phillip's careful supervision, at Port Jackson between 1788 and 1792, a steadily increasing band of colonists laid the basis of a rich and various production, where grains, fruits, vegetables, and flowers from four continents flourished. As they did so, they learned the movement of the native seasons, and established the outlines of what would become the Australian farmer's year, as they sowed wheat in June and reaped it in November; as they sowed maize between July and September, and harvested it the following autumn; as they raised sheep which lambed in July, August, and September; as they grew fruit trees which might bear two crops in a year; as they cultivated gardens which offered vegetables most of the time. Townsmen and watermen followed their pursuits as the landsmen did theirs. Despite the earliest development of the colony's economy remaining obscure, it seems that a basis had also been laid by the end of 1792, with ex-convicts building small boats and carrying goods between Sydney and Parramatta, or between shore and the ships that had begun to enter the harbour in greater numbers; and with a few persons, most of them ex-convicts, acting as middlemen for the ships' captains and the officers who had goods to sell. So began to develop the life of the city which now, in its favoured suburbs, exemplifies beyond all others the magical possibilities of an urban mingling of land, air, and water, and of a society organized on different principles to that from which the colonists had come. Inevitably, there remained inequalities in position or possession, but there was no necessary inequality in essence. No person was forever blighted by his or her past, nor was anyone beyond the censure of the law. Adults had prospects. Children had childhood, and a future. In short, Phillip's New South Wales elaborated ideals towards which modern Australia still strives.

Arthur Phillip was first a practical man, but he was also capable of entertaining larger and more extensive views. He knew from the first that the New South Wales venture involved more than the simple disposal of convicts. He 'would not wish Convicts to lay the foundation of an Empire', he observed in considering the venture in September 1786.[60] He hoped he would not leave the colony, he told Nepean in October, 'till it is in such a State as to repay Government the Annual Expence, as well as to be of the greatest consequence to this Country'.[61] And in July 1788, he described Sydney as the future 'Seat of Empire'.[62] These were muted expressions of an expectation that underlay British consciousness of the colony, and which flew in the face of its obviously unpromising beginnings. From some clay which Phillip sent to Banks, Wedgwood made a medallion showing 'Hope encouraging Art and Labour, under the influence of Peace, to pursue the employments necessary to give security and happiness to an infant settlement'.[63] After seeing this medallion, Erasmus Darwin was moved to have Hope prophesy of Sydney Cove:

> *There* shall broad streets their stately walls extend,
> The circus widen, and the crescent bend;
> *There*, ray'd from cities o'er the cultur'd land,
> Shall bright canals, and solid roads expand.—
> *There* the proud arch, Colossus-like, bestride
> Yon glittering Streams, and bound the chafing tide;
> Embellish'd villas crown the landscape-scene,
> Farms wave with gold, and orchards blush between.—
> *There* shall tall spires, and dome-capt towers ascend,
> And piers and quays their massy structures blend;
> While with each breeze approaching vessels glide,
> And northern treasures dance on every tide![64]

On receiving examples of the medallion, and a copy of the poem, Phillip commented, 'Wedgwood has showed the World that our Welch Clay is capable of receiving an Elegant impression'.[65] We may sense his quiet understanding that he was laying the foundations of more than a convict dump.

Fernando Brambila, 'View of Sydney' (March/
April 1793)

Fernando Brambila, 'View of Parramatta'
(March/April 1793)

Return to England

Phillip had come to New South Wales expecting to make the colony self-sufficient during his term, and his leaving it before he had brought it to that 'state' in which he had 'so long and anxiously wished to see it' caused him considerable disappointment.[1] By the end of 1792 it was clear that the settlement would shortly prosper; and Phillip had cogent reasons for leaving it then. The sheer difficulty of the business—the struggle to overcome the failures of the plantings, the loss of the animals, and the consequent anxieties about future supplies; the long drought; the recalcitrance of the convicts and the dissensions among the officers; the loss of the ships; the failures in relations with the Aborigines—had quite drained him of his energy. The young William Chapman, with whose family Phillip was friendly, reported home in May 1792 that the governor's 'health now is very bad he fatigues himself so much he fairly knocks himself up & wont rest till he is not able to walk'.[2] We may suppose that by this time Phillip was also eager for a respite from the responsibility of being, in the final count, the one person on whose unremitting efforts the success of the whole endeavour depended.

By the end of 1792, Phillip had been in poor health for some years. The precise nature of his illness is unclear. His comment to Banks in July 1790 that 'my complaint is want of Sleep, of which I sometimes dont get more than a few hours in many Nights',[3] suggests that he was suffering from depressive illness brought on by prolonged stress; but there seems also to have been a precise physical cause of his recurrent bouts of pain. It is very likely that he suffered from calcium deposits in his urinary tract, a condition which was then one of the seaman's occupational hazards because of the use of salt to preserve foods. When he began to experience the pain of this condition is not entirely clear. In one letter, he indicates this to have been at the beginning of 1789, but in another he locates it even earlier, after his exploration of Broken Bay in April 1788.[4] What is clear is that the condition grew progressively worse. He told Banks in July 1790 that he had at times 'a severe pain in the Side'. Eighteen months later, he told Sydney that he had lately been suffering more than ever 'from a violent pain in the left Kidney ... [which] renders me at times unable either to ride or walk'.[5] That these were no passing symptoms is shown by Collins's comment on Phillip's departure that 'his health and constitution' were 'much impaired', and particularly by Banks's more forthright report that 'Governor Phillip ... was so ill when he left Sydney as to feel little hope of recovery'.[6]

But it was more than exhaustion of spirit and decay of body that drew Phillip home. He had sailed for New South Wales knowing that his estranged wife was in poor health, and unlikely to live many more years. By early 1790, when he had had no news directly from England for almost three years, he became particularly anxious about what provisions she had made in her will and his attendant legal responsibilities.[7] These were the 'private affairs' to which he referred in his applications for leave to return, even if only temporarily. Knowing how indispensable his services had been to the success of the venture, Grenville was rather coy about granting this, conveying only an implicit permission in the hope that Phillip would decide to stay longer in the colony.[8] In October 1792, in view of this reticence on the part of the Secretary of State, Phillip was inclined to await explicit approval;[9] but the next month his tiredness, his failing health, and his concern for his legal position impelled him to decide to return on the *Atlantic*.[10]

Surveyor of a new world, Phillip left it able to convey its attributes to the old. He took with him two Aborigines, Bennelong and Yemmerrawannie, kangaroos, dingoes, birds, and other animals, plants, and samples of timber and rock, and a portfolio of drawings. And just as ritual had framed his arrival at Sydney Cove, so too did it his departure. As he left to board the ship, he was 'received near the wharf on the east-side ... by Major Grose, at the head of the New South Wales Corps, who paid him, as he passed, the honors due to his rank and situation in the colony'. The *Atlantic* sailed at daybreak on 11 December 1792. By 8 a.m. she was through the Heads.[11] There is no record of Phillip's thoughts precisely as he sailed, but in one of those ironies that so mark his life, he left a planting about to flourish as a desert after rain.

John Easty's journal records the *Atlantic*'s swift passage home. Passing icebergs and running through squalls, she rounded Cape Horn on 17 January 1793, and reached Rio de Janeiro on 7 February. She sailed again on 4 March, and as she proceeded up the ocean from which she took her name, she encountered winds and rain.[12] There is again no record of Phillip's thoughts as each league sailed from the Horn brought him back into the world. We may, however, doubt that he could have conveyed the torrent of feeling inevitable in this homecoming better than Henry Handel Richardson did one hundred years later. Nor can her evocation be improved on by the historian, whose age's technological comforts make it impossible for him to know the old realities of sea and time.

When, having braved the bergs and cyclones of the desolate South Pacific, and rounded the Horn; having lain becalmed in the Doldrums, bartered Cross for Plough, and snatched a glimpse of the Western Isles: when the homeward-bound vessel is come level with Finisterre and begins to skirt the Bay, those aboard her get the impression of passing at one stroke into home waters. Gone alike are polar blasts and perfumed or desert-dry breezes; gone opalescent dawns, orange-green sunsets, and nights when the very moon shines warm, the black mass of ocean sluggish as pitch. The region the homing wanderer now enters is quick with associations. These tumbling crested marbled seas, now slate-grey, now of a cold ultramarine, seem but the offings of those that wash his native shores; and they are peopled for him by the saltwater ghosts of his ancestors, the great navigators, who traced this road through the high seas on their voyages of adventure and discovery. The fair winds that belly the sails, or the head winds that thwart the vessel's progress, are the romping south-west gales adrip with moisture, or the bleak north-easters which scour his island home and make it one of the windy corners of the world. Not a breath of balmy softness remains. There is a rawness in the air, a keener, saltier tang; the sad-coloured sky broods low, or is swept by scud that flies before the wind; trailing mists blot out the horizon. And these and other indelible memories beginning to pull at his heart-strings, it is over with his long patience. After tranquilly enduring the passage of some fifteen thousand watery miles, he now falls to chafing, and to telling off the days that still divide him from port and home.[13]

Avoiding enemy privateers (for England and France were once more at war) she was off Falmouth on 19 May. The next morning, Phillip went ashore to travel overland to London, taking Bennelong and Yemmerrawannie with him.

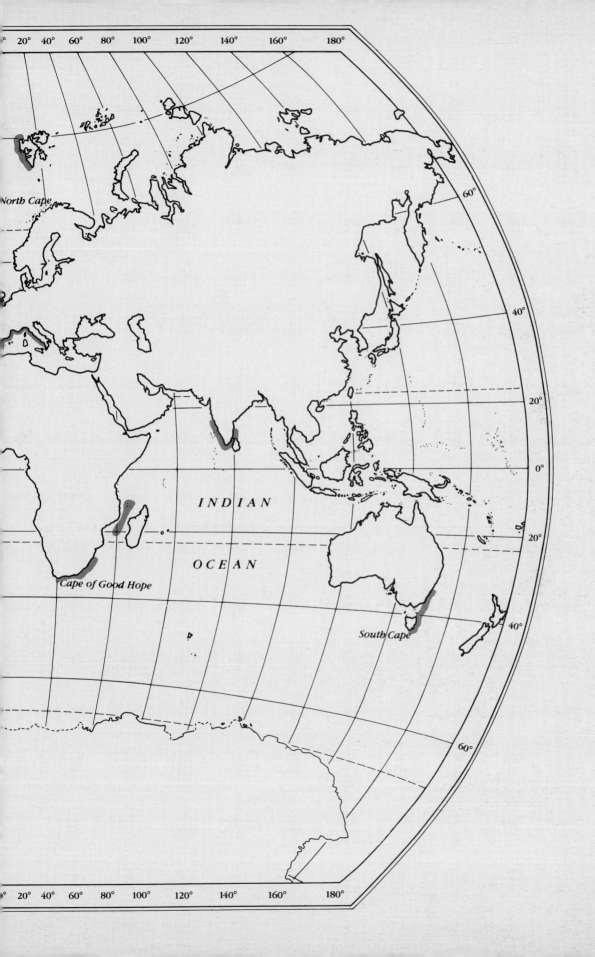

North Cape

INDIAN

OCEAN

Cape of Good Hope

South Cape

PASSING TIME, 1793–1800

I am become a name;
For always roaming with a hungry heart
Much have I seen and known; cities of men
And manners, climates, councils, governments,
Myself not least, but honoured of them all;
And drunk delight of battle with my peers,
Far on the ringing plains of windy Troy.

Tennyson, '*Ulysses*'

Immediately on his arrival in London, Phillip reported to his superiors on the colony's general circumstances and its particular needs. The records of this reporting are sparse, but as much was done in conversation, that is perhaps only to be expected. From casual references, and from actions taken by the administration in the next months and years, we may surmise that Phillip's conversation with officials covered such topics as the need to have suitable ships always stationed at the colony; the need to stock it with animals; the need to contain the rapaciousness of those contracting to transport the convicts; and the need to see that those in authority in the colony pursued the public's interest rather than their own. As part of his reporting, Phillip gave details of the colony's agriculture to Hawkesbury at the Board of Trade; and he discussed New South Wales's natural products with Hawkesbury and Banks.[1] What contact he had with the Aborigines who came with him is unknown. It is reported that Bennelong, at least, was introduced to the King; and that he and Yemmerrawannie disliked London. The pair lived for a time at Eltham in Kent, where Yemmerrawannie died in May 1794. Bennelong returned to New South Wales with Hunter the next year.

The relief from the responsibility of governing the colony, and the long voyage home had not alleviated Phillip's ill-health to any marked degree. He told Hawkesbury on 23 June that he would have presented his returns earlier, 'but that I have been much Indisposed for several days'.[2] At the end of July, after 'being convinced by those I have consulted that the complaint I labour under may in time require assistance which cannot be found in a distant part of the world, and that the time in which such assistance may become necessary is very uncertain', he asked Dundas's and the King's permission to resign his governorship.[3] This he formally did on 10 October, when he was again entered on the Navy's Half Pay lists.[4] In February 1794, he began also to draw the pension of £500 per annum which the administration granted him in recognition of his service in New South Wales.[5]

When he asked for leave to relinquish the governorship, Phillip asked also for 'liberty to leave town' for Bath, saying that while he had given up hope that the waters might remove the pain in his side, he thought they might 'in other respects be beneficial'. In taking this view, he was simply reflecting the limited medical knowledge of his age, which held that the Bath waters helped those afflicted variously with gout, rheumatism, palsies, convulsions, scab, leprosy, scrofula, lameness, colic, consumption, asthma, jaundice, scurvy, scabies, high blood pressure, urinary disorders, piles, deafness, and infertility. Phillip took up residence in Bath in August, at 3 South Parade, and placed himself under the care of Dr Hutton Cooper.[6] The nature of the regimen that Cooper prescribed for his new patient is unknown. If, however, it involved such well-established measures as daily bathing in the vile waters, drinking them, and bleeding, the steady, if slow, improvement that Phillip seems to have experienced over the next months was more a tribute to his body's resilience than it was to the efficacy of the cure. The wonder is not so much that he grew better as that he survived the waters.

One sign of the improvement in Phillip's health is his October 1793 request to the Admiralty to be considered again for active service.[7] Another, perhaps, is the fact of his remarriage. On his arrival home, he had learned that his estranged wife had died the previous year. In her will, she had released him from all the obligations he had entered into when they married and separated; she had freed him of any need to repay debts to the estate; and she had left him a legacy of £100—all provided he did not challenge any other provisions.[8] Wisely, he seems not to have done so. Rather, on 8 May 1794, in London, he took as his second wife Isabella Whitehead.[9] She was the daughter of Richard Whitehead and Elizabeth Sudell, who married at Salmesbury, Blackburn, on 24 January 1744. The Whiteheads and the Sudells were prominent North Country families, with Richard Whitehead possessing seats at Claughton and Blackburn and serving as sheriff of Lancaster in 1759; and the Sudells had been to the fore in Blackburn's economic life for 300 years. Both families were much involved in the cotton and linen weaving industries. During the middle decades of the century, Richard Whitehead and his family lived variously in Blackburn, Preston, and Manchester. Isabella was, seemingly, the second of four children to survive into adulthood; and, being baptized at Blackburn on 2 January 1751, she was presumably born early in December 1750.[10]

Given his associations with the English cloth trade, Phillip's interest in Isabella Whitehead may indicate a previous acquaintance with her family. There is also a simpler explanation of how they may have met. Phillip had something of a scholarly bent—'in him is blended … the Gentleman the scholar and the

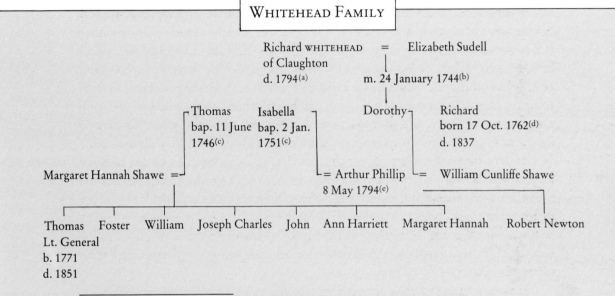

WHITEHEAD FAMILY

Richard WHITEHEAD of Claughton d. 1794[a] = Elizabeth Sudell m. 24 January 1744[b]

Thomas bap. 11 June 1746[c]

Isabella bap. 2 Jan. 1751[c]

Dorothy

Richard born 17 Oct. 1762[d] d. 1837

Margaret Hannah Shawe =

= Arthur Phillip 8 May 1794[e]

= William Cunliffe Shawe

Thomas Lt. General b. 1771 d. 1851   Foster   William   Joseph Charles   John   Ann Harriett   Margaret Hannah   Robert Newton

[a] 'At Bath, Richard Whitehead, esq. of Preston. He was sheriff of the county of Lancaster in 1759', entry for 20 September 1794, *European Magazine* (1794), 310.
[b] St Leonard's, Salmesbury, Marriage register.
[c] Blackburn Cathedral, Baptismal register.
[d] Preston, Lancaster, ADM 107/21:50.
[e] St Mary le Bone, Middlesex Marriage register, Harleian, 53.
This genealogy differs from that of the Whitehead of Claughton family given in Chetham, vol. 105, p. 254, where Isabella does not appear. However, there can be no doubt of Isabella's place. In her will (PROB 11/1668), for example, she mentions her brother Richard, her nephews Lt. Colonel Thomas Whitehead and Joseph Charles Whitehead, her nieces Margaret Hannah (Chadwick) and Ann Harriet Whitehead, and her nephew Robert Newton Shawe, whom she made her sole executor. Despite extensive searches, Richard Whitehead's will has not been found.

seaman', observed one who knew him.[11] Richard Whitehead, then in Bath for the recovery of his health, was a gatherer of books, an interest which his daughter evidently shared. Isabella joined the Bath Circulating Library on 13 August 1793, the day after Phillip did so.[12] It is tempting to entertain the idea that theirs was a romance pursued over books. How intense it was is open to doubt. In attaching himself to Isabella Whitehead, Phillip was following a familiar path. At forty-three she was, as Charlott Denison had been, presumably past child-bearing age. She was also the daughter of a gentleman of affluent means, which soon after became Phillip's, on the death of his father-in-law on 20 September.[13] While Richard Whitehead's will is not to be found, Phillip's references to his father-in-law's effects in his own will indicate that many of these were not conveyed specifically to Isabella.

With his half pay, his pension, and his wife's family's means, Phillip was again in a position to live as a gentleman; and this he proceeded to do, whether in Bath or in London, between which the Phillips oscillated in the middle 1790s at those times when he was not at sea. They mingled with society, entertaining and being entertained by his naval and administration acquaintances and French emigrés, attending card parties, shows, and balls.[14] Amid these pleasures, Phillip involved himself in some serious matters. Most immediately, these concerned the New South Wales colony, in which he continued to be 'greatly' interested.[15] There were the inevitable requests from those who had served under him for help to obtain advancement. This help Phillip gave scrupulously where he thought he justly could, though he tailored the level of his support to his sense of the individual's merit. Between 1794 and 1802, he variously helped Henry Waterhouse, George Johnston, John Hunter, David Collins, Philip Gidley King and Thomas Jamison, as well as lesser officers, to new appointments or to more favourable terms of existing ones.

It was on King's behalf that Phillip made his most strenuous efforts. After unsuccessfully recommending that his protégé should succeed him, he made repeated applications to the administration to have the terms of King's appointment as lieutenant-governor of Norfolk Island altered to compensate him for his loss of seniority in and half pay from the Navy, and to lessen the personal expense of the position. In February 1794 he pointed out to Nepean that King forfeited his naval half pay while he held the civil appointment, and that while the 'Pay & Emoluments' of the lieutenant-governor of the whole colony stood at £1500, that of the administrator of Norfolk Island was only £250. A year later, he extracted a promise from officials that King's salary would be increased to £450, and that he would also have his half pay. But this unusual arrangement required the sanction of the Privy Council, and the wheels of bureaucracy turned slowly. In September 1796, Phillip sought Banks's help to bring the business to a close, pointing out in King's cause that 'he writes badly, but he is an honest man, who is faithfully discharging the trust reposed in him'. In June 1797, when the necessary arrangements had finally been made, King acknowledged to Portland that it was to Phillip's 'representations in my favor that I am indebted to your Lordship's goodness for the increase of my salary'.[16]

At the same time, Phillip continued to offer the administration general advice about the colony. In November 1793, for example, he told John King, Nepean's successor at the Home Office, of the urgency of the need to re-supply the colony and to station a suitable vessel there.[17] As he advised, however, he grew increasingly troubled by reports from the colony, whose life had become more and more dominated by rum. In 1794, he learned that before he had been 'clear of the land, liquor was sent up to Parramatta & the Ewes & Goats I had given to the Settlers to breed from, purchased by those who should have prevented the settlers selling any thing for liquor'. Two years later he told Banks that fresh news indicated that the colonists went on 'as they have done for some time past: [with] individuals making fortunes at the expence of the Crown'. In 1799 he offered the departing Philip Gidley King precise advice about what he needed to do in order to succeed in his governorship, which included 'the sending home those who have been the principal means of ruining the Colony', not granting land to serving officers, and separating the Irish convicts from the rest.[18]

Phillip continued to play these roles of private helper and public adviser into the new century, just as he continued to enjoy life with Isabella. Unlike his first, this marriage seems to have been a happy one, and the social compliments offered by such acquaintances as the Nepeans, the Bankses, the St Vincents and the Nelsons indicate that, though he lacked either the political influence or the social standing or the naval distinction of the one man or the others, he enjoyed their friendship and esteem. Like Tennyson's aging Ulysses, Phillip had seen and known much, 'cities of men/And manners, climates, councils, governments'. Now, as his day began to wane, he found himself 'not least, but honoured of them all'. He also found himself with a hungry heart.

Swiftsure

5

In Search of a Last Glory

Europe, 1793–1805

There lies the port; the vessel puffs her sail:
There gloom the dark broad seas. My mariners,
Souls that have toiled, and wrought, and thought with me—
That ever with a frolic welcome took
The thunder and the sunshine, and opposed
Free hearts, free foreheads—you and I are old;
Old age hath yet his honour and his toil;
Death closes all: but something ere the end,
Some work of noble note, may yet be done,
Not unbecoming men that strove with Gods.

Tennyson, 'Ulysses'

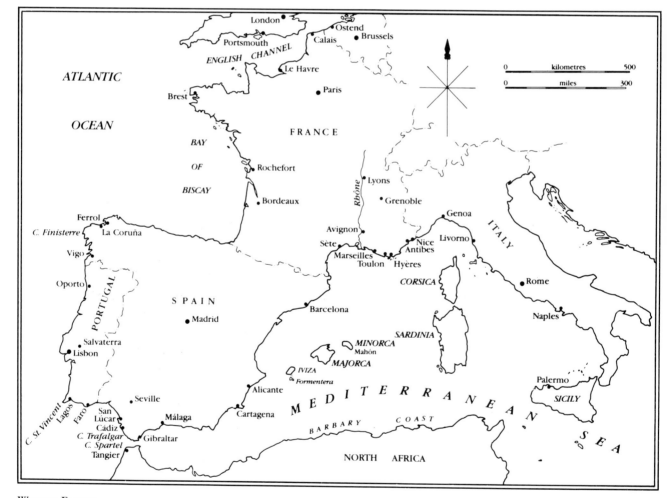

Western Europe

Europe, 1793–1805

In conveying his thanks to Dundas for his pension, Phillip remarked that he hoped in the future to establish another claim for reward, this time for naval service. What he would look to when he had, he said, was a seat on 'either of the Naval Boards, Colonel of Marines, or [governor of] Greenwich Hospital'.[1] This was a not inconsiderable ambition—the great James Cook, for example, had been appointed governor of Greenwich Hospital only after his second voyage; and while it was true that Phillip had done valuable work for previous administrations, particularly in a secret way, it was also true that in 1793 he needed to distinguish himself further before he might offer himself for one or other of the positions he mentioned with any real hope of success. On the other hand, he had certainly done enough to expect, when he recovered his health, the command of a line-of-battle ship. But a peacetime command would not have offered him the opportunity either dramatically to impress his superiors with his worth, or to make his fortune. What he needed to realize his profoundest ambition before old age and general decrepitude forced him into retirement was, to be blunt, war. With a war, he might either distinguish himself in battle, or lead an expedition to capture the enemy's distant colonies, or scavenge sea lanes for rich prizes. Without one, there was very little he might do to brighten his prospects.

Unbeknown to him at the time, Phillip had almost had this opportunity while in New South Wales. In 1789, in assertion of Spain's claim to the exclusive right of trade and navigation along the west coasts of America, the Viceroy at Mexico had sent a small naval force to establish a presence at Nootka Sound, to where British and American traders had begun to go for sea-otter furs. The Spanish commander seized or expelled a number of foreign vessels. When garbled news of this confrontation reached Europe at the beginning of February 1790, the Spanish claimed control of the area as a consequence of first discovery and effective occupation, and argued that the British had no business trading there. In return, the British disputed Spain's priority in discovery and occupation, denied her claim to exclusive control of the northeastern Pacific region, and moved to strengthen their hand by deciding 'to lay the foundation of an establishment for the assistance of His Majesty's subjects in the prosecution of the Fur trade from the North West Coast of America'.[2]

The scheme that Mulgrave and Nepean developed from late February to late March 1790 involved sending the *Gorgon*, a 44-gun ship then being prepared to carry troops and supplies to New South Wales, and the *Discovery*, the sloop intended for a survey of the south Atlantic, to Port Jackson, where Phillip would supply a party to undertake the settlement. These ships would rendezvous in December at the Hawaiian Islands with the frigate which Commodore Cornwallis would simultaneously despatch from India. The squadron would proceed to the northwest American coast in the northern spring, where the officers would demand or enforce satisfaction from the Spanish, establish the settlement, and survey the coast from 40°N to 60°N. When winter came, the *Gorgon* would return to New South Wales, picking up some Maoris en route so that these might instruct the colonists on Norfolk Island in the art of dressing New Zealand flax. Nepean outlined the scheme to the Admiralty at the end of February, and then drafted appropriate instructions for the captains of the ships, for Phillip, and for Cornwallis.[3]

In this scheme, Phillip would have had charge of a small Pacific squadron, and been governor of far-flung imperial outposts. If war had resulted, presumably his zeal would have led him to attempt to ravage the Spanish settlements on the western coasts of the Americas and return like Drake and Anson with treasure. But no sooner did the officials formulate the scheme than they gave it up, when the adventurer John Meares reached London with an inflated account of acts of possession at Nootka. Deciding that these provided an occasion to resolve the issue in Europe, the ministers mobilized the fleet, and demanded that Spain concede. With this change, yet another opportunity of naval distinction slipped by Phillip.

When Phillip returned to England, he found the European situation offered fresh hope to those who dreamed as he did. The French Republicans had declared war on the United Provinces (Holland) and Britain on 1 February 1793, and Pitt and Dundas had already set about the strategy that Pitt's father had used to such effect in the Seven Years War, of subsidizing allies to contain or defeat the French armies in Europe, and of sending naval squadrons and expeditionary forces to destroy France's shipping and to capture her colonies. This strategy initially brought some slight successes, with the British capturing Tobago, and Pondicherry. Simultaneously, Pitt and Grenville brought an allied army together in the Low Countries, which also enjoyed some victories; and arranged joint operations in the Mediterranean with local rulers, which made the resources of Sicily, Sardinia, Corsica, Elba, and Naples available to the British squadron. In August French Royalist forces handed Toulon over to Admiral Hood. Phillip's first offer to return to active service coincided with the British occupation of Toulon.[4] While it is not hard to see why gaining control of the base that was the pride of the French navy might have set him to dreaming again, any dreams he indulged were to no avail, for the Admiralty did not offer him a ship.

Republican forces retook Toulon in December 1793, and events continued to go badly wrong for the British in 1794 as the French mobilized huge armies and progressively defeated the allies. At the end of the year, the British were forced to withdraw their troops from the United Provinces. In 1795 the Dutch Patriots concluded a treaty of offensive and defensive alliance with the French; and the First Coalition collapsed when Prussia and Spain made separate peaces and the Austrians wound down their campaign. There were some naval and colonial victories to weigh against these reverses. Howe defeated a French squadron off the Brittany coast on 1 June 1794; and Sir John Jervis's squadron captured French islands in the West Indies through the year. In 1795 other squadrons captured the Cape of Good Hope, Trincomalee, and Malacca. These losses and gains produced a profound impasse, with Britain in control of the seas and dominant in the West and East Indies, but unable to diminish France's power in Europe.

Such were the political circumstances obtaining when Phillip returned to active service in 1796. After a false start in February, when he travelled from Bath to Portsmouth to take command of the *Atlas*, only to find that she had somehow been given to another, he recommenced active service in March, when he was appointed captain of the *Alexander*, the ship on which he had served as first lieutenant in 1778–79. He joined her in the Hamoaze estuary at Plymouth, remaining there from 16 March to 28 June, when he helped escort a convoy across the Bay of Biscay. He then patrolled until 27 August, when he entered Cawsand Bay. He remained there until 6 October, when he left the *Alexander*[5] to take over, on 20 October, the command of the *Swiftsure*, a 74-gun battleship. She fitted in Portsmouth Harbour until 14 November, when she moved out to Spithead. From 30 November until 12 January 1797, she patrolled with the Western squadron about the Isles of Scilly and Ushant, returning to Spithead via Cawsand Bay on 28 February. As usual, the winter service was arduous, and there was no action of any note to show for it.[6]

The situation in Europe grew steadily worse for Britain during these months, as the French army under Napoleon defeated the allies in Italy. In October, harbouring deeply-felt grievances about Gibraltar, Nootka, and other matters, Spain entered the war on France's side. These developments forced the British to evacuate their land forces from Corsica and Elba, and to withdraw their squadron from the Mediterranean. Gibraltar was thus left extremely vulnerable, and the British squadrons that patrolled in the Atlantic became dependant on access to Portugal's harbours. In February 1797 Sir John Jervis and Horatio Nelson with fifteen ships smashed the much larger Spanish fleet off Cape St Vincent, and blockaded the survivors in Cádiz harbour. The British took advantage of this respite to re-supply Gibraltar; and the *Swiftsure* was one of the warships that escorted the convoy south in April. This service brought Phillip back to the coasts he had first sailed as a youth. This was to be his last opportunity to attain the naval consummation that he dreamed. Like Tennyson's Ulysses, he sailed in search of something before the end; but unlike that archetypal voyager, though he had his wife's brother as his third lieutenant, essentially he sailed without a band of familiar followers, for most of those who had gone with him from ship to ship in the 1780s were dead, or in New South Wales, or serving under other commanders.

The year 1797 was most difficult for the Royal Navy. The immense expansion undertaken to meet the French threat had seen the number of men borne for wages rise from 16 000 in 1792 to more than 118 000. Many of these—perhaps as many as a quarter—were landsmen pressed or otherwise cajoled into the service, some of whom brought with them bitter resentments and democratic notions. In April, disgruntled further by low pay much in arrears and poor food and conditions, the crews of the Channel fleet mutinied at Spithead, and refused to put to sea. Scarcely had the cabinet and the Admiralty met the sailors' reasonable requests when the crews of the North Sea squadron followed suit at the Nore. As Collingwood observed sourly to his sister after these startling events, 'The chief promoters and counsellors in all this business have been what they call Billy Pitt's men, the county volunteers, your ruined politicians, who having drank ale enough to drown a nation, and talked nonsense enough to mad it; your Constitution and Corresponding Society men, finding politics and faction too rare a diet to fat on, took the country bounty and embark'd with their budget of politics and the education of a Sunday's school into the ships, where they disseminated their nonsense and their mischief. Those are the fellows who have done the business, the seamen who suffer are only the cat's paws.'[7]

There were early signs of this unrest on the *Swiftsure*, with Phillip meting out frequent punishments of one or two dozen lashes for drunkenness, theft, and insolence in the first months of the year. But it is another mark of his ability to persuade an unruly group of men to work for the common good that, when it came, the mutiny did not spread to his ship. When Nelson inspected the *Swiftsure* on 9 June, he found a healthy and disciplined crew, with only twenty-six on the sick list, and he reported to Jervis, soon to be made Lord St Vincent in recognition of his victory, that the ship was 'in most excellent Order and fit for any service'.[8] Indeed, the situation on the *Swiftsure* was distinctly superior to that on St Vincent's flagship, where the admiral was forced to severe measures to suppress murmuring.

The *Swiftsure* was off Cape Finisterre on 9 April, and Cape St Vincent seven days later. From then until 27 May, Phillip patrolled into the Atlantic, as far as Madeira. After a four-day break at Lisbon, he sailed for Cádiz Bay where, on 4 June, he joined the blockading squadron under Nelson, and kept this station until 27 September, when he took over the command of the *Blenheim*.[9] Phillip believed that the *Swiftsure* was 'one of the best ships in His Majesty's service';[10] and while, since the *Blenheim* mounted 90 guns, the captaincy of her was notionally a superior appointment, it was in fact a less attractive post. Being in need of repair, the *Blenheim* was distinctly less seaworthy than the *Swiftsure*, and her crew was ill and fractious. The change to her was by no means one that Phillip desired, and it was to prove entirely counter to his interests, as it led to the severest disappointment of his naval life.

From late in 1796, the British had been gravely concerned at the prospect of Spain's overrunning Portugal, with all that that would mean for the Navy's future operations about Atlantic coasts. Following a request from the Portuguese Court for help, the British ministers sent 5000 troops under General Stuart to Lisbon. The simple giving of assistance was not, however, the real aim of the British. From the first, the ministers envisaged that they might rather add Portugal's armed forces to Britain's. Stuart went to Lisbon understanding that the British ambassador there would suggest this change to the Portuguese Court at an opportune moment; and in May and June 1797, St Vincent negotiated for the Portuguese to provide four 'well manned, commanded,

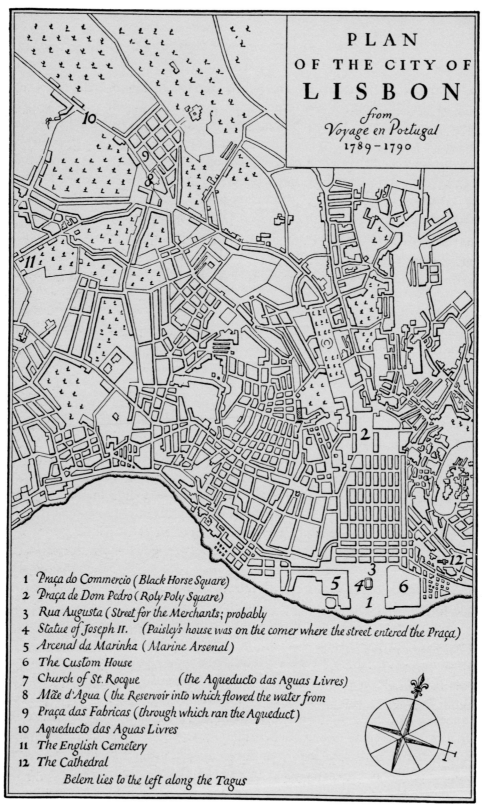

PLAN
OF THE CITY OF
LISBON
from
Voyage en Portugal
1789–1790

1 *Praça do Commercio* (*Black Horse Square*)
2 *Praça de Dom Pedro* (*Roly Poly Square*)
3 *Rua Augusta* (*Street for the Merchants; probably*
4 *Statue of Joseph II.* (*Paisley's house was on the corner where the street entered the Praça*)
5 *Arcenal da Marinha* (*Marine Arsenal*)
6 *The Custom House*
7 *Church of St. Rocque* (*the Aqueducto das Aguas Livres*)
8 *Mãe d'Agua* (*the Reservoir into which flowed the water from*
9 *Praça das Fabricas* (*through which ran the Aqueduct*)
10 *Aqueducto das Aguas Livres*
11 *The English Cemetery*
12 *The Cathedral*
  Belem lies to the left along the Tagus

Artist's impression of Lisbon (*c.* 1790)

and appointed' battleships as 'an Auxiliary Naval Force of Co-operation'. The admiral's idea was, first, to augment this force with three of his ships, so as to form a competent squadron to patrol constantly between the Tagus and Cape St Vincent. His idea was, second, to have this squadron commanded by 'a Native of Great Britain'. At the end of June, in the face of Portuguese resentment, he ostensibly gave this second idea up. When the Portuguese Court announced that the Marquis of Niza would command their squadron, St Vincent replied that 'the moment he appears, I will unite the *Swiftsure, Bellerophon,* and *Audacious* to it, under the Command of Captain Phillip who is an Officer of Merit, and temper, and I am informed gave great satisfaction to the Government of Portugal, while he was employed in the Portuguese Service'.[11] Delay in Portugal's fitting out the ships, though, meant that St Vincent had to approach the matter in another way.

The unrest in the British squadron at this time was not confined to the crews. Charles Thompson, St Vincent's junior admiral, bitterly resented his chief's preference for Nelson; and this resentment burst forth when St Vincent executed two mutinous sailors on a July Sunday. Thompson told his chief publicly that he had 'profaned' the Sabbath; and St Vincent thereupon insisted that the Admiralty choose between him and his deputy. Thompson's consequent recall made vacant the command of the *Blenheim*, and St Vincent told Phillip to take it. The move in fact represented another attempt to establish British control over Portugal's naval forces, for by September the *Blenheim* needed to go at least to Lisbon for repairs, and the admiral sent Phillip in her so that he might be in a position to 'co-operate' with General Stuart there.[12]

Phillip arrived to a most delicate political situation. With Spanish and French forces threatening invasion, there were rumours that the Portuguese might seek a separate peace. In this event, the Pitt administration told their commanders, British forces were to withdraw from Portugal; but if Portugal were to resist the enemies, the British should offer her every assistance.[13] The clear implication was that this latter event would justify Britain's taking control of Portugal's forces. General Stuart would inevitably become commander of the troops, and Phillip's 'merit, and temper', and his reputation with the Portuguese made him a natural choice to command their warships. As commodore of an Anglo–Portuguese squadron, he would have had opportunities to distinguish himself in battle, and to enrich himself with prize money. As he afterwards wistfully told Sydney, 'Lord St. Vincent proposed [the move to the *Blenheim* and Lisbon], it was a compliment he paid me, & had the event then expected in Portugal taken place, my situation would have been more desirable than that of remaining off Cadiz'.[14]

Immediately on his arrival, Phillip set about renewing his links with the

Portuguese authorities, and during the three months he was based at Lisbon he followed St Vincent's orders precisely. These included the taking of secret instructions to Sir John Orde at sea in late November, and preparing the way for expected events. St Vincent praised Phillip warmly for his efforts,[15] which proved to be entirely fruitless. They were so for two reasons. First, the expected Spanish–French attack did not arrive. Second, in February 1798 Phillip was abruptly superseded in his command, when Rear-Admiral Frederick arrived from England with his own captain, and insisted on hoisting his flag in the *Blenheim*. Though St Vincent wished to oblige Phillip, he did not find himself able either to resist Frederick's wish, or to give the *Swiftsure* back to Phillip. Phillip was, as he himself told Nepean, 'obliged to come on shore, under the most mortifying circumstances'.[16] Bitterly disappointed, he returned immediately to England. It was in any event a galling manner in which to end a long naval career; but future ones were to make it even more so, when the *Swiftsure* was one of the squadron under Nelson that destroyed Napoleon's fleet at Aboukir Bay. In one bleak Lisbon day, Phillip's last hopes for naval glory vanished like fine sand through a beachcomber's fingers.

Phillip arrived at Falmouth on 2 March 1787.[17] Four weeks later, the Admiralty found him some compensation, when it appointed him commander of the Hampshire Sea Fencibles.[18] This organization was then being established to provide a home defence force of volunteers from among the 'fishermen and other persons occupied in the ports and on the coast who, from their occupations, are not liable to be impressed'.[19] The members were to be trained in the use of cannon and pike, and were to man the Martello fortifications that the Admiralty established according to a plan by St Vincent, and the signal stations established according to one by Keith. They were to put to sea in small boats if the French attempted an invasion.

Taking a house at the corner of Ashley Lane,[20] from April 1798 until the end of 1803 Phillip based himself at Lymington, the old, narrow-streeted port standing below the New Forest, on the west bank of the Lymington River where it enters the Solent. He had two local captains under him, and in the first twelve months they recruited over 300 men at Lymington, Redbridge, and Gosport, whose training Phillip oversaw with the same attention to detail as that he had shown in New South Wales. In April 1799 he could say that sixty-six men had attended the last exercise at Lymington, and sixty-one at Redbridge. Though only fifteen had appeared at Gosport, he reported that the men enrolled there, 125 in all, wished him to say that 'they are ready to come forward in case of any alarm, although they do not regularly attend on the days of exercise'. Fears of being forced into the Navy went a long way to explaining the reluctance to attend training. Part of Phillip's business was to issue certificates of exemption, but these were not always efficaceous. Thomas Jenkins, for example, an inhabitant of Redbridge, received a protection to sail on the local boat *John and Elizabeth* on joining the Fencibles in April 1798, but was pressed at Plymouth in August. Another part of Phillip's business was therefore to obtain the release of persons wrongly pressed.[21]

Early in February 1801, Pitt suddenly resigned as prime minister. Ostensibly, this was for the reason that historians have long accepted—the King's obstinate refusal to countenance in the slightest way Pitt's promise to the Irish Catholics of electoral and parliamentary reform. Recent research suggests that there was another significant reason, which might also have been the more profound. Pitt's close friend and long-time adviser Henry Dundas, and his cousin William Grenville had become bitter ministerial enemies over questions of objectives and strategy, and he could no longer cope with their enmity.[22] Dr Henry Addington, the speaker of the House of Commons, formed a new ministry; and this began to discuss terms of peace with the French in March 1801. As negotiations proceeded, the new administration disbanded the Sea Fencibles, and closed down the signal stations.

The peace negotiations were protracted, and as they proceeded the Admiralty, of which St Vincent was now head, found other work for Phillip. In April, he and two other officers inspected the ships and hospitals at Portsmouth, Porchester, and Forton where French and Spanish prisoners of war were confined. It was work for which Phillip's knowledge of languages and experience in New South Wales made him well suited; and the reports that he and his colleagues produced show a typical concern for the welfare of the prisoners and a desire to reduce abuses by supervising officers and surgeons, and contractors. They paid particular attention to the cleanliness of the ships and hospitals; and among their recommendations were those that surgeons should stay aboard the ships and not pursue private practice ashore, and that one contractor should stop making bread from inferior flour.[23]

Phillip had risen by seniority to rear-admiral of the Blue in January 1799, and some of his old embers must have continued to glow as he went about his unglamorous work in these years. In May 1801 he again offered himself for a sea command. St Vincent replied that he would take 'great pleasure' in giving him an appointment, and showed his regard for his former captain when he said that he rejoiced 'most exceedingly that the occasion of your offering your Services in a limited Sense is removed'.[24] However, the First Lord does not seem to have found an opportunity to compensate Phillip for the misfortune at Lisbon before the nations reached an uneasy peace in March 1802.

Still, there was further work for Phillip. In July 1801, the Lords Commissioners asked Phillip to undertake a thorough inspection of the Impress Service.[25] The habit of recruiting men for naval service either by offering them a financial incentive (an 'imprest') or by more coercive means, had reached full flower in the eighteenth century, as the Royal Navy's need for crewmen grew ever greater. Legally, only 'seafaring' men—those 'who used the sea'—were liable to be 'pressed' into the King's service, but exemptions for those in 'essential trades' such as fishing, barge traffic, and coastal carriage limited the numbers eligible. Recruits were obtained by 'gangs' who worked the land and coastal waters. Those that scavenged ashore were usually about twenty strong, and were led by a lieutenant and a mate. The gang's first move was to establish a 'rendezvous', to which those wishing to enlist might come, and those unwilling be brought. The rendezvous was almost invariably a tavern, where the enthusiastic or gullible were lulled by drink, and the reluctant confined in a strongly-built room. From the rendezvous, recruits were transferred under guard to a press tender for transport to a warship. The activities of these shore gangs were overseen by 'Regulating' captains, who were usually old naval officers no longer fit for sea command. By the end of the eighteenth century, there was a regulating captain in each major port, and also in a number of lesser ones. There was also pressing, at sea, from among the crews of returning merchant vessels. This was done by tenders manned from ships in commission, under the authority of commanders-in-chief. To have men available to replace those pressed and to see the ships into port, these latter tenders usually had a crew of between thirty and forty, under the command of a lieutenant.

Because of the coerciveness of the business, and of the brutality that often accompanied it, the Impress Service was unpleasant to perform and unpopular with the country, and gangs sometimes encountered comprehensive opposition from the individuals whom they wished to seize and from local populations. In 1779, for example, a midshipman escorting four pressed men from Lymington to Southampton was stopped in the New Forest by armed horsemen, and forced to release his charges.[26] In 1780 the captain of a Liverpool privateer led a party of eighty armed men to free fifteen of their fellows from a press room.[27] In 1803, on learning that a gang had arrived, Portland seamen sought the help of the quarrymen. A pitched battle ensued between the gang under Captain George Wolfe, and the force of 300 locals armed with muskets, pistols and cutlasses. Four of the local men were killed, sixteen of Wolfe's marines wounded, and the captain came away with only five captives.[28] Civil authorities also obstructed, and often actively opposed, the operations of the gangs. In 1744 London authorities imprisoned one entire gang.[29] In 1791 the mayor of Dover personally broke down the doors of a press room to liberate one of the town's freemen.[30] Two of the leaders of the opposition to Captain Wolfe's gang were the mayor of Weymouth's constables.[31] And it was by no means uncommon for officers who led gangs to face charges of assault, manslaughter, and even murder.

Those leading sea-gangs had an even more difficult task, as sailors who had the end of one long voyage in sight went to any lengths to avoid beginning another immediately in a King's ship. The crews of returning Indiamen would abandon their ships in the Downs, so as to avoid the Navy's waiting press tenders. In October 1745, for example, Vernon waited there for the convoy expected from the West Indies. Despite a great sea, he reported to the Admiralty, he had out his squadron's boats, but he feared that they would not take many of the incoming sailors, 'as they are as industrious to avoid [impressment] as we can be to execute it'.[32] The Bristol pilots regularly carried returning sailors ashore surreptitiously.[33] Sailors confronted by press tenders might also resist the ministrations of the gangs strenuously. In 1742 the men on the *John and Elizabeth* repelled the crews of three tenders with crowbars, boathooks, and muskets.[34] In 1779 Captain Dods's gang killed two men in the course of pressing thirty-two from a Greenland whaler returning to Shields. Dods reported to the Admiralty, 'I said everything I could think of to induce them to enter [the Navy], or surrender themselves quietly, but their answer was that they were determined to die rather than be taken and that they would destroy every man that should attempt to come on board; the shores on both sides were lined with people who insulted me and all the officers with me in the grossest manner.' He had fired on the whaler's crew, Dods continued, only as the ship was escaping downstream, and after his men had asked him to; and now he feared for his life if he remained at his station. The Admiralty's advice to its unfortunate servant was to leave England before he was charged with murder.[35]

Dods's story serves to indicate just how unpopular impressment was. Even if they exaggerated, the views were widespread that it ruined trade by carrying off the men needed to promote it; and that, despite what judges might say, it was inherently lawless, violating the tenets of the Magna Carta and being only kidnapping dressed up. One severe critic spoke for many when he said, '[It] sets up numbers of little tyrants in all our seaports, when you shall see droves of these lawless fellows, armed with great sticks, force such as they think proper into the service and knock down any who will not submit to appear before their magistrate, who is sometimes a lieutenant, but oftener an officer of the lowest rank in an alehouse at Wapping or St Catharine's, a midshipman, a boat-swain's mate, or some such like judge of liberty and property'.[36]

Rather than exhibiting scruples about the morality of the business, though, St Vincent and his colleagues were concerned about its cost and effectiveness. In considering how few men were recruited and at what expense, they told Phillip, they suspected that 'either proper exertions have not been made by some of the Officers employed on that service, or that there have been great abuses and mismanagement in the expenditure of the Public Money'. They therefore wished him to investigate the operation of the service in the ports along England's southern coast, and the eastern and western coasts into Scotland.[37] Accompanied by a secretary, Phillip began his inspection in Scotland. In August he travelled south through the ports of Yorkshire, Lincolnshire, Norfolk and Suffolk, and in September and October he moved along England's southern coast, through Deal, Gosport, Southampton, Exmouth, Plymouth, and Falmouth.[38]

Phillip was an appropriate choice for this difficult task. He had seen a good deal of the Impress Service from both sides. As fourth lieutenant of the *Egmont* in 1770–71, he had recruited in London; and as captain of warships in the 1780s and 1790s he had pressed men in his crews. Then, as commander of the Sea Fencibles in Hampshire, he had supervised men anxious to avoid impressment. Also, his years in New South Wales had given him a wealth of experience in the management of a large body of men and large and intricate accounts, and of subordinates who benefited from abusing a system and who were therefore unwilling to co-operate in investigating it.

The comprehensive report which Phillip produced at the end of the year shows his customary diligence.[39] Prominent among the ways of avoiding impressment, he had found, were the false registering of young men as apprentices, and the having civil authorities issue warrants for debt against those seized, which precluded their being sent to sea. He deprecated the current practices of parish officials getting rid of undesirables by reporting them as deserters from the Navy or sailors, for these generally proved to be as useless to the service as they were to the parish; and of 'Officers attending the Quarter Sessions, Petty Sessions, and Magistrates', when they were liable to be 'persuaded to receive a Man who is soon after turned out of the Service as unfit for it, and who they would not have received at the Rendezvous', and when attendance 'occasions an expence and loss of time'; and that of 'detaining the Men raised at the Rendezvous, a longer time than what is absolutely necessary', which led to the loss of many.

Among the reforms Phillip proposed were changes in methods of bookkeeping and the reconciliation of accounts, and the standardization of expenses allowed to the regulating captains. He suggested that central registers of 'protections' (i.e., exemptions) be set up, and all apprentices exempted be listed at the Admiralty office. He thought that group exemptions might be offered to boats' crews in return for one volunteer for every five or six men. He also thought that it would be better to draw the officers who ran the service from guard ships, for they might then be the more easily 'exchanged if it was necessary'; and that there should be greater discipline amongst gang members. How much attention the Admiralty paid to these suggestions is unclear.

Isolated in Europe, and with her naval resources stretched to breaking point by the Second Armed Neutrality, Britain desperately needed peace in 1801. The terms which Napoleon insisted on required that Britain restore what she had captured in the colonies, but allowed her no counterbalancing gains in Europe or influence in European affairs. In agreeing to peace, the First Consul was in reality only giving himself and France a breathing space in which to prepare for further expansion. This he immediately set about doing, and his preparations soon impelled the anxious British to counter ones. As the naval historian William James observed, from the commencement of the peace, 'the activity which reigned on the ocean ... [was] much greater than any which had been witnessed during the last two or three years of the war, [and] gave to the treaty the air of a truce, or suspension of arms, in which each of the belligerents, some of whom signed it for no other purpose, was striving to gain an advantageous position, in order, when the tocsin should again sound, to be ready for the recommencement of hostilities. French, Dutch, and Spanish fleets were preparing to put to sea; and English fleets, to follow them and watch their motions: who, then, could doubt that, although the wax upon the seals of the treaty concluding the last had scarcely cooled, a new war was on the eve of bursting forth?'[40]

Amid this welter of anticipation, Phillip again brought himself to notice. In January and October 1802 he lent his charts of the harbour at Rio de Janeiro, of Rio Grande, and of Colonia do Sacramento to the Hydrographic Office for copying. His providing this information about South American locations presumably relates to the advancing of invasion schemes by Craig, Abercromby, Colnett, Popham and others in the preceding years, schemes which were revived immediately on the resumption of war. As Popham's, especially, provided for part of the force destined to liberate Spanish America to sail via New South Wales, we may assume that Phillip's was one of the opinions sought by the officials who considered the idea.[41]

In July 1802 Phillip once more offered his services to St Vincent, asking specifically to be appointed Admiral in the Leeward Islands. This was a position for which his experience in the Seven Years War and his seniority equipped him well. The First Lord replied that the post would 'be filled up as soon as the conquered Colonys are restored to France and Batavia, and I shall have great pleasure in naming you to the King as a fit person to succeed to it, if that command suits your ambition'. In the event, Phillip did not receive this post, but early the next year St Vincent asked him if he would like the command of the warships based in Ireland. Given the widespread unrest in that island in the previous years and Napoleon's attempts to forge links with the rebels, this was an important, if unspectacular, position. Phillip's failure to accept it presumably indicates that for some reason it was not to his taste.[42]

By the beginning of 1803 it was clear to the governments of both Britain and France that the renewal of war might not be much further delayed. Among its many preparations, the Admiralty revived the Sea Fencibles under the general command of Admiral Keith, with Phillip commencing *ad hoc* inspections of the force in southern England in January.[43] At the end of the year, the Lords Commissioners appointed him inspector of the whole force, as well as of the Impress Service.[44] Again accompanied by a secretary, he travelled repeatedly between December 1803 and January 1805, inspecting centres in Kent, Essex, Suffolk, Norfolk, Lincolnshire, Yorkshire, Northumberland, Scotland, Lancashire, Wales, Somerset, Devon, Cornwall, and Hampshire. It was an anxious time for Britain, as Napoleon once more gathered invasion forces in northern French ports, and ordered boats and barges to carry them across the Channel; and the officers of both services redoubled their recruitment efforts. In his comprehensive return of February 1805, Phillip reported that since December 1803 5128 men had been pressed into the Navy, 5978 seamen had volunteered for service, together with 3211 landsmen and 1285 boys, and the magistrates had sent 559 vagrants and criminals.[45] While such exact figures are not available for those enrolled in the Sea Fencibles in the same period, it is likely that these numbered approximately 20 000.[46]

In the absence of any detailed study of the Sea Fencibles, it is difficult to know how to appraise Phillip's work in these years, particularly as contemporary opinions are contradictory. At the end of 1803 Pitt, for example, considered that this corps' branches were 'calculated to answer every object for which they were first formed,' that 'they will be found superior to any flotilla they may have to encounter,' and that the men's 'exertions will prove such as to gratify the expectations of the Country'.[47] Two years earlier, though, Nelson had thought that its members would 'come forth when the country prepares for fighting and all business stands still,' but that they were 'no more willing to give up their work than their superiors'. And by mid-1803 St Vincent himself had decided that the corps as then expanded was of little use other than 'to calm the

[Port Jackson Painter], 'A New South Wales native striking fish while his wife is employed fishing with hooks & lines in her Canoe'

[Port Jackson Painter], 'A woman of New South Wales curing the head ache, the blood which she takes from her own gums she supposes comes along the string from the part affected in the patient. This operation they call Bee an ee.'

[Port Jackson Painter], 'The Governor making the best of his way to the Boat after being wounded with the spear sticking in his Shoulder'

[Port Jackson Painter], 'Ban nel lang meeting the Governor by appointment after he was wounded by Wille ma ring in September 1790'

fears of the old ladies'.[48] Typically perhaps, Phillip's opinion lay somewhere between these poles. By 1805, because at many centres of recruitment there were 'neither Ships of Force, Gun Boats, or Batteries,' he did not see what useful service numbers of the men might be able to perform; but 'where there are Batteries at which they have been exercised, they will in every respect answer the purpose of a Corps of Artillery: and in Gun Boats, or Ships of War, their great utility cannot be doubted'.[49]

While we might incline to value the opinion of the admirals over the politician's, none the less the organization of a coastal defence force on a national scale was an innovation. Phillip's work as inspector of both the Impress Service and the Sea Fencibles led to more efficient and more widely spread recruiting, and the results, at least in terms of numbers, were impressive. But the very success of the Sea Fencibles scheme brought a serious problem. No matter how much the presence of tens of thousands of trained defenders might allay the populace's anxiety about invasion, it did little to help the Navy meet its ever greater need of men to work its ships. Indeed, in a particular way it mitigated against the meeting of this need, for many who volunteered for the Sea Fencibles did so to gain immunity from impressment. Phillip himself saw this conflict early. After his first term as inspector of the Impress Service, he had observed that 'the receiving as Sea Fencibles, Shipwrights and men employed on the water prevented a great number of good men from being brought into the Service, during the last three Years of the War'.[50] When inspector of both services between 1803 and 1805 he was particular to distinguish from the generality of the Sea Fencibles those 'who reside within the District: but who are not married, or have families,' and who were therefore prime candidates for the impressment that the Admiralty tried to achieve.[51] In December 1803, in reporting on the prospects of establishing an impressment rendezvous at Newhaven on the Sussex coast, Phillip suggested that if the two services were to operate there, they should do so under a single command.[52] And in February 1805, he thought that the numbers of Sea Fencibles might be reduced so as to free seafaring men for naval service proper.[53] At the end of the year, the Admiralty acted on this advice, deciding to amalgamate the two services so as to remove the conflict.[54]

By the time this had happened, though, Phillip was well-ensconced in retirement. He had risen by seniority to rear-admiral of the White Squadron in April 1804, but there could only be a limited number of flag appointments and his days of commanding at sea were clearly over. Then in his mid-sixties, he must have found his work of inspection increasingly arduous, with its constant travel, often in uncomfortable coaches over rudimentary roads. It also allowed him only brief respites in which to enjoy domestic comfort. At least for some of this time Mrs Phillip lived at Bathampton, on the eastern edge of Bath, where the couple had friends; and Phillip was able to spend a few weeks there in June and July 1804. He had other breaks when in London to report to the Admiralty, which allowed him to see old friends such as Nepean, Osbert Standert, and the Lanes. Welcome as these breaks must have been, they could scarcely have been sufficient to succour his health, which his periodic reports of 'accidents' indicate to have been growing increasingly fragile. Still, it seems that Phillip did not retire voluntarily. In December 1804 the Admiralty replaced him as inspector of the eastern half of the country with Admiral George Berkeley; and the following February the Lords Commissioners told him to close his accounts and to consider his appointment 'at an end'.[55] A week later, when he offered to continue inspections in the 'Western District, or any part thereof', they evidently did not accept this offer.[56]

It is difficult to know what to make of this dismissal. It might simply reflect a change of heart about the Sea Fencibles. Keith's advice to Berkeley suggests that the latter was appointed to reduce the Force 'to a limited number which would not only decrease the expense but throw many reliable men into one or other of the services'—a policy rather antithetical to that Phillip had pursued for the previous six years.[57] It is true, however, that a new Admiralty Board under Henry Dundas, now Lord Melville, had been formed on Pitt's retaking office in May 1804, so that Phillip had lost St Vincent's patronage. Yet he was no stranger to Dundas, who had warmly praised his work in New South Wales,[58] and Pitt had simultaneously appointed Evan Nepean a Lord Commissioner, so that we might suppose that his 'interest' at the Admiralty had been strengthened. The continuance of his appointment to the end of the year suggests that this was so, at least for a time. But what also seems likely is that Phillip stayed too long. In December 1803, responding to the Lords Commissioners' instructions to begin his second tour of inspection, he told Nepean 'I have to request that you will please to represent to [them] ... that in case an Enemy should attempt to land on that part of the Coast where I may be in the execution of the Service on which I am directed to proceed: my situation would ... be very unpleasant, unless their Lordships are pleased to Authorise me to take the Command of such Armed Vessels, Gun Boats, & Sea Fencibles, as may be there for the defence of the Coast; on the Appearance of an Enemy. Should my flag be hoisted onboard any Armed Vessel, on such an occasion, it would be for such particular Service only, immediately after which I should proceed according to my Instructions.' He ended this request with the hope that 'their Lordships will not see any impropriety in my making [it]'. But their Lordships did indeed consider it improper, for it would have usurped the authority of those to whom they had given the major commands; and they saw 'no grounds whatever for complying with [it]'. Presumably feeling the chagrin that a blunt admonishment would cause his old friend, Nepean diminished the Lords Commissioners being 'not a little surprized that it should have been made to them' to their directing him 'to confine himself solely to the objects pointed out in his Instructions'.[59] Only a week later, however, Nepean had to issue another caution over a different matter, telling him that 'applications upon subjects unconnected with the Duty on which he is employed, ought not to be received or transmitted by him'.[60] Twelve months further on, the new Lords Commissioners seem to have acted to retire a long serving and meritorious officer whom old age was making frail, and whose frustrated ambition to win naval glory was increasingly clouding his judgement. It was a dismissal which hurt Phillip deeply. As he was, he remarked in his letter to Melville, 'desirous of taking up as little of your Lordship's time as possible', he reported only briefly on the Sea Fencibles. When, five days later, he reported on the Impress Service, he observed that he did so even though he had closed his accounts and considered his appointment at an end; and he concluded with: 'I will not take up their Lordships time with any further observations and remarks.'[61] It could not but be a disappointing career's end for someone who had ranged the coast of Europe and drunk the heady wine of battle in northern and southern hemispheres, who had doubled the world's great capes, who had once returned from planting the Antipodes.

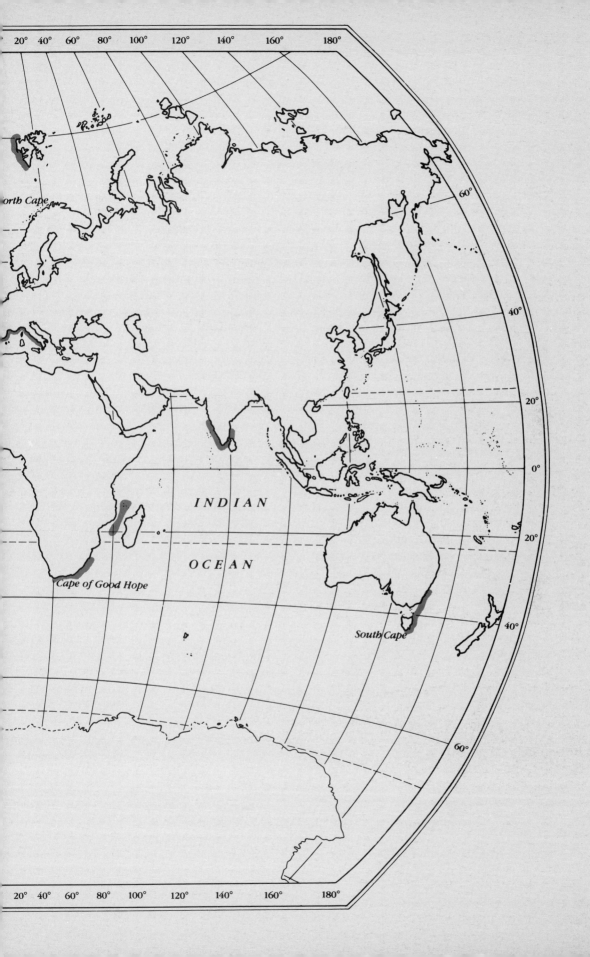

AMONG HIS PEOPLE, 1805–14

Heureux qui, comme Ulysse, a fait un beau voyage,
Ou comme celui-là qui conquit la toison,
Et puis est retourné, plein d'usage et raison,
Vivre entre ses parents le reste de son âge!

Happy is the person who, like Ulysses, has made a good journey,
or, like Jason, has gained the Golden Fleece,
and then returned, full of experience and wisdom,
to enjoy the comfort of his family the rest of his days.

Joachim du Bellay, 'Heureux qui, comme Ulysse'

The details of Phillip's life for most of 1805 and 1806 are largely unknown. A local tradition says that he and his wife passed some weeks or months at Bathampton during these years,[1] and it may be that they effectively resided there, for they were subsequently buried in the parish church.

In December 1806 the couple purchased the dwelling at 19 Bennett Street, Bath, for £2200. Designed by John Wood the Younger, this had been built in 1744, and consisted of three substantial floors, with a basement below and attic above. The basement held a kitchen, scullery, pantry, housekeeper's room, and cellar. On the ground floor there was an entrance hall, and breakfast and dining rooms. A stone staircase led to the three drawing rooms on the first floor, then to the four bed- and dressing-rooms on the second floor. The attic was divided into four servants' rooms.[2] The contemporary description of 19 Bennett Street as a 'Commodious and Gentlemanly Dwelling House' is an apt one.[3] Gathering about them a more than adequate stock of linen, china, silver plate, wines and liqueurs, and books the Phillips made the house also a comfortable one. It was an eligible address, from which they might very conveniently promenade to mingle with the like-minded souls in the Circus, the Royal Crescent, and the Park, and enjoy the musical entertainments at the adjacent Assembly Rooms. In Bath, in short, Phillip lived the life of a retired gentleman.

Almost none of Phillip's own papers from this period survives, and the absence of Isabella's papers is total. Still, references scattered through the diaries of Christina Fanny Chapman allow us to glimpse the nature of the couple's life then. Isabella received and returned visits from a circle of women friends, visits in which Phillip participated so long as his health permitted. One can assume that he himself enjoyed the company of other naval officers retired to Bath, such as Admirals Alexander Christie and Robert Mann. From time to time, too, he saw old friends who travelled to the city, such as Philip Gidley King in November 1807.

As we lack Phillip's father-in-law's will and his own and his wife's papers, we cannot be certain precisely from where the couple had the resources to underwrite this life. Clearly, the Whitehead family was one of considerable means; and Phillip himself now had a more than useful income, with his pension of £500 and his admiral's half pay of £750 per year. But while all these factors no doubt significantly contributed to their prosperity, in the absence of others such as large prize money, they do not entirely explain it. The value of Phillip's estate on his death approached £20 000, with his being able to leave his wife £8300 in Old South Sea Annuities, and substantial legacies to other members of his family.[4] Perhaps he had made some investments earlier in his life which bore good fruit in the high inflation of the French wars, but this is only a guess. Certainly, though, he had not returned from New South Wales enriched; and his first wife had only barely remembered him in her will.

In New South Wales, in an extreme moment, Phillip had professed himself ready to meet his fate, 'let it be whatever it would'.[5] Then, Fate had kindly deferred their ultimate encounter. Now, it gave fresh notice of its intent. On Saturday 20 February 1808, he suffered a stroke, and hovered near death for twenty-four hours. After showing some improvement, he survived another crisis two weeks later, but by the beginning of April he was well enough to see visitors again.[6] While he retained his intellect, the stroke had serious physical effects, leaving him paralysed throughout his right side. Aged seventy, his future could not but be bleak. As Philip Gidley King remarked after seeing him in May, 'He may linger on some years under his present infirmity, but, from his age, a great reprieve cannot be expected.'[7]

Weakened though he was, Phillip was to live another six years, during which he did rather more than linger. He had an iron railing fitted to the staircase wall, so that he might haul himself up the stairs. As he recovered somewhat physically, he received old acquaintances. Henry Waterhouse came to see him in March, and Philip Gidley King in May and September 1808.[8] John Hunter came in July 1811.[9] These visits must have given him considerable satisfaction, bringing him as they did news of a prospering colony and memories of his time there a quarter of a lifetime ago. He appeared again when Isabella had company, and mostly with her, but sometimes alone, he resumed social calls, and such concomitant activities as dinners and card games. From time to time he even ventured beyond Bath, as when he travelled to Oxford in November 1809, and when he and Isabella spent the summer of 1810 on the coast at Charmouth, near Lyme Regis. The next year they spent two summer months at Clifton, near Bristol, 24 kilometres away, where he met the architect Francis Greenway, whose talents Macquarie was shortly to employ to give the New South Wales colony a permanence previously lacking; and they seem to have departed Bath also in the summer of 1812.[10]

While Phillip's health was better at some times than at others in these years, clearly it was in general precarious; and it is a mark of his determination that he lived as long as he did after the stroke. It is possible, however, that his courage failed at the end. There are rumours that he committed suicide by pushing himself from the window of an upper floor. These rumours seem to have arisen only in the twentieth century, and there is no evidence to support them, but it is not impossible that they convey the bleak reality of the final moment of an old man tired of his decrepit body.[11] Phillip died on 31 August 1814, as he was approaching seventy-six, and was buried in the Church of St Nicholas at Bathampton on 7 September 1814,[12] three months after he had risen by seniority to admiral of the Blue Squadron.[13]

Isabella Phillip continued to live at 19 Bennett Street after her husband's death. While almost all details of her life there are unknown, it seems that her means progressively diminished. In 1815 and 1816 she approached the administration for the continued payment of her husband's pension, as had been earlier promised,[14] and when she died on 7 March 1823, the value of her estate did not exceed £5000. There is no ready explanation for this loss of prosperity. At her request, she was buried beside her husband in the Bathampton Church.

In her will,[15] Isabella Phillip left the portrait of her husband painted by Francis Wheatley to Harriet Lane, and his diamond ring to Lady Nepean; and she appointed her sister Dorothy's son Robert Newton Shawe the sole executor of her estate. The portrait went from the old Lane house at Peckham to the National Portrait Gallery in 1907; the Nepean family has lost trace of the ring; and the whereabouts of whatever of her effects Shawe may have taken from the house are unknown. On Isabella's death, in short, Arthur Phillip's papers and effects vanished, not—with only a very few exceptions—to be recovered. The absence now teases the would-be biographer out of thought as does eternity.

Francis Wheatley, Governor Arthur Phillip (1786)

Arthur Phillip, 1738–1814

'Fortune smiles when we least think of it', Edward Spain wrote years after Arthur Phillip had dismissed him as boatswain of the *Europe*, and continued sourly, 'Who would have thought it that Captain [Phillip] a man of no great family without any connections should be appointed comodore and governor of a new Colony to be established in new holland?'[1]

Though not that of a Cook or a Nelson, Phillip's career was certainly distinctive. He was born the son of an obscure German wanderer and a London woman of ordinary family; he was educated at the Charity School at Greenwich Hospital; and he made a slow way in the Royal Navy. As a sailor and colonizer, he ranged further about the world than all but a handful of his contemporaries; and between his voyages he travelled in Europe. He observed the world carefully as he went, and educated himself. What is now known about him amply justifies the assessment of two contemporaries, that he was a person 'who has seen much of the Service, and much of the World; and has studied it. He is posses'd of g^t good Sence, [and is] well inform'd'; that in him was blended that 'which is not common with Captains the Gentleman the scholar and the seaman'.[2]

Despite the best efforts of this writer and his predecessors, much desirable information about Phillip is still lacking. When precisely did he first go to sea? How did he spend his time in France in the early 1770s? Did he then train as an artillery officer or an engineer? What are the facts behind the strange story of the convict voyage to South America? Did he—as seems more likely than not—never love romantically? Did he, having no need of that permanency which children bring, marry mostly for money? What caused him and his first wife to separate? Was he indifferent to religious impulses? How did he view his world, and what did he think of his place in it? No doubt his private papers would cast light on these matters, but the fate of these and his personal effects remains obscure. One would suppose that the Whitehead family would have had sufficient sense of his significance to preserve them, but they are not to be found. And it is a cause for wonder that though he was 'longer on the seas than on the land',[3] only one letter of an entirely private nature survives, and that from a seventeen-year-old youth after his first battle. There is not one private letter from the adult man to any friend or business associate, just as there is not a single letter from him to either of his wives or to members of their families, nor from them to him. Even the letters to his enduring friend Evan Nepean, though from time to time containing private information or views, are not fundamentally private communications; and they therefore allow only fleeting glimpses of his personality and outlook. Time has removed much of the man from our view.

But if much of Arthur Phillip is now lost, a real presence does remain. Though we have no precise height, he was a small man physically. Illness and the privations of the seafarer's life progressively removed his youthful plumpness, so that by the time of New South Wales his face was 'shrivelled', his 'thin' nose prominent, and his figure 'little'. In his maturity his voice was 'powerful', if 'sharp', and his presence evidently one that commanded attention and respect.[4] Given his responsibilities and the difficulties he faced, particularly in New South Wales, it would not be surprising had he become unremittingly serious. It is therefore an unexpected pleasure of the quest for the person behind the strained exterior to find that he had a warm sense of humour. One of his men related how, during an expedition to Broken Bay, they 'ketched the Largest Mullett I ever Saw[.] at this place Dinner being Ready they turned too, Doc'r White, said to the Govenor, I am amazing fond of those Mullet, the Govenor being in a jokus youmor, Answered him, so I purceive, for you have eat Six of them as you Say, & we must allow that the least of them, weigh Three Pound and by Calculation, the whole must weigh Eighteen Pounds, which Created a deal of Sport, and Deversion'.[5] Another example is his pleasure, during one stay in Plymouth, in explaining to companions that the dramatic loss of weight shown by certain women was due to their having deposited their smuggled cargoes of gin.[6] No doubt this sense of humour contributed largely to his wry acceptance of such flawed helpers as Henry Brewer and Billy Sutton.

He was an honest man. In an age when corruption was rife, he was, as the Viceroy of Brazil put it, 'very clean-handed', never being accused of any malfeasance.[7] Throughout his stay in New South Wales—and there is no reason to suppose that he did otherwise at other periods of his life—he also took pains to represent things as they were. He was not helped in this task by the biassed and highly unfavourable descriptions sent back by his disillusioned or disgruntled companions, who indeed misrepresented with their claims that the region was a rocky waste, the outcast of God's works, 'a country and place so forbidding and so hateful as only to merit execration and curses'.[8] Such claims gave Phillip considerable trouble, for while he knew them to be untrue, he also knew that the English public would give them credence. In an attempt to counter them, he had David Burton, the gardener sent out by Banks in 1791, survey the districts about Parramatta. 'That the Soil of this Country has been much misrepresented', he told Sydney, 'the inclosed report will satisfy your Lordship. It is made by a man who was bred a Gardener, & sent out as a Superintendent, & who has been employed in the marking out allotments of land for Settlers; nor do I believe that his report of the nature of the soil, will lead your Lordship to form a better opinion of the country for some few miles round Parramatta than what it deserves, for he was very particularly directed to make his report in such a manner, that the ground might be found to be to the full as good in every part, on any future examination, as could be expected from the opinion he was to give.'[9]

To Banks, he made the point in a different way. 'I would wish you to shew Burton's letter to Lord Mulgrave, for it is probable that he will have a very different account of the Country, from some of those Gentlemen who are on their passage home; Major Grose met some of the Officers of the late *Sirius* at the Cape, & to use the Majors expression, the Country was most infamously misrepresented to him, I believe by the Surgeon & Capt. Clerk. The few Cattle we have, grow exceeding fat, & the Cape Ewes too fat to breed, although they are kept up the greatest part of the day & all night. All our fruit trees thrive well, & I have this year gathered about three hundred weight of very fine grapes, the quantity next year will be very considerable, I have Oranges but they are not yet ripe, the soil round the trees having been moved too late in the season. All the plants sent out in the *Gorgon* will do very well, & we have now vegetables in abundance. at Parramatta they are now served daily to the Convicts, still you may be told that the Country will not produce a Cabbage.'[10] It was as a consequence of Phillip's care in this regard that Banks later observed that 'I never had the smallest opportunity of calling [his perfect veracity] in question' and that the administration placed 'a full reliance on his reports'.[11]

Phillip's actions in the Portuguese navy and in New South Wales show him to have been a physically brave man, and one respectful of others. As the Viceroy again said, he was 'an Officer of education and principle, he gives way to reason, and does not, before doing so, fall into those exaggerated and unbearable excesses of temper which the majority of his fellow-countrymen do, more especially those who have been brought up at sea ... [he] is no flatterer, saying what he thinks, but without temper or want of respect.'[12] And when a decision was taken, and orders issued, he followed them diligently, even if he disagreed with them. Nelson's instruction to his wife about to go to London, 'Governor Phillip is a good Man remember me kindly to him ther',[13] reflects a firm perception of his worth as an officer.

He was also a humane man. No 'Tartar' who ruled his ships with a savage lash, he enjoyed the respect of his crews, even their affection; and his quiet resolution allowed him to weld them into effective working units. While he may have been somewhat unusual in this, he was not entirely so, for a sense of the advantages of humane treatment of crews slowly permeated the Royal Navy during his time. What perhaps distinguished him more was that his concern for his crew's welfare did not end with their being paid off, as is shown by his representing to the Admiralty on the *Europe*'s return to England the cause of the Irish volunteers who had been promised a passage home.[14] He was also unusual for his eagerness to undertake service in 'whatever part of the World',[15] for many of his colleagues shied from the unhealthy West Indies, or from more distant waters where their opportunities to take prizes were fewer.

He was a kindly man. When Philip Schaffer reached New South Wales with his ten-year-old daughter in 1790, the girl's health had been ruined by the ordeal on the *Guardian*. Phillip took her in and fed her until Schaffer was able to provide for her comfort.[16] He offered his kindness to those about him, excusing the sick convicts from labour, feeding hungry Aborigines and caring for sick ones. Nor was this humanity a matter of easy paternalism, for Phillip was not someone who showed different colours when circumstances squeezed. In May 1790, for example, when the colony was very short of supplies, 'declaring that he wished not to see any thing more at his table than the ration which was received in common from the public store, without any distinction of persons', he put three hundredweight of his own flour into the government store;[17] and he steadfastly declined to view the Aborigines in ways that would have permitted the Europeans to treat them with indiscriminate violence.

[Port Jackson Painter], 'A view of Sydney Cove, Port Jackson, March 7th 1792'

[Port Jackson Painter], 'A view of Government Farm at Rose hill N.S. wales 1791'

It is clear that Phillip tried by all available means to prevent his colonists from harming the Aborigines, and the habits of a naval captain gave him much greater control of events than that possessed by later authorities.[18] It is also clear that he excused the harm the Aborigines did the colonists whenever there were the slightest grounds for suspecting that this had been provoked. Unduly harsh as they may seem now, even his responses to McIntyre's murder and Balloderry's attack are not signs of a residual racism. And while we may certainly see these as aberrations, the rather impetuous gestures of a man racked by physical pain and driven to desperation by yet another stupidity, they also had a certain logic. Just as Phillip would not tolerate theft or acts of wanton violence from the Europeans, so too would he not tolerate dishonesty or mindless violence from the Aborigines, for whom his government had made him also responsible. To have done so would have made his task of establishing an orderly settlement impossible, both because of the inherent havoc, and because of the bitter resentment that would have been engendered in the colonists by a governor who excused in the blacks what he fiercely punished in them.

It is true that Phillip's views were those of an educated European who believed instinctively in order. In the light of differences now visible between the cultures, this may be a less than satisfactory premise on which to have had contact between those at Port Jackson proceed, but to criticize Phillip for lacking a knowledge that has taken another 200 years to develop is to miss an important historical point.[19] Phillip was the first European to begin to develop a competent understanding of Aboriginal culture; and, whatever its flaws, the information which he and his officers gathered between 1788 and 1792 is an invaluable record of that culture as it began to experience a world of which it had previously had no conception.

Again, it is not helpful to the development of a sound understanding of Australia's past or of Phillip's personality to enshroud him with what doubts we may have about the merits of civilization and the morality of colonization. Phillip was an eighteenth-century European, not a twentieth-century one. He came to New South Wales as the representative of his King and government, and the colonization he pursued was, in contemporary terms, a legal and a moral act.[20] His self-esteem and his future career depended on his succeeding with it; and he accepted the superiority of civilization. But if his imagination was inevitably constrained in certain ways, so too was it unusually flexible in others. His efforts to establish harmonious relations between the races at Port Jackson were one very significant result of this flexibility. The Aborigines there had a better friend in Phillip than they could possibly have known, or than historians have lately allowed.

Opposite: Francis Wheatley, 'Captain Arthur Phillip' (1786)

If we need—as we should not—any counterbalancing details to confirm that Phillip was not a 'racist', his decision concerning the Polynesian women, and his treatment of 'Black Caesar' suffice. In England he had had doubts about the scheme to bring women from Polynesia to redress the sexual imbalance among the colonists, and within four months of settling at Sydney, he had abandoned it, on the grounds that to bring them 'in our present situation, would answer no other purpose than that of bringing them to pine away in misery'.[21] A black from America, John Caesar was endowed with great physical strength but little percipience, and gave constant trouble. In June 1789 he absconded into the bush, whence he ventured to rob the gardens until he was recaptured a few weeks later. Collins tells the story nicely: 'This man was always reputed the hardest working convict in the country; his frame was muscular and well calculated for hard labour; but in his intellects he did not very widely differ from a brute; his appetite was ravenous, for he could in any one day devour the full ration for two days. To gratify this appetite he was compelled to steal from others, and all his thefts were directed to that purpose. He was such a wretch, and so indifferent about meeting death, that he declared while in confinement, that if he should be hanged, he would create a laugh before he was turned off, by playing off some trick upon the executioner. [He also believed that, after death, 'he would go to his own Country and see his friends'.] Holding up such a mere animal as an example was not expected to have the proper or intended effect; the governor therefore, with the humanity that was always conspicuous in his exercise of the authority vested in him, directed that he should be sent to Garden Island, there to work in fetters; and in addition to his ration of provisions he was to be supplied with vegetables from the garden.'[22]

This same consideration and patient understanding characterized Phillip's treatment of the convicts at large. He excused bad behaviour wherever he saw any grounds to justify his doing so. He mitigated sentences, or pardoned, when he thought there was any prospect of the offenders thereby benefiting. He rewarded when it was appropriate to do so. Examples of these habits are, variously, his reprieve of five of the six convicts condemned to death for stealing from the stores in February 1788; his granting of land and assistance to James Ruse and others, so that they might become farmers; his emancipation of James Bloodworth for 'his very meritorious behaviour and the great service he has rendered the colony by his own labour, and by instructing others, in the business of a bricklayer'; his emancipation of John Ascott, for putting out a fire on the wrecked *Sirius* before her stores had been unloaded.[23] As carefully as he judged his indulgences to the convicts, Phillip assessed the prospects of those applying to become settlers, granting land and offering help only to those convicts who possessed the knowledge and exhibited the character and industry necessary for success. He applied the same criteria to the marines and seamen who offered themselves. In March 1791, on learning that a number of the *Sirius*'s crew desired to stay, he told them to present themselves at Government House. 'The Whole Ships Company Turned out Excepting about Ten of us ... However the Govenor found there was but few that could Expect to improve in the Farming Business.'[24] In the end, Phillip permitted eight seamen and two marines only from the *Sirius* to become settlers on Norfolk Island.

All this is not to say that Phillip's character was flawless. Ross complained bitterly about what he took to be Phillip's failure to inform him fully—really, to have confidence in him; and Campbell made the same criticism.[25] The marine officers were certainly no friends of Phillip, and much of their criticism was clearly ill-informed, but the Viceroy of Brazil remarked that he was 'distrustful', and even Hunter made a muted comment to this effect,[26] so that there may have been something to it. Phillip certainly did at times delegate some of his authority, but there may have been a pattern to his doing so. The situation is not clear-cut, but he seems mostly to have put his trust in junior officers who were less likely to pursue independent paths. It does seem that he tended not to confide in, or much to consult, senior officers who were more likely to maintain divergent views. Given the quickly-rising antagonism of the marine officers, perhaps he had little real choice in New South Wales; but we may also suspect that he tended to become impatient with those, like the marine officers, who did not see as far into situations as he did and therefore understand the need of unconventional approaches, or with those, like Hunter, who could not come to a decision as readily as he could.

There was another complaint about Phillip in New South Wales, made by junior officers who considered that he did not promote them as he should. Daniel Southwell was one who felt much aggrieved on this point.[27] He had sailed thinking that his mother's friendship with the Lane and Everitt families gave him a claim on Phillip's attention. During the voyage out he entertained a highly favourable opinion of Phillip—'the Governor is certainly one of a Thousand'; but in New South Wales this approval changed progressively to bitterness, as Phillip assigned him to duty at the lookout on South Head and favoured others, and Southwell sprinkled his letters home with such phrases as 'pompous despot' and 'a fickle Man's Caprice'. Southwell's resentment centred on Phillip's promoting Henry Waterhouse, several years his junior, to lieutenant ahead of him; but apart from the matter of intrinsic merit, about which there is evidence to suggest that Phillip's preference was soundly based, Southwell failed to understand two salient points. First, in aligning himself with such as Campbell and Dawes, he joined with Phillip's professed enemies. Second, Phillip was as much a subject of the patronage system as he was a principal. Waterhouse had come recommended by the wife of George III's younger brother Henry, Duke of Cumberland.[28] It was an interest Phillip could not fail to satisfy if he himself were to realize his naval ambitions after New South Wales.

Phillip also had a certain tendency to act impetuously—as the Viceroy reported, 'he is a little headstrong, but can easily be brought to reason'.[29] The first sign of this in the available record of his life comes in his 1756 letter describing Byng's behaviour. His firing on the *guardacostas* at Colonia, and his running up to the *San Agustin* in the much smaller *Pilar* are instances of this impulse, as is his 1803 request to the Admiralty to be empowered to assume local sea command in an emergency. His punitive expedition against the Aborigines after their murder of McIntyre is another example. However, the wonder is not that he may have acted impulsively on one occasion in New South Wales, but that he did so once only (when Tench quickly 'brought him to reason'). It is a mark of his achievement that, when ill and tired and tried beyond what would normally be the limits of even an exemplary patience, he showed so little impulsiveness. To be able so to contain an important aspect of personality is a sign of a very considerable imaginative capacity.

The precise conformation of Phillip's imagination, to use the term somewhat in Coleridge's sense,[30] is uncertain. Not written with any literary intent, and with his private perceptions most often deliberately excluded from them, his letters from New South Wales lack a distinctive literary character, and their mass of details makes them rather dour reading. As Phillip travelled widely, and as his age was greatly interested in geographical detail, though, it would be inherently surprising if he never thought to give his perceptions a literary form. There are clear indications that he indeed did so. The fragment of his Brazilian journal that survives was evidently written up after the event with an eye to publication;[31] and that he also gathered information systematically in New South Wales, with the intention of later working it up into a coherent account, is shown by his March 1791 comment to Nepean, 'As I have hitherto sent home an account of those little circumstances which I thought might tend to give any information respecting this country or the natives, I have now, as usual, inclosed an extract from a book in which the occurrences of the day are set down. They are such as may not merit the attention of the Minister, and as they never were intended, so they certainly are not calculated, for the eye of the publick, having been put down in haste, and merely for the information of a friend; and so far from having had time to make any correction, they have been more than once, as they will now be, sent away without my having time to read them over.'[32]

Fragments only of this New South Wales journal are now extant. Phillip copied some early entries from it into his July 1788 letter to Lansdowne; and he clearly drew on it regularly for the information he sent to Banks.[33] The accounts of, especially, the Aborigines and the fauna and flora published under his name in *The Voyage of Governor Phillip to Botany Bay* and Hunter's *An Historical Journal* must also be based largely on his daily entries, but it is now impossible to know how much the editors of these works altered what he wrote. In this hiatus, the seven surviving pages of the Brazilian journal offer the best insight into his literary production. They show that he had an eye for interesting detail, an ability to sketch the context of a particular event and to organize material, and an utilitarian but not an accomplished style. But even if they might lack literary elegance, Phillip's worked-up journals of his times in Brazil and New South Wales would be of great interest and historical importance. It is much to be hoped that someone will one day chance upon them.

If Phillip's imagination did not give rise to striking literary productions, it was none the less both particular and expansive. These characteristics must have served him well on a number of occasions, but they did so particularly where New South Wales was concerned. Given the general habits of the age, and the rudimentary knowledge of New South Wales, he possessed before he sailed extraordinarily realistic expectations of conditions the colonists were to encounter, and of their likely progress. His and Nepean's estimate of the time the voyage would take, for example, proved quite accurate. He understood clearly that his party would find none of 'the necessarys of Life' there, and would therefore need to be equipped to meet this exigency. He suspected that the Aborigines might be much more numerous than Cook's and Banks's reports indicated, and so they turned out to be.

Indeed, we may suppose that Phillip could not have succeeded in New South Wales without this imaginative capacity. In discussing the 'repeated failure' of British attempts at colonization in North America to 1630, Kenneth Andrews stresses a larger cause than those of poor organization, unsuitable colonists, hunger and illness, and Indian resistance. 'Much more important than all these faults,' he argues, 'was [the colonists'] inability to adapt, to learn how to survive, to live off the country, to cope with a hostile environment. And they found it so hard to adapt because they began with false ideas both about America itself and about the kind of life they could lead there. Such false ideas were in part the results of deliberately deceptive promotional propaganda, much of it naive and pernicious nonsense, and in part the natural assumptions of men who had almost no means of imagining a world different from their own.'[34] In assessing the success of the New South Wales endeavour one must of course make allowance for the late eighteenth-century British having had another 200 years' experience of the non-European world, and for advances in the control of disease. Still, there is a singularity to New South Wales, for the consequences of the failure to imagine well which Andrews points to in North America— depression, disillusionment, and death—did not appear on nearly the same scale there. That they did not must have been due in large part to Phillip's capacity to conceive of circumstances realistically, and to convey his understanding to others who needed it.

The extent and flexibility of Phillip's habits of imagination are most evident in his treatment of the convicts. Before he began the voyage to New South Wales, thinking as he did that they should be kept forever apart, he seems largely to have shared the age's prejudices about common people who transgressed the law. Yet, immediately he became involved in the details of the business, his attitudes seem to have changed. Nepean's view that the 'banditti' embarked on the transports at Portsmouth did not deserve the same allowance of 'sick' rations as seamen,[35] for example, was never Phillip's, who badgered officials until all on the First Fleet were fed 'indiscriminately'. It may be that at first Phillip's concern was as much for his reputation as for the convicts in themselves— consider his March 1787 comment to Sydney that he feared 'that it may be said hereafter the officer who took charge of the expedition should have known that it was more than probable he lost half the garrison and convicts, crowded and victualled in such a manner for so long a voyage'.[36] Later, though, his concern was qualitatively different. In July 1788, he told Sydney that he was 'satisfied to remain [in New South Wales] as long as my services are wanted: I am serving my country, and serving the cause of humanity'; and commented to Grenville about those who arrived on the Second Fleet: 'I will not, sir, dwell on the scene of misery which the hospitals and the sick-tents exhibited when those people were landed, but it would be a want of duty not to say that it was occasioned by the contractors having crowded too many on board those ships, and from their being too much confined during the passage.'[37] Between the one set of remarks and the other, Phillip has come to see the convicts as people as well as objects to be transported successfully. We may speculate that this sea change might have begun in those early days at Port Jackson, when, in the face of the marine officers' refusal to supervise the convicts at their work, he developed the habit of moving among them, praising effort and criticizing indolence. Yet there is no real need to locate its onset so precisely: it is sufficient to understand that it developed in New South Wales, to see that the New World gave rise to new perceptions, called forth new sympathies in someone flexible enough to entertain them.

Yet, no matter how diligently Phillip went about his work, what reach of understanding he showed in it, and how actively he sought opportunities to make his mark, somehow he always missed the main chance. When he at last gained a superior ship in the Portuguese navy, the war with Spain ended. During that with the American colonies, France, and Spain, Sandwich kept him about England, and when opportunity finally arose, in the shape of the expedition against Montevideo, peace again removed it. Through no fault of his own, he lost the command of the *Swiftsure*, and with it the opportunity to participate in Nelson's victory of the Nile. Simultaneously, his prospects at Lisbon vanished. His complaint to Townshend from Rio de Janeiro in April 1783—'You will Sir, easily suppose how much I must be mortified in being so near & not at liberty to Act'[38]—might well stand as a coda to his whole naval life.

Ostensibly, it might also seem to epitomize his experience in New South Wales. Phillip himself was painfully aware of how much more he might have done there had he received additional supplies and skilled supervisors sooner; and, in keeping with his general luck, it was only after he left the colony that it really flourished—as John Macarthur said without rancour in August 1794, 'the changes that we have undergone since the departure of Governor Phillip are so great and extraordinary that to recite them all might create some suspicion of their truth'.[39] Yet the colony could have had no existence without his work; and it is for what he did there that we most remember him. There are good grounds for considering this great work. The decision to found the colony reflected Enlightenment perceptions that a change in environment might lead to desirable alterations in behaviour, and non-Calvinist Christian ones that human nature was redeemable. Time has shown the wisdom of these views. From Phillip's beginning with the convicts has come a nation refreshingly free of Old World constraints and distinguished by the opportunities it offers to its members. Viewed in the context of the resurgence of European culture in Australia and New Zealand, the colonization of New South Wales was one of the striking events of eighteenth-century British history. Phillip might justly have taken considerable satisfaction from his part in this 'diffusion of [a] great and surprizing people of a remote European isle, in the most distant extremities of the navigable ocean'.[40]

He might have: but did he? This is perhaps the most intriguing of all the questions that remain about Arthur Phillip. Did he understand that posterity would find his effort in New South Wales the most significant aspect of his life? Did he somehow understand that he was laying the foundations of a new society? Considering that his over-riding ambition was to achieve naval greatness, much of what he did in New South Wales must have seemed mundane or not to his taste—as he told Banks in November 1788, 'people talk here of Mines, my

Dear Sir, I am at an Age when three or four Years are of some value & [wish] to be better employ'd than in looking after a Silver Mine'.[41] And such comments as those that he did not wish convicts 'to lay the foundations of an Empire', and that 'when this Colony is the Seat of Empire, there is room for Ships of all Nations'[42] might, after all, have only reflected conventional perceptions of what was involved in colonization, rather than shown an insight into the future. They might have: but there are hints that they did convey something more, that Phillip did indeed have a sense of the historicity of the business he was about. His July 1788 remark to Lansdowne that 'this country will, hereafter, be a most valuable acquisition [to Great Britain from its situation]' is that of a man with a distinct perception of future possibility.[43] Subsequent ones, such as that of March 1791 to Banks that he remained very much 'interested' in the colony despite the 'many anxious hours' it had given him, and that of April 1792 to Sydney that he would leave it with 'regret' because he would not 'leave it independant, as to the necessaries of life', suggest that he maintained this perception.[44] And the desire he expressed to return when his health had improved seems to have been genuine.

Perhaps the best glimpse of Phillip's own sense of the significance of New South Wales is provided by his having kept until his death his 'drawings' done there. Who the artist was is not certain. Henry Brewer, his clerk, seems the most likely candidate, though there are others. If, as seems likely, these works are those by the 'Port Jackson Painter' now in the British Museum (Natural History) in London, of the coasts about Port Jackson, of the plants, animals, and Aborigines of the Sydney region, and of the settlements at Sydney and Parramatta, then Phillip retained a matchless visual record of the colony in its first five years; and his doing so shows both a sense of the works' historical importance, and an attachment to the experience which produced them.

Arthur Phillip lived into the second decade of the nineteenth century, but his was the eighteenth-century maritime rather than the developing industrial age. His technology was that of horse and cart, of handlooms, of ships framed and planked with oak, masted with pine, worked by hemp and propelled by wind on canvas. This age was effectively over by the time he died, though it is most unlikely that he would have realized it. By 1810, Baudin and Flinders had essentially concluded that great period of Pacific exploration which began in the 1760s and which Cook so massively carried forward. By 1810, too, the Navy had begun seriously to experiment with iron and steel; and Wellington's Peninsular campaign, leading as it would to the defeat of Napoleon on the continent, had marked the implementation of a new strategy to replace that naval one which had held sway all of Phillip's life, of reducing the enemies' capacity to fight by destroying their shipping and capturing their colonies. The victories of his contemporaries, St Vincent and Nelson especially, were in fact the last auroras of an old dispensation even then fading.

Accomplishment in battle eluded Phillip, but he did, with his planting of New South Wales, contribute significantly to the maritime and geographical accomplishment of his age. Lord Howe termed the venture a 'Voyage of discovery & Settlement',[45] and in a straight-forward sense it was indeed so. To bring the ships of the First Fleet and their human cargoes safely to New South Wales, and to establish the colony were very considerable achievements; and from them came a mass of geographical, ethnographical, biological, and botanical knowledge about a hitherto scarcely-imagined region. But Phillip's voyage to New South Wales was one of 'discovery' in another sense too, for no one had previously done what he came to do; and in his success in establishing a viable colony from a mass of initially reluctant members he raised the possibility of an important renewal and development of European culture, one based on principles of material comfort, equality, and opportunity, rather than on birth and inherited wealth or power.

Were Phillip now to take ship again, to stretch canvas from the spars of one of those great eighteenth-century men-of-war, and to sail again the western European coasts he once knew so well, were he to come past Cape Finisterre and down the green coast of northern Portugal to Lisbon, were he to come past the rocky escarpments of Cape St Vincent and through the long wash off Cape Trafalgar to Cádiz, to go again between the pillars of the Mediterranean and up the bleached coast to Barcelona, to cross the blue water to Nice and Livorno, he would find eucalypts overspreading the littorals and coastal hills, and black swans tranquil in the pleasure gardens. And were he to strike out again beyond western stars, and make again the long voyage to the Antipodes, he would find in the transformation of New South Wales his 200-year-old hope and Erasmus Darwin's prophecy fulfilled, and a society of persons born to, or come in search of, that new life whose promise he had first articulated. It is in the perception of these relationships and continuities that we may understand how much Arthur Phillip quietly enlarged the world into which he was born.

Bibliographies and Notes

KEY

1 *Form of the citation of documents*

Writer   Report/to recipient   date $\begin{cases} \text{Archive file: page, folio, item} \\ \text{Printed source, (volume), page} \end{cases}$

2 *Locations of unpublished manuscripts*

AGI	Archivo General de Indias, Seville
AGNBA	Archivo General de la Nación, Buenos Aires
	Sala IX Gobierno Colonial
AGM	Arquivo Geral da Marinha, Lisbon
AHU	Arquivo Histórico Ultramarino, Lisbon
	RJ Rio de Janeiro
	Colonia Colonia do Sacramento
ANTT	Arquivo Nacional da Torre do Tombo, Lisbon
	MNE Ministério dos Negócios Estrangeiros
ANRJ	Arquivo Nacional, Rio de Janeiro
	SPE Seção do Poder Executivo
AONSW	Archives Office of New South Wales, Sydney
BNL	Biblioteca Nacional, Lisbon
	CP Colecção Pombalina
BNRJ	Biblioteca Nacional, Rio de Janeiro
(BL)	The British Library, London
	Add. ms Additional manuscripts
BM(NH)	British Museum (Natural History), London
CMCM	Collection of Sr Marcos Carneiro de Mendonça, Rio de Janeiro
Cape	Cape Archives Depot, Cape Town
Clements	William L. Clements Library, University of Michigan
	Sackville-Germain Germain Papers
	Nepean Nepean Papers
	Shelburne Shelburne Papers
	Sydney Sydney Papers
Dixson	Dixson Library, State Library of New South Wales, Sydney
Guildhall	Guildhall Library, London
Huntington	Huntington Library, San Marino

Hydrographic   Hydrographic Department, Ministry of Defence, Taunton
IOR   India Office Records, London
                 H   Home Miscellaneous series
                 L/P & S   Political and Secret
IHGB   Instituto Histórico e Geográfico Brasileiro, Rio de Janeiro
Sandwich   Mapperton Manor House, Dorset
Mitchell   Mitchell Library, State Library of New South Wales, Sydney
MM   Museu da Marinha, Lisbon
NLA   National Library of Australia, Canberra
NMM   National Maritime Museum, Greenwich
NHL   Naval Historical Library, Ministry of Defence, London
(PRO)   Public Record Office, London
                 ADM   Admiralty
                 BT   Board of Trade
                 CO   Colonial Office
                 FO   Foreign Office
                 HO   Home Office
                 PRO   Chatham Deposit
                 PROB   Prerogative Court of Canterbury
                 PC   Privy Council
                 SP   State Papers
                 T   Treasury
                 WO   War Office
Kew   Royal Botanic Gardens Library, Kew
York Gate   York Gate Library, Royal Geographical Society of Australasia (South Australian
                 Branch), Adelaide
Château de   Service Historique de l'Armée, Paris
  Vincennes
Hamburg   Staatsarchiv, Hamburg
Sutro   Sutro Library, San Francisco
                 Banks   Banks Papers
Turnbull   Alexander Turnbull Library, Wellington

3 *Printed sources (and two analogous manuscripts)*

Journal   [Anon.], *An Authentic Journal of the Expedition under Commodore Phillips to
                 Botany Bay* (London: C. Forster, 1789)
Barnard   M. Barnard Eldershaw, *Phillip of Australia: An Account of the Settlement at
  Eldershaw   Sydney Cove* (1938; Sydney: Angus and Robertson, 1977)
Becke and   Louis Becke and Walter Jeffery, *Admiral Phillip: The Founding of New South
  Jeffery   Wales* (London: T. Fisher Unwin, 1899)
Bradley   William Bradley, *A Voyage to New South Wales: The Journal of Lieutenant Wil-
                 liam Bradley RN of HMS Sirius* (Sydney: The Trustees of the Public Library of
                 New South Wales in association with Ure Smith, 1969)
Clark   Ralph Clark, *The Journal and Letters of Lt. Ralph Clark 1787–1792*, ed. P.G.

	Fidlon and R.J. Ryan (Sydney: Australian Documents Library in association with the Library of Australian History, 1981)
Collins	David Collins, *An Account of the English Colony in New South Wales* (1798), ed. B.H. Fletcher (Sydney: A.H. and A.W. Reed in association with the Royal Australian Historical Society, 1975)
Easty	John Easty, *Memorandum of the Transactions of a Voyage from England to Botany Bay 1787–1793* (Sydney: The Trustees of the Public Library of New South Wales in association with Angus and Robertson, 1965)
EHR	*English Historical Review*
Harleian	Publications of the Harleian Society
HAHR	*Hispanic American Historical Review*
HRA	*Historical Records of Australia*, series I, IV (Sydney: The Library Committee of the Commonwealth Parliament, 1914–22)
HRNSW	*Historical Records of New South Wales*, ed. A. Britton and F.M. Bladen, 7 vols (Sydney: Government Printer, 1892–1901)
Hunter	John Hunter, *An Historical Journal of Events at Sydney and at Sea 1787–1792* (1793), ed. John Bach (Sydney: Angus and Robertson in association with the Royal Australian Historical Society, 1968)
JRAHS	*Journal* of the Royal Australian Historical Society
King	Philip Gidley King, *The Journal of Philip Gidley King: Lieutenant, RN 1787–1790*, ed. P.G. Fidlon and R.J. Ryan (Sydney: Australian Documents Library, 1980)
Mackaness	George Mackaness, *Admiral Arthur Phillip: Founder of New South Wales 1738–1814* (Sydney: Angus and Robertson, 1937)
Nagle	Jacob Nagle, Manuscript *Journal*, William L. Clements Library
Phillip	[Arthur Phillip], *The Voyage of Governor Phillip to Botany Bay* (1789), ed. J.J. Auchmuty (Sydney: Angus and Robertson in association with the Royal Australian Historical Society, 1970)
RIHGB	*Revista* do Instituto Histórico e Geográfico Brasileiro
Scott	James Scott, *Remarks on a Passage to Botany Bay 1787–1792* (Sydney: The Trustees of the Public Library of New South Wales in association with Angus and Robertson, 1963)
Spain	Edward Spain, Manuscript *Journal*, Mitchell Library ms C 266
Smyth	Arthur Bowes Smyth, *The Journal of Arthur Bowes Smyth*, ed. P.G. Fidlon and R.J. Ryan (Sydney: Australian Documents Library, 1979)
Tench	Watkin Tench, *A Narrative of the Expedition to Botany Bay* (1789) and *A Complete Account of the Settlement at Port Jackson* (1793), reprinted as *Sydney's First Four Years*, ed. L.F. Fitzhardinge (1961; Sydney: Library of Australian History in association with the Royal Australian Historical Society, 1979)
White	John White, *Journal of a Voyage to New South Wales* (1790), ed. A.H. Chisholm (Sydney: Angus and Robertson in association with the Royal Australian Historical Society, 1962)
Worgan	George Worgan, *Journal of a First Fleet Surgeon* (Sydney: The Library of Australian History in association with the Library Council of New South Wales, 1978)

Trained up to a Seafaring Life

Bibliography

The vignette of life in London in the 1730s and 1740s is partly based on my reading of parish and other records of the times. *The London Encyclopaedia*, ed. Ben Weinreb and Christopher Hibbert, Macmillan, London, 1983, is a very convenient mine of information about the city. The essays by Douglas Hay and his colleagues in *Albion's Fatal Tree: Crime and Society in Eighteenth-Century England*, Allen Lane, Harmondsworth, 1975, and those in J.S. Cockburn, ed., *Crime in England 1550–1800*, Princeton University Press, Princeton NJ, 1977, provide many insights into the nature of the society. J.C. Drummond and Anne Wilbraham, *The Englishman's Food: A History of Five Centuries of English Diet*, rev. Dorothy Hollingsworth, Jonathan Cape, London, 1957, offer an extended account of diet and disease. Many of the nineteenth-century circumstances described by F.B. Smith, *The People's Health 1830–1910*, Croom Helm, London, 1979, also existed in the eighteenth. R.W. Malcolmson, *Life and Labour in England 1700–1780*, Hutchinson, London, 1981, summarizes the results of recent labour and demographic studies.

Notes

1 Archdeacon of London's Court, Marriage allegations, 29 November 1728, Guildhall ms 10091/68.
2 Harleian, 65.
3 The phrasing is from the standard will printed for the benefit of illiterate seamen, of which there is an example in ADM 96/3:352.
4 PROB 6/108; PROB 11/653.
5 *Tartar*, Musterbook, ADM 36/4179.
6 *Tartar*, Captain's log and journal, ADM 51/969.
7 PROB 6/108; PROB 11/653.
8 [Anonymous], 'Anecdotes of Governor Phillip', Phillip, p. xvii.
9 Enquiries in Germany and extensive searches in England have proved fruitless.
10 All Hallows, Bread Street, Baptismal register, Guildhall ms 5033.
11 All Hallows, Bread Street, Poor Rate register, Guildhall ms 5038/3, 4.
12 ADM 73/416, 404.
13 Lavradio to Mello e Castro, 10 May 1778, AHU RJ caixa 115:9.
14 ADM 73/416; ADM 73/404. ADM 67/239 ('Minutes of the Admission of Boys') gives 22 June 1751 as the date Phillip's application was accepted. The details of his application are not to be found in ADM 6/223 ('Candidates for Admission to Greenwich Hospital').
15 [John Cooke and John Maule], *An Historical Account of the Royal Hospital for Seamen at Greenwich*, London, 1789, p. 128; *Articles and Instructions for the better Government of His Majesty's Royal Hospital for Seamen at Greenwich*, 2nd ed., London, 1741, pp. 109–24; and [The Chaplains], *A Description of the Royal Hospital for Seamen, at Greenwich*, Greenwich Hospital, 1801, pp. 46–8.
16 *An Historical Account of the Royal Hospital for Seamen at Greenwich*, p. 126; and *A Description of the Royal Hospital for Seamen, at Greenwich*, pp. 46–8; *Articles and Instructions*, pp. 109–24.

17 *A Description of the Royal Hospital for Seamen, at Greenwich*, pp. 14–24.
18 Quoted in Felix Barker, *Historic Greenwich*, Jarrold & Sons, Norwich, 1981, p. [8].
19 ADM 73/390, i ('Binding out of Boys') and ADM 73/416 ('Entry and Binding out of Boys')
    give the date as 1 December 1753; ADM 67/240 ('Minutes of the Admission of Boys') gives 8
    December 1753.

1 ABOUT NORTHERN CAPES

The Arctic Ocean

Bibliography

The following offer accounts of Arctic navigation and whaling from the seventeenth into the
nineteenth centuries: Tancred Robinson, comp., *An account of the Several Late Voyages & Dis-
coveries to the South and North*, Sam. Smith and Benj. Walford, London, 1694; [Anonymous], 'A
Journal of a Voyage undertaken by order of His Present Majesty, for making Discoveries towards
the North Pole', in *An Historical Account of all the Voyages round the World*, ed. D. Henry,
F. Newbery, London, 1773, IV, supplement; John Laing, *A Voyage to Spitzbergen*, 4th ed., The
Author, Edinburgh, 1822; and the extracts from William Scoresby's journals printed by Tom and
Cordelia Stamp in *Greenland Voyager*, Caedmon, Whitby, 1983.

   Lloyd's List gives details of the whaling fleet's (and other ships') arrivals at and departures
from London from 1742 onwards.

   J.T. Jenkins, *A History of the Whale Fisheries*, H.F. & G. Witherby, London, 1921, and
Gordon Jackson, *The British Whaling Trade*, Adam & Charles Black, London, 1978, are detailed
modern studies of the industry.

Notes

1 ADM 73/390.
2 Quoted in Jackson, p. 55.
3 Laing, p. 54.
4 See ibid., p. 49.
5 'A Journal of a Voyage ... for making Discoveries towards the North Pole', in Henry, IV,
   supplement, pp. 63–4.
6 ADM 68/199.
7 Phillip to Nepean, 29 March 1792, HRNSW, I, ii, 613.

The European Coasting Trade

Bibliography

Augustus Hervey's Journal, ed. David Erskine, William Kimber, London, 1953, offers much immediate detail of navigation about, and social circumstances in, the ports of southern Europe. For

details of the coasting trade, I have drawn on the following modern studies: L.S. Sutherland, *A London Merchant 1695–1774*, Oxford University Press, Oxford, 1933; Allan Christelow, 'Great Britain and the Trades from Cádiz and Lisbon to Spanish America and Brazil', HAHR, 27 (1947), 2–29; Ralph Davis, *The Rise of the English Shipping Industry*, National Maritime Museum, London, n.d. [1962]; H.E.S. Fisher, 'Lisbon, its English merchant community and the Mediterranean in the eighteenth century', in *Shipping, Trade and Commerce*, ed. P.L. Cottrell and D.H. Aldcroft, Leicester University Press, Leicester, 1981; C.R. Boxer, *The English and the Portuguese Brazil Trade, 1660–1780*, La Trobe University, Institute of Latin American Studies, Melbourne, 1981.

Notes

1 Quoted in Davis, pp. 234–5.
2 BT 6/93: 116.
3 *Lloyd's List*, 21 February 1755; ADM 7/89, Pass no. 285; ADM 68/199; *Lloyd's List*, 21 February and 22 April 1755.

The Seven Years War: Europe

Bibliography

The following are valuable for the light they cast on conditions in the Royal Navy in the age: Michael Lewis, *England's Sea-Officers: The Story of the Naval Profession*, George Allen & Unwin, London, 1939; Daniel A. Baugh, *British Naval Administration in the Age of Walpole*, Princeton University Press, Princeton NJ, 1965; Christopher Lloyd, *The British Seaman 1200–1860: A Social Survey*, Collins, London, 1968; Sir James Watt, 'Medical aspects and consequences of Cook's voyages', in *Captain James Cook and his Times*, ed. Robin Fisher and Hugh Johnston, Australian National University Press, Canberra, 1979, pp. 129–57; and various of the essays in *Starving Sailors: The Influence of nutrition upon naval and maritime history*, ed. Sir James Watt, E.J. Freeman, and W.F. Bynum, National Maritime Museum, London, 1981.

There are any number of studies of the Seven Years War in general and of British naval strategy in particular. Some I have found useful are: Julian Corbett, *England in the Seven Years' War*, 2nd ed., 2 vols, Longmans, Green and Co., London, 1918; Sir Herbert Richmond, *Statesmen and Sea Power*, Clarendon Press, Oxford, 1946; O.A. Sherrard, *Lord Chatham, II: Pitt and the Seven Years War*, The Bodley Head, London, 1955; Eric Robson, 'The Seven Years War', in *The New Cambridge Modern History, VII: The Old Regime 1713–63*, ed. J.O. Lindsay, Cambridge University Press, Cambridge, 1957, pp. 465–86; Geoffrey Marcus, *A Naval History of England, I: The Formative Centuries*, George Allen & Unwin, London, 1961; and Richard Pares, *War and Trade in the West Indies 1739–1763*, Frank Cass & Co., London, 1963 [1936].

Brian Tunstall, *Admiral Byng and the Loss of Minorca*, Phillip Allan & Co., London, 1928, offers a portrait of a failed admiral; and R.F. Mackay, *Admiral Hawke*, Clarendon Press, Oxford, 1965, a portrait of a successful one. C.H. Firth, ed., *Naval Songs and Ballads*, The Navy Records Society, [London], 1908, provided the ballad of Admiral Byng.

Notes

1 ADM 68/199.
2 Hardwicke used the phrasing in his letter to Newcastle, 14 July 1755, which Sherrard quotes in describing the ministers' manoeuvrings, pp. 60–1; see also Mackay, pp. 114–43.
3 *Buckingham*, Musterbooks, ADM 36/5004; Paybook, ADM 33/535.
4 Everitt to Clevland, 30 June 1755, ADM 1/1758.
5 The details of the cruise are from *Buckingham*, Captain's log and journal, ADM 51/4132.
6 Quoted in Tunstall, p. 53.
7 Cited in Baugh, p. 375; see also Lloyd, p. 254, and *Starving Sailors*, p. 10.
8 Quoted in Mackay, p. 121.
9 Arthur to [Rebecca] Phillip, 21 June 1756, PRO 30/8/52.
10 *Princess Louisa*, Musterbooks, ADM 36/5946-8; Captain's log and journal, ADM 51/4301.
11 *Ramilles*, Musterbooks, ADM 36/6464; Captain's log and journal, ADM 51/4304.
12 *Neptune*, Musterbooks, ADM 36/6217–18; Captain's log and journal, ADM 51/632.
13 [Anonymous], 'Biographical Memoir of Arthur Phillip, Esq: Vice-Admiral of the Red Squadron', *Naval Chronicle*, 27 (1812), 1–9. *Union*, Musterbooks, ADM 36/6945; Captain's log and journal, ADM 51/1019.
14 *Jason*, Musterbooks, ADM 36/5889.
15 *Aurora*, Musterbooks, ADM 36/4936; Captain's log and journal, ADM 51/76.

The Seven Years War: West Indies

Bibliography

Richard Pares, *War and Trade in the West Indies 1739–1763*, Frank Cass & Co., London, 1963 [1936], and J.H. Parry, 'Rivalries in America, 1: The Caribbean', and Frank Thistlethwaite, 'Rivalries in America, 2: The North American Continent', in *The New Cambridge Modern History, VII*, pp. 514–40, survey the progress of the war in the American hemisphere. The documents in *The Siege and Capture of Havana 1762*, ed. David Syrett, The Navy Records Society, [London], 1970, give much graphic detail of one campaign. *Naval Songs and Ballads* again supplied the ballad of the attack on El Morro.

Notes

1 *Stirling Castle*, Musterbooks, ADM 36/6735-9.
2 These cruising details are from *Stirling Castle*, Captain's log and journal, ADM 51/934.
3 Pares, pp. 265–325, Parry, pp. 521–5, and Sherrard, *passim*, summarize this strategy and describe the campaign.
4 For Phillip's commission of 7 June 1761, see ADM 6/62. The Navy Board confirmed this appointment on 24 March 1763, ADM 6/19. Phillip's Passing certificate has evidently been lost.
5 The cruising details are now from Phillip's own log and journal—*Stirling Castle*, Lieutenants' logs and journals, NMM ADM/L/S/447.

6 The *Dragon* had sixteen killed and thirty-seven wounded; the *Cambridge* twenty-four/ninety-five; the *Marlborough* two/eight; the *Stirling Castle* two/eight—see Pocock to Clevland, 14 July 1762, Huntington ms 1000.

7 Hervey to Keppel, 3 July 1762, printed in Syrett, p. 222.

8 The decision, but not minutes of the hearing, is in ADM 1/5301.

9 Pocock to Clevland, 17 July 1762, Huntington ms 1000.

10 Quoted in Syrett, p. xxix.

11 Keppel, Journal entry of 9 July 1762, printed in Syrett, p. 228.

12 Pocock to Clevland, 17 July 1762, printed ibid., p. 247.

13 Pocock to Clevland, 9 October 1762, printed ibid., p. 302.

14 These details are from Phillip's log and journal—*Infanta*, Lieutenants' logs and journals, NMM ADM L/J/59.

15 Phillip, Memorandum of c. September 1786, CO 201/2:92.

16 Spain (pp. 53–4) says that Phillip had a woman on board the *Europe* in 1783–84. It is difficult to know what to make of this story, for Spain is not a trustworthy witness, and there is nothing to confirm his claim.

Peacetime Pursuits

Bibliography

Alicia Amherst, *London Parks and Gardens*, Archibald Constable & Co., London, 1907, pp. 56–82, describes the St James's Park scene in the mid-eighteenth century.

The details of England's weather in the 1760s are from reports in the *Gentleman's Magazine*, and from J.M. Stratton and J.H. Brown, rev. R. Whitlock, *Agricultural Records AD 200–1977*, 2nd ed., John Baker, London, 1978, pp. 80–2. Gilbert White's journals give details of particular conditions at Selbourne, further to the east in Hampshire—see *Gilbert White's Selbourne*, ed. R.B. Sharpe, S.T. Freemantle, London, 1900. Charles Vancouver, *General View of the Agriculture of Hampshire*, 2nd ed., Sherwood, Neely, and Jones, London, 1813, gives details of production at the turn of the nineteenth century. I am grateful to Professor E.L. Jones and Mr Colin Tubbs for advice on this subject.

The social history otherwise is based generally on R.W. Malcolmson, *Life and Labour in England 1700–1780*; and E.P. Thompson, *Whigs and Hunters: The Origin of the Black Act*, Penguin, Harmondsworth, 1975. Particular studies of the food riots are: R.B. Rose, 'Eighteenth century Price Riots and Public Policy in England', *International Review of Social History*, 6 (1961), 277–92; and W.J. Shelton, *English Hunger and Industrial Disorders: A Study in social conflict during the first decade of George III's reign*, Macmillan, London, 1973.

Julius Goebel, *The Struggle for the Falkland Islands*, Yale University Press, New Haven, Conn., 1982 [1927], describes the first Falkland Islands crisis in great detail.

Notes

1 ADM 6/19, ADM 25/64.

2 ADM 25/66; Syrett gives details of the divisions of the Havana prize money, pp. 305–13.

3 St Augustine, Watling Street, Marriage register, Guildhall ms 8875/1. The details are variously from the *Gentleman's Magazine*, 29 (1759), 392; John Denison's will, proved 4 June 1760, PROB 11/856; the executors' statement of his estate, and accompanying affidavits, 4 August 1764, PROB 31/491/699, 700; indenture of release and settlement signed by Charlott Denison, 21 October 1762, PROB 31/491/697; and the authority given to Charlott Phillip's executor, October 1792, PROB 8/185. The marriage agreement, which was dated 18 July 1763, has not been found, but some of its details are repeated in the authority given to Mrs Phillip's executor in 1792, where it is also stated that she died without issue.

4 Information kindly supplied by the Bank of England. The firm of Thomas and John Lane (later Lane, Son & Fraser), of 10 and 11 Nicholas Lane, appears in city directories of 1730–1800.

5 This is a family tradition, the reliability of which is uncertain—see James Logan's affidavit, Mitchell ms Ap 13/1:1.

6 There are photographs of the entries in Mitchell uncatalogued ms 440, and ms Ap 13/2:4; see also Mitchell document 1701b; and the Vicar of Lyndhurst to Cotterell, 17 October 1937, Bath Library, Phillip packet.

7 Tithe Survey, Lyndhurst, c. 1841, Hampshire Record Office.

8 [London] *Observer*, 15 December 1793.

9 'Anecdotes of Governor Phillip', Phillip, p. xvii.

10 [London] *Observer*, 15 December 1793.

11 Despite widespread searching, the separation agreement has not come to light, but some details of it are given in the authority granted to Mrs Phillip's executor in 1792, PROB 8/185. Such formal agreements were not common, and an application for one had to be supported with detailed evidence concerning the couple's circumstances. The discovery of the Phillips' agreement would doubtless significantly enlarge our knowledge of his life at this time, and earlier.

12 ADM 106/2972.

13 The details are from Phillip's journal—*Egmont*, Lieutenant's logs and journals, NNM ADM L/E/52.

14 ADM 6/213.

15 ADM 106/2972.

16 Ibid.

17 [London] *Observer*, 15 December 1793.

18 Augustus Hervey to Pinto de Souza, 25 August 1774, Becke and Jeffery, pp. 263–4.

19 Lavradio to Mello e Castro, 10 May 1778, AHU RJ caixa 115:9 (Becke and Jeffery, p. 319).

20 G.T. Landmann, *Adventures and Recollections of Colonel Landmann*, Colburn and Co., London, 1852, I, 121. This speculation is not to be confirmed or disproved by reference to the (very few) relevant papers in French army archives at the Château de Vincennes. The discovery of Isaac Landmann's papers, which were in his son's possession in 1850, presumably would also add significantly to our knowledge of Phillip.

21 See Stephens to Denis, 24 April 1773, ADM 2/1333; Grantham to Rochford, 27 April 1773, SP 94/192; and various letters April–June 1773 in SP 94/193.

22 Rochford to Stormont, 20 April 1773, printed in *British Diplomatic Instructions: France, 1745–1789*, ed. L.G. Wickham Legg, The Royal Historical Society, London, 1934, p. 135.

23 Suffolk to St Paul, 23 July 1773, in *Colonel St Paul of Ewart*, ed. G.G. Butler, The St Catherine Press, London, 1911, I, 181–2.

2 BEYOND WESTERN STARS

Bibliography

I have drawn on published sources for details of the places Phillip saw while in the Portuguese navy, and manuscript ones for the details of his service.

[Janet Schaw], *Journal of a Lady of Quality, Being the Narrative of a Journey from Scotland to the West Indies, North Carolina, and Portugal, in the years 1774 to 1776*, ed. E.W. Andrews, Yale University Press, New Haven, 1921, and William Dalrymple, *Travels through Spain and Portugal, in 1774*, J. Almon, London, 1777, describe Lisbon and its environs much as we may suppose Phillip saw them. An anonymous French traveller recorded a visit to Salvaterra de Magos in January 1766 in 'Journal historique de mon voyage d'Espagne et Portugal en 1765 et 1766', in *Notícia de uma viagem a Portugal em 1765–1766*, Arquivo Histórico de Portugal, Lisboa, 1960. José-Augusto França, *Lisboa Pombalina e o Iluminismo*, Livraria Bertrand, Lisboa, 1977, gives much detail about the city in the 1770s.

Louis de Bougainville, *A Voyage round the World*, J. Nourse, London, 1772, describes Rio de Janeiro a few years before Phillip saw it. Gilberto Ferrez, *O Rio de Janeiro e a Defesa do seu Porto 1555–1800*, Serviço de Documentação Geral da Marinha, Rio de Janeiro, 1972, reproduces many plans and views of the port. Somewhat later descriptions of Rio de Janeiro, and of Brazil more generally, are to be found in: White; John Mawe, *Travels in the Interior of Brazil*, Longman, Hurst, Rees, Orme, and Brown, London, 1812; and Robert Southey, *History of Brazil*, 3 vols, Longman, Hurst, Rees, Orme, and Brown, London, 1819.

Allan Christelow, 'Great Britain and the Trades from Cádiz and Lisbon to Spanish America and Brazil', HAHR, 27 (1947), 2–29, gives many details of the commerce between Europe and the South American colonies.

Visconde de Carnaxide, *O Brasil na Administração Pombalina*, Companhia Editora Nacional, São Paulo, 1940, gives a modern account of the Marquis of Lavradio's administration. Pedro Calmon offers another in *História do Brasil: IV*, 2nd ed., Livraria José Olympio Editôra, Rio de Janeiro, 1963. Jonathas da Costa Rego Monteiro, *A Colônia do Sacramento 1680–1777*, 2 vols, Livraria do Globo, Porto Alegre, 1937, gives an extended account of the Portuguese outpost on the northern bank of the Plate estuary. The major study in English of Brazil in this period is Dauril Alden, *Royal Government in Colonial Brazil*, University of California Press, Berkeley and Los Angeles, 1968, which is most valuable both for its details and for the accompanying extensive account of sources.

Pablo Blanco Acevedo, *El Gobierno Colonial en el Uruguay y los orígenes de la nacionalidad: I*, Biblioteca Artigas, Montevideo, 1975, describes the development of Spanish occupation of what is now Uruguay. (I am grateful to Dr Luis Carresse for pointing me to this work.)

The original records are to be found in the archives listed in the Key. Some—but by no means all—of this material has been printed, as follows:

- 'Documentos sobre a Colonia do Sacramento', 'Cópia: Carta regia ...', and 'Documentos sobre o Rio Grande de S. Pedro, Santa Catarina e Colonia do Sacramento', RIHGB, 31 (1868), 161–212, 265–349.
- 'Instituto Histórico e Geográfico Brasileiro: Arquivo do Conselho Ultramarino: Correspondência do Marquês do Lavradio (1776–7)', RIHGB, 255 (1962), 231–356.

- José d'Almeida, Marquês do Lavradio, *Vice-reinado de D. Luiz d'Almeida Portugal 2.º marquês de Lavradio*, Editora Nacional, São Paulo, 1942.
- 'Correspondência passiva do T.ᵗᵉ G.ᵃˡ João Henrique do Böhm', *Boletim do centro rio-grandense de estudos históricos*, I (1939), 10–160.
- 'Appendix II: Documents from the Archives at Lisbon relating to Phillip's Service with the Portuguese Navy (1775–1778)', Becke and Jeffery, pp. 259–323.
- 'Inventário dos Documentos Relativos ao Brasil existentes no Arquivo da Marinha e Ultramar de Lisboa, I: Bahia, 1762–1785', *Annaes da Biblioteca Nacional do Rio de Janeiro*, 32 (1910), 286–391.

Rather than from these printed sources, though, I have worked from the originals, which I have succeeded in locating in all but a few instances. For convenience, I have quoted from the translations in Becke and Jeffery, the accuracy of which has been checked by Miss Isabel Moutinho. Otherwise, Miss Moutinho has translated passages quoted.

Notes

1 Sandwich to Bristol, 28 April 1777, NMM SAN/T/8.
2 My account of the political background to Phillip's Portuguese service is based largely on Alden's account, which I have augmented at some points by reference to archival sources and other studies.
3 Lords Commissioners of the Admiralty, Minutes of 2 May 1763 and 5 April 1765, ADM 3/71, 73. There has been a good deal of confusion over the spelling of M'Douall's name. The form used here is the one he used in his letters to the Admiralty—see, e.g., those in ADM 1/2123.
4 At different times, Funck was a Lieutenant Colonel in both the Swedish and British armies, and he also served in the English East India Company—see his memorial concerning his services in BNL CP ms 611:102–9. It is tempting to speculate that Phillip may have acquired some of his military knowledge under Funck at the siege of Havana, but there is no evidence to confirm this.
5 The armaments of these ships vary from source to source. Those given are from 'Mapa das Naus e Fragatas de guerra Portuguezas q' se encorporarão na Esquadra do Sul, no tempo em que Surgio no porto de S. Catharina, com as entradas e sahidas q' fizerao de d.º', MM G5-30-1. The correspondence between Pombal and Mello e Castro and Lavradio, the Viceroy of Brazil, gives details of the ships' departures and arrivals—see particularly Pombal to Lavradio, 15 July and 18 September 1774, RIHGB, 31 (1868), 180–212; and Lavradio's letters in BNL codex 10624. Lavradio's 'Quadro das forcas de mar e terra . . .', RIHGB, 21 (1858), 166–72, gives some additional details, as does the Lavradio correspondence printed in RIHGB, 255 (1962), 231–356.
6 The details of these negotiations appear in the June–December 1774 letters which passed between, on the one hand, Pombal and Luis Pinto de Souza, ANTT MNE maço 138, and on the other, Rochford and Suffolk and Robert Walpole, SP 89/83, 84.
7 Hervey had visited Portugal on a number of occasions, and had an extensive range of acquaintances there—see his *Journal*, passim.
8 See, e.g., Glyndwr Williams, ' "The Inexhaustible Fountain of Gold": English Projects and Ventures in the South Seas, 1670–1750', in *Perspectives of Empire*, ed. J.E. Flint and Glyndwr Williams, Longman, London, 1973, pp. 27–53.

9 Quoted in Christelow, p. 5.

10 Cited ibid., pp. 24–5.

11 Hervey to Rochford, 10 May 1771, SP 89/71:108, 110.

12 Hervey to Pinto de Souza, 25 August 1774, Becke and Jeffery, pp. 263–4.

13 Pinto de Souza to Mello e Castro, 30 August 1774, ibid., pp. 260–2.

14 Mello e Castro to Pinto de Souza, 15 October 1774 (two letters), ANTT MNE maço 61 (Becke and Jeffery, p. 269).

15 Pinto de Souza to Mello e Castro, 8 November 1774, Becke and Jeffery, p. 270; and same to same, 9 November 1774, BNL codex 11225:10.

16 Lords Commissioners, Minute of 1 December 1774, ADM 3/80.

17 Mello e Castro to Pinto de Souza, 25 November 1774, Becke and Jeffery, pp. 273–6.

18 Pinto de Souza to Mello e Castro, 22 December 1774, ibid., pp. 276–8.

19 Ibid., and Hervey to Mello e Castro, 22 December 1774, ibid., pp. 278–9.

20 Dom José, Decree of 14 January 1775, ANTT Conselho de Guerra, Decretos maço 134:3; Letters Patent of 16 January 1775, Becke and Jeffery, pp. 3–4; Entry of 17 January 1775, AGM codex 371:83.

21 Entry of 25 January 1775, AGM codex 371:83.

22 Entries of 6 and 9 February 1775, ibid.: 85, 86.

23 Lavradio reported the *Belém*'s arrival in his letter to Mello e Castro, 22 April 1775, BNL codex 10624:50ff.

24 Z. Nuttall, 'Royal Ordinances concerning the laying out of new towns', HAHR, 4 (1921), 743–53, 5 (1922), 249–54.

25 Mawe, p. 97.

26 Lavradio to Pombal, 23 and 26 June 1775, BNL codex 10624:71, 73.

27 Mello e Castro to Lavradio, 24 January 1775, ANRJ SPE codex 67/5:161–2.

28 Lavradio to Mello e Castro, 23 April 1775, to Pombal, 23 and 26 June 1775, BNL codex 10624:57, 71, 73.

29 Ibid.; and Lavradio to M'Douall, 2 May and 19 July 1775, AHU ms 1252; to Böhm, 15 July 1775, BNRJ codex 13/4/2:23; to Phillip, 18 July 1775, ANRJ codex 70/8; to Mello e Castro, 21 July 1775, BNL codex 10624:83.

30 Lavradio to Pombal, 23 June 1775, BNL codex 10624:71.

31 Quoted in Alden, p. 50.

32 Nagle, pp. 38–9.

33 This is Phillip's annotation to his copy of the chart, which is now in Hydrographic S 96- Af 1.

34 Mello e Castro to Lavradio, 5 April 1775, ANRJ SPE codex 67/5: 168–70.

35 Pombal to Lavradio, 9 May 1775, ibid.: 170–4.

36 Lavradio to Pombal, 20 August 1775, BNL codex 10624:91.

37 Lavradio to M'Douall, 26 August and 22 September 1775, AHU ms 1252.

38 The following give some details of the *Pilar*'s movements: 'Mapa das Naus e Fragatas ...', MM G 5-30-1; M'Douall to Böhm, 6 and 22 October 1775, BNRJ codex 13/4/5:71, 73; Rocha to Lavradio, 12 October 1775, CMCM codex 29:91; Lavradio to Pombal, 13 December 1775, BNL codex 10624:98–103.

39 Lavradio to Pombal, 13 December 1775, BNL codex 10624:98–103; and see Alden, pp. 160–8.

40 Rocha to Lavradio, 9 April 1776, AHU CS caixa 6:10.

41 Rocha to Lavradio, 20 April 1775, CMCM codex 29:37.

42 Ibid.

43 Rocha to Lavradio, 1 December 1775, ibid.: 94.

44 These and the details following are from: Nicolas Garcia to Orduy, 16 December, Orduy to Vertiz, 16 and 17 December, Vertiz to Orduy, 18 December, Orduy to Vertiz, 25 December, Orduy to Rocha, 26 December, Rocha to Orduy, 27 December, Vertiz to Orduy, 30 December 1775, all of which accompanied Vertiz to Arriaga, 3 January 1776, AGI Legajo Buenos Aires caja 56:486; Rocha to Lavradio, 20 December 1775, AHU RJ caixa 107:15; Orduy to Rocha, 2 January, Rocha to Orduy, 3 January 1776, AGNBA sala IX 4/3/8.

45 Lavradio, 'Mappa dos Officiaes e Embarcacoens de Guerra, que servem na Esquadra', 27 November 1776, AHU RJ caixa 109:53.

46 Rocha to Gama e Freitas, 24 February 1776, AGNBA sala IX 3/8/4.

47 Lavradio to M'Douall, 13 December 1775, AHU ms 1252.

48 Rocha to Lavradio, 29 December 1775, CMCM codex 29:127.

49 M'Douall to Böhm, 3 February 1776, BNRJ codex 13/4/5:77.

50 M'Douall to Lavradio, 31 March 1776, AHU RJ caixa 107:35.

51 Lavradio to M'Douall, 17 April 1776, ibid.: 20 (Becke and Jeffery, pp. 286–9).

52 Lavradio to Mello e Castro, 18 August 1776, ibid.: caixa 108:65 (Becke and Jeffery, ibid.).

53 Ibid. (Becke and Jeffery, p. 290).

54 Rocha to Lavradio, 9 April 1776, AHU CS caixa 6:10.

55 Lavradio to Mello e Castro, 21 February 1776, AHU RJ caixa 107:13; to Pombal, 17 April 1776, BNL codex 10624:147.

56 Lavradio to Mello e Castro, 18 August 1776, AHU RJ caixa 108:65 (Becke and Jeffery, p. 290).

57 Ibid. (Becke and Jeffery, p. 291).

58 Lavradio to M'Douall, 17 April 1776, AHU RJ caixa 107:20; to Mello e Castro, 18 August 1776, ibid. caixa 108:65.

59 Lavradio, 'Mappa dos Officiaes …', 22 October 1777, AHU RJ caixa 113:15 (Becke and Jeffery, p. 317).

60 Rocha to Lavradio, 4 August, to Böhm, 14 August 1776, AHU RJ caixa 108:76; Lavradio to Mello e Castro, 18 August and 16 October 1776, BNL codex 106:166, 178; Lavradio to Rocha, 30 October 1776, BNL codex 10631; Phillip to Lavradio, 22 September and 8 November 1776, BNL mss caixa 236:87, 84, and 18 November 1776, CMCM maço 31:41; Lavradio to Pombal, 21 November 1776, AHU RJ caixa 109:49.

61 See Phillip to Lavradio, 8 November 1776, BNL ms caixa 236:84.

62 Phillip to Sandwich, 17 January 1781, Sandwich F/26/23.

63 Ibid.; and [M'Douall], Memorandum concerning the Plate settlements, undated but c. October 1780, FO 95/7/4:517–24.

64 Lavradio to Mello e Castro, 11 August 1775, ANRJ codex 69/2:113; and Lavradio, 'Relatorio … apresentado ao seu Successor Luiz de Vasconcellos e Souza', 19 June 1779, ANRJ SPE caixa 746:1.

65 Phillip, Journal, Clements Sydney 17.

66 Lavradio to Rocha, 10 December 1776, BNL codex 10631.

67 Lavradio to M'Douall, 11 December 1776, ibid.

68 Lavradio to Pombal, 20 November 1776, BNL codex 10624:191 (Becke and Jeffery, p. 295);

Lavradio, 'Mappa dos Officiaes …', 27 November 1776, AHU RJ caixa 109:53 (Becke and Jeffery, p. 296), and 'Mappa dos Officiaes …', 22 October 1777, ibid. caixa 113:15 (Becke and Jeffery, p. 317).

69 Mello e Castro to Lavradio, 21 August, 29 September, and 9 October 1776, AHU codex 570.

70 M'Douall to Lavradio, 19 February and 9 March 1777, AHU RJ caixa 110:30, 56; Alden, p. 228; Lavradio, 'Mappa dos Officiaes …', 22 October 1777, AHU RJ caixa 113:15 (Becke and Jeffery, p. 317).

71 Lavradio to Pombal, 10 March 1777, AHU RJ caixa 110:57 (Becke and Jeffery, p. 303–4).

72 Five captains, Opinion of 20 February 1777, AHU RJ caixa 110:36 (Becke and Jeffery, pp. 304–5).

73 Jacintho da Costa Freire, Opinion of 20 February 1777, ibid.: 35 (Becke and Jeffery, pp. 305–6).

74 Jose dé Mello, Opinion of 20 February 1777, ibid.: 37 (Becke and Jeffery, pp. 308–9).

75 Phillip, Opinion of 20 February 1777, ibid.: 34 (Becke and Jeffery, pp. 306–7).

76 Sá e Mello to Pinto de Souza, 21 June 1777, ANTT MNE maço 61.

77 Lavradio to Pombal, 10 March 1777, AHU RJ caixa 110:57.

78 Lavradio to Böhm, 7 March 1777, ABNRJ, 32 (1910), 347–8; to Mello e Castro, 19 March 1777, AHU RJ caixa 110: (unnumbered, but between items 65 and 66). See also the list of supplies put on board the *Pilar*, 6–25 March 1777, AHU RJ caixa 111:20.

79 Lavradio to M'Douall, 31 March 1777, BNL codex 10631.

80 M'Douall to Lavradio, 26 April 1777, Lavradio to [Cunha Menezes], 5 May 1777, ABNRJ, 32 (1910), 353–4, 366–7; to Mello e Castro, 2 June 1777, AHU RJ caixa 111:56; to Böhm, 4 June 1777, BNL codex 10631.

81 Lavradio to Mello e Castro, 2 June 1777, AHU RJ caixa 111:56 (Becke and Jeffery, p. 313).

82 Lavradio to M'Douall, 27 May 1777, BNL codex 10631.

83 Lavradio to M'Douall, 7 July, to Böhm and M'Douall, 10 August 1777, ibid.

84 Mello e Castro to Lavradio, 22 December 1777, RIHGB, 31 (1868), 348–9; Lavradio to M'Douall, 16 February 1778, BNL codex 10631.

85 Lavradio to the Spanish captain of the *San Agustin*, 5 April 1778, BNL codex 10631.

86 This summary is based on: 'Do descubrimento dos Diamantes …', and 'Dos Servissos, ou Lavras Diamantinas, e modo com que nellas se trabalha', BNL codex 746:2–34, 36–43; on the accounts in Mawe, pp. 137ff, and Southey, III, 634–43; and on Phillip's account, cited following.

87 Southey, ibid., pp. 634–5.

88 Phillip, Journal, Clements Sydney 17.

89 York Gate ms 5c.

90 Phillip, Journal, Clements Sydney 17.

91 AGM codex 371:212, 213, 214.

92 Lavradio to Mello e Castro, 10 May 1778, AHU RJ caixa 115:9 (Becke and Jeffery, pp. 319–20).

93 Walpole to Weymouth, 19 September 1778, SP 89/85:456.

94 Mello e Castro to Pinto de Souza, 14 September 1778, ANTT MNE maço 61.

95 Lords Commissioners, Minute of 2 September 1779, ADM 3/89; Weymouth to Pinto de Souza, 9 September, Pinto de Souza to Weymouth, 10 September, Weymouth to Walpole, 14 September 1779, SP 89/86:222, 224, 226.

Awaiting Opportunity

Bibliography

As Phillip took so little part in the naval war of 1776–83, I have not attempted to describe it broadly. Those wishing details should first consult such old standards as John Campbell and Dr Berhenhout, *Lives of the British Admirals: V*, rev. H.R. Yorke, C.J. Barrington, London, 1813, and Joseph Allen, *Battles of the British Navy*, 2 vols, Henry G. Bohn, London, 1852, which describe many voyages and actions. The papers of such principals as the Earl of Sandwich and Sir Charles Middleton (Lord Barham), Augustus Viscount Keppel, Sir Hugh Palliser, Richard Earl Howe, Sir George Rodney, and Sir Edward Hughes, many of which have been published by the Navy Records Society, cast much light both on proceedings at sea, and on behind-the-scenes manoeuvrings.

Piers Mackesy, *The War for America, 1775–1783*, Longmans, London, 1964, and Sir H.W. Richmond, *The Navy in India 1763–1783*, Ernest Benn, London, 1931, present accounts of activities in two spheres. A.T. Mahan, *The Influence of Sea Power upon History 1660–1783*, 10th ed., Little, Brown, and Company, Boston, 1895, and R.G. Albion, *Forests and Sea Power: The Timber Problem of the Royal Navy 1652–1862*, Harvard University Press, Cambridge, Mass., 1926, draw attention to broad underlying considerations. J.R. Dull, *The French Navy and American Independence: A Study of Arms and Diplomacy, 1774–1787*, Princeton University Press, Princeton NJ, 1975, describes the progress of the war from the French point of view.

Daniel A. Baugh, *British Naval Administration in the Age of Walpole*, Princeton University Press, Princeton NJ, 1965, describes the naval bases on England's southern coasts that Phillip frequented in these years. V.T. Harlow, *The Founding of the Second British Empire 1763–1793, I: Discovery and Revolution*, Longmans, Green and Co., London, 1952, offers a very detailed account of the negotiations for peace, in which naval considerations loomed large.

Notes

1 Phillip to Stephens, 5 October 1778, SP 42/53:198.
2 These and the details of cruising which follow are from Pakenham, 'Journal of the Proceedings of his Majesty's Ship *Alexander*', 2 June 1779–24 December 1782, NMM PAK 2; and Phillip, Lieutenant's log and journal, NMM ADM L/A/95.
3 Campbell, V, 463.
4 Lords Commissioners, Minute of 2 September 1779, ADM 3/89, and Commission of 2 September 1779, ADM 6/62; Lord Commissioners, Orders of 27 August and 2 September 1779, ADM 2/250:155, 184.
5 Phillip to Stephens, 26 February 1780, ADM 1/2306.
6 Phillip to Sandwich, 5 September 1779, Sandwich F/21/22.
7 *Basilisk*, Master's log and journal, ADM 52/1595; Half Pay register, July–December 1780, ADM 6/214.
8 Phillip to Stephens, 25 March 1780, ADM 1/2306.
9 Phillip to Sandwich, 19 July 1780, ADM 1/2306.
10 Phillip to Stephens, 20 and 23 October, 11 and 25 November, 4, 11, 14, and 26 December 1780, ADM 1/2306.

11 Half Pay register, ADM 6/214.
12 Sandwich, Appointment Book, c. 1780–82, NMM SAN 6:18.
13 Lords Commissioners, Order of 10 October 1781, ADM 2/111.
14 Phillip to Stephens, 3, 4, and 27 November 1781, ADM 1/2306; *Ariadne*, Lieutenant John Stevens's log and journal, NMM ADM L/A/181.
15 Lords Commissioners, Commission of 30 November 1781, NLA ms 1599; Order of 29 November 1781, ADM 2/111.
16 The details of the *Ariadne's* cruising are from Phillip, Captain's log and journal, 30 November 1781–25 December 1782, which is misplaced in NMM ADM L/A/181.
17 Phillip to Stephens, 20 December 1781, ADM 1/2306. The details which Phillip gives of the ships' situation and of the mutiny are confirmed by various documents in the archives of the Senat der Freien und Hansestadt, Hamburg—see Amt Ritzebüttel I, Abteil VII, Fach 8, vol. C, and Amt Ritzebüttel, Abteil I, Fach 14Q. I am grateful to Dr Gabrielsson of the Staatsarchiv, Hamburg, for locating these documents, and to Professor Karl Guthke of Harvard University for reading them.
18 Phillip to Stephens, 25 March 1782, ADM 1/2307.
19 Phillip to Stephens, 12 and 14 June 1782, ibid.
20 Douglas to Sandwich, 13 April 1782, *The Private Papers of John, Earl of Sandwich*, G.R. Barnes and J.H. Owen, Navy Records Society, London, 1932–38, IV, 257.
21 Phillip to Stephens, 25 August 1782, ibid.
22 Phillip to Stephens, 19 April 1782, ibid.

3 TO INDIAS OF MINE AND SPICE

Bibliography

Glyndwr Williams indicates the general context of British interest in Spanish America in '"The Inexhaustible Fountain of Gold": English Projects and Ventures in the South Seas, 1670–1750', in *Perspectives of Empire*, ed. J.E. Flint and Glyndwr Williams, Longman, London, 1973, pp. 27–53. Williams's Introduction to his edition of Richard Walter and Benjamin Robins, *A Voyage round the World*, Oxford University Press, London, 1974, focuses on Anson's striking development of this interest. G. Rutherford, 'Sidelights on Commodore Johnstone's Expedition to the Cape', *Mariner's Mirror*, 28 (1942), 189–212, 290–308, describes another such attempt (though there is now much more light to be cast upon the details and intentions of this expedition). V.T. Harlow, *The Founding of the Second British Empire 1763–1793, II: New Continents and Changing Values*, Longmans, London, 1964, pp. 615–61, takes the story into the nineteenth century.

The description of the Comoro Islands in Thomas Bankes, *A New ... System of Universal Geography*, J. Cooke, London [1786], pp. 451–4, indicates what Phillip would have seen there. Some eighteenth-century descriptions of the Dutch colony at the Cape of Good Hope are: Francois Valentyn, *Description of the Cape of Good Hope with Matters concerning it* [1726], ed. P. Seton et al., Van Riebeeck Society, Cape Town, 1971; Abbé da la Caille, *Journal Historique du Voyage au Cap de Bonne-Esperance*, Guillyn, Paris, 1763; Anders Sparrman, *A Voyage to the Cape of Good Hope, towards the Antarctic Polar Circle, round the World, and to the Country of the Hottentots and the Caffres from the year 1772–1776*, trans. and ed. V.S. Forbes, J. and I. Rudner, Van Riebeeck Society, Cape Town, 1975; and James Cook, *The Journals of Captain James Cook on his Voyages of Discovery*, ed. J.C. Beaglehole, 4 vols, Hakluyt Society, Cambridge, 1955–67.

Valuable too are the First Fleet narratives listed above, and cited in the next chapter. M.C. Karsten, *The Old Company's Garden*, Maskew Miller, Cape Town, 1951, offers wonderful details of the organization of the town and gardens. Robert Ross, 'Oppression, Sexuality and Slavery at the Cape of Good Hope', *Historical Reflections*, 6 (1979), 421–33, and 'The "White" Population of South Africa in the Eighteenth century', *Population Studies*, 29 (1975), 217–30 gives insights into the nature of the society that developed there. Spain is an interesting source for what Phillip did there, but not altogether a trustworthy one.

Abbé Raynal, *A Philosophical and Political History of the Settlements and Trade of the Europeans in the East and West Indies*, 3rd ed., T. Cadell, London, 1777, offers a contemporary sense of European colonizing.

Notes

1 See Glyndwr Williams, '"The inexhaustible Fountain of Gold"'; and Admiralty Memorandum, 1749, Clements Shelburne 75.

2 Call summarized this proposal at the opening of that for a colonization of New South Wales, HO 42/7:50. Hippisley's proposals are printed in *Memoirs and Correspondence of Viscount Castlereagh*, William Shoberl, London, 1848–53, VII, 262–7. White gives details of the history of his scheme in his letter to Archibald Campbell, 25 October 1790, PRO 30/8/120:58–60.

3 The later correspondence indicates that Dalrymple first wrote to Germain in June—see Sir John Dalrymple, *Memoirs of Great Britain*, new ed., A. Strahan and T. Cadell, London, 1790, III, 284–314, and Historical Manuscript Commission, *Stopford-Sackville*, London, 1904, II, 153–8; see also Dalrymple to Germain, 31 July 1779, Clements Sackville–Germain 9, 10, 11; and Dalrymple to Grenville, 20 October 1806, Huntington STG 141, ii.

4 Fullarton, 'Proposal of an Expedition to South America by India', 3 June 1780, IOR L/P & S/1/6. (There is an incomplete copy of this document in WO 1/178.)

5 John Hippisley used these phrases in a letter to Loughborough, 7 July 1779, in *Memoirs and Correspondence of Viscount Castlereagh*, VII, 261.

6 M'Douall, Memorandum, undated but before 30 October 1780, Sandwich F/26/24; and [M'Douall], Memorandum, undated but before 30 October 1780, FO 95/7/4:517–24.

7 Johnstone to Sandwich, 30 October 1780, Sandwich F/25/28.

8 Cabinet, Minutes of 2 and 25 November, and 16 December 1780, *Correspondence of George III*, ed. Sir John Fortescue, Frank Cass & Co., London, 1967 [1928], V, 145, 155–6, 162.

9 Lords Commissioners, Orders of 9 and 22 December 1780, ADM 3/91.

10 Cabinet, Minute of 29 December 1780, *Correspondence of George III*, V, 173–4.

11 Ibid.

12 Phillip to Sandwich, 17 January 1781, Sandwich F/26/23.

13 Pinto de Souza to Sá e Mello, 6 and 13 February 1781, ANTT MNE caixa 15.

14 Reported by Francisco Antonio de Espana y Menezes to Vasconcellos, 7 May 1781—see ANTT MNE Letters of Sá e Mello to Pinto de Souza 2 (1781–86).

15 Johnstone, Instructions to M'Douall, 31 March 1781, ADM 1/2123.

16 M'Douall to Stephens, 13 October 1781, ADM 1/2123; to Sandwich, 13 October 1781, Sandwich F/28/101.

17 Johnstone to Sandwich, 22 August 1781, Sandwich F/28/49.

18 Johnstone to Pasley, 22 November 1781, to Shelburne and Nepean, 11 May, Shelburne to Lords Commissioners, 16 May 1782, and report, 29 May 1782, HO 28/2:75–82.

19 See the Portuguese and English documents printed by Eduardo Marques Peixoto in *Ilha da Trinidade: Memoria Historica*, Publicaçoes do Arquivo Nacional #28, Rio de Janeiro, 1932, pp. 31–51, 355–70.

20 Phillip to Sandwich, 17 January 1780, Sandwich F/26/23.

21 *St James Chronicle*, 2 February 1787.

22 E.M. Green, 'Arthur Phillip: An Unwritten Chapter', *United Empire*, n.s. 12 (1921), 732–5.

23 Menezes to Vasconcellos, 7 May 1781, ANTT MNE Letters of Sá e Mello to Pinto de Souza 2 (1781–86).

24 See Walpole to Hillsborough, 16 June 1781, FO 63/1; 1, 7, and 8 July 1781, FO 63/2; and 23 March 1782, FO 63/3.

25 NMM SAN 5 and 6.

26 Oswald, 'Minutes Relative to the Situation of England in the Present War', 26 June 1782, and Supplement, 5 July 1782, Clements Shelburne 72:26, 28; and Oswald to Shelburne, 12 July 1782, in *Memorials and Correspondence of Charles James Fox*, ed. Lord John Russell, Richard Bentley, London, 1857, IV, 256–7. See also Harlow, II, 640–1, and R.A. Humphreys, 'Richard Oswald's Plan for an English and Russian Attack on Spanish America, 1781–1782', HAHR, 18 (1938), 95–101.

27 See, e.g., 'Carta do Rio de Janeiro em 20 de Junho de 1781', FO 63/2; 'A true and impartial Account of the present state of Peru', 30 July 1781, FO 63/3; 'Intelligence enclosed in a Letter from John Stables Esqr dated Rio de Janeiro, 3d July 1782, received by him from Capt. McDouall, of His Majesty's Ship *Africa*, who Speaks Portuguese', PRO 30/8/345: 280. There are precis and translations of numerous intercepted 1781 letters from Spanish authorities in America in Clements Shelburne 67.

28 *St James Chronicle*, 30 July/1 August 1782.

29 Pinto de Souza to Sá e Mello, 6 and 13 August 1782, ANTT MNE caixa 16:545, 546.

30 Pinto de Souza to Sá e Mello, 13 August 1782, ibid.: 548.

31 The Portuguese government had been alarmed at the prospect of a British attack against the Plate settlements for the previous twelve months and more—see Sá e Mello to Pinto de Souza, 17 March and 15 August 1781, and Pinto de Souza to Sá a Mello, 18 September 1781, ANTT MNE Legaçao Portuguesa em Londres (1781).

32 Blankett, 'Force proposed for an Expedition to Buenos Ayres, & to the Sth Seas conditionally', August 1782, Clements Sydney 9.

33 Keppel to Townshend, 25 September 1782, Clements ibid.

34 Pinto de Souza to Sá e Mello, 1 October 1782, ANTT MNE caixa 16:560.

35 Middleton to Shelburne, 25 September 1782, NMM MID 2; Sydney, Draft of instructions to Oswald, September/October 1782, Huntington HM 25760; and see Harlow, I, 312–407.

36 Middleton, 'Preparations necessary for a Secret Expedition', 26 September 1782, Clements Shelburne 151:28.

37 Shelburne, Memorandum, undated but c. 27 September 1782, ibid.: 29.

38 Middleton to Shelburne, 3 October 1782, ibid.: 30, 31.

39 Middleton to Shelburne, 23 November 1782, ibid.: 36.

40 Nepean, Draft to Lords Commissioners, undated but November 1782, SP 42/66:408.

41 Lords Commissioners, Order of 17 December 1782, ADM 2/113:522–3.

42 Townshend to Parker, 21 December 1782, NHL ms 205:239.

43 Lords Commissioners, Order of 21 December 1782, ADM 2/113:533–4.

44 See *Europe*, Musterbooks, ADM 36/9517.

45 Kingsmill to Stephens, 11 December 1782, ADM 1/2015.

46 *Elizabeth*, Captain's log and journal, NMM KIN 11.

47 The details of the voyage are from *Europe*, Captain's log and journal, ADM 51/324; from Spain; and from the letters cited hereafter.

48 Phillip to Stephens, 7 March and 25 April 1783, ADM 1/2307.

49 Vasconcellos to Mello e Castro, 24 April 1783, AHU RJ caixa 131:44.

50 Phillip to Stephens, 25 April 1783, ADM 1/2307.

51 Phillip to Townshend, 25 April 1783, IOR H 175:237.

52 Phillip to Nepean, 2 September 1787, HRNSW, I, ii, 114.

53 Banks, pp. 451–4.

54 Spain, p. 55.

55 Ibid., p. 56.

56 Hughes, Journal entries of 18 July, 17 and 19 August, and 26 September 1783, ADM 7/739; to Sir Richard King, 30 September 1783, ADM 7/735:115–18.

57 King to Plattenburg, 9 December 1783, Cape Inkomende Brieven C 556:97–9; Governor and Council, Minutes of 9 and 10 December 1783, ibid., Resolusies C 165:364–6, 368–75; and King to Stephens, 25 December 1783, ADM 1/54.

58 Spain, pp. 58–62: *Europe*, Captain's log and journal, ADM 51/324.

59 Governor and Council, Minutes of 21, 23 and 31 January 1784, Cape Resolusies C 166:62–7, 76–9, 107–8.

60 Cook, I, 465.

61 Sparrman, I, 47.

62 Unless otherwise indicated, these details are from Karsten; and from various of the First Fleet narratives.

63 'Letters of David Blackburn', JRAHS, 20 (1934), 322–3.

64 Quoted in Ross, 'Oppression, Sexuality and Slavery at the Cape of Good Hope', p. 430.

65 *London Magazine*, 51 (1782), 364; and Ross, pp. 421–3.

66 King to Stephens, 18 February 1784, ADM 1/54.

67 Phillip to Stephens, 23 April 1784, ADM 1/2307.

68 Phillip to Townshend, 25 April 1783, IOR H 175:237.

69 Phillip to Nepean, 28 October 1786, HO 42/9:83.

Private Affairs

Bibliography

There are a number of studies of the whole or of part of the British Secret Service in the eighteenth century, viz.: A. Cobban, 'British Secret service in France 1784–1792', EHR, 69 (1954), 234–7, and *Ambassadors and Secret Agents: The Diplomacy of the First Earl of Malmesbury at the Hague*, Jonathan Cape, London, 1954; Richard Deacon, *A History of the British Secret Service*, Taplinger Publishing Company, New York, 1970.

Nonetheless, its operations remain shrouded in mystery, and crucial details are quite unclear. While it casts no light on earlier operations and any part Phillip may have had in them, the ledger which Evan Nepean kept of secret service payments, now in the Clements Library, is very valuable for the operation of the service from the mid-1780s. Indeed, Nepean's role in the development of the modern service is an unwritten chapter. Papers in the HO 42 series and in the Clements Library indicate that he began to expand operations immediately Shelburne installed him as Undersecretary in March 1782; the results of his vigilance were central to British decisions during the Nootka Sound crisis in 1790, with many of the reports of Spanish naval preparations which survive being copies in his hand; and various Admiralty papers show that he continued this role through the 1790s.

[John Mullard?], *The Gentleman's Guide, in his Tour through France*, S. Farley, Bristol, [1770] and Tobias Smollett, *Travels through France and Italy*, ed. Frank Felsenstein, Oxford University Press, Oxford, 1979, have each left vivid accounts of journeys to the south of France in search of health. R.T. Sussex gives a particularly evocative description of the Camargue in 'Joseph d'Arbaud, Poet of the Camargue', AUMLA, 42 (1974), 175–6.

Notes

1 [Anon.], 'Military Memoranda of Spain, & c., intended for Mr Chamier', SP 94/254:288. The author is likely to have been Sir John Dalrymple, who was for many years consul at Cádiz.

2 See Oakes's correspondence with Nepean and Shelburne, HO 42/1, FO 95/5, and Clements Shelburne 168, ii.

3 See the documents in NMM NEP 2.

4 This summary is based on the numerous papers in ADM 1/4352, ADM 1/3967, 3968, 3969, and FO 27/4, 14.

5 See R. Lacour-Gayet, *A Concise History of Australia*, Penguin Books, Ringwood, 1976, p. 81.

6 See Nepean's copy book, WO 1/405.

7 See Egmont to Grafton, 20 July 1765, SP 94/253.

8 See SP 37/15:145–55.

9 ADM 1/3969.

10 Colpoys to Lindsay, 22 September 1784, ADM 1/388.

11 Fraser to Stephens, 7 October 1784, ADM 1/4151:61.

12 Enclosed with Fraser to Stephens, 15 October 1784, ADM 1/4151:65.

13 Enclosed with Fraser to Stephens, 25 October 1784, ADM 1/4151:66.

14 Mevrow Wolters, Report of 1 October 1784, ADM 1/3969.

15 Dundas to Sydney, 2 November 1784, PRO 30/8/157:7.

16 See *Convicts and Empire*, pp. 88–92.

17 Carmarthen to Dorset, 19 October 1784, FO 27/13:1158–9.

18 Nepean, Entry of 11 November 1784, Secret Service Ledger, Clements Nepean.

19 Phillip to Stephens, 14 October 1784, ADM 1/2307; and Register of Officers on leave abroad, ADM 6/207.

20 Nepean, Entry of 11 November 1784, Secret Service Ledger, Clements Nepean.

21 [Mullard?], p. 58.

22 Smollett, p. 329.

23 Phillip to Nepean, January and 21 March 1785, FO 95/4/6:499–500, 501. Nepean annotated the second of these reports 'Nᵒ 5'. It is much to be regretted that the others in the series seem not to have survived.

24 Phillip, Report of 21 March 1785, ibid.

25 ADM 6/207.

26 Ibid.

27 Nepean, Entry of 2 November 1785, Secret Service Ledger, Clements Nepean.

4 OUT OF THE WORLD

General

The literature of the early years of the British colonization of Australia is now extensive. A good point to begin surveying it is Victor Crittenden, *A Bibliography of the First Fleet*, Australian National University Press, Canberra, 1982. While it is impossible that someone writing now should not have general debts to predecessors, I have sought to avoid writing in immediate consciousness of what others have said. Rather than to the historical literature, I have gone to the original sources, in an attempt to write freshly. The more substantial of these sources are listed above. Lesser ones are cited in the notes. Since fresh appraisal does not necessarily lead to fresh insights, many of my conclusions will none the less be familiar. Where I have borrowed particular points, I have indicated the sources in the appropriate notes. Kerry Agnew, Gwen Bailey, and Judith Renton will recognize adaptations of ideas they formulated. The epigraphs are from Cook's letter to John Walker, 20 November 1772, Turnbull ms P COO, and Phillip's letter to Sydney, 24 September 1788, Dixson ms Q 162:15.

The Decision to Colonize

Bibliography

The precise reasons for the colonization of New South Wales have become a matter of very considerable controversy, with writers pursuing three fundamental directions in argument, viz.: the 'dumping of convicts' one (Eris O'Brien, C.M.H. Clark, A.G.L. Shaw, Mollie Gillen, David Mackay); the 'trade' one (H.T. Fry, Ged Martin, Margaret Steven); and the 'strategic' one (Geoffrey Blainey, Alan Frost). Readers interested in details should first consult Ged Martin, ed., *The Founding of Australia: The Argument about Australia's Origins*, Hale & Iremonger, Sydney, 1978. The major pieces published subsequently are Alan Frost, *Convicts and Empire: A Naval Question 1776–1811*, Oxford University Press, Melbourne, 1980; Mollie Gillen, 'The Botany Bay Decision, 1786: Convicts not Empire', EHR, 97 (1982), 740–66; Margaret Steven, *Trade, Tactics and Territory*, Melbourne University Press, Carlton, 1983; David Mackay, *A Place of Exile: The*

European Settlement of New South Wales, Oxford University Press, Melbourne, 1985; and Robert J. King, '"Ports of shelter and refreshment ...": Botany Bay and Norfolk Island in British naval strategy, 1786–1808', *Historical Studies*, 22 (1986), 199–213.

Inevitably, I am not a disinterested observer in this matter, but it does seem to me that numbers of those who have criticized the views which Blainey and I have advanced have not sufficiently understood the imperatives of eighteenth-century naval and colonial warfare, and the context which imperial rivalry created for any such venture as the Botany Bay one. It is one of my intentions that the telling of Phillip's life will bring a greater understanding of these imperatives and this context. Any reader inclined to find this view of the Botany Bay expedition hopelessly idiosyncratic should consult Catherine Gaziello, *L'Expédition de Lapérouse 1785–1788: Réplique française aux voyages de Cook*, C.T.H.S., Paris, 1984, who from a study of previously unused French manuscript sources emphasizes a similar political background.

Notes

1 Quoted in Phillip, p. 340.
2 Ibid., p. 3.
3 These comments are based on a study of Duncan Campbell's letterbooks, Mitchell mss A3227–32, and his returns in various Public Record Office files.
4 For details, see *Convicts and Empire*, pp. 33–49.
5 Edward Thompson, diary entry of 31 July 1783, Add. ms 46120:7.
6 William Dalrymple to Devaynes, undated but September 1785, PRO 30/8/128:64–5.
7 As argued by James Matra, Sir George Young, Sir John Call—see *Convicts and Empire*, pp. 10–28.
8 See ibid., pp. 88–141.

The First Fleet

Bibliography

The mounting of the First Fleet has yet to be adequately described and analysed. It is a commonplace of Australian historiography that the expedition was poorly equipped. Whether the commonplace is true is another matter. All who have so pronounced have based their comments on the one hundred or so relevant documents published in *Historical Records of New South Wales*, I, ii, and the few additional ones printed in *Historical Records of Australia*, series 1, vol. 1, and in Owen Rutter, *The First Fleet*, The Golden Cockerel Press, London, 1937. This documentary record is a grossly inadequate one, which scarcely begins to show the complexity of the business, and the officials' attention to detail. There exist in archives in England and North America, and in private hands, something like 800 relevant documents. Wilfred Oldham, who saw a good deal more than the published ones, strongly refuted the view that the expedition was poorly mounted—'The Administration of the System of Transportation of British Convicts 1763–1793', unpublished Ph.D. thesis, University of London, 1933, pp. 365–73. It will be clear that this is also my view, though confirmation must await a thorough survey of all the documents. I am presently gathering these. Dr R.J.B. Knight, of the National Maritime Museum, is preparing an analysis.

The voyage itself has been better, but not perfectly, described. Eris O'Brien, *The Foundation of Australia*, 2nd ed., Angus and Robertson, Sydney, 1950, pp. 279–84, discusses in detail the complements of the ships. Charles Bateson, *The Convict Ships 1787–1868*, A.H. & A.W. Reed, Sydney, 1974 [1959], pp. 94–119, discusses the voyage from specific points of view. Two recent general accounts (to which mine is not indebted) are Victor Crittenden, *The Voyage of the First Fleet 1787–1788*, Mulini Press, Canberra, 1981, and Jonathan King, *The First Fleet: The Convict Voyage that Founded Australia 1787–1788*, Macmillan, Melbourne, 1982.

Notes

1 The letter was backdated to 18 August 1786. For this and the following details, see *Convicts and Empire*, pp. 126–35.

2 See, e.g., *Whitehall Evening Post*, 1, 4, and 8 September 1786.

3 See *Convicts and Empire*, pp. 190–1.

4 King, p. 5.

5 Howe to Sydney, 3 September 1786, HRNSW, I, ii, 22–3.

6 See *Convicts and Empire*, p. 129.

7 Pinto de Souza to Sá e Mello, 3 October and 14 November, Sá e Mello to Pinto de Souza, 26 October 1782, ANTT MNE caixa 16; C.R. Freire to Sá e Mello, 31 August and 7 September, Mello e Castro to C.R. Freire, 2 October 1784, ibid., caixa 17 and maço 61; and Freire to Nepean, 17 November 1784, HO 42/5:382.

8 Southwell to Butler, 2 August 1787, Butler to Southwell, 25 May 1789, Add ms 16381:22, 40–1.

9 This memorandum is in CO 201/2:88–93. It is undated, but as Phillip refers to the *Berwick*, he was clearly writing before 12 October 1786, when the ship was recommissioned as the *Sirius*.

10 See Nepean, Memorandum of c. January 1787, Dixson ms Q 522.

11 See Alan Frost, 'New South Wales as *terra nullius*: the British denial of Aboriginal land rights', *Historical Studies*, 19 (1981), 513–23.

12 Phillip, Comments on a draft of his instructions, c. 11 April 1787, CO 201/2:130.

13 Middleton to Nepean, 11 December 1786, HRNSW, I, ii, 35–6.

14 Teer to Navy Board, 4 December 1786, ADM 106/243.

15 Tench, p. 12; and cf. White, pp. 49–50.

16 Phillip to Sydney, 12 March 1787, HRNSW, I, ii, 56–7.

17 Teer to Navy Board, 7 December 1786, ADM 106/243.

18 Phillip to Nepean, 28 October 1786, HO 42/9:83–4.

19 Phillip to Sydney, 1 November 1786, Dixson ms Q 162:1–2.

20 See Nepean to Sackville Hamilton, 26 October 1786 (draft), HO 100/18:372.

21 George III, Commission of 12 October 1786, HRNSW, I, ii, 24–5.

22 See ibid., pp. 25–8.

23 See Nepean to Sydney, 9 November 1786, Dixson ms Q 522.

24 Camden to Pitt, 29 January 1787, PRO 30/8/119:149–50.

25 Sydney, Draft Notes concerning provision for trials in Senegal and Gibraltar, undated, Dixson ms Q 522.

26 Macdonald to Nepean, 25 March 1787, HO 48/1B:119–20 specifically cites this precedent.

27 George III, Commission of 2 April 1787, HRNSW, I, ii, 61–7.

28 George III, Letters Patent of 2 April 1787, ibid., pp. 70–6.

29 William Blackstone, *Commentaries on the Laws of England*, 5th ed., Clarendon Press, Oxford, 1765–9, IV, 277.

30 27 Geo III, c. 2, as printed in HRNSW, I, ii, 67–70.

31 Lords Commissioners to Privy Council, 28 March 1787, and Minute of 4 April 1787, PC 1/62:16; the various minutes of the Committee of Trade, April 1787, Add. ms 38390:127–34 and Add. ms 38394:23–4; George III, Letters Patent of 5 May 1787, HRNSW, I, ii, 95–100.

32 Solicitor General to Nepean, 30 March 1790, HO 48/1B:351.

33 Attorney General, 'Warrant for a Commission authorizing the Gov. of New South Wales to remit Sentences', 30 March 1790 (draft), ibid.: 345–50; 30 Geo III, c. 47; George III, Letters Patent of 8 November 1790, HRNSW, I, ii, 410–13.

34 *Whitehall Evening Post*, 4 January 1787.

35 [Nepean], Memorandum of c. January 1787, Dixson ms Q 522.

36 Phillip to Stephens, 27 December 1786, Stephens to Phillip, 23 February, Phillip to Nepean, 1 March, Sydney to Phillip, 20 April 1787, HRNSW, I, ii, 40–1, 48–9, 54–5, 82–3.

37 The earliest draft of Phillip's instructions has not appeared. Phillip's comment on it, c. 11 April 1787, are in CO 201/2:128–31. A revised version was then sent to the Privy Council, which referred it to the Committee of Trade on 20 April. The Committee (Hawkesbury, Sydney, W.W. Grenville) considered this on 24 April, 'making some Amendments and alterations therein' (Add. ms 38390:134). On 25 April, the Privy Council instructed Sydney to issue a fair copy (PC 2/132:167), which was dated the same day as the amended instructions, which are evidently those in CO 201/1:29–40. This fair copy was evidently dated 25 April 1787 (CO 202/5:28–38).

38 Phillip, Comments on his instructions, c. 11 April 1787, CO 201/2:131.

39 Phillip used this or similar phrasing a number of times—see, e.g., his letter to Nepean, 28 October 1786, HO 42/9:84.

40 Bradley, p. 11.

41 Ibid., p. 12.

42 Smyth, p. 16.

43 Collins, p. lvii.

44 Phillip to Sydney, 5 June 1787, HRNSW, I, ii, 106; and Clark to Hartwell, 10 June 1787, Clark, p. 251.

45 Phillip to Nepean, 5 June 1787, HRNSW, I, ii, 108.

46 F. Fernandez-Arnesto, *The Canary Islands after the Conquest*, Clarendon Press, Oxford, 1982, gives the Spanish history of the islands.

47 Phillip to Nepean, 5 June and 2 September 1787, HRNSW, I, ii, 107, 114; Bradley, p. 38; Tench, p. 17; White, p. 54.

48 Phillip to Nepean, 2 September 1787, HRNSW, I, ii, 113: Bradley, p. 38.

49 Nagle, pp. 38–9; King, p. 15; Phillip to Nepean, 3 September 1787, HRNSW, I, ii, 116.

50 King, p. 15; Smyth, pp. 29–30; Bradley, pp. 37–9; Nagle, p. 39; White, p. 73; Phillip to Sydney, 2 September, to Nepean, 2 September 1787, HRNSW, I, ii, 110, 112–13; to Banks, 31 August 1787, Sutro Banks (uncatalogued) and 2 September 1787, Mitchell ms C 213:3–5.

51 E.g., Smyth, pp. 28–36; Tench, pp. 21–5; White, pp. 72–88.

52 Governor and Council, Minute of 19 October 1787, Cape Resolusies C 176:92–5; Tench, p. 27; White, pp. 90–3; Smyth, p. 43.

53 Smyth, p. 42; White, p. 90; King, p. 21.

54 White, p. 90; Smyth, p. 41; 'Letters of David Blackburn', pp. 322–3; White, p. 91; Tench, p. 27; Smyth, p. 42; Southwell to Butler, 11 November 1787, Add. ms 16381:25.

55 Tench, p. 26; White (of Rio de Janeiro), p. 81.

56 Bradley, pp. 44–5; Collins, pp. lxxx–lxxxi.

57 Bradley, p. 46; Smyth, p. 40.

58 Phillip to Nepean, 28 October 1786, HO 42/9:83.

59 Worgan, p. 1.

60 Southwell to his mother, 11 November 1787, Add. ms 16381:23.

61 Cook to Walker, 20 November 1771, Turnbull ms P COO; Collins, p. lxxxvi.

62 White, p. 101.

63 Tench, p. 28.

64 Worgan, p. 1; Masson to Banks, 13 November 1787, Sutro Banks (uncatalogued); Banks to Masson, 3 June 1787, BM(NH) DTC 5:173.

65 King, pp. 24–31; Phillip to Middleton, 6 July 1788, (in private hands).

66 E.g., Smyth, pp. 47, 50, 53; Hunter, pp. 22–7.

67 Tench, p. 31.

68 Blackburn to his sister, 5 June 1787, Australian Joint Copying Project M970.

69 Phillip to Middleton, 6 July 1788, (in private hands); Collins, 'Return of men, women, and children belonging to the settlement that have died since the 13th of May, 1787', HRNSW, I, ii, 193.

70 See Bateson, pp. 98–117.

71 Nagle, p. 47.

72 Shapcote to Navy Board, 24 April, Phillip to Grenville, 17 July 1790, HRNSW, I, ii, 334–5, 362.

73 Phillip, Memorandum, c. September 1786, CO 201/2:88.

74 Phillip to Sydney, 12 March 1787, HRNSW, I, ii, 56–7.

75 Nepean to Middleton, 13 February 1787, (in private hands); Middleton to Nepean, 20 February 1787, HRNSW, I, ii, 91–2 (where it is misdated); Phillip to Nepean, 18 March 1787, ibid., pp. 58–9; White, p. 50.

76 See above, pp. 27–9.

77 Smyth, p. 18.

78 White, pp. 67–8.

79 See Sir John Pringle, 'A Discourse upon some later improvements of the means for Preserving the Health of Mariners', in James Cook, *A Voyage Towards the South Pole and Round the World*, W. Strahan & J. Cadell, London, 1777, II, 369–96.

80 Sir James Watt, 'Medical Aspects and Consequences of Cook's voyages', in *Captain James Cook and his Times*, ed. Robin Fisher and Hugh Johnston, Australian National University Press, Canberra, 1979, pp. 129–57 (particularly pp. 144–6); C.C. Lloyd, 'Victualling of the Fleet in the eighteenth and nineteenth centuries', I.M. Sharman, 'Vitamin Requirements of the Human Body', G.J. Milton-Thompson, 'Two hundred years of the sailor's diet', in *Starving Sailors*, ed. Sir James Watt et al., National Maritime Museum, London, 1981, pp. 1–15, 17–26, 27–34.

81 Easty, p. 30; Hunter, p. 12; Nagle, p. 38; Smyth, p. 29; White, p. 73.

82 White, pp. 64–6.

83 Collins, p. 1. The difference between the number of deaths Collins gives and that deriving from other records of the voyage (see above, p. 162) arises from the one figure dating from departure from England, and the other from embarkation—see John Cobley, 'The Convicts who Died in the First Fleet', JRAHS, 51 (1965), 249–53.

Planting New South Wales: Difficulties

Bibliography

The most relevant published documentary sources are the First Fleet narratives listed above; HRNSW, I, ii; and the selection John Cobley published as *Sydney Cove, I (1788), II (1789–90), III (1791–2)*, Hodder & Stoughton, London, 1962, Angus & Robertson, Sydney, 1963, 65. The three previous major studies of Phillip all pay great attention to his time in New South Wales— L. Becke and W. Jeffery, *Admiral Phillip: The Founding of New South Wales*; George Mackaness, *Admiral Arthur Phillip: Founder of New South Wales 1738–1814*; and M. Barnard Eldershaw, *Phillip of Australia: An Account of the Settlement at Sydney Cove*. Peter Taylor, *Australia: The First Twelve Years*, George Allen & Unwin, Sydney, 1982, offers a more general account.

Notes

1 King, pp. 32–3.
2 Hunter, p. 28.
3 Phillip, Comments on a draft of his Instructions, c. 11 April 1787, CO 201/2:128. Phillip's reference to islands in Port Jackson is puzzling, for neither Cook nor Banks mentions them in his journal of the *Endeavour*'s voyage. We can only assume that those on board her noticed more than Cook and Banks recorded, and that Phillip had access to this additional information.
4 Sydney to Phillip, 20 April 1787, HRNSW, I, ii, 83.
5 Hunter, p. 29; Phillip to Sydney, 15 May 1788, HRNSW, I, ii, 122.
6 Gaziello, *L'Expédition de Lapérouse*, pp. 47–65; Lapérouse, *A Voyage Round the World*, ed. L.A. Miler-Mureau, G.G. and J. Robinson, London, 1799, I, 27; Phillip, Comments on his instructions, c. 11 April 1787, CO 201/2:131; Hunter, p. 29; Smyth, p. 63; Worgan, p. 30.
7 King, p. 36; Collins, p. 4; Bradley, pp. 64–5; Worgan, p. 33; White, pp. 112–13.
8 Andrew Miller, 'An Account of Live Stock in the Settlement', 1 May 1788, HRNSW, I, ii, 151; and Robert Brown, Journal entry, 30 January 1788, HRNSW, II, 409.
9 Collins, p. 5.
10 Worgan, p. 34.
11 Smyth, p. 67; Tench, p. 39.
12 It is much to be regretted that Phillip's own notes for his speech have not survived. My account draws on Bradley, pp. 80–1; Clark, p.96; Collins, pp. 6–7; Easty, p. 96; [An Officer], pp. 20–1; Smyth, pp. 67–9; Tench, pp. 41–2; Waterhouse, Mitchell FM 4/63; White, p. 114; Worgan, pp. 34–5.
13 Clark, p. 96; Smyth, p. 69.
14 Worgan, p. 8.

15 Phillip to Sydney, 15 May 1788, HRNSW, I, ii, 123.

16 Ibid., p. 128; Collins, p. 23.

17 Phillip to Sydney, 28 September 1788, HRNSW, I, ii, 190.

18 White, pp. 113–14; Worgan, pp. 12–13, 42–3; Phillip to Sydney, 28 September 1788, HRNSW, I, ii, 188.

19 Collins, p. 15.

20 Smyth, pp. 70, 79; White, pp. 119, 173–7; White to Sydney, July 1788, HRNSW, I, ii, 175; 'Letter from an Officer at Sydney', ibid., II, 744–5; Bryan Gandevia, 'A-going for greens', in *Plants and Man in Australia*, ed. D.J. and S.G.M. Carr, Academic Press, Sydney, 1981, pp. 256–65.

21 Sydney to Lords Commissioners, 31 August 1786, HRNSW, I, ii, 22.

22 Phillip to Sydney, 16 May, to Nepean, 9 July 1788, HRNSW, I, ii, 138, 153; to Sydney, 5 July 1788, Dixson ms Q 162:6.

23 Smyth, p. 70; Clark, p. 96.

24 Ross to Stephens, 10 July 1788, HRNSW, I, ii, 169; Campbell to Ducie, 12 July 1788, Mitchell ms AC 145:1–2; Smyth, pp. 44–5.

25 Campbell to Ducie, 12 July 1788, Mitchell ms AC 145:3–4; Ross to Nepean, 10 July and 16 November 1788, HRNSW, I, ii, 176, 212–13; 'Letter from an Officer at Sydney', 12 July 1788, HRNSW, II, 745; Southwell to his mother, 27/30 July and 7 August 1790, Add. ms 16381: 77–84, 85–8.

26 See the various papers in HRNSW, I, ii, 156–65; Ross to Stephens, 1 October 1788, ibid., 194–9; and Phillip to Sydney, 5 July 1788, Dixson ms Q 162:6.

27 Nagle, p. 50.

28 White to Skill, 17 April 1790, HRNSW, I, ii, 333.

29 Ross to Nepean, 10 July 1790, ibid., p. 176; 'Letter from an Officer at Sydney', 12 July 1788, ibid., II, 745.

30 Phillip to Banks, 26 July 1790, Mitchell ms C 213:59.

31 Quoted in Anne McCormick and Derek McDonnell, *The Riou Papers*, The Authors, Sydney, 1985, pp. 46–7.

32 Phillip to Banks, 26 July 1790, Mitchell ms C 213:55, 56.

Planting New South Wales: Solutions

Notes

1 'Letter from a Female Convict', 14 November 1788, HRNSW, II, 747.

2 Phillip to Sydney, 24 September 1788, Dixson ms Q 162:14, and 28 September 1788, HRNSW, I, ii, 190.

3 Phillip to Sydney, 16 November 1788 and 12 February 1790, HRNSW, I, ii, 211, 296, 299.

4 Ibid., pp. 211, 300; and King, passim.

5 Smyth, pp. 70, 79; White, pp. 145–6, 151, 155; Collins, p. 5.

6 Phillip to Sydney, 12 February 1790, HRNSW, I, ii, 298.

7 Ibid.

8 Phillip to Middleton, 6 July 1788, (in private hands).

9 Phillip to Sydney, 16 May, to Nepean, 28 September 1788, HRNSW, I, ii, 138, 184; Collins, p. 7.

10 Collins, pp. 63–4, 70; Phillip to Sydney, 1 February 1790, HRNSW, I, ii, 288–9.

11 Tench, p. 71.

12 Phillip to Nepean, 12 February, to Sydney, 1 February 1790, HRNSW, I, ii, 301–4, 288. Nagle's vignette of life on Norfolk Island under Ross is instructive:
   'Lieut Govenor Ross was a Merciless Commander to either free Man or Prisoner, he laid us Under Three differint Laws, the Seamen ware still under the Naval Laws, the Soldiers under the Military Laws, beside the Sivil Laws, & a Marchal Law of his own directions with strict orders to be Attended to for the Smallest Crime Whatever, or neglect of duty' (p. 52).

13 Elizabeth Macarthur to Eliza Kingdon, 7 March 1791, *Some Early Records of the Macarthurs of Camden*, ed. S.M. Onslow, Rigby, Adelaide, 1973 [1914], p. 28.

14 Hunter, p. 117.

15 Tench, pp. 168–70.

16 Phillip, Memorandum of c. September 1786, and Comments on a draft of his Instructions, c. 11 April 1787, CO 201/2:90–1, 128.

17 Phillip to Banks, 2 July 1788, Mitchell ms C 213:17.

18 See Alan Frost, '"A Strange Illumination of the Heart": James Cook, Tahiti, and Beyond', *Meanjin Quarterly*, 29 (1970), 446–52; and Glyndwr Williams, '"Far more happier than we Europeans": Reactions to the Australian Aborigines on Cook's voyage', *Historical Studies*, 19 (1981), 499–512.

19 King, p. 32.

20 White, p. 109.

21 Worgan, p. 3.

22 Bradley, pp. 59–60; King, p. 35; Smyth, p. 58; Worgan, p. 6.

23 Worgan, p. 33.

24 Ibid., pp. 23, 33.

25 Nagle, p. 43.

26 Phillip to Lansdowne, 3 July 1788, HRNSW, II, 411.

27 Nagle, p. 43.

28 Worgan, p. 41.

29 Bradley, p. 85; Collins, p. 13; Phillip to Banks, 2 July 1788, Mitchell ms C 213:12. The cause of this incident is unclear. Bradley says that the French were 'obliged to fire on the Natives at Botany Bay to keep them quiet' some time before 9 February 1788. Two weeks later, French officers told the British that the Botany Bay Aborigines were 'exceedingly troublesome', that 'wherever they meet an unarmed Man they attack him' (Bradley, pp. 81, 85).

30 Phillip to Banks, 2 July 1788, Mitchell ms C 213:19; Tench, p. 40.

31 Collins, p. 13.

32 Bradley, p. 126.

33 Collins, p. 24.

34 Collins, pp. 24–5; Phillip to Sydney, 9 July 1788, HRNSW, I, ii, 148–9.

35 Phillip to Sydney, 18 May 1788, HRNSW, I, ii, 131–5; to Banks, 2 July 1788, Mitchell ms C 213:9–11, 18–21, 21–2.

36 Phillip to Banks, 2 July 1788, Mitchell ms C 213:11, 20; to Nepean, 10 July 1788, HRNSW, I, ii, 178.

37 Tench, p. 138.

38 Phillip to Sydney, 12 February 1790, HRNSW, I, ii, 298; Bradley, pp. 161–3; Collins, p. 40; Hunter, pp. 92, 270–4; Tench, pp. 138–51; Fowell to his father, 31 July 1790, HRNSW, I, ii, 376. Desperate as this action may now seem to us, it is worth noting that it was a time-honoured European procedure—see, e.g., C. Macknight, *The Farthest Coast*, Melbourne University Press, Carlton, 1969, p. 43. Both Cook and Bougainville took Polynesians to Europe with the idea of learning more of their culture, and of showing them the merits of civilization—but both Tupia and Autourou did go voluntarily.

39 Tench, p. 151.

40 Collins, p. 71; Tench, pp. 159–61, 167; Phillip to Banks, 26 July 1790, Mitchell ms C 213:58.

41 Phillip to Sydney, 11 November 1791, Dixson ms Q 162:29–41.

42 Ross, Report of c. December 1790, HRNSW, I, ii, 416–20.

43 Phillip to Dundas, 2 and 4 October 1792, HRNSW, I, ii, 645, 653–60.

44 Grose to Nepean, 2 April 1792, ibid., p. 613.

45 Collins, pp. 120, 161, 217.

46 Phillip to Grenville, 5 November 1791, to Dundas, 19 March 1792, HRNSW, I, ii, 538, 596; Collins, pp. 143, 145–6, 149–50.

47 See, e.g., Grimes to Grimes, 21 October 1792, HRNSW, I, ii, 672.

48 Collins, pp. 91, 163, 193; Phillip to Grenville, 5 November 1791, HRNSW, I, ii, 537.

49 Phillip to Banks, 17 November 1788, 13 April and 22 August 1790, 24 March 1791, 4 April 1792, Mitchell ms C 213:49–51, 53–4, 62–8, 70–8, 90–4; to Grenville, 14 December 1791, HRNSW, I, ii, 566.

50 Phillip to Banks, 15 October 1792, NLA ms 9/134.

51 Elizabeth Macarthur to Eliza Kingdon, 7 March and 18 November 1791, *The Macarthurs of Camden*, pp. 39, 42.

52 Collins, pp. 110–12; Hunter, pp. 140–3; Nagle, p. 46; Tench, pp. 177–80. It is significant that even in this extremity Phillip fired his pistol to frighten the Aborigines, not to harm them—see Waterhouse's description, Mitchell ms AW 109.

53 Tench, p. 208.

54 Collins, pp. 110–12; Tench, pp. 181, 183–90; Hunter, p. 139.

55 Hunter, pp. 313, 319–23; Tench, pp. 200–3.

56 Collins, pp. 117–19; Hunter, pp. 326–9; Tench, pp. 205–6.

57 Tench, pp. 207–11.

58 Phillip to Banks, 24 March 1791, Mitchell ms C 213:76.

59 Harris to [   ], 20 March 1791, Mitchell ms A 1597:6.

60 Collins, pp. 137–9, 146.

61 Ibid., p. 211.

62 See, e.g., Hunter, pp. 143–5.

63 Report, Museo Naval (Madrid), ms 318:11–37 (NLA film B 415, G 425). I am grateful to Mr Robert King for this translation.

64 Phillip to Dundas, 19 March 1792, to Grenville, 20 June 1790, HRNSW, I, ii, 598, 351.

65 Phillip to Sydney, 11 November 1791, Dixson ms Q 162:31; to Grenville, 21 November 1791, to Dundas, 2 October 1792, HRNSW, I, ii, 559, 645–6.

Founding Australia

Bibliography

There are many general studies which consider the beginning of modern Australia, which the interested reader can easily discover. The following more specialized studies, though, discuss at greater length a number of the aspects I mention: Bryan Gandevia, *Tears Often Shed: Child Health and Welfare in Australia from 1788*, Pergamon Press, [Sydney], 1978; Portia Robinson, *The Hatch and Brood of Time: A Study of the first generation of native-born white Australians 1788–1828*, *I*, Oxford University Press, Melbourne, 1985; and J.B. Hirst, *Convict Society and its Enemies*, George Allen & Unwin, Sydney, 1983. The epigraph is from Butler to Southwell, 30 January 1791, Add. ms. 16381:99.

Notes

1 Phillip to Sydney, 15 May 1788, HRNSW, I, ii, 122.
2 E.g., 'we got Save to ane Anchor in one of the finest harbours in the world—I never Saw any like it'—Clark, p. 93; 'This is Certainly in the Opinion of everyone one of the finest Harbours in the World, not excepting that of Trincamale in the East Indies'—Smyth, p. 62; 'Having passed between the capes which form its entrance, we found ourselves in a port superior, in extent and excellency, to all we had seen before'—Tench, p. 38; 'Port Jackson I believe to be, without exception, the finest and most extensive harbour in the universe, and at the same time the most secure, being safe from all winds that blow'—White, p. 112; 'it is not easy to describe adequately the beauty of this harbour and the admiration it should arouse in any seafarer who enters it'—Francisco Xavier de Viana, 'Diario', in *The Spanish at Port Jackson*, Australian Documentary Facsimile Society, Sydney, 1967, p. 24.
3 This assessment is based on the discussion in [   ], *The Portsmouth Guide*, R. Carr, Portsmouth, 1775, pp. 65–8.
4 See above, p. 68.
5 See above, pp. 7–8, 65, 68–9, 120–1, 132.
6 Phillip to Sydney, 15 May 1788, HRNSW, I, ii, 122.
7 Phillip to Sydney, 9 July 1788, ibid., p. 148.
8 Ibid., p. 147.
9 Collins, p. 17.
10 Phillip to Sydney, 9 July 1788, HRNSW, I, ii, 147.
11 Waterhouse to his father, 11 July 1788, Mitchell film FM 4/63.
12 Phillip to Sydney, 28 September 1788, HRNSW, I, ii, 186–7.
13 Phillip to Nepean, 12 February 1790, ibid., p. 302.
14 Navy Board, Minute of 8 November 1786, ADM 106/2622.
15 King, p. 37; Smyth, p. 66; Worgan, p. 34.
16 Phillip to Sydney, 15 May 1788, HRNSW, I, ii, 136.
17 Smyth, p. 68.
18 Forbes to Horton, 6 March 1827, HRA series, 4, I, 688.
19 Ross to Stephens, 10 July 1788, HRNSW, I, ii, 174; Harris to [   ], 20 March 1791, Mitchell

ms A 1597:3; Collins, p. 82; Hill to Wathen, 26 July 1790, HRNSW, I, ii, 369; Phillip to Grose, 4 October 1792, ibid., p. 652; Grose to Dundas, 16 February 1793, ibid., II, 13–14; *The Macarthurs of Camden*, p. 20.

20 Hirst develops this point in detail.

21 Collins, pp. 11, 34. For a description of the system in the English dockyards, see Baugh, *British Naval Administration in the Age of Walpole*, pp. 308ff.

22 Collins, pp. 82, 98, 216.

23 Robinson develops this point in detail.

24 See Phillip to Nepean, 12 February 1790, HRNSW, I, ii, 301.

25 Nagle, p. 44.

26 See the accounts based on his journals in Hunter, pp. 319–21, 325, 339.

27 Nagle, p. 36.

28 Entry of 20 February 1783, *Europe*, Captain's log and journal, ADM 51/324.

29 Spain, pp. 64–5.

30 Nagle, pp. 35–6.

31 Ibid.

32 Clark, p. 96.

33 Collins, p. 66.

34 Collins, p. 49; Tench, p. 145.

35 See Phillip to Sydney, 1 February 1790, HRNSW, I, ii, 288–93.

36 Collins, p. 70.

37 George III, Instructions to Phillip, 25 April 1787, HRNSW, I, ii, 90.

38 Details of Ruse and Elizabeth Perry (or Parry) are from articles in the *Dictionary of Australian Biography*, John Cobley, *The Crimes of the First Fleet Convicts*, Angus & Robertson, Sydney, 1982 [1970], and elsewhere.

39 Collins, p. 75.

40 Tench, pp. 197–8, 256.

41 Ibid., pp. 256–7.

42 Collins, p. 136.

43 Tench, p. 198.

44 This calendar of the weather is based partly on the details recorded in Hunter, pp. 50–2, and partly on the annotations to various of the Port Jackson Painter's works in the British Museum (Natural History).

45 William Kent, 'Remarks on His Majesty's Settlement in New South Wales', [1806?], Mitchell ms A 78/3:284; Roger Therry, *Reminiscences of Thirty Years' Residence in New South Wales and Victoria*, Sydney University Press in association with the Royal Australian Historical Society, 1974 [1863], p. 37.

46 Phillip to Sydney, 15 May 1788, HRNSW, I, ii, 128.

47 Tench, p. 65.

48 Phillip to Sydney, 9 July and 24 September 1788, HRNSW, I, ii, 150 and Dixson ms Q 162:13; to Sydney, 12 February 1790, HRNSW, I, ii, 298.

49 Hunter, p. 12.

50 For example: The first Roanoke colony (1585) consisted of 108 men, the second (1586) was a holding party of fifteen, the third (1587) consisted of 117 men, women, and children. Only one of the 132 persons in the second and third attempts survived two years. The first Virginia

Company settlement at Jamestown in 1607 involved about 100 persons, half of whom died before the year was out. The Pilgrims who founded Plymouth Plantation in 1620 numbered 101, and half of them died in the first winter.

51 Tench, p. 267.

52 The claim that the First Fleet colonists lacked potatoes is another of the myths of Australian historiography. The list of seeds which Banks drew up in October 1786 included '1 Jar potatoe Seed' (T 1/639); and there can be no doubt that the colonists brought this with them. Worgan, for example, planted vegetables in February 1788; and in June he 'opened one of my Potatoe Beds, & Found 6 or 7 at each Root' (p. 13). There is no reason to think that the cultivation of the root was not general in the colony from the first year. In November 1791, for example, Phillip reported that he had two acres of potatoes at Parramatta (to Sydney, 11 November 1791, Dixson Q 162: 34). The situation was similar on Norfolk Island. King sowed potatoes immediately on his arrival in March 1788, and continued to do so seasonally. In September 1789, he harvested '5 Bushells of very fine Potatoes' (King, pp. 52, 54, 224, 289, 291, 297, 305, 308). In 1790, from two of the three acres King had planted, Ross obtained four bushels, and from the third, 167 bushels. In January 1791, he reported 'Potatoes thrive remarkably well, and yield a very great increase. I think two crops a year of that article may be got with great ease' (Ross, Reports of December 1790 and January 1791, HRNSW, I, ii, 418, 431).

53 The establishing of accurate demographic statistics before about the middle of the nineteenth century is notoriously difficult. Portia Robinson discusses the particular problems concerning New South Wales in its first forty years at the beginning of *The Hatch and Brood of Time* (pp. 23–6). While not disagreeing in general, I have supposed that the figures available for Phillip's years are reliable enough to permit some detailed analysis, given that 1) settlement was not then nearly so dispersed as it later became; 2) Phillip and his subordinates were therefore able to know circumstances of birth and death much more accurately than their successors; and 3) they were manifestly concerned to do so. While the figures offered by Collins and in the various returns printed in HRNSW and HRA, and elsewhere, are reasonably accurate, they are not complete, and they therefore need to be augmented from other sources. As Bryan Gandevia and Simon Gandevia have done so in 'Childhood mortality and its social background in the first settlement at Sydney Cove, 1788–1792', *Australian Paediatric Journal*, 11 (1975), 9–19, their figures are a convenient basis for discussion.

Considering 'infants' and 'children' together for the present purpose, it appears that 36 children disembarked from the First Fleet (O'Brien, p. 284); that none arrived in 1789, 33 in 1790, 11 in 1791, and five in 1792. In the same period, there were 247 births in the colony. Deaths from all causes (i.e., including accidents) were: 1788–12, 1789–8, 1790–8, 1791–116, 1792–33: a total of 77.

Counting as children still all those who reached the colony as children, these figures give the following approximate mortality rates: 1788—19%, 1789—9%, 1790—5%, 1791—7%, 1792—12%. Though it is not really congruous to do so, if for the purpose of having a rough comparison we translate these percentages into proportions per 1000 births, we have a range from 50 to 190.

The British rates with which we might compare the New South Wales ones are even rougher. The general figures—150–180 per 1000 births—of infant and child mortality there which the standard authorities offer for the late eighteenth and earlier nineteenth centuries are not very reliable, partly because the extant records do not include the deaths of infants immediately after birth or in the first month, when baptism was not usual. (See B.R. Mitchell and P. Deane, ed., *Abstract of British Historical Statistics*, Cambridge University Press, Cambridge, 1962, and F.B. Smith, *The People's Health*, Croom Helm, London, 1970, pp. 68–9, 119.) None the less, the clear implication is, particularly as the New South Wales figures include *all* births, that the children in the colony had a distinctly better chance of survival than those in England generally, and a very much better one than those in London, where the death rate among infants and children might have averaged one in two.

54 Palmer, Return of 8 December 1792, HRNSW, I, ii, 676–7.
55 Robinson (pp. 41–3, 121) makes the point strikingly, but does not apply it specifically to the colony in Phillip's time.
56 Cf. e.g., Rennell's:
  '... the progress of population is too rapid to be opposed by human means, and will soon outgrow, in America, that of France, with all her conquests and fraternizations. The colony of New South Wales, too, will probably be able to take care of itself. The rising generation there is said to be very numerous, and it is pretty obvious that on the care of their religion and morals the character of the future nation will depend.'
  —quoted in C.R. Markham, *Major James Rennell and the Rise of Modern English Geography*, Cassell & Co., London, 1895, p. 104.
57 George III, Additional Instructions to Phillip, 29 August 1789, HRNSW, I, ii, 259.
58 Johnson to Morice, 21 March 1792, quoted in Cobley, III, 231–2; and see V.W.E. Goodwin, 'Public Education in New South Wales before 1848', JRAHS, 36 (1950), 1–14.
59 See Phillip to Dundas, 2 and 4 October 1792, HRNSW, I, ii, 645, 653–61.
60 Phillip, Memorandum of c. September 1786, CO 201/2:92.
61 Phillip to Nepean, 28 October 1786, HO 42/9:84.
62 Phillip to Middleton, 6 July 1788, (in private hands).
63 Phillip, p. xii.
64 Ibid., p. xxiii.
65 Phillip to Banks, 26 July 1790, Mitchell ms C 213:57.

Return to England

Bibliography

Easty's is the only known account of the *Atlantic*'s return voyage. Phillip does not refer to it in any of his extant letters.

Notes

1 Phillip to Grenville, 11 October 1792, HRNSW, I, ii, 666.
2 Chapman to his mother, 5 May 1792, Mitchell ms A 1974:22.
3 Phillip to Banks, 26 July 1790, Mitchell ms C 213:59.
4 Phillip to Banks, 24 March 1791, ibid.: 77, to Nepean, 12 February 1790, HRNSW, I, ii, 301; and cf. White, p. 127.

5 Phillip to Banks, 26 July 1790, Mitchell ms C 213:59, to Sydney, 11 November 1791, Dixson ms Q 162:35.
6 Collins, p. 211; Banks to Paterson, 31 March 1797, Dixson ms Q161:67.
7 Phillip to Nepean, 15 April 1790, HRNSW, I, ii, 330.
8 Grenville to Phillip, 19 February 1791, ibid., pp. 463–4.
9 Phillip to Banks, 15 October 1792, NLA ms 9/134.
10 No discussion by Phillip of his reasons for doing so is extant, but see Collins, pp. 207–11.
11 Collins, ibid., p. 211.
12 Easty, pp. 142–73. See also Rudy Bauss, 'The Critical Importance of Rio de Janeiro to British Interests, with Particular Attention to Australia in her Formative Years, 1787–1805', JRAHS, 65 (1979), 168, and the *Dublin Chronicle*, 28 May 1793.
13 Henry Handel Richardson, *The Fortunes of Richard Mahoney*, Heinemann, London, 1954, p. 345.

Passing Time

Bibliography

John Kenny gives an account of the Aborigines in England in *Bennelong*, Bank of New South Wales in association with the Royal Australian Historical Society, Sydney, 1973, pp. 54–7. R.S. Neale, *Bath 1680–1850: A Social History*, Routledge & Kegan Paul, London, 1981, describes the city at the turn of the nineteenth century; and Sir Frederick Chapman, *Governor Phillip in Retirement*, Halstead Press, Sydney, 1962, gives some details of Phillip's activities there.

Notes

1 Phillip to Hawkesbury, 27 June 1793, Add. ms 38229:44; to Dundas, 21 October 1793, HRNSW, II, 74.
2 Phillip to Dundas, 21 October 1793, ibid.
3 Phillip to Dundas, 23 July 1793, ibid., p. 59.
4 Phillip to Stephens, 11 November 1793, ADM 1/2310.
5 Phillip to Dundas, 23 July and 21 October 1793, and Chinnery to [   ], 14 December 1795, HRNSW, II, 60, 74–5, 342–3.
6 Mackaness, p. 417.
7 See Stephens to Phillip, 21 October 1793, HRNSW, II, 75.
8 Charlott Phillip, Will, dated 21 December 1781, proved PCC 6 October 1792, PROB 11/1224.
9 St Mary le Bone, Marriage register, Harleian 53; and *Gentleman's Magazine*, 64 (1794), 480.
10 Pedigree, Whitehead of Claughton, Chetham Society 105: 254. Curiously, this does not include Isabella, but her will (PROB 11/1668) makes it clear that she was the daughter of Richard Whitehead and Elizabeth Sudell. The date of her birth conflicts with that deduced from her age at marriage and death; but it does seem correct.

11 Quoted in Chapman, p. 18.

12 Joining register, Bath Circulating Library (photograph in Mitchell uncatalogued ms 440).

13 *European Magazine and London Review*, 13 (1794), 310.

14 See Chapman, pp. 23–4.

15 Phillip used this phrasing in his letter to Dundas, 23 July 1793, HRNSW, II, 59.

16 Phillip to [Dundas?], 26 October 1793, HRNSW, II, 75–6; to [Nepean?], 19 February 1794, CO 201/1:117; to Banks, 7 September 1796, Mitchell ms C 213:95–7; King to Portland, 15 June 1797, HRNSW, III, 221–2.

17 Phillip to John King, 26 November 1793, HRNSW, II, 99.

18 Phillip to Banks, 13 March 1794, Mitchell ms A 81:195–6; to Banks, 7 September 1796, Mitchell C 213:95; to King, 4 October 1799, Mitchell ms Ap 13/2:7.

5 IN SEARCH OF A LAST GLORY

Bibliography

David Mackay, *In the wake of Cook: Exploration, Science & Empire, 1780–1801*, Victoria University Press, Wellington, 1985, pp. 57–120, describes the events leading to the Nootka Sound crisis from the British point of view, and the aftermath; Warren L. Cook, *Flood Tide of Empire: Spain and the Pacific Northwest, 1543–1819*, Yale University Press, New Haven, 1973, pp. 146–249, does so from the Spanish point of view as well; J.M. Norris, 'The Policy of the British Cabinet in the Nootka Crisis', EHR, 70 (1955), 562–80 gives details of the British preparations for war (though there is more to be said about these).

J.H. Rose, *William Pitt and the Great War*, G. Bell and Sons, London, 1911, and John Ehrman, *The Younger Pitt, [II]: The Reluctant Years*, Constable, London, 1983, describe the general progress of the war in the 1790s. As before, Joseph Allen, *Battles of the British Navy: I*, Henry G. Bohn, London, 1852, and Geoffrey Marcus, *A Naval History of England: II: The Age of Nelson*, George Allen & Unwin, London, 1971, give details of sailings and engagements. Piers Mackesy, *War without Victory: The Downfall of Pitt, 1799–1802*, Clarendon Press, Oxford, 1984, shows the consequences of failure.

Daniel A. Baugh, *British Naval Administration in the Age of Walpole*, Princeton University Press, Princeton, NJ, 1965, pp. 147–79, and N.A.M. Rodger, 'Stragglers and Deserters from the Royal Navy during the Seven Years' War', *Bulletin of the Institute of Historical Research*, 57 (1984), 56–73, discuss manning in the mid-eighteenth century. Michael Lewis, *A Social History of the Navy 1783–1815*, George Allen & Unwin, London, 1960, pp. 85–140, and Christopher Lloyd, *The British Seaman 1200–1860*, Collins, London, 1968, pp. 112–72, offer brief analyses of it at the turn of the nineteenth century.

Notes

1 Phillip to Dundas, 22 October 1793, CO 201/8:289.

2 See Alan Frost, 'New South Wales as *terra nullius*: the British denial of Aboriginal land

rights', *Historical Studies*, 19 (1981), 517–18. The quoted passage appears in Nepean's draft to Phillip, March 1790, CO 201/1:20.

3   Mackay, *In the wake of Cook*, pp. 87–93.

4   Stephens to Phillip, 21 October 1793, HRNSW, II, 75.

5   Phillip to Lords Commissioners, 26 February 1796, ADM 1/2313; entry of 10 March 1796, *Alexander*, Captain's log and journal, ADM 51/1123; ADM 6/25.

6   Entry of 29 September 1796, *Swiftsure*, Captain's log and journal, ADM 51/1192.

7   Collingridge to his sister, quoted in Lloyd, p. 200.

8   *Swiftsure*, Captain's log and journal, ADM 51:1192; Nelson to St Vincent, 9 June 1797, ADM 1/396.

9   *Swiftsure*, Captain's log and journal, ADM 51/1192.

10   Phillip to Nepean, 17 February 1798, ADM 1/2317.

11   Dundas to Stuart, 3 December 1796, 6 May 1797, WO 6/40:1–7, 20–7; to Grenville, 22 November 1796, WO 6/163:147–9; St Vincent, Letters of May and June 1797, Add. ms 31166:158, 168, 171; to Nepean, 26 June 1797, to Souza Coutinho, 26 June 1797, ADM 1/396; Lords Commissioners to St Vincent, 4 November 1797, ADM 2/1352:173–4.

12   St Vincent to Nepean, 29 August and 28 September 1797, ADM 1/396.

13   Dundas to Stuart, 19 August 1797, WO 6/40:67–80; Grenville to Walpole, 24 November 1797, FO 63/26:28, 29.

14   Phillip to Sydney, 7 October 1798, quoted in Mackaness, p. 430.

15   *Blenheim*, Captain's log and journal, ADM 51/1200; St Vincent to Phillip, 13 and 17 October, and 17 November 1797, Add. ms 31166:144, 147, Add. ms 31160:73.

16   Phillip to Nepean, 17 February 1798, ADM 1/2317.

17   Phillip to Nepean, 2 March 1798, ibid.

18   'A List of Post Captains appointed to superintend the Enrollment of Sea Fencibles', and Lords Commissioners to Navy Board, 6 April 1798, ADM 28/147:16, 18.

19   *The Keith Papers*, ed. Christopher Lloyd, The Navy Records Society, London, 1955, III, 133.

20   Land Tax Assessments 1800–03, Lymington Borough, Hampshire Record Office; and Edward King, *Old Times re-visited in the Borough and Parish of Lymington, Hants.*, 2nd ed., Simpkin, Marshall & Co., London, 1900, p. 304 and plate 120.

21   ADM 28/145:114; and Phillip's letters to the Admiralty, 1798–99, ADM 1/2317.

22   See Mackesy.

23   The relevant letters and reports are in ADM 105/44.

24   St Vincent to Phillip, 18 May 1801, Add. ms 31168:38.

25   Lords Commissioners to Phillip, 8 July 1801, ADM 2/141:525–30; and Instructions of 26 August 1801, ADM 2/142:125–6.

26   Lloyd, p. 169.

27   Ibid.

28   Lewis, p. 111.

29   Baugh, p. 161.

30   Lloyd, p. 162.

31   Lewis, p. 111.

32   Baugh, p. 158; and cf. Lloyd, p. 143.

33   Baugh, p. 162.

34 Lloyd, p. 168.

35 Ibid.

36 Quoted in Lloyd, p. 154.

37 Lords Commissioners to Phillip, 8 July and 26 August 1801, ADM 2/141:525–30, ADM 2/142:125–6.

38 'Account of the movements of Governor Phillip, as far as they can be traced, from his return to England in 1793 to his death in 1814', Mitchell ms A 2000/4:969.

39 Phillip, Report of 5 December 1801, ADM 1/579.

40 William James, *The Naval History of Great Britain*, Richard Bentley, London, 1837, III, 162.

41 These charts are in Hydrographic S 83/16-Af3, 96-Af1. Details of Craig's and Abercromby's schemes appear in WO 1/178:103–94. Colnett's 1801 proposal is in ADMI/5121:22. Popham's memorandum to Pitt and Melville of 16 October 1804 is in WO 1/161:39–66.

42 St Vincent to Phillip, 8 July 1802, 28 February 1803, Add. ms 31168:116, 135.

43 Phillip to Nepean, 24 January 1803, ADM 1/580; and Keith, III, 133–53.

44 Lords Commissioners to Phillip, 5 and 6 December 1803, ADM 2/146:335–6, 330–4.

45 Phillip, Return of 26 February 1805, ADM 1/581:86–9.

46 See Lloyd, pp. 206–7.

47 Quoted in *Letters of Lord St Vincent*, ed. D.B. Smith, The Navy Records Society, London, 1922–27, II, 45.

48 Quoted in Keith, III, 133–4.

49 Phillip to Melville, 21 February 1805, ADM 1/581:79–80.

50 Phillip to Nepean, 5 December 1801, ADM 1/579.

51 See, e.g., Phillip to Nepean (private), 31 December 1803, ADM 1/580; and Lords Commissioners, Order of 6 September 1803, Keith, III, 138.

52 Phillip to Nepean, 26 December 1803, ADM 1/580.

53 Phillip to Melville, 21 February 1805, ADM 1/581:79–80.

54 See Lloyd, p. 207.

55 Lords Commissioners, Order to Berkeley of 8 December 1804, NMM WYN 109/8; Marsden to Phillip, 19 December 1804 and 11 February 1805, ADM 2/1092:10, 25.

56 Phillip to Marsden, 18 February 1805, ADM 1/581:78.

57 Keith, III, 137–8.

58 Dundas to Phillip, 10 January 1792, HRNSW, I, ii, 585.

59 Phillip to Nepean, 5 December 1803, and Nepean, annotation thereto, ADM 1/580.

60 Nepean, annotation to Phillip's letter of 12 December 1803, ibid.

61 Phillip to Melville, 21 February, to Marsden, 26 February 1805, ADM 1/581:79–80, 83–4.

Among his People

Bibliography

As before (Chapter 5), R.S. Neale, *Bath 1680–1850: A Social History*, gives details of the city; and Sir Frederick Chapman, *Governor Phillip in Retirement*, is the only substantial source of information about Phillip's life then.

Notes

1 From a conversation with Mr John Vivian, of Bath.
2 Information supplied by Mr Vivian.
3 Quoted in Mackaness, p. 442.
4 Phillip's will, dated 20 May 1814, proved PCC 14 October 1814, PROB Bridport 579.
5 Waterhouse, Description of Phillip's wounding, undated, Mitchell ms Aw 109:2.
6 See Chapman, pp. 33–4.
7 King to his son, quoted in Chapman, p. 35.
8 Ibid., pp. 34, 35, 47.
9 See Hunter and Phillip, Testimony in favour of George Johnstone, 2 August 1811, NLA ms 4271.
10 This summary is based on information in Chapman, passim. See also Mackaness, p. 452.
11 J.F. Meehan, 'Admiral Arthur Phillip, First Governor and Founder of New South Wales', *Beacon*, April 1911, p. 63.
12 *Bath Chronicle*, 1 September 1814; St Nicholas, Bathampton, Burial register, 1814, entry 61.
13 Lords Commissioners, Commission of 4 June 1814, NLA ms 1613.
14 Treasury Minute, 24 October 1815; and Isabella Phillip to Lushington, 12 November 1816, Add. ms 38269:381, 383.
15 Isabella Phillip's will, dated 15 October 1822, proved PCC 18 March 1823, PROB 11/1668.

6 ARTHUR PHILLIP

Notes

1 Spain, p. 70.
2 Southwell to Butler, 2 August 1787, Add. ms 16381:22; and quoted in Chapman, p. 18.
3 G.T. Landmann, *Adventures and Recollections of Colonel Landmann*, Colburn and Co., London, 1852, I, 123.
4 Ibid.
5 Nagle, p. 44.
6 Landmann, I, 122.
7 Lavradio to Mello e Castro, 10 May 1778, AHU RJ caixa 115:9 (Becke and Jeffery, p. 320).
8 White to Skill, 17 April 1790, HRNSW, I, ii, 333.
9 Phillip to Sydney, 2 April 1792, Dixson ms Q 162:43–4.
10 Phillip to Banks, 2 April 1792, Mitchell ms C 213:87–8.
11 Banks to Nicol, 22 July 1793, Turnbull ms 155/20.
12 Lavradio to Mello e Castro, 10 May 1778, AHU RJ caixa 115:9.
13 Nelson to his wife, 7 April 1798, (in private hands).
14 Phillip to Stephens, 14 May 1784, ADM 1/2307.
15 Phillip to Sandwich, 19 July 1780, ADM 1/2306.
16 Schaffer to Nepean, [1790?], quoted in Anne McCormick and Derek McDonnell, *The Riou Papers*, p. 73.
17 Collins, p. 88.

18 I am grateful to Professor Glyndwr Williams and Dr Campbell Macknight for this suggestion. I disagree strongly with the view that W.E.H. Stanner expressed in 'The History of Indifference thus begins', *Aboriginal History*, 1 (1977), 11, 16–17, 20, 21, 22, 25, and in *White Man Got No Dreaming*, Australian National University Press, Canberra, 1979, pp. 144, 191, that Phillip's actions (and those of the British more generally) at Port Jackson began what later became the pattern of race relations in Australia. Phillip particularly, but also numbers of his officers, arrived without highly developed prejudices, with a lively desire to enquire into the details of Aboriginal life, and with genuine concern to establish peaceful relations. Of course they had preconceptions, on which Stanner lays much stress. In doing so, though, he fails to perceive his own, which is that these officers were inflexible in their habits of thought. They were distinctly not so. They changed their views of the Aborigines repeatedly in the early years, according to the knowledge they gained. Phillip's centralizing of authority and control of events in a confined area, which constrained the wilful or ignorant who might have been disposed to act vengefully, also makes this period of colonial history different from those which followed. Instructive comparisons are Stirling's and Bourke's failures in the 1830s to see that colonists observed government policy towards the Aborigines.

19 In speaking of the response of some English reviewers to the second volume of his biography of Smuts, Sir Keith Hancock said that they 'violated what I once called "the rule of contextual congruity". According to this rule it is wrong—in every sense of that word—to measure the thoughts and actions of people in the past by a measuring rod of knowledge and experience which did not come into existence until after those people were dead'—*Professing History*, Sydney University Press, Sydney, 1976, p. 61.

It is on this ground that I most strongly disagree with Stanner's view of Phillip as an imperceptive person—see, e.g., *White Man Got No Dreaming*, pp. 168, 174, 190–1.

20 See Alan Frost, 'New South Wales as *terra nullius*: the British denial of Aboriginal land rights', *Historical Studies*, 19 (1981), 513–23.

21 Phillip, Queries concerning his Instructions, c. 11 April 1787, CO 201/2:130; to Sydney, 15 May 1788, HRNSW, I, ii, 127.

22 Collins, pp. 58–9. The detail inserted is from Nagle, p. 50.

23 Phillip to Grenville, 5 March 1791, HRNSW, I, ii, 472.

24 Nagle, p. 58.

25 See above, pp. 174–5.

26 E.g., Hunter, p. 22.

27 See Southwell's letters to his mother and uncle, Add. ms 16381:13–104.

28 Phillip to Middleton, 4 March 1791, Mitchell film FM 4/63.

29 Lavradio, Mappa dos Officiaes e Embarcacoens, 27 November 1776, AHU RJ caixa 109:53 (Becke and Jeffery, p. 296).

30 'The IMAGINATION then, I consider either as primary, or secondary. The primary IMAGINATION I hold to be the living Power and prime Agent of all human Perception, and as a repetition in the finite mind of the eternal act of creation in the infinite I AM ...'—*Biographia Literaria*, ed. J. Shawcross, Oxford University Press, Oxford, 1979, I, 202.

31 'Extract from the Journal of Capt. Arthur Phillip', Clements Sydney 17.

32 Phillip to Nepean, 26 March 1791, HRNSW, I, ii, 484.

33 Phillip to Lansdowne, 3 July 1788, HRNSW, II, 410–11. There is a five page extract in Mitchell ms C 213:23–7.

34 Kenneth R. Andrews, *Trade, plunder and settlement: Maritime enterprise and the genesis of the British Empire, 1480–1630*, Cambridge University Press, Cambridge, 1984, p. 338.

35 Nepean to Middleton, 13 February 1787, (in private hands).

36 Phillip to Sydney, 12 March 1787, HRNSW, I, ii, 56–7.

37 Phillip to Sydney, [10] July 1788, to Grenville, 13 July 1790, ibid., pp. 179, 354.

38 Phillip to Townshend, 25 April 1783, IOR H 175:237.

39 Quoted by Elizabeth Macarthur in her letter to Eliza Kingdon, 23 August 1794, in *The Macarthurs of Camden*, p. 45.

40 John Pinkerton, *Modern Geography*, T. Cadell and W. Davies, London, 1802, II, 471.

41 Phillip to Banks, 16 November 1788, Mitchell ms C 213:46.

42 Phillip, Memorandum of c. September 1786, CO 201/2:92; to Middleton, 7 July 1788, (in private hands).

43 Phillip to Lansdowne, 3 July 1788, HRNSW, II, 411.

44 Phillip to Banks, 24 March 1791, Mitchell C 213:77; to Sydney, 2 April 1792, Dixson ms Q 162:43.

45 Howe to Blankett, 19 August 1786 (draft), NMM HOW 3.

Sources of Illustrations

For permission to reproduce the works indicated, my thanks are due to the following:

PRIMARY SOURCES

The Library Council of New South Wales, Sydney:

Francis Wheatley, 'Captain Arthur Phillip' (1786) (Mitchell Library ZML 124)

William Bradley, 'Santa Cruz on the SE side of Teneriffe; *Sirius* & Convoy in the Roads. June 1787' (Safe 1/14)

William Bradley, 'Botany Bay. *Sirius* & Convoy going in: *Supply* & Agent's Division in the Bay 21 Jan.ʸ 1788' (Safe 1/14)

William Bradley, 'Tracks of the *Sirius* & *Waakzaamheydt* in the Southern Hemisphere, 1787–1792' (Safe 1/14)

George James, 'Lieutenant Arthur Phillip' (1764) (Dixson Galleries ZDG 233)

George James, 'Charlott Phillip' (1764) (Dixson Galleries ZDG 235)

The Director, National Library of Australia, Canberra:

Augustus Earle 1793–1838
Negro fandango scene, Campo St Anna, Rio de Janeiro
Watercolour, 21 × 34 cm
NK12/98
Rex Nan Kivell Collection

Augustus Earle 1793–1838
A catamaran, Madras Roads
Watercolour, 14.6 × 26.3 cm
NK12/126
Rex Nan Kivell Collection

Francis Fowkes (attrib.)

[Port Jackson Painter], 'New South Wales. Port Jackson from the Entrance up to Sydney Cove taken in Oct.ʳ 1788'

[Port Jackson Painter], 'A New South Wales native striking fish while his wife is employed fishing with hooks & lines in her Canoe'

[Port Jackson Painter], 'A woman of New South Wales curing the head ache, the blood which she takes from her own gums she supposes comes along the string from the part affected in the patient. This operation they call Bee an ee.'

[Port Jackson Painter], 'The Governor making the best of his way to the Boat after being wounded with the spear sticking in his Shoulder'

[Port Jackson Painter], 'Ban nel lang meeting the Governor by appointment after he was wounded by Wille ma ring in September 1790'

[Port Jackson Painter], 'A view of Sydney Cove, Port Jackson, March 7th 1792'

[Port Jackson Painter], 'A view of Government Farm at Rose hill N.S. wales 1791'

George Raper, 'His Majesty's Ship *Sirius* in Sidney Cove 1789'

George Raper, 'Entrance of Rio de Janeiro (Brasil) from the Anchorage without the Sugar Loaf bearing in N.W.½N. off Shore 2 miles'

George Raper, 'View of the Table Land from the Anchorage in the Bay Cape Good-hope. (1) Devil's Mount S. b W. (2) Sugar-loaf W.S.W. (3) Green Point W.N.W.'

The Controller of Her Majesty's Stationery Office, and the Hydrographer of the Royal Navy:

'Porto e Entrada de Rio de Janeiro' (*c.* 1776)

Arthur Phillip, 'Nova Collonia do Sacramento' (1775)

Captain Scott, 'Johanna Bay' (October 1785)

'Fort St George, Madras' (1780)

The Controller of Her Majesty's Stationery Office, and the Keeper of the Public Record Office:

Page 1 of Phillip's memorandum concerning the colonization (CO 201/2:88)

Sir George and Lady Raper:

George Raper, 'Plan of Table Bay Cape of Good Hope' (1787)

George Raper, 'A North & South Chart from the Lands End to the Equator' (1787)

George Raper, 'Carreening Cove Nᵒ Side Port-Jackson' (1789)

The Director, Musée de la Marine, Paris:

Claude-Joseph Vernet, 'Vue de la Rade d'Antibes' (1756)

Claude-Joseph Vernet, 'Vue de l'Intérieur du Port de Marseille prise du Pavillon de l'Horloge du Parc' (1754)

Claude-Joseph Vernet, 'Vue du vieux Port de Toulon prise du coté du Magasin aux Vivres' (1756)

Claude-Joseph Vernet, 'La Ville et la Rade de Toulon vues a mi-côte de la montagne qui est derrière' (1756)

The Director, Museo Naval, Madrid:
Fernando Brambila, 'Vista de la Colonia Inglesa de Sydney en la Nueva Gales Meridional' (March/April 1793) (ms 1724/15)

Fernando Brambila, 'Vista de la Colonia de Paramata en la Nueva Gales Meridional' (March/April 1793) (ms 1723/24)

The Director, Arquivo Histórico Ultramarino, Lisbon:
Jean Massé, 'Planta da Cidade de São Sebastião do Rio de Janeiro, com suas fortifficaçoins' (1713) (ms 1066)

The Director, Museu da Marinha, Lisbon:
'Nᵃ Sᵃ do Pilar e S. João Baptista' (G5–30–7)
'Mapa das Naus e Fragatas de guerra Portuguezas q.' seemcorporaraõ na Esquadra do Sul' (G5–30–1)

Câmara Municipal de Lisboa, Palácio Galveias:
(Segundo Carlos Mardel?), 'Vista imaginária da Praça do Comércio'

The Director, Arquivo Nacional do Brasil, Rio de Janeiro:
'Planta da Costa e Ilha de Santa Catharina' (1776)

The Director, Museu Histórico Nacional, Rio de Janeiro:
Leandro Joaquim, 'Largo do Paço, por ocasião de uma revista militar' (1780s?)

Jean Baptiste Réville, 'Vista de uma parte da cidade e do grande Aqueduto do Rio de Janeiro' (mid-eighteenth century?)

Leandro Joaquim, 'Vista de uma Esquadra Inglesa' (1780s?)

The Director, Museu Nacional de Belas Artes, Rio de Janeiro:
Leandro Joaquim, 'Pesca da Baleia na baía de Guanabara' (1780s?)

The Director, Cape Archives Depot, Cape Town:
F.C. Brink, 'Plan en Caart van het Fort en Vlek au Cabo de Goede Hoop' (1767) (M3/18)

PUBLISHED SOURCES

Robert Seymour, *A Survey of the Cities of London and Westminster* (1734): 'Bread Street Ward'

An Historical Account of all the Voyages round the World, *IV* (1773): 'Spitsbergen or New Greenland'

Brian Tunstall, *Admiral Byng and the Loss of Minorca* (1928): The diagrams of the battle off Minorca

[An Officer], *An Authentic Journal of the Siege of the Havana* (1762): 'A Plan of the Siege of the Havana'

[Janet Schaw], *Journal of a Lady of Quality* (1921): 'Plan of the City of Lisbon'

The Voyage of Governor Phillip to Botany Bay (1789) (Arthur Phillip/John Hunter/William Dawes), 'Sketch of Sydney Cove, Port Jackson, in the County of Cumberland, New South Wales. July 1788'

Index

180° 160° 140° 120° 100° 80° 60° 40° 20°

ARCTIC CIRCLE

60°

40°

TROPIC OF CANCER
20°

ATLANTIC

PACIFIC

EQUATOR 0°

OCEAN

20°
TROPIC OF CAPRICORN

OCEAN

40°

Cape Horn

60°

the Commodore
navigated ever
the severest h
longer on the

ANTARCTIC CIRCLE

180° 160° 140° 120° 100° 80° 60° 40° 20°